DEVELOPMENT CENTRE DOCUMENTS

To CAROline,
With thanks for
the encouragement
your invitation to
the Economic Council
gave me to
continue working
on partnering +
networking activity.

SOUTH-SOUTH CO-OPERATION IN A GLOBAL PERSPECTIVE
Edited by Lynn K. Mytelka

COOPÉRATION SUD-SUD : PERSPECTIVES GÉNÉRALES
sous la direction de Lynn K. Mytelka

D1406707

PUBLISHER'S NOTE

The following texts have been left in their original form to permit faster distribution at lower cost.

NOTE DE L'ÉDITEUR

Les textes reproduits ci-après ont été laissés dans leur forme originale pour permettre pour un coût moindre, une diffusion plus rapide.

ORGANISATION FOR ECONOMIC CO-OPERATION AND DEVELOPMENT

ORGANISATION FOR ECONOMIC CO-OPERATION AND DEVELOPMENT

Pursuant to Article 1 of the Convention signed in Paris on 14th December 1960, and which came into force on 30th September 1961, the Organisation for Economic Co-operation and Development (OECD) shall promote policies designed:

— to achieve the highest sustainable economic growth and employment and a rising standard of living in Member countries, while maintaining financial stability, and thus to contribute to the development of the world economy;

— to contribute to sound economic expansion in Member as well as non-member countries in the process of economic development; and

— to contribute to the expansion of world trade on a multilateral, non-discriminatory basis in accordance with international obligations.

The original Member countries of the OECD are Austria, Belgium, Canada, Denmark, France, Germany, Greece, Iceland, Ireland, Italy, Luxembourg, the Netherlands, Norway, Portugal, Spain, Sweden, Switzerland, Turkey, the United Kingdom and the United States. The following countries became Members subsequently through accession at the dates indicated hereafter: Japan (28th April 1964), Finland (28th January 1969), Australia (7th June 1971) and New Zealand (29th May 1973). The Commission of the European Communities takes part in the work of the OECD (Article 13 of the OECD Convention).

The Development Centre of the Organisation for Economic Co-operation and Development was established by decision of the OECD Council on 23rd October 1962.

The purpose of the Centre is to bring together the knowledge and experience available in Member countries of both economic development and the formulation and execution of general economic policies; to adapt such knowledge and experience to the actual needs of countries or regions in the process of development and to put the results at the disposal of the countries by appropriate means.

The Centre has a special and autonomous position within the OECD which enables it to enjoy scientific independence in the execution of its task. Nevertheless, the Centre can draw upon the experience and knowledge available in the OECD in the development field.

THE OPINIONS EXPRESSED AND ARGUMENTS EMPLOYED IN THIS PUBLICATION ARE THE SOLE RESPONSIBILITY OF THE AUTHOR AND DO NOT NECESSARILY REFLECT THOSE OF THE OECD OR OF THE GOVERNMENTS OF ITS MEMBER COUNTRIES

*

* *

ORGANISATION DE COOPÉRATION ET DE DÉVELOPPEMENT ÉCONOMIQUES

En vertu de l'article 1er de la Convention signée le 14 décembre 1960, à Paris, et entrée en vigueur le 30 septembre 1961, l'Organisation de Coopération et de Développement Économiques (OCDE) a pour objectif de promouvoir des politiques visant :

— à réaliser la plus forte expansion de l'économie et de l'emploi et une progression du niveau de vie dans les pays Membres, tout en maintenant la stabilité financière, et à contribuer ainsi au développement de l'économie mondiale ;

— à contribuer à une saine expansion économique dans les pays Membres, ainsi que les pays non membres, en voie de développement économique ;

— à contribuer à l'expansion du commerce mondial sur une base multilatérale et non discriminatoire conformément aux obligations internationales.

Les pays Membres originaires de l'OCDE sont : l'Allemagne, l'Autriche, la Belgique, le Canada, le Danemark, l'Espagne, les États-Unis, la France, la Grèce, l'Irlande, l'Islande, l'Italie, le Luxembourg, la Norvège, les Pays-Bas, le Portugal, le Royaume-Uni, la Suède, la Suisse et la Turquie. Les pays suivants sont ultérieurement devenus Membres par adhésion aux dates indiquées ci-après : le Japon (28 avril 1964), la Finlande (28 janvier 1969), l'Australie (7 juin 1971) et la Nouvelle-Zélande (29 mai 1973). La Commission des Communautés européennes participe aux travaux de l'OCDE (article 13 de la Convention de l'OCDE).

Le Centre de Développement de l'Organisation de Coopération et de Développement Economiques a été créé par décision du Conseil de l'OCDE, en date du 23 octobre 1962.

Il a pour objet de rassembler les connaissances et données d'expériences disponibles dans les pays Membres, tant en matière de développement économique qu'en ce qui concerne l'élaboration et la mise en œuvre de politiques économiques générales ; d'adapter ces connaissances et ces données d'expériences aux besoins concrets des pays et régions en voie de développement et de les mettre à la disposition des pays intéressés, par des moyens appropriés.

Le Centre occupe, au sein de l'OCDE, une situation particulière et autonome qui lui assure son indépendance scientifique dans l'exécution de ses tâches. Il bénéficie pleinement, néanmoins, de l'expérience et des connaissances déjà acquises par l'OCDE dans le domaine du développement.

Also available in English under the title:

*
* *

Foreword

This study is a product of the Development Centre's 1990-92 research programme on Globalisation and Regionalisation, directed by Charles Oman.

Avant-propos

Cette étude s'inscrit dans le cadre du programme de recherche 1990-92 du Centre de Développement sur la Globalisation et la régionalisation, sous la direction de Charles Oman.

Contents

Preface

This study was carried out as part of the Development Centre's research project on Globalisation and Regionalisation, one of the themes of its 1990-1992 Research Programme. The project seeks to provide a better understanding, for policy makers in both developing and OECD countries, of the forces that are working for, and against, the formation of regional economic groupings, and how those forces interact with those driving globalisation today.

Much attention is being paid to the *de jure* and/or *de facto* processes of regionalisation involving OECD countries in Europe, North America and Pacific Asia. In parallel, the late 1980s and early 1990s have also witnessed a major resurgence of interest in regional co-operation and integration among developing countries. The latter is stimulated as much by the current dynamics of globalisation — and the risk perceived by many developing countries of being isolated from those dynamics — as by the moves by OECD countries toward the formation or strengthening of regional economic groupings.

This study focuses on the potential role of South-South co-operation as an instrument for developing countries to strengthen their international competitiveness in the current context of globalisation. Going beyond conventional explanations in its analysis of the numerous and largely unsuccessful schemes for regional integration among developing countries that emerged between the 1950s and 1970s, it highlights the importance of breaking with traditional theory, and practice, in the promotion of South-South co-operation today. Contrary to the earlier period, when regionalisation in the South was largely pursued as a substitute for increased integration with the North, the study emphasizes the importance of South-South co-operation today as a means to strengthen such integration.

Particularly important, the study argues, is the need to actively involve private-sector and other non-governmental economic actors in the design and launching of new forms of South-South co-operation, and for policies that foster networking for innovation among such actors across national boundaries in developing countries. It is also important to recognise that there is considerably more to South-South co-operation than trade.

In drawing attention to how diverse actors and interests can interact to support, or constrain, effective South-South co-operation, in clarifying the policy agenda for promoting such co-operation in a way that strengthens developing countries' ability to compete in global markets, and in highlighting the importance of such co-operation for improved North-South economic relations, this study constitutes a major contribution to the Development Centre's research on Globalisation and Regionalisation. Edited by an expert and policy advisor on regional integration among developing countries, the study comprises chapters by specialists in their fields from both OECD and developing countries. This volume is important for policy makers in the South, but also for aid donors, policy officials in OECD countries, as well as for students of co-operation among developing countries in the new context of globalisation.

Jean Bonvin
President
OECD Development Centre
December 1993

Préface

Cette étude a été réalisée dans le cadre du projet de recherche du Centre de Développement sur la globalisation et la régionalisation, l'un des thèmes de son programme pour 1990-92. Ce projet vise à apporter aux décideurs des pays en développement et de ceux de l'OCDE une meilleure compréhension des forces qui favorisent ou entravent la constitution de groupements économiques régionaux, et des mécanismes d'interaction entre ces forces et celles qui régissent le processus actuel de mondialisation.

Une attention particulière est prêtée aux processus de régionalisation *de jure* et/ou *de facto* qui concernent les pays d'Europe, d'Amérique du nord et de l'Asie/Pacifique Membres de l'OCDE. En parallèle, la fin des années 80 et le début des années 90 ont également connu un regain d'intérêt sensible pour la coopération régionale et l'intégration entre les pays en développement. Cette dernière est stimulée aussi bien par la dynamique actuelle de mondialisation — et la crainte de nombreux pays en développement d'être tenus à l'écart de cette dynamique — que par les efforts de pays de l'OCDE pour créer ou renforcer les groupements économiques régionaux.

Cette étude montre que, dans le contexte actuel de mondialisation, la coopération sud-sud peut jouer un rôle très important dans l'amélioration de la compétitivité des pays en développement sur les marchés internationaux. Au terme d'une analyse qui dépasse les explications classiques de l'échec des nombreux projets de coopération régionale entre ces pays dans les années 1950-80, les auteurs plaident pour une rupture avec la théorie et les pratiques traditionnelles pour encourager la coopération sud-sud aujourd'hui. Alors que, par le passé, les efforts d'intégration régionale du sud représentaient essentiellement une alternative à la poursuite de l'intégration avec le nord, les contributions de cet ouvrage soulignent *a contrario* l'importance de la coopération sud-sud dans le renforcement de cette intégration aujourd'hui.

Dans cette perspective, il est essentiel de faire participer activement le secteur privé et d'autres acteurs économiques non gouvernementaux à l'élaboration et à la mise en œuvre de nouvelles formes de coopération sud-sud, ainsi que de politiques encourageant la coopération entre les acteurs des différents pays en développement dans le domaine de l'innovation. Il est également important d'admettre que la coopération sud-sud ne saurait se limiter aux échanges commerciaux.

En attirant l'attention sur la manière dont l'interaction entre les intervenants et les intérêts peut favoriser, ou entraver, la coopération sud-sud, en proposant un calendrier pour la définition de politiques permettant de renforcer la compétitivité des pays en développement sur les marchés mondiaux par le biais de cette coopération et en soulignant le rôle qu'elle peut jouer dans l'amélioration des relations économiques nord-sud, cette étude représente un apport majeur pour les recherches que mène le Centre de

Développement sur la mondialisation et la régionalisation. Supervisée par un expert et conseiller politique en matière d'intégration régionale des pays en développement, elle comprend les contributions de spécialistes des domaines étudiés, originaires aussi bien de pays de l'OCDE que de pays en développement. Elle présente un grand intérêt pour les décideurs des pays du sud, mais également pour les organismes d'aide et d'autres institutions de l'OCDE, ainsi que pour tous ceux qui se préoccupent de la coopération entre les pays en développement dans le contexte nouveau de la mondialisation.

Jean Bonvin
Président
Centre de Développement de l'OCDE
Décembre 1993

The Contributors

Lynn K. Mytelka is a Professor of Political Economy at Carleton University, Ottawa and a senior research associate at the Centre de Recherche sur les Entreprises Multinationales, Université de Paris-X. She has published extensively in the areas of regional integration and inter-firm technological collaboration, among others.

Carlota Perez has specialised on the impact of the present wave of technical and organisational change on development prospects. Her professional experience includes a combination of government policy work in Venezuela, academic research and independent consultancy for governments, industry associations and international organisations. Currently she is affiliated part-time with SPRU, University of Sussex and the Instituto de Ingenieria, Sartenejas, Caracas.

Dieter Ernst is currently a Senior Fellow at the Berkeley Round Table on the International Economy, University of California, Berkeley. He has previously directed international projects on the electronics industry while at the OECD, the Institute for Development Studies in the Hague and UNIDO. Dr. Ernst has written extensively on technology transfer and accumulation, the strategy of multinational firms and competition in the global economy.

Linda Yuen-Ching Lim, a native of Singapore, teaches Asian economic development and international business at the University of Michigan in Ann Arbor, where she is also Research Director of the Southeast Asia Business programme.

Daniel Chudnovsky is Director of the Centro de Investigaciones para la Transformación (CENIT]) and Professor of Development Economics at the University of Buenos Aires. His previous work experience includes seven years as an Economic Affairs Officer in the Technology Division of UNCTAD. He has also served as a consultant to UNIDO, UNCTC, INTAL, SELA, UNDP and the IDRC. Professor Chudnovsky has written extensively on trade and technology issues.

Alyson Warhurst is a geologist and social scientist. She is currently a Senior Fellow at the Science Policy Research Unit (SPRU) of the University of Sussex and Director of the international Mining and Environment Research Network. She has previously worked on mining technology development in the Andean Group countries and as a Programme Officer for the International Development Research Centre (IDRC) of Canada, responsible for technology policy projets in Latin America and China. Dr. Warhurst currently manages a network on environmental management in mining and mineral processing.

Clive Thomas is Director of the Institute of Development Studies, University of Guyana. He has written extensively on regional integration in the Caribbean, technological change and innovation.

Les auteurs

Lynn K. Mytelka est professeur d'économie politique à l'université de Carleton, Ottawa, et est directeur de recherche associé au Centre de Recherche sur les Entreprises Multinationales de l'Université de Paris-X. Elle a beaucoup publié, entre autres, sur les thèmes de l'intégration régionale et de la collaboration inter-entreprises en matière de technologie.

Carlota Perez est une spécialiste de l'impact du progrès technique et organisationnel sur les problèmes du développement. Ses fonctions successives l'ont amenée à participer à l'élaboration de la politique économique du gouvernement vénézuélien, à mener des travaux de recherche et à travailler comme consultante auprès de gouvernements, de groupes d'industriels et d'organismes internationaux. Elle partage actuellement ses activités entre le Science Policy Research Unit (SPRU) de l'université du Sussex et l'Instituto de Ingenieria, Sartenejas, Caracas.

Dieter Ernst est actuellement *Senior Fellow* à la Berkeley Round Table on the International Economy de l'université de Californie, Berkeley. Auparavant, il a dirigé des projets internationaux sur l'industrie électronique dans le cadre de ses travaux à l'OCDE, à l'Institut d'études du développement de la Hague et à l'ONUDI. Le Dr Ernst a beaucoup publié sur l'accumulation et les transferts de technologie, la stratégie des firmes multinationales et la concurrence internationale.

Linda Yuen-Ching Lim est originaire de Singapour, elle enseigne les affaires internationales et le développement économique des pays asiatiques à l'université du Michigan, Ann Harbor, où elle est également directeur de recherche du Southeast Asia Business Program.

Daniel Chudnowsky est directeur du Centro de Investigaciones para la Transformacion (CENIT) et professeur en économie du développement à l'université de Buenos Aires. Il a passé sept ans en tant que responsable des affaires économiques à la division technologique de la CNUCED. Il a été également consultant pour l'ONUDI, le CNUST, l'INTAL, le SELA, le PNUD et le CERDI. Le professeur Chudnowsky a beaucoup publié sur le commerce et les problèmes de technologie.

Alyson Warhurst est géologue et sociologue. Elle est actuellement *Senior Fellow* au SPRU de l'université du Sussex et directeur de l'International Mining and Environment Research Network. Auparavant, elle s'est consacrée au développement des technologies minières pour les pays du Pacte andin et elle a été chargée de programme au CERDI (Canada), ainsi que responsable de projets dans le domaine des politiques technologiques en Amérique latine et en Chine. Le Dr Warhurst dirige actuellement un réseau sur la gestion de l'environnement dans les secteurs minier et de la transformation des minerais.

Clive Thomas est directeur de l'Institute of Develoment Studies de l'université de Guyana. Il a beaucoup publié sur l'intégration régionale dans les Caraïbes, le progrès technique et l'innovation.

Executive Summary

Since the 1970s, new forms of global competition and collaboration among firms have emerged in which innovation in products, processes and organisational practices play a central role. These changes are signalling the need for continuous economic, social and political transformation in both developed and developing countries. They also expose the inadequacies of earlier conceptions of development as a finite process, bounded by the experience of a small number of European and North American countries, and put into question the practice in developing countries of imitating product, process and organisational norms developed in other times and other contexts. This has been particularly evident in the developing countries' pursuit of regional integration, which has mainly taken the form of preferential trading arrangements among neighbouring countries.

From the late 1950s to the early 1970s, many such arrangements were established among developing countries, but few achieved their development goals. Chapter 1 describes the "exchange driven" and "production specialisation" models of regional integration that dominated during that period. It points up the anomalies in conventional explanations, which attribute the failure of regional integration among developing countries to government policies and a lack of political will, and clarifies the underlying causes of those policies and apparent lack of political will. Particularly important were the zero-sum trade-offs within regional integration schemes that resulted from a unique historical conjuncture in which the import-substituting industrialisation strategies of states and the internationalisation strategies of multinational corporations (MNCs) combined to undermine both the rationale for and the gains from regional integration. The approach developed in Chapter 1, and on which the volume as a whole is based, draws attention to the way in which different actors and interests can interact to support or constrain particular integration efforts.

The late 1980s and early 1990s have witnessed a resurgence of interest in South-South co-operation that owes much to two developments: the impact of changes in technology on the competitive strategies of MNCs, and the search for new development strategies in the South prompted by the difficult economic situation in which most of those countries found themselves during the 1980s. Combined, these two developments have opened a window of opportunity for a new focus on innovation-driven co-operation both within and across countries in the South, and between the North and the South.

For such efforts to succeed, however, the interests, capabilities and strategies of domestic actors must be taken into account. As the chapters on regional integration in the Caribbean and in South America (Mercosur) illustrate, non-governmental organisations, labour and farmers' associations, private companies, consumer groups and researchers traditionally have been brought into the process only sporadically, and even then their role has remained subject to institutional direction from above. Indeed, the traditional models of South-South co-operation have often operated as *disincentives* to forms of regional co-operation outside their formal ambit. Such structures are clearly anachronistic in a world economy in which competitiveness is increasingly a function of organisational changes that involve close linkages between clients and suppliers, collaboration between firms in R&D, production and marketing, and networks between producers and the scientific and technological infrastructure. There is thus a pressing need to innovate in the very forms that regional integration takes, and that of South-South co-operation more generally. Particularly needed is an alternative to the traditional state-centric view, one that brings participants more meaningfully into the process of regional co-operation.

Once a user orientation is adopted, moreover, it quickly becomes apparent that there is more to South-South co-operation than trade. Going beyond trade, the papers in this volume suggest a number of new directions which South-South co-operation might take. The latter begin from a set of common observations concerning the growing knowledge-intensity of production and the role of innovation in international competition. From this perspective, modernisation and competitiveness are no longer conceived solely as a process of moving away from raw materials production to manufacturing. To the contrary, new technologies are today capable of upgrading all economic activities, and not only the high-technology sectors.

Furthermore, with innovation as a focus, positive-sum games are possible even among competitors. In Latin America, for example, collaboration between private-sector mining companies has generated considerable learning opportunities for all participating firms. In ASEAN, the designation of frontier regions as growth triangles has stimulated the role that intra-regional direct investment can play in the development process.

On a wider scale, for regional co-operation to strengthen the ability of developing countries to adjust to continuous changes in international tastes, prices and competitive conditions, networking for innovation must become central to the process. Although such linkages must begin at home, and strengthening the domestic system of innovation is thus clearly important, increasingly ties must also be forged across national borders. They must be forged regionally, because proximity is important for user-producer links, and because regional networks reduce the enormous co-ordination costs involved in global sourcing and marketing. They must also be forged among developing countries more generally, because developing countries face many common problems, for example in minerals processing, in the development of environmentally sound technologies and in agriculture. And they must be forged with the developed countries, especially in dynamically evolving sectors such as electronics and biotechnology.

Developing innovation-driven forms of South-South co-operation is also more feasible in the 1990s than it was in the past, for two important reasons. First, the need to pool resources has become evident to states and other social and economic actors in the South. Second, technological accumulation within Asian, Latin American and Caribbean public and private sector enterprises, research institutions and universities has progressed in a wide variety of sectors. As the papers in this volume show, these include the resource industries, electronics, machine tools, auto parts and biotechnology.

The process of technological accumulation is proceeding at a far slower pace in Africa. Yet the need to stimulate firms in Africa to solve restructuring problems, and to innovate in the course of rehabilitation, is critical to the sustainability of development on that continent. Given current financial constraints in Africa, technology transfers from abroad, while vital, cannot fulfil Africa's needs. Moreover, such transfers are generally costly and require recurrent expenditures for the import of capital and intermediate goods, management skills, maintenance services and technical knowhow that Africa can ill afford at present. It has thus become imperative for the enterprise sector in Africa to strengthen its ability to solve its own problems and to overcome bottlenecks in production.

To engage in a process of problem-solving innovation in an environment where firms rarely think strategically or incorporate innovation into their growth strategies will require outside stimulus, and it cannot be done without access to financial and technological resources. These resources can and must come through a process of collaborative research and development involving other domestic actors, including supplier firms, university faculties, engineering consultancy firms and research institutions. The critical density required for such problem-solving innovation is, however, rarely present in any single African country. Regional networking is thus critical here.

African governments have acknowledged the need to develop training that promotes innovation. They are also attempting to put in place a policy environment that is conducive to innovation. To complement these initiatives, a regional mechanism will be needed through which enterprises are encouraged to identify problems and to innovate, and local resources are marshalled in support of that endeavour. In view of Africa's limited financial resources, such a mechanism would also have an important financial role to play in underwriting the costs and risks of innovation. Such initiatives provide important new areas for support from aid donors in helping to build the basis for dynamic North-South partnerships as well.

In a period of intense and rapid technological change, breaking with traditional theory and practice concerning the form and function of South-South co-operation is thus essential. The papers in this volume argue for a wider vision of what needs to be done. In particular, they provide a rationale for innovation-driven models of South-South co-operation, and demonstrate their feasibility through numerous examples of firm-to-firm, university-industry and government-to-government arrangements that are already underway. To strengthen these initiatives, states are increasingly being called upon to play a key steering role even as the private sector's contribution and active participation increases. Policies must be put in place that promote innovation and technological diffusion, that provide an institutional and legal framework which allows and indeed fosters networking for innovation, and that are conducive to the development of the telecommunications, transportation, research and training infrastructure which support such networking. So, too, must creative solutions to the financing of innovation be developed. The agenda for South-South co-operation is thus long, but it is not inchoate if it remains firmly focused on the goal of networking for innovation.

Résumé

Depuis les années 70, de nouvelles formes de concurrence mondiale et de coopération inter-entreprises sont apparues, dans lesquelles l'innovation en termes de produits, de procédés et de pratiques d'organisation jouent un rôle central. Ces évolutions montrent la nécessité de mutations économiques, sociales et politiques permanentes, à la fois dans les pays développés et dans les pays en développement. Elles révèlent également les insuffisances de certains concepts antérieurs qui considéraient le développement comme un processus uniforme, calqué sur l'expérience d'un petit nombre de pays d'Europe et d'Amérique du nord. Les évolutions survenues entre-temps remettent également en cause les pratiques adoptées par les pays en développement consistant à imiter les normes de production, de procédures et d'organisation élaborées à d'autres époques et dans d'autres contextes. Ces pratiques et les dysfonctionnements qu'elles entraînent se manifestent tout particulièrement dans les efforts d'intégration régionale des pays en développement, qui prennent essentiellement la forme d'accords d'échanges préférentiels entre pays voisins.

De la fin des années 50 au début des années 70, nombre de ces accords ont été conclus entre des pays en développement, mais peu ont atteint leurs objectifs. Le chapitre 1 décrit les deux grands modèles d'intégration régionale de cette époque, l'un fondé sur les échanges et l'autre sur la spécialisation de la production. Il met en évidence les insuffisances des théories classiques qui attribuent l'échec de l'intégration régionale des pays en développement aux mesures prises par les gouvernements et à l'absence de volonté politique. Il éclaire également les raisons profondes de ces mesures et de ce manque apparent de volonté politique. Il est important de noter que ces programmes d'intégration régionale ont débouché essentiellement sur des jeux «à somme nulle», du fait d'une évolution historique particulière : la combinaison des stratégies nationales de substitution aux importations et des stratégies d'internationalisation des sociétés multinationales a en effet limité à la fois la raison d'être et la portée de ces programmes. Ainsi, l'approche développée dans ce premier chapitre, sur laquelle se fonde l'ensemble du livre, attire l'attention sur la manière dont différents intervenants et différents intérêts peuvent concourir à soutenir ou entraver les efforts d'intégration.

Deux facteurs expliquent le regain d'intérêt pour la coopération sud-sud à la fin des années 80 et au début des années 90 : d'une part, l'impact du progrès technique sur les stratégies des multinationales en termes de concurrence et, d'autre part, la recherche de nouvelles stratégies de développement dans les pays du sud, accélérée par les difficultés économiques qu'ont connu la plupart de ces pays au cours des années 80. La conjonction de ces deux phénomènes nous donne l'occasion de reconsidérer la coopération fondée sur l'innovation technologique, dans les pays du sud et entre eux, ainsi qu'entre le nord et le sud.

Pour que ces efforts aboutissent, il faut prendre en compte les intérêts, les compétences et les stratégies des acteurs nationaux. Comme le soulignent les chapitres consacrés à l'intégration régionale dans les Caraïbes et en Amérique du sud (Mercosur), les organisations non gouvernementales, les syndicats de travailleurs et d'agriculteurs, les entreprises privées, les associations de consommateurs et les chercheurs ne participent généralement à ce processus que de manière sporadique, encore leur action reste-t-elle soumise à une tutelle institutionnelle. De fait, les modèles classiques de coopération sud-sud présentent souvent un caractère dissuasif pour des formes décentralisées de coopération régionale. Ces structures sont manifestement anachroniques dans un contexte économique mondial où la compétitivité dépend de plus en plus de l'évolution récente de pratiques d'organisation, qui impliquent des relations étroites entre les clients et les fournisseurs, une coopération entre les entreprises dans les activités de recherche, de développement, de production et de commercialisation, ainsi que des réseaux organisés entre les producteurs et les infrastructures scientifiques et techniques. Il est donc urgent d'innover en ce qui concerne les formes mêmes de l'intégration régionale et de la coopération sud-sud en général. Il faut notamment trouver une alternative à l'approche classique centrée sur l'État, qui intégrerait les intervenants de manière plus significative au processus de coopération régionale.

En outre, dès lors qu'on décide d'adopter une approche centrée sur les utilisateurs, il devient rapidement évident que la coopération sud-sud ne doit pas se limiter aux échanges. Les études regroupées dans ce document vont au-delà des questions relatives aux échanges et proposent un certain nombre d'orientations nouvelles pour la coopération sud-sud. Ces études commencent par une série d'observations sur l'importance croissante du savoir dans le processus de production et sur le rôle joué par l'innovation dans la concurrence internationale. Dans cette perspective, la modernisation et la compétitivité ne sont plus considérées uniquement comme moyen de passer de la production de matières premières à l'industrie manufacturière. Bien au contraire, les nouvelles technologies permettent aujourd'hui d'améliorer l'ensemble des activités économiques, et pas seulement les secteurs de pointe.

De plus, en favorisant l'innovation technologique, des «jeux à somme positive» sont envisageables, même entre concurrents. En Amérique latine, par exemple, la coopération entre les entreprises privées du secteur minier permet d'améliorer considérablement les connaissances de toutes les entreprises participantes. Dans l'ANASE, le statut de «triangles de croissance» donné à des régions frontalières renforce le rôle que peuvent jouer les investissements directs intra-régionaux dans le processus de développement.

Plus généralement, si l'on souhaite que la coopération renforce la capacité d'adaptation des pays en développement aux évolutions des préférences, des prix et des conditions de la concurrence sur le plan international, un rôle central doit être donné à la constitution de réseaux pour promouvoir l'innovation technologique. Même si ces relations doivent d'abord être créées à l'intérieur de chaque pays et si le renforcement des systèmes d'innovation nationaux est donc très important, des liens plus étroits doivent également être tissés entre les pays, et plus particulièrement à l'échelon régional. En effet, la proximité est un facteur important pour les liens entre producteurs et utilisateurs. De plus, la création de réseaux régionaux réduit les coûts de coordination très élevés qu'impliquent la commercialisation et les approvisionnements à l'échelle mondiale. De manière plus générale, des liens doivent également être créés entre les pays en développement, dans la mesure où ces pays sont souvent confrontés à des problèmes communs, par exemple en ce qui concerne la transformation des minerais, la mise au point de technologies non polluantes et l'agriculture. Enfin, de tels liens doivent également être noués avec les pays développés, notamment dans les secteurs en évolution rapide, comme l'électronique et les biotechnologies.

Par ailleurs, il est plus facile de mettre en œuvre des formes de coopération sud-sud dans les années 90 que par le passé, et ce pour deux raisons principales. Premièrement, les États et les autres acteurs sociaux et économiques des pays du sud reconnaissent la nécessité de mettre en commun leurs ressources. Deuxièmement, comme le montrent les articles de ce livre, le patrimoine technologique s'est accru dans les entreprises publiques et privées, ainsi que dans les instituts de recherche et les universités des pays d'Asie, d'Amérique latine et des Caraïbes ; ce phénomène concerne un grand nombre de secteurs dont les industries de base, l'électronique, les machines-outils, les pièces automobiles et les biotechnologies.

En Afrique, ce processus d'accumulation technologique se déroule à un rythme beaucoup plus lent. Or, il est indispensable d'encourager les entreprises africaines à résoudre leurs problèmes de restructuration tout en innovant, afin de garantir un développement durable sur le continent. Compte tenu des difficultés financières actuelles de l'Afrique, les transferts de technologies, bien que vitaux, ne peuvent répondre à tous ses besoins. En outre, il s'agit d'un processus coûteux qui nécessite des dépenses répétées pour l'importation de biens d'équipement et de biens intermédiaires, de compétences de gestion, de services de maintenance et de savoir-faire technique, dépenses que l'Afrique peut difficilement supporter à l'heure actuelle. Aussi, il est aujourd'hui impératif que les entreprises africaines renforcent leurs capacités à faire face à leurs propres difficultés et à venir à bout des blocages de la production.

Dans un environnement où les entreprises n'ont pas l'habitude de raisonner en termes de stratégie ou d'intégrer l'innovation à leurs stratégies de croissance, la recherche de solutions par l'innovation passe nécessairement par une dynamisation externe, ce qui est inconcevable sans ressources financières et techniques. Ces ressources peuvent — et doivent — provenir de programmes de développement et de recherche en coopération avec d'autres intervenants des pays concernés, notamment les fournisseurs, les universités, les bureaux d'études et de conseil et les organismes de recherche. Toutefois, peu de pays africains atteignent la masse critique requise pour qu'un système de promotion de l'innovation permette la résolution de leurs problèmes. La constitution de réseaux régionaux est donc nécessaire.

Les gouvernements africains admettent la nécessité de développer des programmes de formation pour promouvoir l'innovation. Ils s'efforcent également de mettre en place des politiques favorables à ce processus. Pour compléter de telles initiatives, il faut instituer un mécanisme régional afin, d'une part, d'encourager les entreprises à cerner les problèmes et à innover, et d'autre part, de canaliser les ressources locales pour soutenir cet effort. L'Afrique disposant de ressources financières limitées, ce mécanisme pourrait également jouer un rôle important pour garantir les coûts et les risques liés aux projets d'innovation. De telles initiatives ouvrent des perspectives nouvelles pour les donateurs, car elles jettent aussi les bases d'une coopération nord-sud dynamique.

Dans un contexte marqué par des progrès techniques importants et rapides, il faut rompre avec la théorie et les pratiques classiques concernant la coopération sud-sud et redéfinir ses méthodes et ses objectifs. Les exposés qui composent ce document plaident en faveur d'une vision plus large des aspects à traiter. Ils soulignent notamment le bien-fondé des modèles de coopération sud-sud basés sur l'innovation technologique et démontrent leur faisabilité par le biais de nombreux exemples de projets actuellement en cours entre entreprises, entre l'université et l'industrie, et entre les pouvoirs publics d'un pays à l'autre. Afin de soutenir ces initiatives, les États sont de plus en plus appelés à jouer un rôle directeur clé, alors même que la contribution et la participation active du secteur privé se renforcent. Il faut mettre en œuvre des politiques de promotion de l'innovation et de diffusion des technologies, créer un cadre institutionnel et juridique permettant et encourageant réellement la coopération sous forme de réseaux, et susciter le développement des infrastructures de télécommunications, de transports, de recherche et de formation pour soutenir cette coopération en réseaux. Des solutions novatrices doivent également être trouvées pour financer l'innovation. Il reste donc beaucoup à faire pour relancer la coopération sud-sud, mais on peut y parvenir à condition de concentrer les efforts sur l'organisation de réseaux encourageant l'innovation.

Chapter 1

REGIONAL CO-OPERATION AND THE NEW LOGIC OF INTERNATIONAL COMPETITION

Lynn K. Mytelka[1]

Au cours des années 80, marquées par l'importance croissante de la connaissance dans le processus de production et par la mondialisation de la concurrence, l'innovation est apparue comme l'élément clé de la compétitivité et comme un lien vital de la relation entre les échanges et le développement. Ce dernier n'est désormais plus conçu comme une fin en soi mais au contraire comme un processus continu de mutations, d'adaptations et d'ajustements. Les entreprises comme les pouvoirs publics ont adopté de nouvelles stratégies pour faire face à ces évolutions. De plus, l'échec des modèles traditionnels d'intégration régionale, qui étaient monnaie courante dans les pays en développement au cours de la période 1960-1980 et s'appuyaient sur les échanges ou sur une spécialisation de la production, a permis de recentrer l'attention sur des modèles de coopération sud-sud et nord-sud fondés sur l'innovation technologique. Ce chapitre décrit ces transformations, analyse les échecs des précédents projets d'intégration et pose les bases théoriques de cette nouvelle approche de la coopération sud-sud.

During the 1980s as production became more knowledge-intensive and competition globalised, innovation emerged as the key to competitiveness and a vital link in the relationship of trade to development, where the latter is conceived not as a finite end, but as a continuous process of transformation, adaptation and adjustment. Both firms and states have adopted new strategies in response to these changes. In addition, the failure of 'exchange driven' and 'production specialisation' models of regional integration common among developing countries in the 1960s through the 1980s has helped to refocus attention on innovation-driven models of co-operation both within and across countries in the South, and between the North and South. This chapter describes these underlying changes, analyses the failures of earlier integration schemes and lays the theoretical basis for this new approach to South-South co-operation.

1. Introduction

During the 1970s, a decline in productivity growth and a rise in inflation and unemployment characterised many advanced industrial countries. These changes, coupled with the growth of manufactured exports from a small number of developing countries and heightened competition from Japanese industry, where the organisation of production differed from established practice in much of Europe and North America, stimulated the emergence of new forms of global competition and collaboration in which technology played a central role[2].

More broadly still, the uncertainty generated by these changes signalled the need for continuous economic, social and political transformation in both advanced industrial and industrialising countries. In so doing it exposed the inadequacies of earlier conceptions of development as a finite process, bounded by the experience of a small number of European and North

American countries. It also put into question the notion of development as "a cumulative unidirectional process, a sort of race along a fixed track, where catching-up is merely a question of relative speed" (Perez [1988], 85). Although speed remains a factor in the ability of developing countries to build the indigenous industrial and technological capacities needed for structural competitiveness[3], as Carlota Perez ([1988], 85) has pointed out, "history is full of examples of how successful overtaking has mainly been based on running in a new direction".

With rare exceptions, however, developing countries have accepted the position of "norm" takers — ineffectually seeking to imitate product, process and organisational norms developed in other times and other contexts[4]. This has been particularly evident in the pursuit of regional integration, a concept mainly employed to describe preferential trading arrangements between neighbouring countries[5]. From the late 1950s to the early 1970s, many such arrangements were established among developing countries that sought to overcome perceived constraints on the local development of manufacturing processes and organisational norms originally developed in the advanced industrial countries. Few of those arrangements, however, achieved their development goals.

Section one of this chapter describes the "exchange driven" and "production specialisation" models of regional integration that dominated during that period. Section two points to the anomalies generated by conventional explanations which attribute the failure of regional integration among developing countries to government policies and a lack of political will. It then goes beyond these approaches to focus on the zero-sum conditions within regional integration schemes that resulted from a unique historical conjuncture in which the import substituting industrialisation strategies of states and the internationalisation strategies of multinational corporations (MNCs) combined to undermine both the rationale for and the gains from regional integration.

The late 1980s and early 1990s witnessed the creation of a MERCOSUR between Argentina, Brazil, Paraguay and Uruguay, the liberalisation of trade within the Andean Pact, the development of intra-regional investment ties within ASEAN, the growth of networking in research and development among firms and institutes within and across regions in the South, the adoption of policies to promote human resource development in SADCC and the exploration of proposals for a Great China economic zone linking China, Taiwan, Hong Kong and Macao. This resurgence of interest in south-south co-operation owes much to a new conjuncture that has been shaped by two developments: the impact of changes in technology on the competitive strategies of MNCs and the search for new development strategies in the south prompted by the difficult economic situation in which most of these countries found themselves during the 1980s. Sections three and four of this chapter explore these changes.

Alone such changes do not provide a sufficiently compelling reason for south-south co-operation nor do they ensure its success once initiated. In section five it will be argued, however, that there are commonalities and complementarities in the south today, new advantages to be derived from proximity and opportunities to develop dynamic comparative advantage in traditional and non-traditional products through south-south co-operation that, taken together and in the context of these changes, lay the basis for new forms of south-south co-operation. The emergence of technological capabilities[6] and new dynamic actors[7] in the south, moreover, have created a broader support base for such initiatives than had existed in the past. In contrast to the narrow pay-off matrices and zero-sum conditions that contributed to destructive conflicts over the distribution of gains in earlier integration schemes, therefore, "innovation driven" models of south-south co-operation that build upon these new capabilities, actors and interests have the potential to generate positive sum outcomes for all of the participants.

To argue, as this chapter does, that new forms of co-operation among regions and countries in the south are both necessary and feasible is not to set the process of south-south co-operation in opposition to the maintenance or the further expansion of north-south linkages as others have done (Amin [1977], [1985]; Havrylyshyn & Wolf [1981]; Lall [1984]). Rather, as section five concludes and other chapters in this volume illustrate, changes in technology and in the mode of competition globally are altering the parameters within which such options must be evaluated and undermining the validity of dichotomising between what, in some instances, have become complementary relationships.

2. Traditional regional integration schemes in the 1960s and 1970s

From the late 1950s through to the early 1970s and with an eye on developments in the European Communities, a number of free trade areas, customs unions and common markets[8] were established among countries in Africa, Latin America, Asia and the Caribbean. Each of these initiatives was motivated by a conception of development as a particular form of industrialisation, the mass production of standardized goods[9] and an identification of small market size as a principal obstacle to the achievement of this goal. All placed intra-regional trade liberalisation at the centre of their integration process.

Theoretically, exchange based regional integration schemes were only to be recommended if they contributed to global welfare by shifting trade away from a higher to a lower cost supplier or what Jacob Viner (1950) called trade creation. However, in developing countries, industrial capacity was limited, for the most part, to the manufacture of finished goods. It lacked economies of scale and was highly dependent upon extra-regional imports for machinery, intermediate goods and other immaterial inputs[10]. This made trade diversion, that is, a shift from a lower cost to a higher cost supplier, a more likely outcome. Were regional integration schemes among developing countries, therefore, to be rejected?

Clearly all such judgements depend upon the alternatives. For Viner the question was posed in terms of increases in world welfare. But, as Gehrels, Meade, Lipsey and Johnson argued[11], assessing the utility of customs unions solely from the perspective of global welfare, ignores the distribution of world-wide income. Taking the latter into consideration, and adjusting for the special characteristics of developing countries, as Massell, Mikesell and Balassa suggested, made it possible to envisage a new set of criteria against which customs unions could be assessed.

First, one could set the gains or losses in global welfare against those accruing to individual countries. Thus accepting for the moment that trade diversion may be detrimental from the perspective of world economic efficiency, it may nevertheless be true that trade diversion would contribute to raising real income in the developing countries concerned, if, as a result of a widening of the market through integration, local industry mobilised unused resources and widened the export base. Kahnert, Richards, Stoutjesdijk and Thomopoulos ([1969], 17), moreover, hypothesised that "in the absence of an integration scheme, trade destroying import substitution might have taken place on the national level" with even more limited effects on growth and specialisation then a customs union would have had, even one involving trade diversion.

Alternatively, one could compare long term gains and losses from integration to those obtaining in the short term. This is particularly relevant for developing countries whose "prime concern" is "to change their factor endowment, their incomes and their consumption patterns" (Stewart: 1984). If the enlarged market opens new opportunities for profitable investment in industry, makes possible greater economies of scale, accelerates technological learning or increases domestic competition thereby improving efficiency, then present costs from trade diversion would be offset by future benefits both for the developing countries and for the world as a whole in the longer term.

It could, of course, be argued, as Mikesell ([1963], 192) pointed out, that the

"gains would be greater if each country broadened its export base by expanding its export of both primary commodities and of manufactures to the rest of the world. This is a good doctrine to preach, but it has not happened and it is not likely to happen until developing countries learn to trade and compete with one another on a regional basis."

If, as many acknowledged at the time, the lack of complementarity, imperfect information and low levels of industrialisation in developing countries foreshadowed a very limited range of opportunities for trade expansion within these regional integration schemes (Balassa & Stoutjesdijk [1975]; Kahnert *et al.* [1969]; and Robson [1972], then it could be anticipated that the process of regional integration would require a sustained effort over the long term. Yet, as we shall see below, such a commitment would not be forthcoming.

During the 1960s, however, these theoretical arguments served to justify a policy of import substitution on a regional scale, advocated by influential economists such as Raul Prebisch (1964), then head of the United Nations Economic Commission for Latin America and William Demas (1965) a founder of the Caribbean Free Trade Association (CARIFTA) and later Secretary-General of the Caribbean Community (CARICOM)[12]. Only the Association of South-East Asian Nations (ASEAN) established in 1967 and the Southern African Development Co-ordination Conference (SADCC) founded in 1980 adopted a functional approach based on political considerations. Elsewhere import substitution on a regional scale was widely embraced and given effect through one of two types of integration schemes: an "exchange driven" model and a "production specialisation" model.

Exchange driven models were based on considerations of static comparative advantage and allocative efficiency derived from traditional neo-classical economics. They involved the adoption of comprehensive external protection and to achieve balance, a step by step negotiated reduction of tariffs and other barriers to trade amongst the member countries. Narrowly focused on intra-regional trade as the driving force, exchange driven models of south-south co-operation rarely required more than light organisational structures. Advancement of the integration process thus depended upon initiatives undertaken by national governments. The Latin American Free Trade Area (LAFTA), established in 1960 and transformed into the Latin American Integration Association (ALADI) in 1981, the Customs and Economic Union of Central Africa (UDEAC) as it was initially set up in 1964, the Customs Union of West African States (UDEAO) and its 1970 successor, the West African Economic Community (CEAO), the Caribbean Free Trade Area (CARIFTA) of 1967, the Economic Community of West African States (ECOWAS) established in 1975 and the Preferential Trade Area for Eastern and Southern African States (PTA) formed in 1982, typify this model. The MERCOSUR whose origins date to the signing of an agreement between Argentina and Brazil in 1986, shares some of these characteristics[13].

In contrast to the "exchange driven" model, the "production specialisation" model of regional integration took as its point of departure the low level of existing industrial capacity and the tendency for production to be concentrated in the manufacture of similar finished goods. To enhance complementarity, correct in advance for intra-regional imbalances that were likely to generate polarisation effects in the course of trade liberalisation (Myrdal [1957]), stimulate economies of scale and create an internal dynamic based on increased domestic linkages, regional planning and regulatory mechanisms were proposed. These last were designed to channel foreign investment towards designated sectors and to ensure an effective transfer of technology transfer. In this model, high levels of external protection were accompanied by a selective reduction in intra-regional trade barriers, although free trade remained the ultimate goal. To accommodate the wide range of activities envisaged by this model, a more substantial institutional structure with some degree of initiative was envisaged. The Central American Common Market (CACM), established in 1961, was an early version, of the "production specialisation" model. UDEAC's second treaty signed in 1974 and the Caribbean Community (CARICOM) which replaced CARIFTA in 1973 moved these two organisations closer to this model. But it was the Andean Group, founded in 1969, that during its first decade represented the apogee of the "production specialisation" model of regional integration.

By the late 1970s, integration groupings of both the "exchange driven" and the "production specialisation" type were stagnating or had collapsed[14]. Trade liberalisation had drawn to a halt or been postponed in LAFTA, CARICOM, UDEAC and the Andean Group. Members had withdrawn — Chad from UDEAC, Chile from the Andean Group — or failed to honour regional commitments, Honduras in the CACM, Nigeria in ECOWAS.

To overcome these problems, old treaties were renegotiated, as in UDEAC and new ones signed, as in CARICOM, ALADI and the CEAO. Where smaller groupings had failed to stimulate intra-regional trade, larger associations, such as the PTA and ECOWAS were put into place. Yet, as the figures in Table 1 illustrate, in all but the CACM and to a lesser extent LAFTA/ALADI, the share of intra-regional trade in total trade remained exceedingly low during the 1960s and 1970s. Worse still, much of the increase in the value of trade during the 1970s simply reflected an acceleration of world inflation in dollar terms and in particular the substantial increase in the price of oil.

3. The failure of traditional regional integration schemes

Much of the conventional literature lays the failure of regional integration schemes at government's doorstep. Two variants of this approach can be found. One emphasizes conflicts over the costs and benefits of integration that bedevil these organisations and the lack of political will to resolve them[15]. Yet this deals only with the most proximate cause of the crisis in regional integration and fails to explain why regional integration generated distributional conflicts that proved so intractable, a point to which we will return later in this section. The other stresses the economic inefficiencies generated by government policy. Thus Mansoor and Inotai write:

"The performance of various groupings formed to promote regional economic integration... has been generally negative because of the inefficient resource allocation that has resulted from the emphasis on regional import substitution and attempts at regional industrial planning... further inefficiencies arose from the politically motivated allocation of investment." (Mansoor & Inotai [1990], 2).

But such arguments cannot explain the exceedingly low level of intra-regional trade in "exchange driven" integration schemes where little or no effort at industrial planning was undertaken and a movement towards trade liberalisation was under way. The Treaty of Montevideo which established LAFTA in 1960 is a case in point. It contained no provisions for regional investment or industrial policy. Instead, it concentrated almost exclusively on economic expansion through balanced trade. To accelerate the process of trade liberalisation, LAFTA relied on the private sector. Thus firms in the member countries were encouraged to propose "complementarity agreements" which allocated specialisations and reduced tariffs for a select number of products. Few of them did, however, giving rise to questions about the strategy of firms during this period. Over the next decade with only a small number of complementarity agreements signed, intra-regional trade flows remained low (Table 1).

Table 1. **Intra-Regional Trade**
(value millions US dollars and share of total trade)

	1960	1970	1980	1985	1986	1987	1988	1989	1990[1]
LAFTA/ALADI									
value	564	1 290	10 217	6 779	8 220	8 574	9 514	10 865	11 670
% of total	7.7	10.2	13.5	9.6	11.5	10.9	10.3	10.5	10.4
CACM									
value	33	299	2 242	671	620	428	539	632	664
% of total	7.5	26.8	22.0	15.9	17.7	13.2	13.9	15.3	15.8
ANDEAN GROUP									
value	25	109	955	672	622	1 028	1 011	961	1 192
% of total	0.7	2.3	3.5	3.1	3.3	5.5	5.3	3.8	3.8
CARIFTA/ CARICOM									
value	27	73	354	340	300	165	187	270	273
% of total	4.5	7.3	6.4	5.5	5.4	3.0	3.6	4.5	4.0
PTA									
value	—	—	482[2]	333	372	487	506	582	na
% of total			9.0	7.5	6.9	8.9	8.0	6.2	na
UDEAC									
amount	3	33	200	50	84	103	119	193	180
% of total	1.6	3.4	4.1	2.0	3.0	3.2	3.7	4.1	4.3
CEAO									
amount	6	73[3]	398[2]	297	300	416	488	500	575
% of total	2.0	9.1	10.1	7.1	6.5	8.4	10.3	11.1	12.1
ECOWAS									
amount	17	—	944[2]	1 018	970	1 132	1 294	1 167	1 280
% of total	3.1	3.8	4.6	5.2	7.5	7.8	9.2	7.8	6.1
SADCC[5]									
amount	—	—	258[2]	200	226	308	304	—	—
% of total			5.7	4.9	5.9	6.1	5.0		
ASEAN									
amount	839	860[4]	11 918	12 713	11 096	14 691	18 277	21 610	26 290
% of total	21.7	14.7	17.8	17.9	16.7	17.6	17.4	17.7	18.5

1. Estimates.
2. 1981.
3. Trade liberalisation began with unprocessed products in 1974 and in selected manufactured goods in 1979. Overall trade was growing relatively slowly during the late 1970s. This figure is for 1976.
4. ASEAN's preferential trading agreement was signed in 1976. In that year its intra-regional trade was $3 619 million. Expansion of intra-ASEAN trade was closely associated initially with changes in the price of petroleum which dominated this trade.
5. SADCC did not involve trade liberalisation during this period.
Sources: For 1960, 1970 and 1980, UNCTAD (1983), p. 132. For 1985-90, UNCTAD (1992) Review of major developments in the area of economic co-operation among developing countries TD/B/CN.3/3, 4th December, p. 27.

UDEAC presents a similar anomaly. In 1959, shortly before independence was granted to the Central African Republic (CAR), Chad, Congo and Gabon — the four members of the former Fédération de l'Afrique Equatoriale Française — they signed a convention creating an equatorial African customs union (UDE). In 1964, the UDE, upon the inclusion of

Cameroon, was transformed into UDEAC. Unlike most integration schemes among developing countries, UDEAC had a common central bank and a common currency directly convertible into French francs. To stimulate industrialisation and intra-regional trade, goods manufactured in UDEAC and sold in more than one of its Member states were subject to a single tax (taxe unique) levied to the exclusion of all import duties and taxes on goods used in the manufacturing process and all domestic taxation on the finished product[16]. The rate of the single tax, fixed by the UDEAC Finance Ministers sitting as the Management Committee, was set lower than that of the customs duties which would otherwise have applied to manufactured goods traded among these countries. Just prior to independence, moreover, all five countries had adopted similar investment codes. These codes guaranteed foreign investors against the risks of nationalisation and non-transferability of profits and capital and granted to foreign firms exemptions from the payment of corporate profits taxes, property taxes and import duties on raw materials, intermediates and capital goods used in the production process. In theory, the existence of a wider market and a liberal investment climate were expected to stimulate production and trade in the region. By 1970, however, intra-regional trade accounted for only 3.4 per cent of total trade (Table 1). Despite a shift towards a more production specialisation driven model of regional integration in the 1974 Treaty revisions, intra-regional trade has not significantly increased.

Indeed, among "exchange driven" integration schemes, only the CEAO is heralded by Mansoor and Inotai as a "...relatively successful union...", where success is measured in terms of the growth in intra-regional trade as a share of total trade (Mansoor & Inotai [1990], 14). Looking behind these aggregate statistics, however, what distinguishes the CEAO from other "exchange driven" integration schemes is the extent to which these small gains in trade were achieved by reinforcing traditional patterns of specialisation in production and exchange, notably "the flow of labour from the poor Sahelian countries (such as Burkina Faso and Mali) to the richer coastal countries (such as Côte d'Ivoire and Senegal) [and the supply of]... goods in the opposite direction." (World Bank [1989], 149)[17].

Efforts within the CEAO to move beyond this singularly undynamic division of labour, however, have been harshly criticised by those who see the heavy hand of government as a principal factor in the failure of integration in Africa and Latin America. Thus the Berg report, in its arguments against ECA proposals to develop basic industries such as chemicals, energy and steel on a regional basis, singled out the West African Cement Mill, CIMAO, a joint venture between the Côte d'Ivoire, Togo and Benin, for particular criticism (ARB [1988], 10). In effect, three years after CIMAO began operations in 1980, production costs were still almost twice those projected in the feasibility study and clinker imported from CIMAO and sold in the Côte d'Ivoire cost 74 per cent more than clinker imported from Europe.

A closer look at CIMAO suggests that this large price differential was due less to the inefficiencies of African governments than to management errors on the part of the project's financier, the World Bank, and its promoter, a private French company whose tasks included preparing the feasibility study, managing the project and operating the plant[18]. Three factors, in particular, lend credence to this argument. First, the feasibility study was based on exaggerated expectations of rising world clinker prices, despite the existence of excess capacity in Europe which, coupled with the tendency of firms in the industry to export only a small percentage of their output and to use marginal pricing for these exports, had kept clinker prices low. This drove international clinker prices down and made it more difficult, though not impossible, for plants in relatively higher cost regions like Francophone West Africa to compete. Second, to offset this difficult competitive environment special attention could have been paid to economies in the choice of plant size and process technology and to the training needed to bring costs down after start up. This was not done. Instead, the plant was overdesigned by its engineers who chose expensive technical solutions. Investment costs thus rose as did the firm's debt. Third, errors in the choice of technique compounded these problems. Use of a coal-fired plant, for example, had been suggested at the outset but rejected in favour of electricity produced from imported fuel oil. The low sulphur content of this fuel, the use of siliceous sand in the production process and the power shortages caused by a scarcity of foreign exchange with which to purchase fuel oil, resulted in the need for frequent rebricking. This in turn led to low capacity utilisation and higher unit costs. When in 1984 the CIMAO plant was shut down, it truncated an industrialisation venture that had generated backward linkages to the extraction and processing of local raw materials, contributed to the building of indigenous technological capabilities in a small least developed country (Togo) and promoted intra-regional trade.

In the "production specialisation" models of regional integration where one would expect the hypothesised relationship between government inspired industrial planning efforts, inefficient production and weak intra-regional trade performance to be strongest, there are also anomalies. Thus the Central American Common Market experienced a boom in regional trade precisely when, through the Integration Industries Regime, efforts where being made to allocate industry within the region. Two things, moreover, stand out about that trade. First, it was accompanied by increases in trade with third parties, in keeping with the "outward growth strategy traditionally associated with the development model" of the five member countries (Rosenthal [1985], 146-8). Second, the pattern of specialisation that emerged in intra-regional trade was based on the import and export of close substitutes — "products differentiated not by primary inputs but rather by style, quality, appearance or `brand image'" (Willmore [1974], 122). It thus resembled the kind of intra-industry trade which had constituted the driving force in world trade since the 1950s.

Clearly the failures of CIMAO cannot be attributed solely to the actions of national governments who, though they were its shareholders, were not its principal decision makers. Nor can governments alone be held responsible for the slow growth of intra-regional trade in LAFTA and UDEAC unless they are also to be credited with the initial gains in trade experienced by the CACM.

As these examples suggest, there is a need to go beyond the narrow focus on government policies that has come to typify conventional explanations for the failure of integration among developing countries and to set government policies in a broader context. The analysis that follows, therefore, focuses upon the dynamic interplay between the state and other actors that led to the adoption of a regional import substituting industrialisation strategy and, it will be argued, contributed heavily to its subsequent failure. It begins by stressing the strategic orientation that states and firms brought to the integration process and it points to changes in the international context that reinforced the negative dynamics flowing from this relationship.

3.1 The development strategies of states

By the 1950s, following in the footsteps of Adam Smith, Karl Marx and Max Weber, development theorists and practitioners had embraced both the notion of industrialisation as progress and the characterisation of industrialisation as the mass production of standardized manufactured goods with all that this implied for the organisation of labour — the regrouping of workers into factories, Taylorisation, increased mechanisation and with its particular requirements for capital, mass markets and sophisticated managerial know-how[19]. Today, with changing forms of international competition giving rise to pressures for flexibility in the manufacturing process and widespread use of inter-firm collaboration in research and development (R&D), production and marketing to achieve critical mass, the dominance of the mass production model is under challenge and new competitive conditions are creating both the opportunity and the need for new forms of industrialisation and of south-south co-operation.

At the time, however, little attention was paid to alternatives that had emerged in Japan, northern Italy and parts of Germany (Brusco [1982], Marshall [1890], Piore & Sable [1984]). As a result, the choice of products for local manufacture was largely determined by the existing range of imports, itself sustained by a pattern of income distribution that favoured the developing countries' small urban population. Mass production of an import reproducing kind thus went hand in hand with what has become known as "industrialisation by invitation," that is, efforts to induce capital, engineering, management and marketing skills associated with the production of these goods, to flow from north to south and to ensure a domestic market for the goods that these imported factors could produce. To that end, tariff, exchange rate, wage, price, tax and credit policies were combined to create an environment within which investments in manufacturing would be profitable for foreign capital.

Integration extended these national policies of import substituting industrialisation to the regional market, reproducing a development strategy that paid little attention to those sectors of the economy in which the vast bulk of the population was employed — agricultural and mining. It thus did little to alter the pattern of income distribution and hence the structure of demand within that market. By insulating the regional market from the world economy, moreover, a disincentive to extra-regional exports of manufactured goods was created. By their very design, traditional models of regional integration, thus, narrowed the pay off matrix for individual member countries to the gains and losses from intra-regional trade. When such gains were not immediately forthcoming or, because of inequalities in wealth and levels of industrialisation at the outset, were distributed unevenly (Myrdal [1957]; Mytelka [1973a], [1979], [1984]), most integration schemes among developing countries took on the form of zero sum games[20].

Poorer or less industrialised Member countries now found themselves in the position of subsidising the inefficient industry of their neighbours and doing so without adequate compensation since the relative wealth of their partners did not permit extensive income transfers. In UDEAC, this led to delays in making annual payments to the Solidarity Fund, set up for this purpose, to protectionist pressures from domestic firms for higher levels and wider variations in the single tax rates on products traded intra-regionally and ultimately to the creation of a "taxe complémentaire" that further segmented the regional market. (Mytelka [1984], 133-137; Hugon [1990a], 33). Interestingly enough protectionist pressures came not only from firms in the less industrialised member-states, Chad and the Central African Republic, but also from those in its most industrialised member-state, Cameroon, whose "single tax" firms accounted for an average of 66 per cent of total intra-regional exports during the 1970s. Attempts to allocate new industries more equitably among the member-states as part of a renegotiated UDEAC treaty were thwarted by the practice of competitive import-substitution which persisted throughout the 1980s (Bela [1990]). Similar stories can be told about ECOWAS, the CACM and the now defunct East African Federation.

3.2 The strategies of firms

The drive to industrialise within national boundaries and thus to maintain and even to increase market segmentation within regional integration schemes, was exacerbated by the role played by key economic actors during this period. Few local entrepreneurs had the size or credibility to penetrate neighbouring markets and the high cost, import-intensive manufacturing sector was itself an impediment to market integration. These actors, therefore, could not provide the support base needed for trade liberalisation.

Foreign-owned firms which, by virtue of their size and scanning capabilities, might have been expected to be among the first to engage in intra-regional trade, failed to rationalise to take advantage of the larger market whether in UDEAC, LAFTA, the Andean Group or CARICOM. A number of factors explain this.

For the most part multinational corporations engaged in manufacturing were purveyors of mature technologies and standardized goods to the developing world in this period. Their principal objective was market penetration rather than overseas production for export (Caves [1982], 253-257). Thus the share of US majority-owned foreign affiliates in developing country exports of manufactures was only 4 per cent in 1966, rising to 6 per cent in 1977 and 7.5 per cent in 1983 (UNCTC [1988], 161).

Within regional integration schemes, market segmentation was the rule. Thus of the 513 US subsidiaries operating in the Andean Group in the late 1960s, "362 had affiliates in at least one other member country and 258 in at least two" (Vaitsos [1978], 732). A similar pattern existed in the UDEAC where some 75 per cent of the "single tax" firms were foreign owned and duplicate production existed in nearly all major manufactured goods — beer, textiles, cigarettes, shoes, industrial gases and aluminium products (Mytelka [1984], 141-142).

On the export-side, this meant that a large proportion of the licensing agreements between parent firms and their subsidiaries or between licensor and nationally owned local firms contained clauses prohibiting exports. This reduced both the incentive to rationalise production (Oxman & Sagasti [1972], Vaitsos [1975], Odle [1979], Grynspan [1982]) and to innovate (Mytelka [1979], 113-137).

On the import-side, regional markets were also of little importance to these subsidiaries since the bulk of their imports came from their parent firm or from other firms in the home country. In a survey of 304 foreign manufacturing firms in six Latin American countries in the mid-1970s, Constantine Vaitsos, for example, found that on average, 56 per cent of their imports came from the parent firm's country of origin and only 8.5 per cent of their imports came from other Latin American countries (Vaitsos [1978], 36). National firms that licensed tended to have a similar pattern of imports (Mytelka [1979], [1984], [1991]; Newfarmer [1985]). This created the opportunity for transfer pricing.

Parallel production by these MNCs was thus a powerful disincentive to intra-regional trade since maintenance of duplicate plants was preferred if intra-firm transfer pricing and higher retail prices compensated for production inefficiencies resulting from continued market segmentation. The point was well put by the top manager of a large foreign automobile subsidiary in Mexico, when he said:

"It might make a lot of economic sense in the long run to merge our operations in the region and to introduce some degree of intra-firm specialisation in respect to final products, parts and accessories, instead of working for a dozen individual markets absorbing annually from 10 000 to 130 000 finished cars each. But such operations would involve a complete overhaul of our productive or assembling facilities within the area with the outlay of perhaps several hundred million dollars... There is little reason for us to engage in such gigantic financial and technological operations as long as we can get fairly satisfactory profits from actual investments with small additional capital outlays and technological adjustments geared to the slow growth of individual domestic markets and the demands of both consumer and individual governments" (quoted in Vaitsos [1978], 732-733).

The results of this strategy were evident quite early on in "exchange driven" integration schemes such as LAFTA. Thus, as Sidney Dell (1966) predicted and the United Nations Economic Commission for Latin America (1977) confirmed, complementarity agreements became little more than government approved arrangements for parcelling out the Latin American market among a set of foreign firms that dominated in the pharmaceutical, electronics, office machines and automobile sectors of LAFTA's big three member-states — Argentina, Brazil and Mexico. Once this created sufficient room for export expansion, the Caracas Protocol of 1969 postponed the establishment of a free-trade area from 1973 to 1980 and slowed down the pace of tariff cuts (Mytelka [1979], 19).

In "production specialisation" integration schemes, such as the Andean Group, where efforts were made to avoid duplication, build indigenous technological capabilities through regional industrial programming and strengthen the locally-owned private sector through provisions for divestment and regulations concerning technology transfer, the situation was more complex but the outcome with regard to trade was remarkably similar. Decision 57 establishing the Andean Metalworking Programme of 1972, for example, illustrates the way in which overtime, the interaction between states and firms reduced the gains from regional planning, exacerbated conflicts over the costs and benefits of regional integration and led ultimately to the reimposition of barriers to intra-regional trade[21].

To speed the process of negotiation and avoid conflict with public and foreign private sector actors[22], the Andean metalworking programme excluded both the main input industry, steel and key user industries such as automobiles, shipbuilding and electronics where rationalisation, cost reduction and quality improvements would have substantially increased the gains from regional programming. For the less industrialised countries, notably Bolivia, this was especially problematic since, without forging capabilities, little could be done other than assemble the tri-cone petroleum drill bits assigned to it under this programme. Thus the design of this first regional industrial programme narrowed the pay-off matrix by reducing the value added and the linkage and technology capacity building effects expected from regional industrial programming.

Subsequently, because the Andean private sector was not involved in the planning process after its second meeting in 1969, it was difficult to find domestic entrepreneurs willing to undertake feasibility studies and invest in the manufacture of products assigned under this programme. This also disproportionately affected less industrialised member countries where some of the more technologically sophisticated products were slated for production in the belief that this would spur industrialisation through a process of technological leapfrogging[23]. Bolivia, for example, had considerable difficulty attracting foreign investment into the metalworking sector since few investors had confidence in the durability of the Andean Group, and most products assigned to that country were viable only if 80 per cent of the output was exported.

With progress slow in implementing the metalworking programme in the less industrialised countries, opportunities for competitive "national" import substitution opened. These were exploited by the large multinational enterprises which alone had the requisite technology. In the case of tri-cone petroleum drill bits, two of the four companies that possessed the technology, Hughes Tool and Smith International, were unwilling to take up the assignment in Bolivia. Smith was in the process of establishing a subsidiary in the Venezuelan market where demand for this product was high. As Venezuela was not then a member of the Andean Group, this did not appear to conflict with the aims of Decision 57. In late 1971, however, anxious to preempt the Peruvian market for petroleum drill bits from its rival Dresser Industries, Smith began negotiations with the Peruvian state to form a joint venture in which that firm would hold 85 per cent of the capital. Shut out of the Venezuelan and Peruvian markets, Dresser agreed to take up the assignment of tri-cone drill bits in Bolivia, but it invested little, assembled but did not manufacture, and made no effort at all to explore markets for its product in the Andean region. Not long after it initiated production in Bolivia, Dresser complained to the Bolivian government that Smith's production of petroleum drill bits in Peru violated Decision 57. Within another year Dresser put additional pressure on the Bolivian government by "temporarily" closing its plant. The Bolivian government was thus driven to seek redress through the Andean Group's chief administrative body, the Junta del Acuerdo de Cartagena. One solution under discussion in 1977 was the creation of two "Andean Multinational" firms, that is joint ventures involving all three foreign firms and the three states concerned. Although ultimately unsuccessful, by using the Bolivian state as its proxy, Dresser Industries, frustrated in its efforts to enter the more lucrative Peruvian and Venezuelan market, thus had hopes of still realising that objective.

Over the next ten years, implementation of this and other industrial programmes was bedevilled by similar conflicts and a series of provisional measures restricting trade were adopted by various of the member countries. In 1987, the Protocol of Quito explicitly recognised the existence of a system of administered trade within the region.

In sum, both "exchange driven" and "production-specialisation" models of regional integration failed not because of government policies or political will but because their very design did not take into account the interests, capabilities and strategies of all key actors in the integration process. Neither model, therefore, anticipated the potentially negative dynamics that flowed from the interaction between a development strategy in the member countries based on national import substitution and an internationalisation strategy on the part of foreign manufacturing firms aimed at securing a foothold in the national markets of developing countries. Combined, these strategies favoured market segmentation over integration and protected regional markets over liberalisation. During the 1960s and 1970s this correspondence, in conjunction with the limited possibilities for rapid gains in trade from integration, generated a zero-sum situation marked by protectionist pressures, by conflicts over the costs and benefits of regional integration and by political efforts to manipulate macro and micro-economic levers to resolve them. What mainstream theorists identify as the causes of failure in traditional regional integration schemes are thus reflections of a deeper structural relationship — among key actors within industrial countries, and between countries' national strategies of import substitution and multinational firms' international strategies of securing positions in national markets — whose change is central to the future viability of regional integration among developing countries.

3.3 North-south ties and traditional models of regional integration

By the early 1970s traditional forms of regional integration had reached their limits and were in decline. Fresh from the early success of OPEC, advocates of "collective self-reliance", "selective delinking" and "selective dissociation" (Addo [1984], Amin [1985], Annerstedt [1980], Dos Santos [1973], Frank [1978], Hveem [1983], Senghaas [1980]) thus shifted their focus from south-south co-operation to a more thorough-going change in north-south relations. From an enlightened self-interest perspective, the Brandt Commission report also favoured a restructuring of north-south relations.

From 1974 when the United Nations General Assembly in its Sixth Special Session formally issued the Declaration and Programme of Action on the Establishment of a New International Economic Order (NIEO) through the mid-1980s, much of the Third World's attention was diverted to north-south negotiations over codes of conduct for multinational corporations (MNCs), the Multifibre Agreement governing north-south trade in textile and clothing products, the UNCTAD Common Fund and Integrated Commodities Programme and an impressive number of north-south meetings, including the north-south Dialogue, UNCSTED and EEC-ACP negotiations within the context of the Lome Convention.

Most of these NIEO-related negotiations took static comparative advantage as their point of departure. Securing price stability for raw materials and market access for labour-intensive manufactured exports were thus their principal goals. Despite the mildness of these reform initiatives, remarkably little was achieved. Indeed, global trends were increasingly less favourable to the developing countries.

Beginning in the mid-1970s, for example, the share of global foreign direct investment (FDI) flows going to the developing countries had stagnated or was in decline. Over the 1980s, the situation of most developing countries deteriorated further. Thus if we exclude the Caribbean offshore tax havens, "the developing countries' share of global FDI inflows fell from roughly 20 per cent in 1980-84 to not much more than 10 per cent in 1985-89" (Oman [1993], 4). Although in current dollar terms FDI flows to the developing countries rose towards the end of the decade, in constant 1988 prices and exchange rates, total FDI flows to the developing countries declined from $11 517 million in 1980-84 to $10 211 million in 1985-89 (Table 2). Moreover, the Asian share in FDI flows to the developing countries rose over this period from 43.6 per cent to 59.1 per cent while the Latin American and African shares declined from 41.3 to 30.1 per cent and from 15.4 to 7.9 per cent respectively. Thus those regions most engaged in the process of integration were receiving a decreasing share of an ever smaller pool of foreign direct investment going to the developing world during the 1980s. Yet during that decade, worldwide flows of FDI were growing "at the unprecedented average annual rate of about 29 per cent, reaching close to $200 billion by the end of the decade... This value corresponds to three to four times the average yearly flow of FDI during the decade 1975-84 [while the]... rate of growth [is]... three to five times that of world exports... [and] ten times that of world output." (Oman [1993], 3). This figures point to the extent to which much of the developing world was being marginalised from what had become the dominant flows in the world economy during the 1980s.

Table 2. **Foreign Direct Investment flows from OECD to developing countries** (US $ million in constant 1988 prices and exchange rates)

	1980	1981	1982	1983	1984
Total DC	8 360	18 080	11 083	7 735	12 325
Latin America	7 274	6 069	4 073	1 498	4 893
Asia	3 179	8 954	2 550	4 283	6 164
Africa	1 931	2 491	3 209	1 097	109
	1985	1986	1987	1988	1989
Total DC	3 387	5 984	12 409	13 129	16 144
Latin America	1 290	1 461	2 983	3 957	5 696
Asia	844	2 741	9 073	7 945	9 556
Africa	1 089	749	474	934	761

Source: Derived from data supplied by the OECD Development Co-operation Directorate.

Foreign aid policies did not alleviate this problem since they rarely supported joint ventures between integration partners (Mytelka [1973b]). Both the decline in FDI and the role of foreign aid thus intensified the competitive pressure on developing countries during the 1970s and 1980s, reinforcing the zero-sum nature of regional integration processes between them.

As the global economic crisis of the 1970s and 80s worsened, slower growth in demand for the commodity exports of the south, high unemployment and inflation followed by monetary policies that dramatically pushed interest rates up, compounded the already severe balance of payments problems of many developing countries and reduced their ability to service, what over the lavish years of petrodollar recycling, had become heavy debt burdens[24]. In the search for immediate solutions to their balance of payments problems, decision makers in developing countries abandoned efforts at longer term planning. Under pressure from international lenders, policies were designed to attract new investors at almost any cost while the adoption of market liberalisation and austerity measures further cut into demand, reducing the ability of the domestic market to serve as a stimulus for new investment and innovation[25]. Within a weakening domestic market, the success of structural adjustment policies such as these thus hinged critically upon north-south ties, particularly those permitting market access, debt rescheduling and injections of fresh capital through direct foreign investment or, in the case of the least developed countries, concessional aid. Total net flows of financial resources from DAC countries to the developing world, however, declined radically in this period (Table 3). For many of the poorest countries, therefore, real resource transfer which the United Nations measures as the difference between the current account balance and net interest payments, deflated by the import unit value index, "... declined by more than a quarter in the 1980s, from about $26 per capita (or 12 per cent of GDP) in 1980-82 to about $19 per capita (or 9 per cent of GDP) in 1985-87. This has created a serious budget problem in the LDCs where there is a close link between these flows and the budgetary position..." (UNCTAD [1990c], p. 4).

Table 3. **Total net flow of financial resources from DAC countries to developing countries and multilateral agencies**
(at 1990 prices and exchange rates) in millions of US dollars

1970	1975	1980	1989	1990
70 043	110 961	119 034	94 022	68 365

Source: OECD, Development Co-operation 1992 Report, p. A-32.

The result was a widening gap between the advanced industrial countries, a small number of predominantly Asian newly industrialised economies and the remaining countries in the developing world. Over the years 1970-87, for example, Gross Domestic Product (GDP), grew by a record 40 per cent in the developed market economy countries (DMECs), by 26.7 per cent in all developing countries (DCs) including the Dynamic Asian Economies but by only 8.6 per cent in the 42 countries classified as least developed (UNCTAD [1990c], A-3). In the period 1980-87, average annual growth rates of per capita real GDP declined by 0.2 per cent in the developing countries and rose by 2.1 per cent in the Developed Market Economy Countries. Population which grew by 2.3 per cent in the DCs and 0.6 per cent in the DMECs do not explain this gap in growth (UNCTAD [1990c], A-3, A-4). What this meant in practice was a radical decline in purchasing power as gross national income per capita in sub-Saharan Africa fell from its 1980 peak of just under $600 to below its 1967 low of $450. Latin American purchasing power also contracted though not as severely in this period (South Commission Report [1990], 63).

In the context of significantly diminished net financial resource flows into the developing countries, structural adjustment programmes (SAPs) thus contributed to a reduction in intra-regional trade in the CACM, UDEAC, ECOWAS and the Andean Group. In part this resulted from the imposition of austerity measures that weakened domestic markets in the south. But it was also due to the attempt to restore debt servicing capacity as quickly as possible by cutting imports and refocusing exports on northern markets (UNCTAD [1989], 5-7). For the developing countries the timing was particularly poor as a persistently high commodity concentration of merchandise exports increased the vulnerability of these economies to price fluctuations for their exports. The dramatic decline in intra-regional trade within CARICOM during the 1980s largely can be explained in these terms (Intal [1990], 160-182). Similarly in the CACM, "... when commodity prices collapsed in the late 1970s and foreign financing became unavailable in the early 1980s, the earlier gains were reversed" (Mansoor & Inotai [1990], 5). In the Andean Group"... a general feeling of discouragement and... a real reduction in trade... made the sense of crisis more acute" (Salgado [1985], 175).

In addition, as Philippe Hugon pointed out with reference to Africa, SAPs tended to destabilise the domestic economic environment because, in practice, despite their attempt at optimal sequencing, for both political and economic reasons

> only some of the measures are applied and these only partially, while others are subsequently reversed.... (This gives rise to a context of instability and uncertainty in which economic actors focus on the short term, with the result being a decline in imports of machinery and equipment, and in overall investment, despite structural adjustment loans, and a tendency to move towards commercial, even speculative activities at the expense of production (Hugon [1990b], 10).

The tendency towards speculative activities is particularly destructive for production and trade within a given region, when countries devalue at different times[26]. The devaluation of the naira in Nigeria, for example, produced a dramatic increase in transit trade with negative effects on both domestic producers and government revenues in neighbouring Niger and Cameroon (Hugon [1990b], 12-15).

From a dynamic perspective, the adjustment pattern of the 1980s was far from desirable. With import capacity low, capital goods imports declined in both Africa and Latin America (UNCTAD [1991], 4). This was particularly devastating for African countries where import stability is positively correlated with economic growth rates (Helleiner [1986]). In the Caribbean, investment per worker measured in 1980 US dollars fell to a level below that in 1970 (Thomas [1991], 67). Never a strong point in the developing countries, transportation infrastructure degenerated and the new transportation and communications linkages required for competitiveness[27] in the 1990s were not constructed.

With the radical fall in prices for petroleum, sugar, sisal, copper and other major developing country exports and the contraction of demand in the advanced industrial countries for these products, merchandise trade of the developing world, with the exception of south and south east Asia, fell in value from a high of US$421 billion in 1980 to a low of US$222 billion in 1986, rising to only $301 billion by 1989. The gap between the NIEs and other developing countries widened dramatically in this period as Figure 1 illustrates. Even in the Caribbean where the United States launched its Caribbean Basin Initiative, trade between these countries and the United States declined from US$9.2 billion in 1983 to US $6.2 billion in 1987.

US imports from CBI beneficiaries which represented 3.4 per cent of its total imports in 1983 was more than halved — down to 1.5 per cent. At the same time, US direct investment in the CBI countries, which was 1.6 per cent of its total overseas investments in 1980, had been reduced to 1.1 per cent by 1983 and to 0.9 per cent by 1985 (Thomas [1991], 59).

Figure 1. **Share of developing countries in world merchandise trade 1980 - 1990 (in value)**

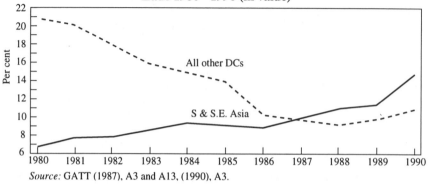

Source: GATT (1987), A3 and A13, (1990), A3.

As crisis conditions deepened in much of the south, trade, aid and investment links to the north thus narrowed pay-off matrices within these traditional integration schemes still further. This contributed to pressures for a reconceptualisation of both the development process in the south and of the role that intra-regional trade might play in it.

4. Towards an innovation driven model of south-south co-operation: rethinking regional trade

Initially efforts aimed at a rethinking of regional trade were confronted with a large body of literature in the north that laid emphasis on export-oriented development as the engine of growth where the exports in question were those directed towards the north (Little *et al.* [1970]; Havrylyshyn & Wolf [1981]; Havrylyshyn & Alikhani [1982]). A delegitimisation of south-south ties flowed from these arguments since the logic of the Heckscher-Ohlin-Samuelson approach predicted greater gains from trade amongst economies with different factor endowments and in products having different factor proportions.

This view of the direction and gains from trade, however, has been challenged by a number of developments in the real world of international trade and competition. Since World War II, for example, trade has increased much faster between the advanced industrial nations which have similar factor endowments and in goods whose production involves similar factor proportions. (Stewart [1976]; Michalet [1976], [1982]; Krugman [1988]; Porter [1990]). Newer theories of international trade have attempted to deal with this change and in so doing are providing a rather different basis from which to assess the role that south-south trade and co-operation might play in shifting competitive advantage.

In these theories, differentiated products are understood to embody the factor proportions of their market of origin and they tend to be traded to countries with similar preferences where such preferences are primarily determined by income levels (Linder [1961], Lancaster [1971], [1980]; Krugman [1980] and Helpman & Krugman [1989])[28]. In theory, Frances Stewart argues, because of different factor costs and lower income levels countries in the South would not buy such products at all. When they do, because income inequalities enable the rich to develop preferences similar to those in the North or because there are no alternative products available, then "the combination of characteristics offered gives less welfare than a specifically designed South-product would" (Stewart [1984]). "The main lesson for the South from this theory "she concludes," is that potentially the South could enjoy preference-similarity trade with other South economies but only if the South innovates and produces its own products " (Stewart [1984]).

As Willmore (1974) noted in the case of intra-regional trade in the Central American Common Market, Dahlman and Sercovich (1984) have illustrated in the case of selected exports from Argentina, Brazil, India, Korea and Mexico and Fransman (1984), has pointed out with regard to the export of machinery from Hong Kong, welfare generating trade of this sort has emerged in south-south trade. The higher skill-intensity of south-south manufactured exports when compared to south-north trade (Amsden [1980]), moreover, suggests that there are opportunities for learning by doing and for innovation to be realised from such trade[29]. In contrast to Havrylyshyn and Wolf's findings (1981) that south-south trade did not intensify during the period 1963-77 and that northern markets, therefore, continue to provide the key to the South's export growth, Sanjaya Lall has demonstrated that the share of south manufactured exports absorbed by the south over the period 1973-81 rose from 28.5 to 37.3 per cent (Lall [1984], 290). Combined with the characteristics of this trade, this suggests that south markets could once again play an important role in south development particularly where, as we shall see in Section 5, competitiveness involves a continuous process of adjustment that requires a capacity to solve problems and to innovate. Moreover, as Amsden (1989), Westphal, Rhee & Kim (1984), and others have emphasized "because the gains from capability building are unpredictable and dynamic (and so are unlikely to be fully financed by capital markets, especially in developing countries), and also because there may be strong externalities (from technical and skill spillovers) and complementarities with other investments, which markets cannot take into account "(Lall [1989], 13), there is a case to be made for selective protection as part of a larger intervention package. It is precisely this margin that regional integration could afford industry in the south.

Linked to the dynamics of intra-industry trade is the growth of intra-firm trade that has reinforced it (Helleiner [1981]; UNCTC [1988]). This, too, has relevance for south-south co-operation. With the growing internalisation of international trade, "in many industries competitive advantage seems to be determined neither by underlying national characteristics, nor by the static advantages of large-scale production, but rather by the knowledge generated by firms through R&D and experience" (Krugman [1988], 8). In attracting foreign partners, therefore, externalities have become central. Taking the point further, Porter argues

> "that competition is dynamic and evolving... In a static view of competition, a nation's factors of production are fixed. Firms deploy them in industries where they will produce the greatest return. In actual competition, the essential character is innovation and change. Instead of being limited to passively shifting resources to where the returns are greatest, the real issue is how firms increase the returns available through new products and process. Instead of simply maximising within fixed constraints, the question is how firms can gain a competitive edge from changing the constraints" (Porter [1990], 20-21).

Many of the insights contained in the new theories of international trade and industrial organisation influenced a reconceptualisation of the role of regional trade in south-south co-operation. Two summit meetings held in 1989, one in Latin America among Andean Group presidents and the other in Africa among SADCC heads of state and the more recent summit of ASEAN leaders reflect this new discourse. Collectively, they suggest a convergence of views in the South on the need for a new "innovation driven" model of south-

south co-operation in which trade is based less on static comparative advantage than on innovation and acquired competitive advantages.

At their Galapagos summit, for example, the Andean Heads of State endorsed a new approach to south-south co-operation in which regional integration was no longer to be viewed as an alternative to north-south ties but rather as a means to change the production patterns in Latin American and Caribbean countries by "strengthening the countries' insertion into the international economy" (Intal [1990], 107; ECLAC [1990], 158). Abandoning traditional import substitution strategies, the Andean Group thus embraced a new "openness to the world, based fundamentally upon its own enlarged market and an increased capacity for technological research, product development and negotiation..." (Intal [1990], 107).

This new approach to integration represents a major reversal in earlier thinking and brings the strategies of states in the Andean region more into line with the kind of dynamic to which Porter alluded above. The ability to redefine the function of regional trade from one of stimulating national import substitution to one of promoting international trade competitiveness, had the added advantage of transforming a closed regional market, within which gains for some were losses for others, into a lightly protected economic space within which firms can hone their ability to compete in the world economy. It thus lifted the zero-sum conditions that characterised earlier models of integration. This, in turn, precipitated a rapid reversal in trade policy within the region. After more than a decade of increasing protectionism, less than three years after the elaboration of its new *Diseno Estrategico para la Orientacion del Grupo Andino*, the Andean Group had moved towards complete liberalisation of intra-regional trade.

Like the Andean Group, domestic markets in the SADCC and ASEAN countries were highly protected during the 1970s and 1980s. Unlike the Andean Group in neither SADCC nor ASEAN was trade liberalisation even nominally a goal. This was due to two main factors. First, both were conceived primarily as functional groupings serving a political purpose. Second, external conditions were a major determinant in shaping the economic content given to their particular form of co-operation. SADCC, for example, brought together nine independent countries in southern Africa as a bulwark against the apartheid regime in South Africa. This goal was given functional content through a series of projects aimed at progressively reducing the region's dependence on South African transportation, communications and energy resources. ASEAN, which links six Asian countries, was initially conceived as part of a cold war regional security arrangement and had limited economic content. Because of their low wages and trained workforce, moreover, the ASEAN countries attracted export oriented investment from Japan, Europe and North America as domestic production in these countries lost competitiveness during the 1970s and 1980s. One consequence of this export orientation was the ability to maintain high levels of domestic market protection which, however, limited the growth of intra-regional trade[30].

In both SADCC and ASEAN, as in the Andean Group, the earlier disinterest in promoting intra-regional trade, however, is changing. Thus at their Harare summit in 1989 the Presidents of SADCC recommended a move towards the creation of a single regional market within which freer movement of capital, goods, services and people would take place. This, they argued,

"is essential, not fundamentally because a quantitative increase in the existing type of intra-regional trade is likely to yield major returns. This trade is, in the short run at least, likely to remain modest. Rather, the creation of a single regional market is important because it can provide an environment conducive to new types of investment in more productive and competitive industries, oriented towards supplying the entire regional market; or producing manufactured goods for export, or in industries processing or benefiting products destined for export to the entire region". (SADCC [1991], 24).

In the case of ASEAN, as Goh Chok Tong, prime minister of Singapore remarked, the creation of larger markets in Europe and North America "are defining the new operating environment for ASEAN... Unless ASEAN can match the other regions both as a base for investments as well as a market for their products, investments by multinational companies are likely to flow away from our part of the world." (International Herald Tribune: 28 January, 1992). At the Singapore summit in January 1992, the ASEAN member states thus signed a free trade agreement. Although the treaty stipulates that trade would be liberalised over a 15 year period, both Indonesia's industry minister and its foreign minister suggested that a full free trade area could be brought about more quickly. Like the Andean countries, this represented an important reversal for Indonesia which previously had been the most reluctant of the ASEAN countries to lower trade barriers.

Following the logic outlined in section three of this chapter, south-south co-operation would be both necessary and feasible only if domestic and international change altered the correspondence between those strategic objectives of states and firms that had earlier given rise to the negative dynamics of the "exchange driven" and the "production specialisation" models of regional integration. Insofar as governments are concerned, it is evident that a process of rethinking south-south co-operation is currently under way. This involves a reconceptualisation of the function of regional trade so that stress is placed on the links between innovation and trade and between intra-regional trade and international competitiveness.

Two factors seem to have influenced this radical shift in the strategies of states particularly in Latin America and to a lesser extent in Africa. These are, the negative impact of indebtedness and structural adjustment programmes on their domestic development potential, and the marginalisation from major flows of finance, trade and technology that had sustained national import substitution strategies in these countries during the 1960s and early 1970s. As in Africa and Latin America, external factors have had a major impact on decision making within ASEAN where concern about the potential for marginalisation resulting from regional initiatives undertaken elsewhere appears to have catalysed a move towards trade liberalisation within the region. But what can be said about the strategies of firms?

Over the 1970s and 1980s a number of factors have also altered the strategic options available to economic and other actors whose participation is essential if an innovation-driven process of south-south co-operation is to be launched and sustained. Three changes in particular bear mentioning here: (i) the increased knowledge-intensity of production, where knowledge is understood to include research and development, design, engineering, maintenance, management and marketing; (ii) the growing uncertainty resulting from the process of continuous innovation and from intensified international competition that has rendered planning by firms more difficult and (iii) and the need for flexibility to which these changes have given rise[31].

5. A changing role for the south in the new innovation based strategies of multinational corporations

The increased knowledge intensity of production is reflected as much in agriculture, forestry, fishing and mining[32] as in the manufacturing sector and within that sector across industries from textiles to telecommunications. This can be seen from OECD data on the number of scientists and engineers engaged in R&D and on the rising share of R&D in Gross Domestic Product and in manufacturing value added, especially in countries such as Japan and Germany where strategies of international competitiveness based on technological innovation and diffusion are being pursued.

Even more revealing, however, are data for the manufacturing sector that show that R&D expenditure has grown at three times the rate of tangible investment over the past two decades. Going beyond R&D, non-material investments in design, engineering, management, maintenance, and marketing capabilities, for training and for the purchase of software, patents and trademarks have been growing rapidly both as a share in the GDP of the major advanced industrial countries over the past ten (OECD [1991], 177-215) and in the balance sheets of individual corporations. Traditional calculations of productivity growth do not take such changes into consideration and thus do not provide us with an accurate picture of the transformations in the system of production currently under way. Yet understanding these changes is crucial in the development of new approaches to south-south co-operation.

As production became more knowledge-intensive, the pace of innovation began to quicken. Product life cycles in dynamic knowledge-intensive industries, for example, began to shorten as the very nature of the products, their uses and the manufacturing techniques required for their production differed substantially from one product generation to the next. With shortened product life cycles, firms were obliged to spend increasing amounts on R&D to remain at the technological frontier in their industry. To amortize these costs, companies required wider markets. Competition thus globalised but as it did, earlier strategies aimed at securing national markets for products with high research and development costs through tariffs, domestic procurement policies and intellectual property rights came under increasing pressure.

The uncertainties generated by the rising costs and risks in knowledge-intensive industries were exacerbated by the segmentation of demand growing out of the economic crisis of the 1970s and early 1980s and by the slow pace of productivity growth that began in the late 1960s and led to a loss of competitiveness by firms in many of the advanced industrial countries (Aglietta [1976]; Baily & Chakrabarti [1988]). With slower growth in domestic purchasing power in the advanced industrial countries and crisis conditions in much of the Third World persisting into the present, markets that depended upon the sale of consumer durables became saturated. These changes undermined the strong linear relationship that had been established between a rapidly growing market, defined in terms of a range of goods, a heavily equipped manufacturing base that permitted economies of scale, and a set of R&D activities primarily oriented toward product differentiation. During the 1950s, this relationship had given rise to a pattern of competition characterised by the setting of a big firm on a big market and the building of an oligopolistic position within it. In this way, market shares were stabilised and oligopoly rents were secured. Within such a competitive framework, new technology was developed primarily to penetrate a previously identified market.

Beginning in the late 1970s, shifts in demand in the context of the growing potential for rapid technological change, undermined this type of competitive behaviour. New products, combining both new manufacturing processes and new goods, stimulated the rise of new industries and brought new entrants into existing industries (including the arrival of the newly industrialising economies), thus shaking the position of established leaders while market segmentation placed new pressures on the model of mass consumption based on the manufacture of standardized goods. With markets under pressure, vertical integration linking the market to manufacturing and to R&D activities, once the formula for growth, now threatened to impair the ability of firms to adapt to change.

By the 1980s, it was evident that traditional product-based oligopolies were no longer as effective in reducing uncertainty when the very conception of what might constitute the market for a new technology or product was unclear and when major discontinuities in formerly incremental technological trajectories and the erosion of frontiers between industries made it difficult to identify from where, geographically or sectorially, new competitors might emerge. The rapid pace of innovation, heightened uncertainty and the mosaic-like structure of segmented demand gave rise to a need for flexibility. At the same time, however, rising costs for R&D and wider sales networks required critical mass.

To achieve the twin goals of critical mass and uncertainty reduction without adding to the inertia of the firm, new competitive strategies have been developed alongside more traditional practices such as mergers and acquisitions. Three of these have direct consequences for innovation in the south and for south-south co-operation.

First, these strategies involve a shift away from competition solely or even primarily based on price and towards the development of value-based competitive advantages through innovation, quality and close ties to clients and suppliers. For the developing countries, this puts a premium on the revival of markets in the south and the creation of a denser network of user-producer linkages within and across those markets than existed in the past[33]. Because of the continuous ability of immaterial inputs to erode the static comparative advantage of countries in all products and the rapidity with which such changes are coming about, at no time has strengthening the knowledge base in developing countries assumed such critical importance.

Second, these new strategies seek to exploit the systems properties of new technologies and of new products by combining generic technologies, often from hitherto distinct disciplines, using networks as a means to access knowledge resources from as wide a range of disciplines and geographical areas as possible. In contrast to earlier assumptions concerning the importance of firm size for R&D, critical mass can thus be conceived quite differently today, notably in terms of the size of the "system" needed to acquire the knowledge rather than the size of the firm itself. This applies to activities all along the value chain from conception to the market, and along with the need for flexibility, it has led a number of firms to decentralise R&D to overseas subsidiaries and to engage in a growing number of strategic partnerships in research and development linking firms to each other and to research institutions. Where the scientific and engineering infrastructure exists, some MNCs have also decentralised research and especially product development activities to subsidiaries in developing countries, and have entered into collaborative activities with research institutions and universities there.

Strategic partnerships, however, merit special attention because they differ from traditional forms of linkage between firms, such as joint ventures, licensing or sub-contracting arrangements, by their focus on joint knowledge production and sharing as opposed to a one-way transfer of knowledge and by their contractual nature. Even when such partnerships include an equity arrangement, the intent most often is not to control the partner firm, but to help finance its share of the joint R&D[34]. These changes in firm strategies have opened new windows of opportunity for innovation in the developing countries and they are laying the basis for the kind of north-south linkages that could complement south-south ties.

Third, in both the advanced industrial and the developing countries, MNCs have been turning their subsidiaries into independent profit centres. This encourages local firms to specialise, to source inputs from least cost suppliers and to export; thus reversing the incentives that had shaped their behaviour in the 1960s and 1970s. In addition, international subcontracting, particularly of the Original Equipment Manufacturer (OEM) variety[35], has led to a more effective transfer of technology to local firms, thus strengthening their ability to innovate in the future. Because of balance of payments constraints and a shortage of foreign exchange, there are, moreover, greater pressures on local firms to absorb technology in order to reduce costs, to source locally and to export. Local firms are in many cases, through licensing over the years and through subcontracting activities, better able to absorb new technology and to adjust to changes in competitive conditions than in the 1960s. This is particularly notable in Asia[36] and in a number of Latin American countries. For these firms trade liberation within a region now plays a more positive role in stimulating innovation for competitiveness.

6. Innovation and competitiveness through south-south co-operation

Earlier models of regional integration among developing countries, it was argued, had been grafted upon a set of national import substitution policies that coincided with MNC market segmentation strategies. As we saw in the preceding sections, debt problems and technology requirements in the former, and the need for continuous innovation and the globalisation of competition for the latter, are eroding these positions and the correspondence between them.

These changes provide the basis for elaborating a quite different rationale for south-south co-operation, one that moves away from trade as the mechanism whereby specialisation and economies of scale can develop, despite the small size of domestic markets, and towards a more dynamic perspective — one in which knowledge, linkages and flexible structure are fundamental building blocks. Unlike earlier "exchange" or "production" driven models of regional integration, the new model of south-south co-operation can thus be described as "innovation" driven, where innovation implies the introduction of a product or a process that is new to that firm or that country whether or not it is new to the world, and where it is understood to be a key element in the competitiveness of firms and by extension, of nations. The value of south-south co-operation in the present conjuncture thus increases the more it contributes to the launching of a virtuous circle of learning and technological change. The basic features of an "innovation" driven model of south-south co-operation are sketched out in Figure 2.

In this new model of south-south co-operation, trade is not an end in itself but rather a reflection of and a stimulus to a process of continuous innovation. The focus, in innovation driven models of south-south co-operation thus will be:

i) less on specific firms and products and more on building the underlying knowledge capabilities that facilitate the creation of imaginative solutions to bottlenecks in production or in the distribution of goods and services;

ii) less on scale economies and more on creating opportunities for the flexible combination of knowledge assets and the development of economies of scope in production particularly wherever networking is feasible and

iii) less on allocative efficiency and more on learning, on x-efficiency and on other forms of increasing returns under conditions of uncertainty.

South-south co-operation of this sort, moreover, will require the maintenance and in some instances even the strengthening of north-south ties, since much of the technology upon which such innovations will be based initially will come from the north. To the extent that such ties provide an effective transfer of technology, therefore, north-south co-operation could provide the externalities that make gains from south-south co-operation more likely. For this to take place, however, such ties must be complemented by increased attention to "the learning and dissemination of internationally available know-how; a possibility which has not been sufficiently exploited by the region in the past" (ECLAC [1990], 14). It is here that local, national and regional states have a crucial role to play in shaping an incentive system that stimulates the demand for innovation and catalyses the linkage between users

Figure 2. **Models of South-South co-operation**

Type	Model I Exchange Driven	Model II Production Specialisation	Model III Innovation Driven
driving force	intra-regional trade	industrial specialisation	user demand
rationale	allocative efficiency with some economies of scale made possible by the enlarged market, post-hoc compensation offered to less-developed member states, trade based on static comparative advantage	creation of an internal dynamic through increased domestic linkages made possible by regional planning, with the latter also serving to correct for intra-regional imbalances that lead to conflicts over the distribution of costs & benefits	induce shifts in comparative advantage and the creation of competitive advantages using networks to create economies of scale and scope in R&D, production & marketing, to spread the costs & risks of innovation & to enhance the conditions for a dynamic process of problem-solving & apprenticeship
degree of openness	comprehensive external protection with gradual intra-regional trade liberalisation	high levels of external protection, selective reduction in intra-regional trade barriers	selective external protection with an emphasis on phasing-in competition
role of FDI	non-descrimination between foreign & nationally owned companies	regional regulation of foreign investment & technology transfer	shift in attention from ownership of the producer to value added in production
organisational structure	light, formal structure with narrow objectives	heavy formal structure, very comprehensive macro-economic harmonisation & planning objectives	a combination of formal and informal structures with the latter involving projects having a narrower focus but linked to broader long-term "process" objectives

and suppliers located in the domestic productive system and in the local science and technology infrastructure.

Innovation driven models of south-south co-operation are thus a complement to the strengthening of domestic markets and national systems of production and innovation. By contributing to the building of structural competitiveness, moreover, they create the capacity for continuous adjustment to changes in tastes, prices and competitive conditions that is central to the competitiveness of firms in today's global economy. This is partly due to the new role that intra-regional trade will play in enhancing the potential for change, by enabling the firm to move more rapidly down its learning curve and by generating the kind of competitive environment in which mastery of imported technology is stimulated and problem solving leads to innovation in quality, design and cost reduction. In addition, however, innovation driven models of south-south co-operation provide a springboard for a more dynamic insertion into the world economy because they offer a reconceptualisation of the process of development which abandons the earlier view of development as diversification out of agriculture and raw materials production and into manufacturing in favour of an approach that stresses the application of knowledge to all sectors. This opens opportunities for building upon the natural resource base and it points to the importance of strengthening the human resource component of the development process so as to be able to innovate by adopting technology to new uses.

From this perspective, a user oriented approach to south-south co-operation is likely to prove more effective than earlier top down models of regional integration for at least two reasons. First, because it involves key actors in the planning process. This ensures that the design for co-operation corresponds more closely to the needs of those who must carry it out. It thus creates a commitment to south-south co-operation that was missing from traditional models of regional integration. Second, it is a more flexible process, one through which opportunities can be spotted faster and translated more quickly into action.

While there is no single organisational form that such models of south-south co-operation must take, the ability of innovation based models to generate positive sum games requires, as Rosenthal observed with regard to integration more generally

> "a high degree of flexibility in the application of regional commitments, and levels of consultation which permit countries to take account of what regional co-operation has to offer in achieving their national development goals. It also requires regional institutions that can identify projects and programmes susceptible to co-operation and that can promote their implementation" (Rosenthal [1984], 156).

Innovation driven models of south-south co-operation, however, do not require a proliferation of new formal institutions. To the contrary, where, as in Africa, there are more than 200 organisations of which more than 160 are inter-governmental, streamlining is clearly needed. Not, however, as the World Bank believes, because fewer institutions is part of the package of "less government involvement in the economy", but because flexibility requires a reduction in the inertia represented by formal institutions. It implies the development of networks through which coordination can take place. A strategy such as this does not get government out but puts government in, where it is needed, closer to the economic agents who are the users of its services, playing the role of catalyst in the process of developing locally suitable alternatives. Institution-building in an innovation driven model thus consists in the creation of coordinating structures which, through scanning and networking, build knowledge about knowledge assets, facilitate international technology brokerage functions, provide financing for technology acquisition and trade, and ensure channels for participation, reflection, consensus-building and the mobilisation of support.

Networking has still other advantages for cash-strapped governments such as those in Africa, since it reduces infrastructural costs that were a factor in the collapse of many of Africa's agricultural research and early warning systems such as locust control and remote sensing facilities. In the past, as Elliot Berg has noted, conflicts over the costs and benefits of such institutions arose because "... countries in which the centre is headquartered or has a testing centre usually benefit the most. Testing is done by regional scientists at the centre and thus released varieties are more likely to best match host country conditions. Moreover, close ties are built with the host country scientists, and it becomes easier to dovetail regional and national research programs" (Berg [1988], 40). Decentralising to smaller centres and linking them through networks, as envisaged in an innovation driven model of south-south co-operation, both increases the direct applicability of the research to the local environment and it transforms these ventures into positive sum games for all participants[37].

If the 1980s were recognised as the lost development decade in much of the south, the publication of ECLAC's study *Changing Production Patterns with Social Equity* and the South Commission's report, *The Challenge to the South* make it clear that the discourse in the south has shifted towards the need to build for the future. Science and technology, the development of skills, the creation of financing mechanisms for investment and trade, all feature prominently in both reports. What distinguishes the South Commission's report from early attempts to lay a conceptual basis for a development strategy, however, is its basic underlying philosophy that the South needs to develop its own vision, rely more on itself than it has in the past, and consciously promote the "acceptance of south-south co-operation as a strategic objective" (South Commission [1990], 158). In contrast to the World Bank's view that donors can contribute to south-south co-operation, notably in Africa, by "funding regional structural adjustment programs" (World Bank [1989], 162), the role of donors is seen as complementary to South designed initiatives in the *South Report*. The *South Report* thus takes a small step away from the traditional role of the South as "norm takers". By refocusing the debate on south-south co-operation in this fashion, it is evident that there is much that developing countries can do for themselves; and indeed to build commitment to the process, the ground work for co-operation can only be laid by those who will be its participants.

Notes

1. I would like to thank Colin Bradford, Havelock Brewster, Ernst Haas, Charles Oman, Carlota Perez and Peter Robson for their helpful comments on earlier drafts of this chapter.

2. These include, *inter alia*, changes in the content of sub-contracting and supplier-client relationships, the development of strategic partnering activity, notably in R&D, and the emergence of technology-based oligopolies. For a detailed discussion see the Introduction and Chapter 1 in Mytelka (1991), Ernst & O'Connor (1989) and OECD (1991), Chapter 3.

3. Going beyond traditional definitions of international competitiveness based on export performance, the concept of structural competitiveness (OECD [1991], Chapter 9) emphasizes the way in which structural characteristics of a domestic economy or a particular local industry influence the performance of firms.

4. For a detailed discussion of "norm-taking" in the design of development models in Africa see Mytelka (1989). Among late industrialisers, Japan is the classic example of "running in a new direction".

5. A process which some have argued might over time lead to the harmonisation of macroeconomic policies and ultimately to political union (Balassa [1961]; Haas [1958], [1964]).

6. Several of the chapters in this volume, for example, point to the emergence of research and development capacity, technical expertise and production know-how in electronics (Ernst), in the exploration and processing of minerals (Warhurst) and in biotechnology for agriculture (Thomas).

7. As the chapters by Lim and Chudnovsky reveal, small and medium sized nationally-owned enterprises, multinational corporations, and senior researchers in universities and research institutes are among the actors promoting new south-south co-operation initiatives.

8. Free trade areas involving the lowering of tariff and non-tariff barriers between the member states. Customs unions add to the free trade area a common external tariff. Common markets widen the scope of co-operation beyond the trade sphere and involve free factor movements, common monetary policy as well as fiscal harmonisation. For a review of these definitions see Balassa (1961).

9. See Piore and Sabel (1984) for a discussion of this model in the context of the advanced industrial countries and Mytelka (1989) for an analysis of the negative impact of its application in the African context.

10. Immaterial inputs include disembodied technology such as process know-how, maintenance, management and marketing.

11. Selections from many of these authors can be found in Robson (1971). The debates themselves are well summarised in Kahnert *et al.* (1969), Balassa (1961), Diouf (1984), Ethier and Horn (1984), and de Melo, Panagariya and Rodrik (1992).

12. Under Prebisch, the UN Economic Commission for Latin America heavily influenced the formation of the Latin American Free Trade Association (LAFTA) in 1960 and the Central American Common Market (CACM) in 1960, preparing the background documents upon which these organisations were founded. CARIFTA was founded in 1967 and replaced by the Treaty of Chaguaramas creating CARICOM in 1973.

13. For a complete list of all contemporary integration schemes see UNCTAD (1990a).

14. Among the groupings to collapse were the Regional Co-operation for Development set up in 1964 by Iran, Pakistan and Turkey, the East African Community which revamped the colonial Federation between Tanzania, Kenya and Uganda and the Arab Common Market created in January 1965.

15. Both political scientists and economists have focused on this issue. See, for example, Axline (1977), Mazzeo (1984), Mytelka (1973a), UNCTAD (1973).

16. The single tax also enabled the member-states to recover a certain percentage of the revenues it otherwise would have earned through tariffs imposed on third party imports. This was particularly important as over 50 per cent of total government revenues in the UDEAC countries during the 1960s came from import and export taxes.

17. Put more graphically, given the structure of production in West Africa and the elasticities of demand for agricultural commodities, "... could one really expect a growth of trade in groundnuts between Senegal, Mali, Niger and Upper Volta... (or) the constitution of a Customs Union... (to) induce an increase in trade of coffee for groundnuts between the Ivory Coast and Senegal..." (Diouf [1984], pp. 35-6).

18. Material for this case study is drawn from the World Bank, Project Performance Audit Report CIMAO Regional Clinker Project (Operations Evaluation Department, Report No. 7328, 23 June 1988, IBRD, Washington, D.C.) and République de Côte d'Ivoire, DGCTX, Plan National de Transport, Monographie sectorielle ciment (avril 1988).

19. This and the following paragraph are based upon arguments advanced in Mytelka (1989), particularly pages 77-88.

20. As Myrdal argued "if things were left to market forces... industrial production, commerce, banking, insurance, shipping and, indeed, almost all those economic activities which in a developing economy tend to give a bigger than average return... would cluster in certain localities and regions, leaving the rest of the country more or less in a backwater" (Myrdal [1957], 26). The availability of externalities adds to the problem of polarisation. See also Dell (1963), pp. 238-243.

21. This and the following paragraphs are drawn from Mytelka (1979), pp. 141-167.

22. In this it differed from the European Economic Community, which launched its integration process through the creation of an iron and steel community. In the Andean Group, the steel sector was excluded because the heavy capital investments it required would have necessitated further public-sector funding and Christian democratic governments of the late 1960s preferred a sector in which private national capital could participate. Both experts and government delegates negotiating the Andean Metalworking Programme were also disinclined to tackle the rationalisation of production in the automobile, shipbuilding and electronics industries where duplicate production was already widespread. The result was a narrower focus on the machinery and tools industries, particularly those related to mining, food processing, textiles and aircraft.

23. While leapfrogging has worked under some circumstances in the diffusion of sophisticated technology (see Antonnelli [1991]), there have been serious problems in leapfrogging in production (Bhalla & James [1988], Ernst & O'Connor [1989] & Mytelka [1991a]).

24. In this connection it is important to remember that "the cost of developing countries' borrowing in world capital markets is largely determined by the financial policies of the industrial countries, since there is a close relationship between domestic interest rates in industrial countries and the rate at which banks lend to developing countries. Furthermore, since a high proportion of developing country debt is denominated in US dollars, an appreciation of the dollar increases the value of debt and debt service payments in terms of the currencies of other industrial countries." It should also be noted that a number of institutional changes "... in the domestic banking systems of the industrial countries lowered the risk on deposit liabilities of the money-centre banks, which enabled the major banks to become the largest recipients of international loanable funds. Furthermore, financial innovations — notably the growth of syndicated loans and the increased use of cross-default clauses, together with the greater use of variable interest rate loans — reduced perceived levels of risk in lending to developing country borrowers, resulting in a significant rise in the volume of private bank lending." (Goldsbrough and Zaidi [1986], 174).

25. Following Friedrich List, such policies perpetuate "the chronic deformation of such economies (which) consists in the non-development of the internal market" (Senghaas [1980], 568).

26. This has led the European Commission to work with the World Bank on a first regional structural adjustment programme to be developed for the UDEAC countries.

27. See Antonelli (1991) for details on the importance of communications.

28. Good summaries of these theories and their consequences for south-south co-operation can be found in Stewart (1984), Venturas-Dias (1985) and Chudnovsky & Porta (1990).

29. Such findings contradict the more commonly held view, expressed by Sir W. Arthur Lewis (1980), a proponent of south-south co-operation, who in his talk on the receipt of his Nobel prize in economics, nevertheless suggested that south-south co-operation was a strategy that could be used to surmount the crisis but that it is less efficient and satisfactory than a strategy which leads to a more advantageous insertion of the third world into a more open and dynamic world economy. The two, we will argue below, are not contradictory.

30. See the chapter by Linda Lim for further details on ASEAN integration.

31. Much of this argument is drawn from L.K. Mytelka "Crisis, technological change and the strategic alliance" in Mytelka (1991a), pp. 7-34.

32. Finland is exemplary in this regard. See, for example, TEKES (Technology Development Centre of Finland), *Views on Finnish Technology*, No. 2, 1991, devoted to "Hitech spin-offs from traditional industries".

33. See Perez (1990) and her chapter in this volume for details. Some of the consequences of these changes are already evident in a number of newly industrialised economies (Mytelka [1990]).

34. On strategic partnerships see Mytelka (1991).

35. See the ASEAN experience in chapter 4 for a contemporary example.

36. See Dieter Ernst's chapter in this volume.

37. There is some evidence that SADCC's institutional structures were of this kind. The Inter-American Development Bank supported the Simon Bolivar programme linking nine Latin American countries in an attempt to promote innovation through strategic partnering activity is another possible example. More research is required to learn how such a structure might be adapted to an innovation driven model of south-south co-operation.

Bibliography

ADDO, H. ed. (1984), *World-Economy? Nine Critical Essays on the New International Economic Order*, Hodder & Stoughton in associations with the United Nations University, London.

AGLIETTA, M. (1976), *Régulation et crise du capitalisme*, Calmann Lévy, Paris.

AMIN, S. (1985), *La déconnexion*, La découverte, Paris.

AMIN, S. (1977), "Self-Reliance and the New International Economic Order", *Monthly Review*, 29:3, July/August, pp. 1-21.

AMIN S., D. CHITALA and I. MANDAZA, eds. (1987), *SADCC Prospects for Disengagement and Development in Southern Africa*, Zed Book for the United Nations University and the Third World Forum, London.

AMSDEN, A. (1989), *Asia's Next Giant, South Korea and Late Industrialisation*, Oxford, New York.

AMSDEN, A. (1980), "The Industry Characteristics of Intra-Third World Trade in Manufactures," *Economic Development and Cultural Change*, Vol. 29, No. 1, October, pp. 181-219.

ANTONELLI, C. (1991), *The Diffusion of Advanced Telecommunications in Developing Countries*, OECD, Paris.

APPLIED DEVELOPMENT ECONOMICS (ADE) (1988), *Regionalism and Economic Development in Sub-Saharan Africa*, Vol. 1, Regional Co-operation in Africa, prepared for the United States Agency for International Development (The Berg Report).

AXELROD, R. (1984), *The Evolution of Co-operation*, Basic Books, New York.

AXLINE, A. (1977), "Underdevelopment, Dependence and Integration: The Politics of Regionalism in the Third World", *International Organisation*, XXI, pp. 83-105.

BAILY, M.N. and A.K. CHAKRABARTI (1988), *Innovation and the Productivity Crisis*, The Bookings Institution, Washington, D.C.

BALASSA, B. (1961), *The Theory of Economic Integration*, Richard D. Irwin, Homewood, Ill.

BALASSA, B. and A. STOUTJESDIJK (1975), "Economic Integration among Developing Countries," *Journal of Common Market Studies*, 14 (Sept.), pp. 37-55.

BELA, L. (1990), "Identification des industries compétitives dans les pays membres de l'Union douanière et économique de l'Afrique centrale", paper prepared for the meeting of the IDRC sponsored *Réseau sur les politiques industrielles et les incitations sectorielles en Afrique francophone*, (Lomé: décembre).

BID/INTAL (1990), *El Proceso de integración en America Latina en 1989*, Instituto para la Integracion de America Latina, Buenos Aires.

BIENEFELD, M. (1982), "The International Context for National Development Strategies: Constraints and Opportunities in a Changing World," in M. Bienefeld & M. Godfrey, eds., *National Strategies in an International Context*, John Wiley, New York, pp. 25-64.

BHAGWATI, J.N., ed. (1972), "Economics and World Order from the 1970s to 1990s: The Key Issues" in *Economics and World Order from the 1970s to the 1990s*, Free Press, New York, pp. 1-28.

BHALLA, A.S. and D. JAMES (1988), "Some Conceptual and Policy Issues," in A.S. Bhalla & D. James, eds., *New Technologies and Development Experiences in "Technology Blending"*, Lynne Reiner, Boulder, Co., pp. 28-50.

BREWSTER, H. (1973), "Caribbean Economic Integration — Problems and Perspectives," *Journal of Common Market Studies*, Vol. 9, (June), pp. 282-298.

BREWSTER, H. and C.Y. THOMAS (1969), "Aspects of the Theory of Economic Integration," *Journal of Common Market Studies*, Vol. 8, No. 2.

BRUSCO, S. (1982), "The Emilian Model: Productive Decentralisation and Social Integration," *Cambridge Journal of Economics*, Vol. 6, No. 2, (June), pp. 167-184.

CAVES, R.E. (1982), *Multinational enterprise and economic analysis*, Cambridge University Press, Cambridge.

CHUDNOVSKY, D. and F. PORTA (1990), "On Argentine-Brazilian Economic Integration", *Cepal Review*, No. 39, pp. 115-134.

DAHLMAN, C.J. and F. SERCOVICH (1984), *Local Development and Exports of Technology: The Comparative Advantage of Argentina, Brazil, India, the Republic of Korea and Mexico*, World Bank Staff Working Papers, No. 667, Washington, D.C.

DELL, S. (1966), *A Latin American Common Market?*, Oxford University Press, London.

DEMAS, W. (1965), *The Economics of Development in Small Countries with Special Reference to the Caribbean*, McGill University Press, Montreal.

DEMAS, W. and J. SCOTLAND (1985), "Experiences in regional integration and co-operation: the case of the Caribbean Community and Common Market" in Altaf Gauhar, ed., *Regional Integration: The Latin American Experience*, Westview Press, Boulder, Co.

DIOUF, M. (1984), *Intégration économique: perspectives africaines*, Publisud & Dakar: nouvelles éditions africaines, Paris.

DOS SANTOS, T. (1973), "The Crisis of Development Theory and the Problem of Dependence in Latin America" in H. Bernstein, ed., *Underdevelopment and Development*, Penguin, UK, pp. 57-80.

DOSI, Giovanni, Laura TYSON and John ZYSMAN (1988), "Technology, Trade Policy and Schumpeterian Efficiencies" in John De la Mothe & Louis Marc Ducharme, eds., *Science, Technology and Free Trade*, Pinter Publishers, London, pp. 19-38.

ENOS, J.L. and W.-H. PARK (1988), *The Adoption and Diffusion of Imported Technology: The Case of Korea*, Croom Helm, London.

ERNST, Dieter & David O'CONNOR (1989), *Technology and Global Competition. The Challenge for Newly Industrialising Economies*, OECD, Paris.

ERNST, Dieter & David O'CONNOR (1991), *Competing in the Electronics Industry — The Experience of Newly Industrialising Economies*, OECD Development Centre, Paris.

ETHIER, Wilfred & Henrik HORN (1984), "A New Look at Economic Integration" in Henryk Kierzkowski, ed., *Monopolistic Competition and International Trade*, Clarenden Press, Oxford, pp. 207-229.

FRANSMAN, M. (1984), "Some Hypotheses Regarding Indigenous Technological Capability and the Case of Machine Production in Hong Kong," in M. Fransman and K. King, eds., *Technological Capability in the Third World*, Macmillan Press, London, pp. 301-317.

FREEMAN, C. & C. PEREZ (1988), "Structural Crises of Adjustment, Business Cycles and Investment Behaviour" in G. Dosi, C. Freeman, D. Nelson, G. Silverberg & L. Soete, eds., *Technical Change and Economic Theory*, Pinter Publishers, London, pp. 38-66.

GATT (1987), International Trade 1986-1987, General Agreement on Tariffs and Trade, Geneva.

GATT, (1990), International Trade 1989-1990, General Agreement on Tariffs and Trade, Geneva.

GOLDSBROUGH, David and Iqbal ZAIDI (1986), "Transmission of Economic Influences from Industrial to Developing Countries," in *IMF Staff Studies*, (July), pp. 150-195.

GRYNSPAN, Devora (1982), "Technological Transfer Patterns and Industrialisation in LDCs: A Study of Licensing in Costa Rica," *International Organisation*, Vol. 36, No. 4 (Autumn), pp. 795-806.

HAAS, Ernest (1958), *The Uniting of Europe — Political, Social and Economic Forces 1950-57*, Stevens, London.

HAAS, Ernest (1964), *Beyond the Nation State: Functionalism and International Organisation*, Stanford University Press, Stanford.

HAVRYLYSHYN, Oli & Martin WOLF (1981), "Trade Among Developing Countries: Theory, Policy Issues and Principal Trends", World Bank Staff Working Paper, No. 479.

HAVRYLYSHYN, Oli & I. ALIKHANI (1982), "Is there Cause for Export Optimism? An Inquiry into the Evidence of a Second Generation of Successful Exporters", World Bank, Washington, D.C.

HELLEINER, Gerald, K. (1981), *Intra-firm Trade and the Developing Countries*, Macmillan Publishers, London.

HELLEINER, Gerald, K. (1986), "Outward Orientation, Import Instability and African Economic Growth: an Empirical Investigation" in S. Lall and F. Stewart, eds., *Theory and Reality in Development*, Essays in Honour of Paul Streeten, Macmillan, London, pp. 139-153.

HELPMAN, E. and P. KRUGMAN (1989), *Market Structure and Foreign Trade, Increasing Returns, Imperfect Competition and the International Economy*, The MIT Press, Boston.

HOFFMAN, Kurt and Raphael KAPLINSKY (1988), *Driving Force: The Global Restructuring of Technology, Labour and Investment in the Automobile and Components Industries*, Westview, Boulder.

HUGON, Philippe (1990a), *Les différentes formes d'intégration régionale en Afrique sub-saharienne et les programmes d'ajustement structurel*, report prepared for the Ministère de la Coopération et du Développement, Paris.

HUGON, Philippe (1990b), "Programme d'ajustement structurel et intégration régionale en Afrique sub-saharienne", paper presented at the Journées du Larea, 22-23 janvier, Université Paris-X, Nanterre.

HVEEM, Helge (1983), "Selective Dissociation in the Technology Sector" in John G. Ruggie, ed., *The Antinomies of Interdependence*, Columbia University Press, New York, pp. 273-316.

INSTITUTO PARA LA INTEGRACION DE AMERICA LATINA (INTAL), (1990), *El proceso de integración en America Latina en 1989*, BID, INTAL, Buenos Aires.

KAHNERT, F., P. RICHARDS, E. STOUTJESDIJK & P.THOMOPOULOS (1969), *Economic Integration Among Developing Countries*, OECD Development Centre, Paris.

KAPLINSKY, R. (1984), "The International Context for Industrialisation in the Coming Decade", *Journal of Development Studies*, 21 (1), pp. 75-96.

KRUGMAN, Paul (1988), "Introduction: New Thinking about Trade Policy" in Paul R. Krugman, ed., *Strategic Trade Policy and the New International Economics*, The MIT Press, Cambridge, Mass., pp. 1-46.

KUMAR, Krishna & Maxwell G. McLEOD (1981), *Multinationals from Developing Countries*, Lexington Books, Lexington, Mass.

LALL, Sanjaya (1989), "Explaining Industrial Success in the Developing World" for *Current Issues in Development Economics* edited by V.N. Balasubramanyam and Sanjaya Lall, Macmillan, London.

LALL, Sanjaya, ed. (1983), *The New Multinationals: the Spread of Third World Enterprises*, John Wiley & Sons, Chichester.

LALL, Sanjaya (1984), "South-South Economic Co-operation and Global Negotiations" in J.N. Bhagwati & M.C. Ruggie, eds., *Power, Passion and Purpose*, The MIT Press, Cambridge, Mass., pp. 287-321.

LANCASTER, K.J. (1971), *Consumer Demand: A New Approach*, Columbia University Press, New York.

LANCASTER, K.J. (1980), "Intra-Industry Trade under Perfect Monopolistic Competition", *Journal of International Economics*, 10, pp. 151-176.

LEWIS, Sir W. Arthur (1980), "The Slowing Down of the Engine of Growth", *American Economic Review*, (September).

LINDER, S.B. (1961), *An Essay on Trade and Transformation*, Almqvist and Wiksell International, Stockholm.

LITTLE, Ian, Tibor SCITOVKSY & Maurice SCOTT (1970), *Industry and Trade in Some Developing Countries*, Oxford University Press, London.

MANSOOR, Ali and Andras INOTAI (1990), "Integration Efforts in Sub-Saharan Africa: Failures, Results and Prospects — A Suggested Strategy for Achieving Efficient Integration", paper prepared for the African Economic Issues Conference, 5-7 June, Nairobi.

MARSHALL, Alfred (1890), *Principles of Economics*, Macmillan, London.

MAZZEO, Domenico, ed. (1984), *African Regional Organisation*, Cambridge University Press, Cambridge.

MELO, Jaime de, Arvind PANAGARIYA and Dani RODRIK (1992), "The new Regionalism: A Country Perspective", paper presented at the World Bank and CEPR conference on New Dimensions in Regional Integration, Washington, D.C., 2-3 April, Revised July.

MICHALET, Charles-Albert (1976), *Le capitalisme mondial*, second enlarged edition 1985, PUF, Paris.

MICHALET, Charles-Albert (1982), "From International Trade to World Economy: A New Paradigm" in H. Makler, A. Martinelli and N. Smelser, eds., *The New International Economy*, Sage, Beverley Hills, Ca., pp. 193-230.

MIKESELL, R.F. (1963), "The Theory of Common Markets and Developing Countries", reprinted in R. Robson, ed., *International Economic Integration*, Penguin, UK., 1971, pp. 166-194.

MYRDAL, Gunnar (1957), *Economic Theory and Underdeveloped Regions*, Duckworth, London.

MYTELKA, Lynn K. (1973a), "The Salience of Gains in Third World Integrative Systems", *World Politics*, Vol. XXV, No. 2, pp. 236-250.

MYTELKA, Lynn K. (1973b), "Foreign Aid and Regional Integration: The UDEAC Case", *Journal of Common Market Studies*, Vol. XII, No. 2, (December), pp. 138-158.

MYTELKA, Lynn K. (1979), *Regional Development in a Global Economy: The Multinational Corporation, Technology and Andean Integration*, Yale University Press, New Haven.

MYTELKA, Lynn K. (1984), "Competition, Conflict and Decline in the *Union douanière et économique de l'Afrique centrale*" in D. Mazzeo, ed., *African Regional Organisations*, Cambridge University Press, Cambridge.

MYTELKA, Lynn K. (1991a), "Ivorian Industry at the Crossroads" in Frances Stewart, Sanjaya Lall and Samuel Wangwe, eds., *Alternative Development Strategies in Sub-Saharan Africa*, Macmillan, London.

MYTELKA, Lynn K. (1990), "New Modes of Competition in the Textile and Clothing Industry: Some Consequences for Third World Exporters", in Jorge Niosi, ed., *Technology and National Competitiveness*, McGill-Queen's University Press, Montreal.

MYTELKA, Lynn K., ed. (1991b), *Strategic Partnerships: States Firms and International Competition*, Pinter Publishers, UK.

MYTELKA, Lynn, K. (1989), "The Unfulfilled Promise of African Industrialisation", *African Studies Review*, Vol. 32, No. 3, pp. 77-137.

NEWFARMER, Richard (1985), *Direction on Trade Flows of Transational Corporations and Domestic Firms in Brazil*, paper prepared for an informal symposium on South-South Trade: Obstacles to its Growth, convened by the Deputy Secretary-General, officer-in-charge, 26-29, June, UNCTAD, Geneva.

O'BRIEN, P., HASNAIN, A. & E. LECHUGA-JIMENEZ (1979), "Direct Foreign Investment and Technology Exports Among Developing Countries: An Empirical Analysis of the Prospects for Third World Co-Operation" in *International Flows of Technology*, Vol. 3, 326, 19 December, UNIDO/IOD, Vienna, pp. 111-188.

ODLE, Maurice (1979), "Technology Leasing as the Latest Imperialist Phase: A Case Study of Guyana and Trinidad", *Social and Economic studies*, (March), pp. 189-233.

OECD (1991), *Background Report Concluding the Technology/Economy Programme (TEP)*, C/MIN(91)14, Paris.

OECD (1987), *STI Statistical Indicators*, Paris.

OECD (1990), *Development Co-operation*, Paris.

OMAN, Charles (1984), *New Forms of International Investment in Developing Countries*, OECD, Paris.

OMAN, Charles (1993), "Trends in Global FDI and Latin America", in W. Fritsch, ed., *Latin America in the Global Economy*, Northsouth Institute, Miami, (1993); also published in C. Bradford, ed., *Mobilising International Investment for Latin America*, OECD Development Centre, Paris (1993).

OXMAN, G., and F. SAGASTI (1972), *Transferencia de tecnologia hacia los países del Grupo Andino*, OAS, Washington, D.C.

PEREZ, Carlota (1988), "New Technologies and Development", in C. Freeman and B-A. Lundvall, eds., *Small Countries Facing the Technological Revolution*, Pinter Publishers, UK, pp. 85-97.

PIORE, Michael and Charles SABEL (1984), *The Second Industrial Divide: Possibilities for Prosperity*, Basic Books, New York.

PORTER, Michael, E. (1990), *The Competitive Advantage of Nations*, The Free Press, New York.

PREBISCH, Raul (1964), *Toward a New Trade Policy for Development*, the Secretary-General's Report to the 1964 UNCTAD, United Nations, New York.

ROBSON, P., ed. (1971), *International Economic Integration*, Penguin, UK.

ROSENTHAL, Gert (1984), "The Lessons of Economic Integration in Latin America: the Case of Central America" in Altaf Gauhar, ed., *Regional Integration: The Latin American Experience*, Third World Foundation for Social and Economic Studies, UK, pp. 139-170.

SALGADO Penaherrera, Germanico (1985), "The Andean Pact: Problems and Perspectives", in Altaf Gauhar, ed., *Regional Integration: The Latin American Experience*, Third World Foundation for Social and Economic Studies, UK, pp. 170-193.

SENGHAAS, Dieter (1980), "Dissociation as a Development Rationale. On the Appropriate Location of Technology in the Development Debate", in Dieter Ernst, ed., *The New International Division of Labour, Technology and Under-development*, Consequences for the Third World, Campus Verlag, Frankfurt, pp. 564-591.

SOUTH COMMISSION (1990), *The Challenge to the South: Report of the South Commission*, (3 August).

STEWART, Frances (1976), "The Direction of International Trade: Gains and Losses for the Third World", in G.K. Helleiner, ed., *A World Divided: the Less Developed Countries in the International Economy*, Cambridge University Press, London, pp. 89-110.

STEWART, Frances (1984), "Recent Theories of International Trade: Some Implications for the South", in Henryk Kierzkowski, ed., *Monopolistic Competition and International Trade*, Clarenden Press, Oxford, UK, pp. 84-108.

THOMAS, Clive (1991), "The Economic Crisis and the Commonwealth Caribbean: Impact and Response" in Dharam Ghai, ed., *The IMF and the South: The Social Impact of Crisis and Adjustment*, Zed Books, London, pp. 43-68.

UNITED NATIONS CENTRE FOR TRANSNATIONAL CORPORATIONS (UNCTC) (1988), *Transnational Corporations in World Development*, United Nations, New York.

UNITED NATIONS CONFERENCE ON TRADE AND DEVELOPMENT (UNCTAD) (1990a), *Economic Integration Among Developing Countries: Trade Co-operation, Monetary and Financial Co-operation and Review of Recent Developments in Major Economic Co-operation and Integration Groupings of Developing Countries*, 12 December, Doc. No. TD/B/C.7/AC.3/10, Geneva.

UNCTAD (1989), *Debt and Structural Adjustment Policies of Developing Countries: Impact on Economic Integration*, Report by the UNCTAD Secretariat, 8 March, Doc. No. TD/B/C.7/AC.3/5, Geneva.

UNCTAD (1990b), *Index of Economic Co-operation and Integration Groupings of Developing Countries: Membership and Objectives*, 12 December, Doc. No. TD/B/C.7/AC.3/3/Rev.1, Geneva.

UNCTAD (1973), "The distribution of benefits and costs in integration among developing countries", in *Current Problems of Economic Integration*, prepared by Eduardo Lizano, Doc. No. TD/B/394, United Nations, New York.

UNCTAD (1990c), *The Least Developed Countries 1989 Report*, United Nations, New York.

UNCTAD (1983), *Trade and Development Report, 1983*, United Nations, New York.

UNCTAD (1991), *Transfer and Development of Technology in a Changing World Environment: The Challenges of the 1990s*, 25 January, Doc. No. TD/B/C.6/153, Geneva.

UNITED NATIONS ECONOMIC COMMISSION FOR LATIN AMERICA AND THE CARIBBEAN (ECLAC) (1990), *Changing Production Patterns with Social Equity*, Santiago.

ECLAC (1977), "Complementarity Agreements of LAFTA and the Role of Transnational Corporations", Joint CTC/CEPAL Draft, 5 July, Santiago.

UNITED NATIONS INDUSTRIAL DEVELOPMENT ORGANISATION (UNIDO) (1985), *Industrial Co-operation Through the Southern African Development Co-ordination Conference, (SADCC)*, UNIDO/IS.570, 15 October, Vienna.

VAITSOS, Constantine (1975), "The Process of Commercialisation of Technology in the Andean Pact" in H. Radice, ed., *International Firms and Modern Imperialism*, Penguin, UK, pp. 183-214.

VAITSOS, Constantine (1978), "Crisis in Regional Economic Co-operation, (Integration) Among Developing Countries: A Survey", *World Development*, Vol. 6, pp. 719-769.

VAITSOS, Constantine (1978), *The role of Transnational Enterprises in Latin American Economic Integration Efforts: Who Integrates and with Whom, How and for Whose Benefits?*, Doc. No. TAD/EI/Sem.5/2, UNCTAD, Geneva.

VENTURA-DIAS, Vivianne (1985), "The Theoretical Background for Analysis of South-South Trade", paper presented to an Informal Symposium on *South-South Trade: Obstacles to its Growth* convened by the Deputy Secretary-General, Officer-in-Charge of UNCTAD, 26-29 June, Geneva.

VINER, Jacob (1950), *The Customs Union Issue*, Carnegie Endowment for International Peace, New York.

WESTPHAL, Larry E., Linsu Kim and Carl J. DAHLMAN (1984), *Reflections on Korea's Acquisition of Technological Capability*, Development Resarch Department Report No. DRD77, April, World Bank, Washington, D.C.

WILLMORE, L.N. (1974), "The Pattern of Trade and Specialisation in the Central American Common Market", *Journal of Economic Studies*, 6 November, pp. 113-134.

WOMACK, James (1990), *The Machine that Changed the World*, Macmillan, New York.

WORLD BANK (1989), *Sub-Saharan Africa From Crisis to Sustainable Growth*, A Long-Term Perspective Study, World Bank, Washington, D.C.

Chapter 2

TECHNICAL CHANGE AND THE NEW CONTEXT FOR DEVELOPMENT

Carlota Perez

Ce chapitre explore les conséquences de la vague actuelle de progrès techniques et organisationnels sur les stratégies de développement. Il étudie l'importance croissante des investissements immatériels, des changements dans les pratiques d'organisation, du développement des ressources humaines et de l'accumulation de compétences techniques comme déterminants de la compétitivité des entreprises et des pays. Il met également l'accent sur l'utilité des synergies qui peuvent résulter de l'organisation de réseaux d'entreprises et de stratégies de spécialisation collective dans ce nouvel environnement. Ce contexte en pleine mutation représente un défi en même temps que l'occasion d'élaborer des stratégies de développement appropriées — et plus ambitieuses — et de réévaluer le rôle et les moyens de la coopération sud-sud.

This chapter explores the implications of the present wave of technical and organisational change for development strategies. It looks at the growing importance of intangible investment, organisational change, the development of human capital and the accumulation of technological capabilities for the competitiveness of firms and countries. It emphasizes the value of the synergies to be gained from networking among firms and from collective specialisation, under these new conditions. This changing context is seen as posing a challenge and providing new opportunities both for the design of appropriate — and more ambitious — development strategies and for reassessing the role and means of South-South co-operation.

Introduction

For the past two decades the world has been shaken by three successive waves of change. First there was the all-pervasive impact of information technology on products, production, services and communication. Then there was the managerial revolution with the diffusion of organisational practices pioneered by the Japanese and other challenges to traditional mass production emerging in various countries of Europe and elsewhere. Now, while those two are still unfolding, there is a wave of political and institutional change involving processes as diverse and complex as the dissolution of the Soviet system, the movement towards trade liberalisation, the adoption of market systems and the creation of regional blocs in every continent.

These waves of transformation in technology, management, economics and politics are interrelated. They point to a world in transition where the rules of the game are changing at every level. The conditions under which competition takes place in international markets are moving further and further away from those that prevailed in the 1960s and 1970s or even the early 1980s. In this changing environment, it is wise to reassess afresh every policy, every development strategy, because the previous success or failure of a particular policy is unlikely to be a good predictor of future performance[1].

One of the most striking examples of how a once effective policy can become inadequate under changing conditions is the Import Substitution Industrialisation (ISI) strategy adopted by many developing countries from the 1950s onwards. Although initially it did achieve significant results in developing industrial capacity, infrastructure, skills and managerial competence, by the early eighties to persist in these policies became counterproductive. New policies and strategies have become essential everywhere. A basic necessity for the development of these new strategies is an understanding of the processes of technical, organisational and institutional change which, though starting in the North, are transforming the entire world economy, North, South, East and West. This chapter, therefore, will examine the way in which technical and organisational innovations have changed the context for development strategies and consequently for any complementary actions in terms of co-operation between countries. It will attempt to indicate some of the new opportunities and constraints confronting the developing countries in the 1990s.

The first section looks at intangible investment. The new development strategies will need to increasingly stress knowledge accumulation, in contrast to traditional development strategies which were heavily oriented towards fixed capital accumulation. Among the most important components of intangible investment are education and training, scientific and technical services and technology infrastructure. These are discussed in Sections 3 and 4. However the appropriate scale and direction of these different types of intangible investment must be carefully considered to increase their effectiveness. For this reason Section 2 analyses the organisational changes which are needed at the enterprise level for developing countries to succeed in the new competition. This analysis shows that even though the initial intangible investment in reorganisation may be quite modest, it is an essential pre-condition for the success of the other tangible and intangible investments which may follow. Moreover the pattern of organisational change which is required, with its strong emphasis on flexibility, initiative at all levels and multi-skilling has rather strong implications for the human resource strategies discussed in Section 3 and the technology strategies which are the subject of Section 4.

Successful development strategies in the 1990s and the early decades of the twenty-first century will however depend not only on these kinds of tangible and intangible investments but also on appropriate specialisation within the international economy. Such specialisation must clearly vary a great deal with size of the economy, level of development, human resources, factor costs and of course the endowment of each country in natural resources.

In the past developing countries have been wary of excessive dependence on primary commodity export specialisation because of the extreme vulnerability to price fluctuations and to shifts in the patterns of demand. However the new technologies and the new organisational principles are revitalising and upgrading all branches of the economy, including the primary sector. The resource endowment of each country and the experience accumulated in their exploitation can be a great source of competitive strength provided they are used as a platform for a whole constellation of new developments. The historical examples of Sweden and Finland show that export strength in primary commodities can be the starting point for strengthening many related branches of manufacturing and services which are mutually reinforcing and provide greater security and breadth of development. The question of achieving appropriate strategic specialisation and market targets in the new forms of global competition are the subject of Section 5.

Whatever the specialisation, collaboration with partners in other countries has become an imperative. The importance of global networking for education and technology already emerges in Sections 3 and 4 but Section 5 explores some aspects of global networking in production and marketing. A wide variety of possible forms of international collaboration is opening up, most of which depend on the initiative and flexibility of the relevant enterprises. There are of course many barriers and great difficulties confronting firms in developing countries, not the least of which is the heritage of established and now obsolete attitudes, customs and institutions. The final section sums up the constructive new approaches which can help developing countries to overcome this dead weight from the past and to embark on a new forward trajectory. Some of the emerging possibilities for South-South co-operation are considered in this overall context.

In the advanced countries it is widely recognised that increasing R&D efforts are becoming crucial for competition at the frontier of technology. In certain areas such as semiconductors, super-computers and optoelectronics, these costs are reaching such proportions that both industrial consortia and government support are often considered necessary to share the burden. It is less well known that the overall amount of investment in manufacturing R&D in advanced countries is approaching the level of investment in plant and equipment. In Japan, for example, R&D expenditure by manufacturing companies had already surpassed tangible capital investment in 1986 (See Figure 1). From these and other data Fumio Kodama argues that manufacturing companies are moving "from producing to thinking organisations"[2]. Although the exact significance of these data is open to discussion there is no doubt that they represent an important new phenomenon and that this marks a shift in the usual notions of investment.

1. The growth of intangibles in investment

Figure 1. **Time-series of R&D expenditure compared with capital investment of all Japanese manufacturing companies (Y billion)**

Year	R&D expenditure	Capital investment	R&D/cap. ratio
1980	2 896	4 651	0.62
1981	3 374	5 161	0.65
1982	3 756	5 099	0.74
1983	4 257	4 762	0.89
1984	4 777	5 788	0.83
1986	5 544	6 110	0.91
1986	5 740	4 896	1.17
1987	6 101	4 860	1.26

Source: Taken from KODAMA Fumio, *Analysing Japanese High Technologies: The Techno-Economic Paradigm Shift*, Pinter Publishers, London and New York, 1991.

Yet the growth of research and development, in the traditional sense of financing laboratory research with the purpose of bringing up new products and processes, including technological breakthroughs, is only one aspect and not the most comprehensive way of defining the transformation that affects the role of technology in competitiveness.

An effort to capture the whole range of areas where knowledge investment is becoming important is made in the Report of the OECD's "Technology Economy Programme"(OECD-TEP) which approaches the question of intangible investment in a wide sense[3]. The Report recognises "the increasing importance of technology, skills and organisation in determining competitiveness" and shows that "as these production factors replace previous factors (capital, labour, land) in determining comparative advantage, there has been rapid growth in the intangible components of investment". These include R&D, purchase of patents and licenses, software, market exploration and development, training, human resource management, strategic reorganisation of enterprises, etc[4].

There are also shifts in the composition of intangible investment itself. Surveys by the IFO Institute in Germany, quoted in the same report, not only verify the steady growth of the share of intangibles in innovation-related investment from 1979 to 1988 but also identify, within it, the faster growth of expenditures other than R&D, such as new product training, reorganisation and process improvement[5].

Martin Bell, from the Science Policy Research Unit of the University of Sussex, has discussed this shift in focus, emphasizing not so much the actual structure of expenditure in precise quantities but the relative importance of the effort[6]. After all, the development of human capital could cost many times less than the purchase of the equipment to be operated, but increased mastery of technology can have greater impact not just on potential productivity from machinery but on how soon and how consistently such potential can be realised.

Figure 2 represents the evolution of the relative importance and the increased visibility of the various components of managerial effort and investment. In it Bell is essentially pointing out three things: a) the growing awareness of the centrality of investment in knowledge in relation to physical plant and equipment; b) the invisibility of the whole iceberg of technology-related effort in industry, of which R&D is only the tip and c) the recognition of investment in human and institutional resources as the means to activate the potential for technical change.

Figure 2. **Components of manegerial effort and investment: evolution of relative importance and visibility**

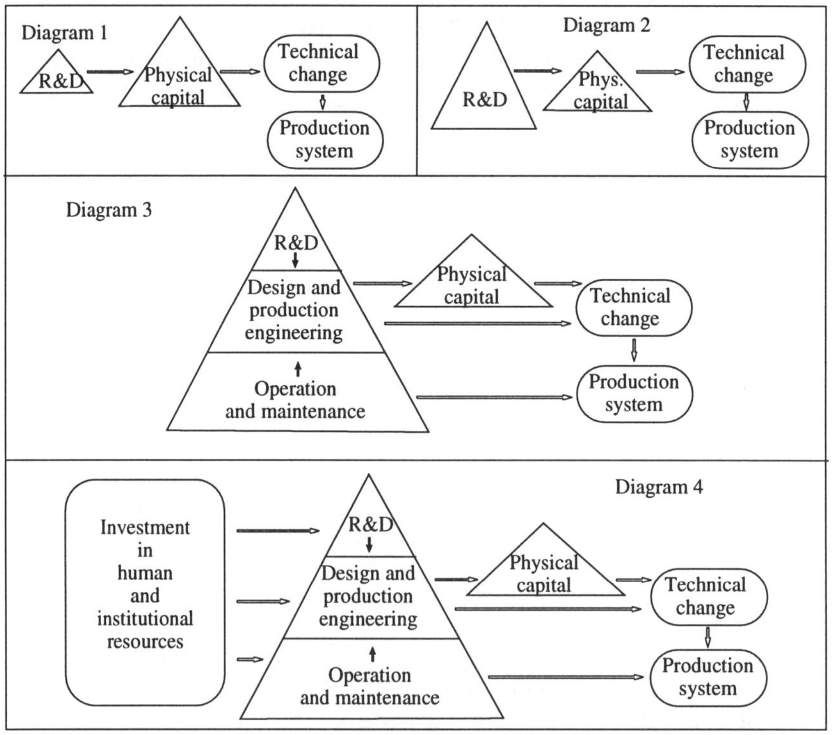

Source: Bell, Martin, *Science and Technology Research in the 1990s: Key Issues for Developing Countries,* paper prepared for the SPRU 25th Anniversary Conference, July 3-4 1991 (forthcoming, Pinter Publishers)

It is interesting to note that Chris Freeman, who drafted the 1963 "Frascati Manual" used by the OECD to gather R&D statistics, had insisted that these indicators be complemented by a range of "related activities". These comprised all of the main components of intangible investment such as geological exploration, design activities, project survey work, information services, training and testing. But it is only thirty years later, in December 1992, that the OECD felt the need to hold a Conference on the measurement of intangible investment. As a result the 1990s are likely to see a big push forward in the area of statistics[7].

The growing role of intangible knowledge-related investment has enormous consequences for developing countries. It obviously needs to be taken into account by firms as they reconvert to become competitive. It is also a key aspect in the design of national strategies and government policies. An understanding of the changes taking place in the world economy and in the factors determining competitiveness is essential both to establish appropriate enabling conditions and to avoid misdirected efforts.

Policy recommendations from a wide range of sources are already drawing attention to technical change as a key element in development strategies under the new conditions. Notably the ECLAC Report "Changing Production Patterns with Social Equity" takes the assimilation of technical change and the development of human resources as the core of its proposals[8]. The World Bank's 1991 World Development Report also highlights the contribution of technology and education as a significant complement to macroeconomic policies in achieving development[9].

The following sections examine three of the main aspects involved in this transition towards a more knowledge centred production system: organisational change, the role of human capital and the mastery of technology. The changes occurring in each of these areas will be described with a view to exploring how they might affect the restructuring strategies of firms and countries in the developing world. Particular reference is made to the ISI policies which were prevalent until recently, notably in Latin America and Africa, and to how this legacy may help or hinder the necessary transformations.

In the early eighties, when awareness of the microelectronics revolution was at its peak and debates raged alternately heralding its promises and fearing its threats, Ingersoll Engineers came up with a set of surprising results from a survey of British manufacturing. When assessing the risk of investment in automated technologies their results showed an inverse relationship between the level of automation and the likelihood of achieving increased productivity. In fact, they found only an 18 per cent rate of success in firms that went for the "high technology" option, in contrast with an 84 per cent success rate in firms that focused mainly on reorganisation, introducing only a few selected changes in equipment (See Figure 3).

2. Investing in organisational change

Rather than conclude that computer integration and flexible manufacturing systems (FMS) cannot yield expected results, what Ingersoll argued is that organisational change is a precondition for reaping the potential benefits offered by the new equipment. They also found that there is considerable leeway to improve production processes through organisational change that can be undertaken before any new equipment is incorporated. In some of the cases they studied as much as 80 per cent of the initial improvements in productivity could be attributed to reorganisation alone[10].

Figure 3. **Assessing the risk of introducing new computerized technologies in manufacturing industry**

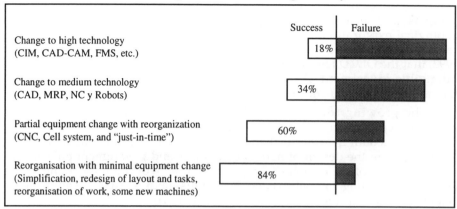

Source: Ingersoll Engineers.

These findings are in line with the increasingly accepted explanation of the productivity paradox in the OECD countries. At a time when investment in modern equipment was growing rapidly and new technologies had been widely applied, instead of the expected increase in efficiency there was a decline in the rate of productivity growth in these economies. The TEP Report locates the main causes of this phenomenon in the "various diffusion barriers including human resources, organisational and management practices and more broadly the surrounding social, economic and institutional environment"[11].

After several years of great interest in microelectronics and the information technology revolution, the centre of concern thus shifted to another wave of equally pervasive but "soft" generic technology. By the mid-eighties the managerial revolution, centred on the new organisational practices developed in Japan, had become the focus of a debate in terms of promises, threats and applicability. Slowly it came to be understood that the greater success of Japanese firms was rooted in an organisational model which allowed them to take much better advantage of modern technologies[12]. Since then there has been a mushrooming of consultancy services in the new organisational practices, various "gurus" in the field have appeared and many books and journals are propagating the new principles, their diverse forms of application and the many specific examples of success or failure in using them.

a. Organisation as the Achilles heel of the traditional technology leader

In 1986 the Massachussetts Institute of Technology set up a special Commission on Industrial Productivity (MIT/CIP) to address the causes of the decline in US competitive performance[13]. It convened more than fifteen top academics in economics, technology management and political science who mobilised dozens of expert researchers to probe into manufacturing companies in eight industries on three continents. Their results point clearly to the organisational issues, rather than to hard technology.

The report groups the causes of the loss of US competitiveness into six categories:

 i) Outdated strategies

 ii) Short time horizons

 iii) Technological weaknesses in development and production *iv)* Neglect of human resources

v) Failures of co-operation (within the firm and with other firms and supporting institutions)

vi) Government and industry at cross-purposes

As can be seen, the great majority are social, organisational and institutional weaknesses. The first two relate to overall managerial attitudes to business. The last two refer to the relationship of firms to other actors in their environment. The fourth is directly related to human capital. Only the third is truly "technological" in nature. And yet, when it is spelled out it, too, is mainly related to management of technology and attitudes towards it. It includes: neglect of manufacturability in product design, lack of teamwork in the product development process, lack of attention to the manufacturing process itself and poor exploitation of the potential for continuous improvement in the quality and reliability of products and processes.

When the MIT Commission analysed the determining features of competitive American firms, it also found that at the root of their achievement were certain common patterns of managerial and organisational practice. Thus, organisational technology seems to underlie competitiveness as much as mastery of specific technologies, product innovation and generic technologies[14].

b. A change in common sense and the difficulty of diffusion

What is happening in the field of management and organisation can be understood as a replacement of the established paradigm for best practice. It is an upheaval in common sense notions of efficiency. The principles that are today recognised as leading to competitiveness are almost all in direct opposition to traditional views. These are presented in two "pure" models in Figure 4.

As regards the shape of the firm, the ingrained ideas of centralised command, pyramidal structures and functional compartments are being replaced by flat flexible networks with increasing decentralisation of decision-making in structures where top management takes on a truly strategic and coordinating role. The goal of standardising and optimising operational procedures and specialising people in clearly defined tasks is being superseded by a trend towards flexible and adaptable systems based on multi-skilled personnel and continuous learning and improvement. Similar contrasts exist for each of the other characteristics.

But this is not just a collection of new management techniques. Rather these trends converge into a coherent system, a model or paradigm of best practice which is proving superior in achieving higher productivity, quality and overall competitiveness in international markets. It is thus generating powerful signals which induce imitation. Even under strong competitive pressures, however, the diffusion of the new organisational patterns from one firm to another faces great obstacles, especially mental blocks and personal or group resistance. A change in mentalities, attitudes and behaviour is far more demanding than the introduction of modern equipment.

Yet the people who occupy leadership positions today and must make the decisions for change are likely to have reached the top by applying the very principles that are now being questioned. It is very difficult to accept that what worked in the past has to be replaced by other practices; that one's competence is threatened with obsolescence. The MIT-CIP report put it very succinctly in relation to the US: "it is the very magnitude of past successes that has prevented adaptation to the new world"[15].

Figure 4. The new vs. the traditional paradigm: contrast between two "ideal types" in managerial common sense

	Conventional common sense	New efficiency principles and practices
Command and control	Centralised command Vertical control Cascade of supervisory levels "Management Knows best"	Central goalsetting & coordination Local autonomy/Horizontal self-control Self-assessing/self-improving units Participatory decision-making
Structure and growth	Stable pyramid growing in height and complexity as it expands	Flat flexible network of very agile units/Remains flat as it expands
Parts and links	Clear vertical links/Separate specialised functional departments	Interactive, cooperative links between functions along each product line
Style of operation	Optimised smooth running organisations Standard routines and procedures "There is one best way" Definition of individual tasks Single function specialisation Single top-down line of command Single bottom-up information flow	Continuous learning and improvement Flexible system/Adaptable procedures "A better way can always be found" Definition of group tasks Multi-skilled personnel/Ad hoc teams Widespread delegation of decision making Multiple horizontal and vertical flows
Personnel and Training	Labour as variable cost Market provides trained personnel People to fit the fixed posts Discipline as main quality	Labour as human capital Much in-house training and retraining Variable posts/Adaptable people Initiative/collaboration/motivation
Equipment and investment	Dedicated equipment One optimum plant size for each product Each plant anticipates demand growth Strive for economies of scale for mass production	Adaptable/programmable/flexible equipment Many efficient sizes/Optimum relative/Organic growth closely following demand Choice/combination of economies of scale, scope or specialisation
Production programming	Keep production rhythm; Use inventory to accommodate variation in demand Produce for stock; shed labour in slack	Adapt rhythm to variation in demand Minimise response time ("Just-in-time") Use slack for maintenance and training
Productivity measurement	A specific measure for each department (purchasing, production, marketing, etc.) Percent tolerance on quality and rejects	Total productivity measured along the chain for each product line Strive for zero defects and zero rejects
Suppliers, clients, and competitors	Separation from the outside world: Foster price competition among suppliers. Make standard products for mass customers. Arms length oligopoly with competitors. The firm as a closed system	Strong interaction with outside world: Collaborative links with suppliers, with customers and, in some cases, with competitors (Basic R&D for instance). The firm as an open system

Source: PEREZ, Carlota, "Technical Change, Competitive Restructuring and Institutional Reform in Developing Countries", SPR Discussion Paper No. 4, The World Bank, Washington, D.C., December 1989.

Certainly, the transition implies that entrepreneurs, managers, labour leaders and government officials must discard a significant part of their accumulated human capital, of their cherished routines, of their hard earned experience. As a result, transformations do not and cannot occur overnight. They take decades.

Elsewhere we have suggested that the delay in implementing change in the old front runners is one of the elements opening a window of opportunity for the lagging countries to accelerate development during paradigm transitions. Another is the availability of generic all-pervasive technologies that are capable of rejuvenating mature technologies and revitalising traditional ones. In so doing, they can reduce an important part of the gap that had been built on the type of experience which is made obsolete by the technical and organisational shift[16].

c. Reorganisation as an effective option in developing countries

Recent experience in developing countries has shown that much ground towards competitiveness can be covered with organisational efforts and modest investment in intangibles. There are many examples of impressive cost reductions and quality improvements, of successful rationalisation and specialisation that have resulted from managerial reconversion[17]. Such cases show that not all modernisation processes involve great expenditures on new equipment.

One particular study that does quantify the initial trade-off between hard and intangible investment is the case of a US paper mill presented in the Harvard Business Review[18]. It is worth summarising it here as an illustration of the type of effort involved and the sorts of results that can be achieved.

In 1983 the mill was losing a million dollars a month and was the last of the five suppliers in their part of the market. Equipment modernisation costs were estimated to be $23 million with at least five years to break-even. The choice was filing for bankruptcy or trying the reorganisation route. They did the latter.

The company decided to turn everyone into a problem solver. "Together, managers and mill workers learned to take the initiative not just for identifying problems but also for developing better processes for fixing problems and improving products... The entire organisation learned how to learn[19]". They established contact with customers, pinpointed the flaws that had to be corrected, went to the root causes in their process and, in the end, not only corrected those problems (going to "zero defects") but actually developed a new thinner grade of paper which created a profitable niche in the market.

In less than two years the mill was profitable. By the third year it had become the number one supplier in its group, with a tenfold rise in prices per share and a capacity to finance expansion out of profits.

This case can be seen as a metaphor for the type of transformation that developing countries might be wise to attempt in this transition. With scarce investment capital and without much time to spare to achieve results, it makes a lot of sense to take the organisational route to modernisation and to concentrate resources on learning.

To start by investing in new equipment means in most cases the highest financial cost although it is probably the line of initial least resistance and minimum effort (See Figure 5). Established practice both in firms and credit institutions assumes this to be the "normal" route[20]. Yet, it is increasingly

Figure 5. **Assimilating the new technologies: optional routes for modernization**

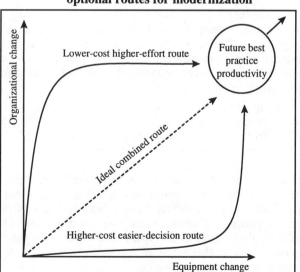

recognised that reorganisation cannot be avoided and is in fact required if full benefits are to be reaped from the introduction of new equipment.

Choosing to begin by reorganising has several advantages, one of which is the trade-off between maximum effort and minimum cost. This is obviously important when investment funds are scarce. But, as the example of the paper mill illustrates, it can be a better route independently of cost comparisons. Increased innovativeness allows each step to be financed by the previous, leading therefore to greater financial autonomy.

Many individual examples show that a sequence of investment moving from intangibles to tangible equipment can optimise both short and long term returns. A process of reconversion that begins with market analysis and focusing and goes on to investment in human capital and technological learning, can be followed by a series of incremental improvements to the existing equipment and process as well as to the products and, by collaboration with suppliers, to improved material and technical inputs. This sequence leads to a full understanding of the potential and limitations of the machinery in place and to a much greater capacity to select the new equipment when the moment comes to incorporate it. Often, as in the case of the paper mill, cash flow from success in the earlier phases can finance each subsequent one[21].

A point worth making is that this sequence is not only applicable to the modernisation of existing plant but helps to avoid waste in hard investment when designing new production facilities. In many instances, the customary practice of estimating market demand for the medium term and setting up a plant of that future scale is no longer advisable. Instead of living with idle capacity (and having capital tied down in it) the lowest possible module is used at start up and capacity is stretched to follow the increase in market demand through incremental improvements, additional shifts or even partial subcontracting. When the next module is finally added, it incorporates the stretching improvements and takes advantage of the people trained in the extra shifts. This is of course not possible in all cases. Bulk production for the standardized portion of any market is likely to remain dependent on a large enough scale of production for cost competitiveness. But as soon as more specialised segments are envisaged, modularity becomes a possibility. Of course in some cases smaller equipment modules are simply not yet available and in certain cases they might never be. Yet, even in steel, minimum scale has already come down from two million tons to 300 000[22]. Therefore, the range of options depends heavily on the market niche being targeted, on the specific product, the particular technology and even the moment in time.

Nevertheless, the principle of avoiding idle capital is generally applicable, sometimes in rather indirect and imaginative ways. For instance, electric utilities in the US have been able to postpone investment by purchasing extra power from large customers who have generating capacity and using it to cover peaks in demand or by financing energy conservation in the clients' premises[23].

Finally a note of warning. The emphasis placed here on the growing importance of organisational issues must be situated within the current period of restructuring and transition. It is not intended to deny the need for new equipment or R&D efforts. In the medium and long term the balance between investing in managerial change or in product and process innovation is biased towards the latter. Once the new managerial principles become the shared common sense and point of departure, a greater effort will be required in product and process technology. Facing these costs, which are likely to grow as the process of restructuring proceeds, is one of the tasks that might more effectively be met through international linkages. Intercountry arrangements established in this transition phase, moreover, might contemplate from the start this probable evolution.

We shall return to the theme of market segmentation and international linkages in Section 5, but we now turn to the issue of human resources without which neither technical nor organisational change can be implemented.

3. Investing in human capital

As the new technologies and organisational principles spread across firms, industries and countries there is a growing realisation that skills and people are becoming central to competitiveness. This heightened role of human resources is being used to explain an important part of the success of firms and countries and has become one of the main criteria for policy recommendations[24]. The new circumstances can be forcefully summarised in the words of Sylvia Hewlett: "In the last decade of the twentieth century, human capital will become the prime source of wealth and power for individuals, corporations and nations"[25].

The irony of this recognition is that hardly more than a decade ago, the main concerns were about the expected negative impacts of the diffusion of information technology on employment and skills. That early simplistic view about massive reduction in manpower needs and widespread deskilling of the workforce was gradually replaced by a deeper understanding of the complex combination of trends and countertrends, job and skill displacement, replacement, extension, redefinition, elimination and creation that accompany the diffusion of an all pervasive wave of technical change[26].

As concerns the impact of new technologies on skills it can be considered that "the debate has largely been settled in favour of upskilling" for most levels of employees and workers, including blue-collar[27]. There are changes in skill profile which vary from industry to industry and from country to country, but the trend with the widest social and economic consequences is the general increase in skill intensity as the new technologies and managerial techniques propagate. This obviously does not mean that every job in the economy of every country will be upskilled. It does mean that most jobs in competitive firms will require higher and growing skills as opposed to the permanent use of unskilled workers by major firms in the mass production system of the past.

Thus an important policy recommendation of the MIT-CIP report is to increase "learning for work and at work" because experience shows that "successful adaptation to the new economic environment involves workers, technicians and managers using technology in ways that require good preparation and continuous learning on the job"[28].

a. From people as cost to investment in people

Companies engaging in the organisational transformation discussed above have found that competitiveness hinges more and more on the capabilities not only of managers, engineers and supervisors but of every single one of their workers. So much so that the most advanced firms no longer consider expenditure in employee and worker training as a cost but treat it explicitly as an investment[29].

Estimates of returns on this very intangible form of asset are hard to come by, but MOTOROLA, a firm that has systematically engaged in a wide range of educational and training activities, has calculated a 30:1 return on such investment[30].

One of the main reasons for this growing need for a skilled — or rather multi-skilled — workforce is the trend towards more segmented and rapidly changing markets. To compete in this shifting world environment, firms need to accelerate their response capability, to augment their rate of assimilation of change and to attain maximum flexibility and adaptability. This is partly achieved through the use of multi-purpose programmable equipment. But to arrive at a thoroughly adaptable process — from variable inputs to segmented markets — a truly flexible type of human organisation is required.

b. The need for a participatory framework

Under the new competitive conditions, the old single-task, single-post type of job in which a worker operates under constant supervision according to the instruction manual is no longer adequate. Upskilling and multi-skilling cannot produce the necessary initiative and creativity if framed in the rigid organisation that characterised mass production. Skill enhancement needs to be complemented by conditions for participation. This is another area where it is critical to abandon the old "common sense" ideas of traditional best practice. But in this case the mental barriers are reinforced by social and ideological ones[31].

The increased role of skills in competitiveness thus involves two complementary aspects: on the one hand, the mastery of technology — both specific and generic — and, on the other, the ability and the incentives to make creative use of those skills. Bell and Richards have proposed the expression "change generating human capital"[32] in order to indicate the type of effort required and the criteria that both governments and companies should apply for investing in people.

It is also possible to see in this heightened role of human resources a basis for attaining true workplace democracy and a better quality of life[33]. The MIT Commission sees "an unprecedented opportunity in the new technologies for enabling workers at all levels of the firm to master their own work environment". They contrast this with "the technologies for mass-producing standard goods" which "consigned workers to tasks that made few demands on their mental capacities or skills". They consider that "the effective use of the new technology will require people to develop their capabilities for planning judgement, collaboration and the analysis of complex systems". If the opportunity is seized "individuals may experience a new measure of mastery and independence on the job that could well go beyond maximising productivity and extend to personal and professional satisfaction and well being"[34]. Of course, if no social processes develop to make such a possibility a consciously pursued goal, this opportunity could largely be wasted.

c. Education and training at the core of development strategies

The implications of this centrality of human resources for developing country firms and governments are of course many and of great importance. Change-generating skills become a key enabling factor both for competitive restructuring and for social equity. This is the central message of the 1990 ECLAC Report, "Changing Production Patterns with Social Equity"[35]. It can also be found in the World Bank Report for 1991 which states that "countries which committed themselves to education and training made great strides in both human development and economic growth"[36].

We would tend to go even further. Education and training have moved from being a complement to the growth process to becoming the most powerful tool at the core of development strategies. It is increasingly clear that the quality of the potential workforce is becoming the determining factor in the achievement of important development objectives[37]. It affects the ability of local firms to successfully compete internationally and domestically, the possibility of confronting some of the unemployment and marginality problems by developing micro-entrepreneurship on a massive scale, and the capacity to attract a significant amount of foreign investment. "In the dynamic and uncertain environment of technological change, more highly educated workers have a big advantage"[38].

But this understanding has been slow to reach the less advanced countries. It is interesting to note that, according to a worldwide survey conducted by Harvard Business Review, developing country managers put relatively less emphasis on the role of worker skills in determining competitiveness than did their counterparts in the industrialised world. One of the analysts suggests that this might reveal an excessive fixation on technology, which they tended to rate quite high among the success factors[39].

Yet among developing countries, those that have truly made a leap forward, such as South Korea and Taiwan, stand out for having made extraordinary efforts in human resource development with levels of participation in education comparable to those of developed countries. Additionally, firms in those countries provide significant amounts of in-house training, often extended to their suppliers[40].

Education and training therefore demand serious strategic attention including a deep reform in the contents, methods and structure of the whole system[41]. Yet it is essential, as both the World Bank and ECLAC Reports recognise, that governments play the key steering role, even as private sector contribution and active participation increase[42].

The role of government will be especially important in stimulating, enabling and financing a variety of forms of South-South collaboration in education and training. The experience of the European Community in its education and research programmes has demonstrated the enormous value of this kind of "networking" between countries. In Section 6 we return to the possible areas for South-South collaboration.

4. Investing in technological capability

The growing knowledge intensity of production and competition is often understood narrowly as pressure towards greater efforts in R&D both inside firms and in universities and institutes. But the discussion so far shows that it is in the combination and interaction of technology, organisation and human capital that the increased knowledge content of production is realised. This has immediate consequences for the direction of technological efforts within firms and for national science and technology (S&T) policies.

a. A new focus on innovation and diffusion

Traditionally S&T policy has focused on strengthening the supply side of the system, especially in the hope of supporting the development of new products and processes. These were expected to lead to breakthroughs for the local firms which might eventually use such results. In doing so, as the OECD-TEP report remarks, these policies "have probably insufficiently paid attention to the capacity of the economic and social system to incorporate such technological changes and transformations"[43]. While a supply-side focus was perhaps acceptable up to the recent past, it is becoming increasingly necessary to deal with the complexity of the innovation process from the perspective of the competing firm. This implies enhancing the firm's capability to absorb and generate technical change and raising its ability to use technologies from wherever they are generated. The time thus has come to shift the balance of concern "from R&D to innovation and diffusion policy"[44].

This change of focus is based in part on a fuller understanding of the role that users play in the process of innovation. Rather than being passive receivers of technology, users, it is now acknowledged, play a very active role in the generation of directly applicable technical change[45]. Indeed, as the MIT Commission pointed out, "simultaneous improvement in quality, cost and delivery" as well as "closer links to customers and closer relationships with suppliers" figured prominently among the factors contributing to competitiveness in successful companies[46].

One consequence of this is for governments to shift from financing innovation outside industry to helping strengthen the processes of technological mastery inside firms and to promoting and facilitating the inter-firm linkages, the exchange of information and all of the other conditions that favour technological interaction between users and producers. These networks of technical collaboration which are woven in a technologically dynamic economy are the core of what has been termed by Lundvall and Freeman the "national system of innovation"[47]. The quality of such a system and its degree of specialisation are crucial in determining the competitive advantage of a national economy.

A second is for firms to reconceptualise the R&D function. The traditional model of innovation within the firm was linear and sequential. People from the research and development department would bring the product or process up to the prototype stage. Then the functions of product engineering would take place and manufacturing and marketing would follow on. This form of compartmentalised effort takes much longer and is much less effective than what is now being called "simultaneous engineering". Researchers, designers, product, process and manufacturing engineers, marketing and salespeople work together in "self-organising development teams". Work is integrated towards a roughly defined product goal, development phases are simultaneous or have broad overlaps. The result is a much quicker response to markets, a significantly shorter time to innovation and increased learning from interaction[48].

Another important change in the traditional notions of technology within the firm is a shift in the focus of attention away from the product or process and towards the whole production system, beginning with the tangible and intangible inputs at the beginning of the chain, through the transformation, packaging and distribution process to servicing the product at the client's premises. Every aspect of the production system — and of the administrative procedures as well — is seen as a target for improvement. The overall result is a visible increase in quality, efficiency and adaptiveness resulting from the additive and systemic effect of minor, medium and major improvements being constantly incorporated at different points in the system.

This incremental attitude to technical change gradually leads to a deeper understanding of the potential and limitations of the technologies in use and points in the direction of more radical change. In short, changes such as this mean that competition is increasingly based on the mastery of technology in an everyday sense; on having production organisations that behave like learning machines.

b. Networks of collaboration

For any given firm, the production system to be improved, however, does not end at its own doors. Technical interaction for the purpose of continuous improvement, system upgrading and new product development requires links outside the organisation to other companies and institutions. Co-operation with suppliers, for example, takes many forms, from the basic exchange of information, through personnel training to collaborative engineering or R&D and joint investment[49]. Clients are also seen as technical partners. They are the source of valuable information about user needs and about the performance of existing products. Direct interaction with customers has been found to be one of the most effective means of guiding technical change[50]. Finally, networks with competitors, involving partial collaboration, patent agreements, joint research, and multiple arrangements for access to complementary assets or for sharing the high cost of some activities, are also becoming a feature of the modern competitive firm[51].

Universities and research institutes are among the most valuable suppliers firms can count upon. Their capacity to provide training, information, technical services and research is important. But for a wide range of reasons there are barriers which prevent a truly intense and fruitful interaction to take place between these institutions and productive units or networks.

c. Networks and the habits of an ISI past

In most developing countries barriers to business collaboration are particularly strong. In relationships between producers and their suppliers there is a long history of confrontation which might need great doses of good will and imagination to overcome.

In order to advance from the mere final assembly stage, most ISI policies included mechanisms to force end product manufacturers to incorporate domestically produced inputs, parts or capital goods, however high the cost or low the quality. The goal of deepening the industrialisation process was often achieved but with the unwanted side-effect of creating mistrust and adversarial relations between producers and their suppliers. It is often said in the developed world that firms have to learn to go from "arm's length relations" with suppliers to stable, technology centred, collaborative links. In developing countries the starting point can be better described as "gun-point confrontation". Overcoming these negative attitudes — reforming their institutional embodiments in ministries and industry associations — is a task facing both the private and the public sector on the road to competitive restructuring.

The experience of technical co-operation with R&D institutes was not very encouraging either. For most countries pursuing an ISI strategy, technology was an input purchased from the foreign originator and put to use by learning established and proven routines. In contrast, the attitude taken by the Japanese and the "catching-up" Asian NICs was to go beyond the mere use of imported technologies according to instructions, and to create a type of organisation and a level of technical skill in the workforce that would purposely lead to full mastery and continued improvement of such technologies.

Elsewhere governments in the developing world tried to compensate for the passive attitude towards technology that characterised local industry by building technological capabilities outside firms, establishing research and development institutes and allocating funds for science and technology to universities. These two worlds remained mainly apart despite constant efforts to build a "bridge" between supply and demand. Yet, as Martin Bell says, "supporting institutions can rarely generate technical change on behalf of industry without significant innovative activity on the part of industrial firms themselves"[52]. In other words, a bridge can only be built if there is a support on each side. But for most firms under the typical ISI regime innovation was not a source of profits. Exogenous factors such as the level of protection or subsidies had a much greater impact on profits than technology, productivity or quality of products.

All this led to another shortcoming: a generalised disdain for everyday engineering. Neither firms nor researchers saw incremental innovation as their concern. With a few notable exceptions[53], the great majority of engineers in developing countries have little experience in the constant improvement of products and processes which is so crucial today. Until recently, engineering graduates were often faced with a stark choice: either the passive operation of foreign technology or research isolated from production.

Competitive restructuring requires activating the links that create a national system of innovation. This depends on establishing a mutually fruitful relationship between industry and technological institutions on new grounds. Such a linkage could begin by the recognition of continuous improvement as an important joint job and of "learning by interacting" as the way to go about it[54].

Those countries that do not show themselves capable of establishing co-operative links among domestic firms and between these and technical institutes are likely to find it equally difficult to collaborate across borders. The experience developed through collaboration between firms within each country can become an invaluable asset for attempting co-operation between firms from different developing countries and making it successful.

The emphasis here on co-operation for incremental technical change is not intended to diminish the importance of R&D for new products and processes. Rather it is a question of timing in the process of learning to be technologically active. As firms and networks acquire greater mastery of technology in their daily practice, they become more capable of pursuing radical product and process change; as they move to more demanding market segments, they are pushed by competition to do so. This means that strengthening the quality and the capacity of the science and technology infrastructure to prepare for the expected increase in requirements is a wise — and indeed an indispensable — exercise in foresight on the part of both firms and governments. Regional co-operation programmes and regional consortia set up to do research about a shared natural resource, product or eco-system is one obvious way to cut the costs for each while increasing the benefits for all. We will return to this below.

5. Market focusing and strategic specialisation

Having seen from Sections 1 to 4 that competitive production rests on a combination of organisation, human capital and technology, we must now look at the ingredient that turns those necessary elements into actual wealth creation. The competitiveness of the firm can only bear fruit through success in the market. This in turn depends on selecting appropriate and realistic market targets. The most creative and efficient firm will fail if its product is unwanted. A company in a developing country trying to compete head-on with a global corporation is not likely to get very far, however much organisational effort it makes. The new approaches discussed above can only be useful for reconversion strategies in developing countries if appropriate market slices are identified by companies, groups of firms or countries and persistently pursued.

a. The collective dimension of specialisation

Another aspect of knowledge-intensive competition is the relationship between static and dynamic comparative advantages. Whereas the first can serve as an initial platform, it is the accumulation of dynamic advantages that determines competitiveness. Whereas the first can provide a basic cost advantage, only superiority in technology or managerial competence can guarantee sustained competitiveness as successive innovations change conditions in the market. Modern specialisation is a direct consequence of knowledge-intensive competition and the greater speed of technical change.

When all technological frontiers are moving, remaining in the race will often require concentration on one or very few areas. Firms must specialise in order to focus learning efforts; dispersion can be weakening.

But the firm cannot specialise in isolation. To be successful it needs to rely on interaction with other specialised firms whose capabilities and core competencies are complementary to its own and also growing. Equally, it must count upon externalities of all sorts, especially those related to the required types of qualified human resources and of technical services and information. Consequently, strategic decisions about specialisation are inevitably collective decisions, especially in countries where resources are too scarce to be squandered.

The question of how these collective decisions are arrived at is another matter. Looking at specific cases it certainly does not seem that they were the result of either pure markets or pure government decision-making. There are countries where geography or history have been decisive, as for instance Iceland's specialisation in fishing. In others, institutional arrangements facilitated the emergence of a consensus strategy, such as that between the Japanese private and public sectors under MITI's aegis. The specialisation of Silicon Valley in microelectronics appears to have been a spontaneous phenomenon driven by the advantages of agglomeration around the first few firms (Hewlett Packard, Intel, etc.) and some of the best university research laboratories in electronics (in Berkeley and Stanford). Informal networks are crucial to pioneering industries. In Chile, the export specialisation in fresh berries and salmon was propelled by the Fundación Chile, a promotional institution set up by ITT, which not only designed the project but organised the initial investment, the transfer of technology and the links with the traders and importers[55]. Both in Italy and in Germany provincial governments have worked together with the local industrial, banking and educational communities to strengthen and modernise the traditional regional speciality, be it engineering, clothing or ceramics[56]. The city of Rochester in the United States, which already had several firms working in optics (Kodak, Xerox, Bausch & Lomb), also arrived at an agreed consensus between the main private and public actors to turn the city into the world centre in optics and imaging technology[57]. The new competition seems to involve a high-tech resurgence of lost artisan attitudes as well as a revitalisation of the advantages of regional specialisation and agglomeration, stressed by Alfred Marshall a hundred years ago[58].

The routes to specialisation are then many and varied. The scale on which it occurs also has a wide range: a city, a province, a small or large geographic region or a countrywide network. A strong focus introduces a bias in the system of innovation, the advantages of which are obvious to all firms connected with that particular focus. That is the main point in Porter's argument about the competitive advantage of nations[59]: the accumulation of experience within each firm, the interaction within specialised networks, the focused research, the concentration of suppliers and services are powerful externalities for enhancing competitiveness.

The free market alone is not likely to lead firms to the sort of long term efforts and investment necessary to remain in dynamic markets. It is precisely to help firms compete better that collective specialisation strategies and a consensus on the need to reinforce the system of innovation, are crucial[60]. As Michael Best shows through his analysis of Japan and Northern Italy, "a healthy industrial sector depends upon combining competition with co-operation". Competition ensures constant innovativeness; co-operation ensures long-term competitiveness. The task of the new industrial policy is to administer this paradox[61].

b. Turning static advantages into dynamic strengths: rescuing the development value of natural resources

The issue of strategic specialisation brings us to the question of comparative advantages and whether they are back at the centre or out of the picture as two extreme positions in the debate would hold. We suggest that in the new circumstances both positions are right. Alone, comparative advantages such as natural resources and other static conditions are no longer a basis for capturing and maintaining market share. But they can become central again and crucially important to development strategies, when they are used as a platform on which to build dynamic advantages.

The new technologies are capable of upgrading and modernising any economic activity from mining, fishing and agriculture, through all branches of manufacturing to finance, distribution and other services[62]. The consequence of this for developing nations and for the firms within them is that the range of economic activities on which to base a process of dynamic growth has broadened. All sectors are capable of becoming technology-intensive. For a long time "development" was almost synonymous with "industrialisation". Manufacturing was seen as the sole generator of technology and progress, primary activities seemed to stagnate and the goal of almost every developing country was to diversify away from natural resources. In the present context, these notions must be revised. The time has come to seriously reconsider resource-based, knowledge-intensive development.

Succeeding in a strategy of turning simple static advantages into truly dynamic and competitive ones will not be easy. It involves intense effort and concentration of local technological capabilities in acquiring and mastering production technology. This demands equivalent and simultaneous efforts in organisation, training and skills, supplier development, continuous improvement of products and processes, effective marketing and technical relations with users. It may also require the establishment of some sort of institutional mechanism to bring together all actors in the system, from initial inputs to markets, in order to develop a consensus strategy and agree on targets and forms of co-operation. The objective would be to become as good at exploiting the potential of natural resources as the Japanese are at electronics[63].

Examples of success in this sort of strategy are the Colombians with fresh flower exports, the Chileans with fresh fruit and the Malaysians in palm products and rubber[64]. All have made intensive efforts at mastering the complexity of handling fresh produce for long distance highly demanding markets. Technology, skills and organisation are constantly being upgraded in agricultural production as well as in post-crop handling, packaging, distributing and marketing. The latter have sometimes required audacious business initiatives. In the case of Colombian flower exports, the resistance of US growers was met by the Colombian Association of Flower Exporters through a coalition with US associations of importers, retailers and supermarkets to resist import quotas. At the same time the Colombians established an alliance with the affected rose growers for a joint strategy to promote an overall increase in the sale of roses[65].

As concerns diversification, there can be a clear advantage in building around natural resources: upstream, to specialised inputs, capital goods and services; downstream, to greater value added and specialised products for "niche" markets. The accumulated technical expertise in the primary product makes for competent users capable of fruitful interaction with suppliers and clients. The growing synergy that can result from these networks of technical interaction can benefit all concerned. Suppliers have demanding customers to specify products and services together with a trial bed for testing and improving before eventual export efforts. Downstream producers can count on the experience of primary producers, with whom they also share an interest in conducting joint research. Finally, the primary producers benefit from the bias of the local system of innovation around their needs and markets. The network thus becomes the basis for a "positive-sum game" among its players.

The idea of following a path of advantage enhancement does not exclude being bold about new options. When building from existing advantages one can identify possibilities for effectively jumping into frontier technology. Biotechnology, new materials and information technology all have vast applicability and can be used as an important additional source of competitiveness in the development of natural resources. Biotechnology is an obvious tool for building dynamic advantages in agricultural activities. It is also useful for managing waste in mineral processing and even as a mining process, through bacterial leaching[66]. The point being made here is precisely that new hard and soft technologies are the tools available for modernising whatever the chosen economic activity. It just makes sense to choose those activities where there are static advantages and accumulated experience as a starting point.

c. Market segmentation and technology focusing

Previous experience can become the basis for the development of a set of "core competencies" in a well specified direction that can lead to dynamic advantages capable of increasing and enduring through time[67]. This is all the more important today when firms and countries are facing much more segmented markets, undergoing frequent technical change[68]. To capture a market position and retain it, firms need to concentrate their continuous improvement efforts in a precisely targeted market slice or range.

It is often said that the new competition involves an increasing number of non-price factors such as quality, reliability, service, timely delivery, flexible response and user-adaptedness. But these features figure in different combinations and with different prominence depending on the chosen market segment. In a specialised "niche", quality and user-adaptedness are much more important than price; for a high volume standard product, timely delivery and price are crucial for competition whereas user-adaptedness and service might not even be pertinent in many cases.

Such variation in the features demanded in each segment implies differences in emphasis for the building of technological capabilities. Figure 6 shows a summary view of these three very rough types of market targets and their characteristics for competitive strengths and technology focus.

Figure 6. **Different competitive and technological accent according to market segment**

	Economies of scale	Economies of scope	Economies of specialisation
Type of market segment	High volume	Multi-product range	User-adapted "niche"
Competitive features			
- Price	* * * * *	* * * *	*
- Quality	* * *	* * * *	* * * * *
- Delivery	* * * *	* * *	* * *
- Service	*	* *	* * * * *
- Flexibility		* * * * *	* * * *
Key area for mastery of technology	Process technology	Organisational technology	Product technology

Targeting the high bulk standard segments of the market for any product (i.e., being a so-called "low cost producer") demands a concentration of effort on the mastery of process technology with a particular emphasis on reliability and cost reduction through the elimination of waste in raw materials, capital, idle inventories, flawed products, by-products, bureaucracy or time.

At the other extreme, the narrow niche markets require the mastery of product technology on the basis of highly specialised and constantly upgraded knowledge and skills, plus very close interaction with the users.

An option located towards the middle part of the spectrum is seeking economies of scope through the multi-product firm operating in the medium volume segments. These, depending on the industry and specific chosen range, can be characterised by higher or lower rates of change in models or technical specifications. Competing in this part of the market demands high flexibility and quick response to variations in demand in terms of product mix (in volume) and product change (in specifications). Handling product variety in this way, which involves avoiding idle capacity through responding "on line" to demand variations in a range of segments, requires special efforts in organisational ("soft") technology.

Thus, the spectrum of options has become wider for almost all product ranges. This demands strategic decisions on the part of each producer. The best choice of location on the market spectrum will depend on many factors including static advantages, the sort of equipment already in place, the level and quality of accumulated knowledge and experience assets, the type of existing or potential market access, etc. There is also the possibility of following a gradual learning path from easier to more demanding market segments.

Whatever the choice, remaining competitive and profitable in fast changing segmented markets demands constant effort. No market position is safe without continuous upgrading of technological capabilities and monitoring of the market. This suggests that even the largest firms cannot remain in isolation. The need to build or join networks, create consortia for research or other purposes, to link up with partners for joint training, marketing, product improvement or other costly activities, to help suppliers and to interact with clients is inherent in the new conditions of competition. Contiguity becomes an asset in developing such networks.

d. Networks and territorial proximity

Proximity is another element to be taken into account when targeting markets and selecting a specialisation. In recent times, developing countries that are geographically closer to the most advanced ones have become the preferred location for foreign investment in export processing or in lower cost manufacturing. East Asian countries are being incorporated in successive concentric waves into the Japanese network[69]. Mexico's contiguity with the US favours it as parts producer for American companies; it also becomes an advantageous location for Japanese or European companies exporting into the US market. So the capacity to attract investment as part of global networks is affected by proximity to core producers or final markets[70].

But this aspect of the proximity issue is in a sense the most traditional. In terms of the new paradigm, knowledge-intensive competition in goods and services fosters frequent interaction and direct human contact in formal and informal networks.

Although the type of interaction varies in accordance with the market segment envisaged, being near certain services or suppliers can in some cases be more important than being close to final markets. So the territorial proximity issue needs to be taken into consideration when targeting markets.

Direct interaction between final producers and suppliers of intermediate goods or services is not so important when the final product is standardised or when the input in question is a basic sort of material. But technical change is increasingly affecting the range of what is considered to be standardised, and the practice of continuous improvement creates the need for direct human contact for technical networking. An organisational technique such as "just-in-time"[71], for instance, tends to favour a strong long-term relationship with a small number of chosen suppliers because it depends upon very quick adaptability and response of the whole chain to changes in demand. This makes physical proximity of suppliers almost indispensable. Equally, "total quality" production implies technical interaction with parts producers in order for the whole system to move towards zero defects. This direct contact often involves "supplier development" programmes where the core firm invests in improving the technical capacity of the chosen suppliers. In the case of very specialised suppliers, direct user-producer links increase the capacity on both sides of the relationship.

This has implications for the way to approach specialisation. A bid to take part in global networks as parts suppliers might be difficult for countries geographically far from the core producer. Next to labour or other cost advantages, attracting this sort of investment would also require great ease of communication and movement of people as well as fluid movement of goods. Physical distance, the quality of the transport and telecommunications infrastructure and the reliability of the services all count towards the competitiveness of suppliers, thus determining the viability of that option.

When the core of the supplier network is local, as when specialising in a natural resource, the quality of the domestically provided goods and services plays an important part in the competitiveness of the main exporters. This is the case when the large oil or mineral companies, the agricultural firms or groups of firms in the developing country, become the core users for supplier networks. The question then is how to attract foreign and local suppliers to give effective support to the core activity. For the local firms, dynamic interaction with the core producers and proven competence in providing the required goods and services may offer a protection equivalent to the old tariff barriers. Fostering the multiplication of these networks as well as the establishment of universities, research centres, consultancy and other technical services is part of the process of rescuing the development value of natural resources. Another aspect of this process is connecting up with foreign sources of information and technology as well as creating conditions to attract investment from highly specialised suppliers. A virtuous circle needs to be unleashed: the stronger the local system of innovation the more attractive it becomes for others, thus reinforcing it further.

A second type of proximity, which overlaps partially with the first, is between producers and final users. In the new competition user-adaptedness is an important characteristic of successful strategies. Locating next to particular key users or in the midst of a large group of users is an advantage in cases where intense interaction with clients is a key element in capturing or keeping markets.

This is obviously the case with customised services but also applies in a range of other cases: when technology is moving very fast and users are highly sophisticated (special materials for the semiconductor industry, for instance); when the main users are themselves very active in developing the technologies they need (as tends to happen with fine chemicals); where environmental factors are essential in determining product or service characteristics (for example, a pest-control system for a tropical crop); where market competition is very fierce in terms of quality, adaptability and functionality (specialised software, for instance); or whenever technical information for development, adaptation and upgrading are a key element in customer satisfaction. In many cases this can be done through a commercial network with technical services but in others direct contact with production engineering, research or design might be necessary.

This again has mixed consequences for specialisation strategies in the developing world. At one extreme, in the high tech sophisticated "niches" there is considerable restriction for successful entry, given that the immense majority of sophisticated users are in the advanced countries. So great care must be exercised when targeting such niches. One obvious recommendation, when aspiring to relatively high-tech products, is to target the needs of the local resource-based industries, when these are — or are trying to become — technologically dynamic and competitive. Linking up with the Venezuelan oil industry, for instance, there is growing expertise in digital image processing services, in certain catalysts and in special chemically treated perforation muds[72]. Analogous examples can probably be found in every country. Other options may involve partners in the advanced countries or technical service "outposts" perhaps in co-operation with other firms.

In contrast to the restrictions encountered when targeting high tech users, the range of opportunities widens wherever the customising or adaptation is related to environmental, cultural or other territorial factors. This is then the case whenever the local market is the initial target and its peculiarities define the "niche". In the case of biotechnology, for instance, Alyson Warhurst has pointed out the difference between closed and open processes[73]. The former take place in an industrial plant or laboratory; the open processes must be carried out in a particular territory and be specific to it. Bacterial leaching as a mining process; some depolluting systems; natural fertilizers, pest control systems, vaccines for local animal or human diseases; and plant or animal varieties adapted to thrive in specific conditions, are some examples of open processes where interaction with the users in the territory allows the development of specialised products. Even in consumer-oriented industries, such as the automobile, global companies locate some of their engineering design centres with a view to adapting to the cultural or climatic requirements of a particular region. This is the policy of Volkswagen in Europe, and at least one Japanese company has declared its intention to set up design centres in several regions of the world to adapt their product to the market[74]. Institutional differences can also be a source of advantages. The electronic banking systems developed in Brazil adapt to the specific type of continental-size, country-wide network, peculiar to Brazilian banks. This gives them an edge in the domestic market and has helped their exports to other countries with similar banking structures[75].

Thus, the capacity of the new technologies to adapt to user-needs gives territorial specificity a more important role to play in defining market segments. Fostering interaction between competent producers and final users, to identify and develop such segments, is an option to consider when developing patterns of specialisation.

6. Internal constraints and windows of opportunity

For a large proportion of developing country firms and governments the idea of striving to become internationally competitive marks a fundamental change in attitude. For decades one of the roles of the State in many countries has been to take compensatory measures for what was understood to be the inevitable lack of competitiveness of firms in their territory. Yet it seems an inescapable fact that the world is going towards open frontiers (whether within trading blocs or globally). To grow and develop, firms and countries will have to become capable of successfully competing in a much wider and much more demanding environment.

The transformation towards knowledge-intensive production and markets is proceeding at different speeds in the various advanced countries and in the "catching-up" NICs. Within most of those countries, it is still only the more dynamic firms and industries that have adopted the new practices. Yet the competitive strength they display in the market makes it likely that technical dynamism and networking will become not only best practice but the normal behaviour of well managed firms everywhere.

a. Obstacles to surmount and opportunities to pursue

Among the developing countries there is a wide variation in terms of the level of awareness of these changing conditions and in the extent to which they are being taken on board in practical terms in strategies and policies. There are, of course, many obstacles in the way of widespread adoption of innovation oriented practices. Some are similar to those faced by firms in the more advanced countries, others are due to underdevelopment itself. But perhaps some of the more intractable ones are the institutional and ideological barriers inherited from the once effective ISI model, including powerful vested interests in the old way of doing things.

The period of industrialising by sheltering the domestic market left a valuable legacy of investment in plant and equipment, development of physical infrastructure, managerial and worker skills and experience, a higher level of education as well as varying amounts of engineering and research capabilities and facilities. This is the platform from which to launch modernisation and reconversion efforts.

But for most countries this positive inheritance carries also a heavy burden. The typical ISI framework, excluding the few cases such as Korea that used it as preparation for competitive exports, remained inward oriented and allowed firms to grow with a particularly passive approach to technology and markets. The combination of high tariff protection, various forms of subsidy, and restrictions to competition[76], made it possible for firms to be highly profitable with little or no effort to increase productivity or quality and with almost no risk of losing what were in fact captive local markets. Even the export promotion policies of later stages carried large subsidies to offset the lower local productivity.

This means that whatever the level of industrialisation attained through an ISI strategy, each country will have to overcome two different sets of weaknesses if it is to become competitive. On the one hand it has to confront changes similar to those identified for US industry by the MIT Commission; in other words, the technologies, the managerial practices, the know-how acquired through traditional technology transfer processes are now as partially obsolete as they are in their countries of origin and must be upgraded and modernised. Additionally, developing country firms need to surmount dependency on state protection and subsidies while they become active in the mastery of technology and in market competition; in other words, firms must endogenise their sources of profitability.

Ironically, the process of weaning firms away from dependency on the state is likely to require support from government. The type of changes to be effected imply access to information, to technical services, training, consultancy and other inputs which must be available in the local environment if they are not to imply excessive expenses. They could also involve transition costs that many firms otherwise capable of surviving might not be able to afford on their own[77].

In sum, while there is no denying that the changes currently underway have mixed consequences for development prospects, this chapter has tried to emphasize some of the positive routes opened for development policies under these new conditions. These include:

i) The possibility of optimising the use of scarce financial resources by reconverting existing plant through reorganisation and by favouring modular growth which reduces the need for new investment in designing new plants;

ii) The potential for reaping high returns from investment in change-generating human capital, while also contributing to greater workplace democracy and social equity;

iii) The advantages that can be created by strengthening the national system of innovation, starting with efforts to bring together the technological capabilities existing outside and inside the productive system to concentrate on incremental innovation and mastery of the technologies already in use;

iv) The possibility of rescuing the development value of natural resources by using these resources as a platform to build competitive advantages and as the core of innovative networks for upstream and downstream spin-offs; and,

v) In general, the opening up of a growing range of options for specialisation stemming from the all-pervasiveness of new technologies, the increasing segmentation of markets and the growth of global networks. This wide spectrum allows each firm, group of firms or country to home in on those market targets that provide an optimal learning route and make the best use of its particular combination of conditions and competitive assets.

b. Some avenues for South-South co-operation

As technology and competitiveness become prominent among the tools and the goals of development strategies within countries, the objects of intercountry agreements will naturally follow along the same route. Even free trade areas, such as the one recently established by the countries of the Andean Pact, now go beyond looking for enlarged markets and explicitly state that a "modern and dynamic insertion in the world economy, reinforcing the competitiveness of Andean economies", is one of the main goals[78]. Given the demands of the new competition, we may be entering, as Lynn Mytelka suggests, a phase of innovation centred co-operation[79].

In fact, collaborative links between firms, regions and countries are likely to multiply rapidly in all directions: North-North, North-South, East-West, South-South, etc. The more prominent of these will naturally be the supranational framework agreements, such as the Free Trade "Blocs". The other innumerable arrangements for partnering and co-operation between firms across borders and in wide international networks or the local initiatives among neighbouring or similar regions will be less visible yet their impact in the long term will perhaps be the most significant. These are likely to be established for specific purposes, by the direct actors, in the context of common or complementary interests and strategies. Here we shall refer to some possible South-South collaboration initiatives to facilitate the processes of modernisation.

i) If enough countries undertake the reorganisation route to modernisation outlined above, regional banks, such as the Inter-American Developing Bank or the CAF and eventually the World Bank, could be convinced to open lines of credit to finance this type of activity in each country and to support public, private or mixed organisations in setting up regional training programmes and mechanisms for sharing experience and information[80].

ii) Investment in human resources could also benefit from co-operation between neighbouring countries, particularly by: sharing the costs of training programmes and of permanent centres in certain technologies; sharing experiences and expertise in relation to educational reform; bringing international specialists for joint courses in areas of common interest; retraining teachers; collectively funding educational material such as video programmes, satellite broadcast and computer teaching aids, etc.; and developing new textbooks between countries with a common language.

iii) As regards the system of innovations, this can develop on an intercountry or regional scale where there are shared eco-systems (Amazon basin, High Andes, African deserts, etc.) or types of natural resources, where there is specialisation in a similar sector or other commonalities such as language, culture, climate. The forms such co-operation might take include networks of technical interaction and various arrangements for joint training, marketing or exports. In regional free trade zones, as trade, communications and movement of people, goods and services increase, possibilities are likely to open for the creation of technical co-operation networks between suppliers, clients and competitors from neighbouring countries. This can be facilitated through financial or institutional agreements.

iv) Countries that take up the idea of knowledge-intensive natural resource development can explore at least three lines of South-South co-operation: extending their supplier networks by profiting from expertise available in neighbouring countries; joining other producers of the same resource to establish a combination of collaboration (for research, information, training, etc.) with competition in final markets; organising with all producers of the same resource to negotiate with consumers and establish positive-sum type rules against violent price fluctuations and other aspects of common interest.

v) Many "intercountry" linkages are likely to develop not between countries as such, but between nearby cities or neighbouring regions[81]. As tariff barriers come down, frontiers become transparent and awareness of shared resources and common interest can grow in border areas. Sharing a port, co-financing a portion of the telecommunications network or other special service, improving or building roads or railways can be joint projects to improve the infrastructure on both sides of a frontier. The same can be said about the technical infrastructure: training services, research centres, testing laboratories, are some of many possible shared projects across borders. Creating an appropriate institutional and legal framework to allow and indeed foster this sort of localised interaction is a task worth pursuing.

vi) Finally, much collaborations will take place between firms from different countries. If firms become the leading actors on the national scene, it is natural to expect this phenomenon to overflow into international co-operation. Again, action to remove obstacles and create a favourable context for such partnerships are worth undertaking.

These collaborative processes cannot be planned in the traditional manner nor will they occur by signing declarations. The actors must be involved, facilitating mechanisms will be better if they are simple and unbureaucratic but, most of all, co-operation is about specific actors joining to perform specific tasks for mutually beneficial results. Much imagination will be needed on the part of policy makers to avoid old style planning and to design schemes that stimulate and support the creativity of the economic actors themselves.

What has been argued throughout is that the present transition involves an upheaval in traditional common sense. This chapter has tried to spell out a few of the main elements of that new common sense and hence to set up some guideposts for viable managerial and institutional creativity. Our intention has been to paint the general background of change on which to locate the possible roles and purposes of intercountry co-operation. Thus, of necessity the chapter has been exploratory and suggestive rather than conclusive or normative. In the uncertain and turbulent world of today much experimenting will take place before a clear difference between successful and unsuccessful strategies can be drawn. There is no doubt, however, that an understanding of the nature of the changes taking place in technology, management and markets is a powerful tool in enhancing the likelihood of achieving positive results on the part of firms, groups of firms, governments or regional organisations.

1. Elsewhere we have suggested that these technological, organisational and institutional changes can be seen as interrelated and constituting a favourable opportunity for a leap in development. See Perez (1989); as well as Freeman and Perez (1988), pp.38-66.

2. See Kodama (1991).

3. See OECD (1991).

4. OECD (1991), Chapter 7. They propose a tentative classification of investment areas, separating two broad categories of intangibles: those directly technological in the conventional sense (R&D, patents and licenses, design and engineering), and those "enabling investment" which includes expenditures in worker training, information and organisational structure. Two other investment areas are singled out as distinct from physical investment: they are software and marketing. For a study of this phenomenon as it relates to a specific industry see Mytelka (1990).

5. Scholtz (1990). Quoted in OECD (1991), Chapter 7.

6. See Bell (forthcoming).

7. As proposed in C. Freeman (1992).

8. ECLAC (1990). Two additional Reports released in 1992 develop this position further: ECLAC (1992a) and ECLAC (1992b).

9. See World Bank (1991), p. 31.

10. Ingersoll Eng. (1985), and Dempsey (1984).

11. L. Soete, "Policy Synthesis" in OECD (1991), Part II.

12. In fact these two waves of change share common features and are strongly complementary. For a discussion of this see Perez (1991).

13. Dertouzos, Lester and Solow (1989).

14. When giving due weight to the various factors determining competitiveness, it must be borne in mind that the US firms being analysed are often at the frontier of "hard" technology which is precisely what makes it paradoxical that they should be losing out in competition.

15. Dertouzos, *et al.*, (1989), Ch. 3, p. 46.

16. See Perez (1989) and Perez and Soete (1988).

17. There is a set of reports on the results of organisational change in Venezuelan firms, which are part of a programme funded by the Andean Development Corp. (CAF) for training consultants in modernisation. They show gains in productivity, reduction of waste and rejects, increases in production, savings in raw material and energy, etc. from efforts in organisational change alone. See FIM-Productividad (1990-1991). For a detailed study of the evolution of a company in the UK and its results, see Kaplinsky (1991).

18. Sirkin and Stalk (1990).

19. Sirkin and Stalk (1990) p. 26.

20. For an example of how this route can yield catastrophic results, see Mytelka (1992a).

21. For a comprehensive textbook discussion of this and other aspects of technical and organisational change, see Bessant (1991).

22. Skezely (1987).

23. See *Business Week* (1984) and Geller (1986).

24. ECLAC, op.cit. (Note 8); Dertouzos *et al.* (1989) and in a more cautious way, also the World Bank (1991).

25. Hewelett (1991).

26. Freeman and Soete, eds. (1987).

27. OECD (1991), L. Soete, Policy Synthesis Part II.

28. Dertouzos *et al.* (1989) p. 135.

29. Wiggenhorn (1990).

30. S. Hooker (1990), cited in OECD (1991), Chapter 7.

31. The difficulty of the change was captured in a statement by K. Matsushita (from a company reputed as most conservative in this area). He notes that the worse obstacle found in the West for adapting to the new conditions, much more than the Tayloristic sort of organisations, is the Tayloristic mentality: "For you management is the art of effectively passing the ideas of the bosses into the hands of the workers... For us, management is the art of mobilising and nourishing the full intelligence of all to be put at the service of the projects of the enterprise" Matsushita (1985). For a discussion from the US point of view on the necessary changes both in managerial practices and in the role of trade unions, see Hoerr (1991).

32. Bell and Richards (1986).

33. Roobeek (1991). See also Freeman (1991a).

34. Dertouzos *et al.*, pp. 134-5.

35. ECLAC (1990) *op. cit.* (Note 8) pp. 61-81 and 103-123.

36. World Bank (1991) p. 52.

37. Even in the most developed countries this is being understood. R. Reich (recently named US Secretary of Labour in President Clinton's cabinet), for instance, suggests that today "American ownership of the corporation is profoundly less relevant to America's economic future than the skills, training and knowledge commanded by American workers", and he goes on to recommend a shift in emphasis towards "a strategy based more on the value of human capital and less on the value of financial capital". Reich (1990).

38. World Bank (1991), p. 57.

39. Austin (1991).

40. This is frequently presented as one of the main factors explaining their economic achievements. Alice Amsden, for instance, suggests that the lack of cheap natural resources, by contrast to the Latin American NICs, forced South Korea to concentrate on the intensive training and the effective deployment of its labour force. See Amsden (1990).

41. See Perez (1992).

42. World Bank (1991) pp. 52-53, ECLAC (1992b) Chapter 5.

43. OECD (1991) PR-Sect. I.

44. OECD (1991) PR-Section I, p. 29.

45. Eric von Hippel's research shows many cases, especially in capital goods, where product development has been done by the user and then passed on to the producer. See Von Hippel (1988).

46. Dertouzos, *et al.*, Chapter 9, pp. 117-128.

47. See Andersen and Lundvall(1988) and Freeman (1987).

48. See Reich (1989); also Best (1990), p. 155 and Imai, *et al.* (1985).

49. For an example from the automobile industry see Lamming (1987).

50. Lundvall (1988), pp. 349-369. See also, for the role of users in innovation, Von Hippel (1988).

51. Hagedoorn and Schakenraad (1990). For an analysis of ESPRIT, one of the CEE programmes to promote inter-firm collaboration, see L. Mytelka "States, Strategic Alliances and International Oligopolies: The European ESPRIT Programme" pp. 182-210 and "Crisis, Technological Change and the Strategic Alliance" pp. 7-34 in Mytelka, ed. (1991). Also Chesnais (1988).

52. Bell (1991) p. 9.

53. Jorge Katz has analysed the patterns of innovative technological behaviour of Latin American firms, in particular in the area of mechanical engineering, during the import substitution period. See Katz (1986).

54. The expression "learning by interacting" was introduced by the Aalborg group in connection with their work on National Systems of Innovation. See Lundvall (1988).

55. See Huss (1991); ECLAC "Cadenas agroexportadoras en Chile: Transferencia Productiva e Integración Social" July 24, 1991, Santiago, Doc. LC-L637 and Mytelka (1992b).

56. See for example: Brusco (1986).

57. Gabor (1991).

58. Marshall (1890).

59. On the notion of competitive (knowledge based) rather than comparative advantage and its attribution to nations and regions, see Porter (1990).

60. In a document to the World Bank, the Japanese Overseas Economic Co-operation Fund refers precisely to the fact that markets mainly reinforce static advantages, and to the need for complementing their working with more directed action. See OECF (1991).

61. Best (1990), p. 19.

62. The fact that the strongest initial impact of new technologies was on certain areas of manufacturing and services (electronics, automobile, information, finance, etc.) stems from a combination of factors, some relevant to the specific conditions of the pioneering countries and firms, others to the conditions of the industries themselves, some of these latter facing severe problems which the new technologies could solve, others finding it particularly easy to take advantage of the new potential. But gradually more and more branches of industry and more and more activities in the primary and tertiary sectors are adopting the new paradigm, both in their production patterns and in their approach to markets. The all-pervasiveness of information technology and the widespread applicability of the new organisational "common sense" give grounds to expect their propagation across sectors. For

a comprehensive review, see Miles, *et al.* (1988). For applications to specific sectors see Walker (1985) and (1986); Hoffman and Rush (1984); Mytelka (1990).

63. This is suggested by Professor Inohara from Sophia University in Tokyo when he remarks that "if nations rich in natural resources were to take advantage of their human resources in the way that the Asian countries of the Pacific basin have done, the results could be extraordinary". H. Inohara, Interview, *Economía Hoy*, Caracas, 11-9-91, p. 20.

64. See Linda Lim's chapter in this volume .

65. ECLAC (Note 8), p. 70.

66. See Clive Thomas' chapter on biotechnology in agriculture and Alyson Warhurst's about minerals, in this volume.

67. About "core competence" see Porter (1985) and Prahalad and Hamel, (1990).

68. For the importance of targeting in a service such as tourism, for instance, see Poon (1990) and Poon (1992).

69. C. Freeman has suggested that proximity to Japan or the United States has influenced the different outcome of the Asian and Latin American countries. See Freeman (1991b).

70. Joining global networks either in "maquiladora" type arrangements or in another specialised role is an option which needs to be considered afresh with reference to the new conditions, even though export processing zones may have had disappointing results in the traditional framework. This issue however will not be discussed here.

71. This system of production, developed in Japan, carries practically no inventories but works at the rhythm of demand. It requires strong links of interaction and trust along the whole chain of supply, which is simultaneously "pulled" by orders received at the downstream end. See Schoenberger (1982) and Bessant (1991).

72. Davila (1991a and 1991b).

73. Warhurst (1984).

74. Avishai (1991) and A. Graves (SPRU), personal communication about Nissan.

75. Cassiolato (1992).

76. Most import substitution policies implemented an entry restriction mechanism which required all investment to be registered in a government department which had to give its official permission for the go-ahead. If the market for the particular product was already satisfactorily covered by the production capacity of existing firms, permission was denied. Though the purpose of this measure was to preserve previous investment and to induce the development of new product areas, the result was often to favour oligopolistic behaviour with rigid high prices and low quality.

77. This need for support in the transition has been understood by governments in both advanced and developing countries. The British Department of Trade and Industry, for instance, set up the "Enterprise Initiative" offering consultancy, information and various technical services to firms wanting to modernise any aspect of their business, especially with a view to the single European market. The Andean Development Corporation (CAF) established a programme for the five member countries with the task of training consultants capable of helping firms to adopt modern managerial practices. Costa Rica has set up a government agency (CEGESTI) with a similar purpose.

78. JUNAC, Documentos de la Reunión de Galapogos, 17-18 Dec., 1989, "Objetivos Estrategicos", Lima, Dic. 1989, p. 43.

79. See Chapter 1 in this volume.

80. Programmes such as joint consultancy training as set up by CAF (see ref. 77) or the UNIDO initiative on capital goods for several countries in Latin America are already underway for joint modernisation efforts. Also, the sectorial loans available from the World Bank have enough flexibility to be used for intangible investment.

81. See Linda Lim's chapter in this volume.

Bibliography

AMSDEN, A. (1990), *Asia's Next Giant*, Oxford University Press, New York.

ANDERSEN, E. and B-A. LUNDVALL (1988), "Small National Systems of Innovation: An Analytic Framework", in C. Freeman and B-A. Lundvall, eds., *Small Countries Facing the Technological Revolution*, Pinter Publishers, London and New York.

AUSTIN, J.E. (1991), "The Boundaries of Business: The Developing Country Difference", HBR, July-August, p. 136.

AVISHAI, B. (1991), "A European Platform for Global Competition: An Interview with VW's Carl Hahn", *Harvard Business Review*, July-August, pp. 102-113.

BELL, M. (1991), "Science and Technology Policy Research in the 1990's: Key Issues for Developing Countries" paper prepared for the SPRU 25th Anniversary Conference, 3/4 July, 1991, Pinter, London, forthcoming.

BELL, M. and P. RICHARDS (1987), "Exploiting the potential of technology: a challenge for innovation policy, institutional development and co-operation", background paper on behalf of TOES/AMPS for the First International Libreville Summit, January, 1987. Mimeo, SPRU, University of Sussex, October 1986.

BESSANT, J. (1991), *Managing Advanced Manufacturing Technology: The Challenge of the Fifth Wave*, NCC/Blackwell, Manchester, England.

BEST, M.H. (1990), *The New Competition*, Polity Press, Cambridge.

BRUSCO, S. (1986), "Small Firms and Industrial Districts: The Experience of Italy", in D. Keeble and E. Wever eds., *New Firms and Regional* Development in Europe, Croom Helm, London, pp. 184-202.

Business Week, (1984), "Are Utilities Obsolete?", 21 May, pp. 60-71.

CASSIOLATO, J. (1992), "The User-Producer Connection in High-Tech: A Case-Study of Banking Automation in Brazil", in H. Schmitz and J. Cassiolato, eds., *High Tech for Industrial Development,*, Routledge, London and New York.

CHESNAIS, F. (1988), "Technical Co-operation Agreements Between Independent Firms: Novel Issues for Economic Analysis and the Formulation of National Technological Policies", *DSTI Review*, No. 4, Summer-Autumn, OECD, Paris.

DAVILA, E. (1991a), "IPQ: Hacer negocio a partir del lobl", *Diario de Caracas*, 2 May, p. 58.

DAVILA, E. (1991b), "Percepcion remota y sus aplicaciones", *Revista Instituto de Ingenieria*, Vol. VII, No. 23, March, p. 1.

DEMPSEY, P.A. (1984), "Flexibility with Prosperity in Manufacturing", Financial Times 2nd Automated Manufacturing Conference, London, March.

DERTOUZOS, M., R. LESTER, and R. SOLOW (1989), *Made in America: Regaining the Productive Edge*, MIT Press, Cambridge, Mass., and London.

DOSI, G. (1988), *Technical Change and Economic Theory*, Pinter Publishers, London and New York.

ECLAC (1990), *Changing Production Patterns with Social Equity*, Libros de la CEPAL, No. 25, Santiago de Chile.

ECLAC (1992a), *Social Equity and Changing Production Patterns: An Integrated Approach*, Santiago de Chile.

ECLAC (1992b), *Education and Knowledge: Basic Pillars of Changing Production Patterns with Social Equity*, Santiago de Chile.

FIM-PRODUCTIVIDAD (1990-1991), "Informes del Convenio CAF-FIM-Prod. para el Desarrollo de Programas Piloto de Mejora de Productividad y Calidad", Caracas.

FREEMAN, C. (1987), *Technology and Economic Performance: Lessons from Japan*, Pinter Publishers, London and New York.

FREEMAN, C. (1991a), "Technology, Progress and the Quality of Life", SPRU 25th Anniversary Papers, *Science and Public Policy*, Vol. 18, No. 6, December, 1991, pp. 407-418.

FREEMAN, C. (1991b), "Catching Up in World Growth and World Trade", SPRU, University of Sussex, December, (mimeo). Forthcoming in book in honour of Alf Maizels, 1993.

FREEMAN, C. (1992), *The Economics of Hope*, Pinter, London.

FREEMAN, C. and C. PEREZ (1988), "Structural Crises of Adjustment, Business Cycles and Investment Behaviour", in Dosi, *et al.*, eds., (1988), pp. 38-66.

FREEMAN, C. and L. SOETE, eds. (1987), *Technical Change and Full Employment*, Blackwell, Oxford and New York.

GABOR, A. (1991), "Rochester Focuses: A Community's Core Competence", *Harvard Business Review*, July-August, pp. 116-126.

GELLER, H.S. (1986), "End Use Electricity Conservation: Options for Developing Countries", Energy Department, Paper No. 32, The World Bank, Washington, D.C.

HAGEDOORN, J. and J. SCHAKENRAAD, (1990), "Inter-Firm Partnerships and Co-operative Strategies in Core Technologies", in C. Freeman and L. Soete, eds., *New Explorations in the Economics of Technical Change*, Pinter Publishers, London and New York, pp. 3-37.

HEWLETT, S.A. (1991), "The Boundaries of Business: the Human Resource Deficit", *Harvard Business Review*, July-August, p. 132.

HOERR, J. (1991), "What Should Unions Do?", *Harvard Business Review*, May-June, pp. 30-45.

HOFFMAN, K. and H. RUSH (1984), *Microelectronics and Clothing: The Impact of Technical Change on a Global Industry*, ILO, Geneva.

HOOKER, S. (1990), "Use of training at Motorola to support the development, acquisition and application of new technologies in six signma quality culture", Conference on Technology and Investment, Stockholm, 21-24 January, 1990. Cited in OECD (1991).

HUSS, T. (1991), "Transfer of Technology: The Case of the Chile Foundation", *CEPAL Review*, No. 43, Santiago, Chile, April.

IMAI, K-I. *et al.* (1985), "Managing the New Product Development Process", in K. Clark, *et al.*, *The Uneasy Alliance*, Harvard Business School Press, Boston.

INGERSOLL Eng. (1985), "Integrated Manufacture", IFS Publications Ltd., Springer-Verlag, Berlin, Heidelberg, New York, Tokyo.

KAPLINSKY, R. (1991), "From Mass Production to Flexible Specialisation: Micro-Level Restructuring in a British Engineering Firm", IDS, University of Sussex, England, April.

KATZ, J. (1986), *Development and Crisis of Latin American Technological Capabilities*, ECLAC, Buenos Aires.

KODAMA, F. (1991), *Analysing Japanese High Technologies: The Techno-Economic Paradigm Shift*, Pinter Publishers, London and New York.

LAMMING, R. (1987), "Towards Best Practice: A report on the UK automotive industry", Innovation Research Group, Brighton Business School, Brighton, England.

LUNDVALL, B-A. (1988), "Innovation as an Interactive Process: From User-Producer Interaction to the National System of Innovation", in G. Dosi, *et al.*, eds., (1988), pp. 349-369.

MARSHALL, A. (1890), *Principles of Economics*, MacMillan, London.

MATSUSHITA, K. (1985), *Science et Techniques*, No. special sur La Revolution de l'Intelligence, p. 11.

MILES, I. *et al.* (1988), *Information Horizons*, Edward Elgar, Aldershot, England.

MYTELKA, L. (1990), "New modes of competition in the textile and clothing industry: some consequences for Third World exporters" in J. Niosi, ed., Technology and

National Competitiveness, Mc-Gill-Queens University Press, Montreal 1990, pp. 225-246.

MYTELKA, L. ed. (1991), *Strategic Partnerships, States, Firms and International Competition*, Pinter, UK.

MYTELKA, L. (1992a), "Ivorian Industry at the Crossroads", in Frances Stewart, Sanjaya Lall and Samuel Wankgwe, eds., *Alternative Development Strategies in Sub-Saharian Africa*, MacMillan, London, pp. 243-264.

MYTELKA, L. (1992b), *Strategic Partnering: Some Lessons for Latin America*, IDRC Social Sciences Division and Montevideo, Ottawa.

OECD (1991), *Technology in a Changing World*, Background report of the Technology Economy Programme (TEP), Paris.

OECF (1991), "Issues Related to the World Bank's Approach to Structural Adjustment: Proposal from a Major Partner", OECF Occasional Paper No. 1, Tokyo, October.

PEREZ, C. (1989), "Technical Change, Competitive Restructuring and Institutional Reform in Developing Countries", SPR Publications, The World Bank, Washington D.C., Discussion paper No. 4, December. (Spanish version in *El Trimestre Economico*, Vol. LIX(1), No. 233, pp. 23-64.)

PEREZ, C. (1991), El Nuevo Patron Tecnologico: Microelectronica y Organizacion", in Carrasquero y Torres, eds., *Topicos de Ingenieria de Gestion*, Editorial Tecnica (EDIT), Caracas.

PEREZ, C. (1992), "New Technological Model and Higher Education: A View from the Changing World of Work", in G. Lopez Ospina, ed., *Challenges and Options, Specific Proposals*, Vol. 2, UNESCO, Caracas, pp. 121-145 (from the original Spanish in G. Lopez Ospina, ed., *Retos Cientificos y Tecnologicos*, Vol. 3, UNESCO, Caracas, pp. 23-49).

PEREZ, C. and L. SOETE (1988), "Catching up in Technology: Entry Barriers and Windows of Opportunity", in G. Dosi, *et al.*, eds., (1988) pp. 458-479.

POON, A. (1990), "Flexible Specialisation and Small Size: The Case of Caribbean Tourism", *World Development*, Vol. 18, No. 1, pp. 109-123.

POON, A. (1992), *Tourism, Technology and Competitive Strategies*, C.A.B. International, Wallingford, England, (forthcoming).

PORTER, M. (1985), *Competitive Advantage: Creating and Sustaining Superior Performance*, The Free Press, New York.

PORTER, M. (1990), *The Competitive Advantage of Nations*, The Free Press, New York.

PRAHALAD, C. and G. HAMEL (1990), "The Core Competence of the Corporation", *Harvard Business Review*, May-June.

REICH, R. (1989), "The Quiet Path to Technological Pre-eminence", *Scientific American*, Vol. 261, No. 4, October, pp. 41-47.

REICH, R. (1990), "Who is Us", *Harvard Business Review*, January-February, pp. 53-64.

ROOBEEK, A. (1991), "Technology and Democracy", Inaugural Address, The Netherlands School of Business, Nijenrode, January, 1991.

SCHOENBERGER, R. (1982), *Japanese Manufacturing Techniques*, The Free Press, New York and London.

SCHOLTZ, L. (1990), "Changing Structure of Investment in Different Industries", paper for the Conference on Technology and Investment, Stockholm, 21-24 January, 1990.

SIRKIN, H. and G. STALK (1990), "Fix the Process, not the Problem", *Harvard Business Review*, July-August, pp. 26-33.

SKEZELY, J. (1987), "Can Advanced Technology Save the US Steel Industry?", *Scientific American*, Vol. 257, No. 1, July, pp. 24-31.

VON HIPPEL, E. (1988), *The Sources of Innovation*, Oxford University Press, New York and Oxford.

WALKER, W. (1985), "Information Technology and the Use of Energy", *Energy Policy*, October, pp. 458-476.

WALKER, W. (1986), "Information Technology and Energy Supply", *Energy Policy*, December, pp. 466-488.

WARHURST, A. (1984), "The Application of Biotechnology for Mining", UNIDO report, March.

WIGGENHORN, W. (1990), "Motorola U: When Training Becomes an Education", *Harvard Business Review*, Vol. 68, No. 4, July-August.

WORLD BANK (1991), *World Development Report*, Washington D.C.

Chapter 3

NETWORK TRANSACTIONS, MARKET STRUCTURE AND TECHNOLOGY DIFFUSION — IMPLICATIONS FOR SOUTH-SOUTH CO-OPERATION

Dieter Ernst

Le mouvement actuel de mondialisation a provoqué l'émergence de réseaux toujours plus denses permettant l'échange et l'élaboration conjointe de connaissances scientifiques, de technologies génériques, de produits et de techniques de production, ou encore la production et le partage d'informations sur les marchés. On estime que ces réseaux devraient avoir des incidences favorables sur la structure des marchés, dans la mesure où ils viennent contrebalancer les fortes tendances à la concentration et à l'oligopolisation de l'économie mondiale. De plus, l'accès aux réseaux internationaux devrait améliorer la situation des pays en développement, aussi bien en termes d'accès aux marchés qu'en termes d'accès aux technologies. Ce chapitre étudie ces hypothèses à la lumière de l'expérience des secteurs automobile et électronique. Il illustre l'émergence de nouvelles barrières à l'entrée pour les entreprises des pays en développement. Cependant, il laisse également penser que la coopération sud-sud, qui encourage la création de réseaux, pourrait élargir la diffusion de certaines connaissances techniques et organisationnelles parmi les entreprises du sud. Les pouvoirs publics de ces pays sont appelés à jouer un rôle important dans le développement de ces réseaux.

A pattern of increasingly dense networks for the exchange and the joint production of scientific knowledge, generic technologies, product design, product technology and market intelligence is characteristic of current globalisation trends. These networks, it is argued, will have a positive impact on market structure by acting as a countervailing force against powerful concentration and oligopolisation trends in the global economy. Access to international networks, moreover, is expected to improve the position of developing countries both in terms of market access and technology acquisition. This chapter explores these propositions with particular reference to the automobile and the electronics industries. It illustrates the emergence of new barriers to entry for firms from developing countries. But it also suggests that South-South co-operation which stimulates the formation of networks could broaden the diffusion of basic technological and organisational capabilities among firms in the South. In developing such networks, states in the South have an important role to play.

1. Expectations

There is a widespread consensus today that prevailing concepts of south-south co-operation need to be revised. Attention has shifted from static comparative advantage to the formation of technological capabilities, organisational competence and competitive advantage[1]. South-south co-operation is increasingly seen as a defensive strategy which would enable developing countries (DCs) to cope with some of the new challenges and opportunities resulting from the globalisation of competition[2]. Among the most prominent challenges are the decreasing scope for domestic development strategies, due to debt-related structural adjustment programmes and the globalisation of financial markets; the proliferation of protectionist policies in major OECD countries; rising entry barriers in a wide variety of industries due to the growing knowledge-intensity of industrial production; a progressive marginalisation of developing countries from international investment and technology flows; and potential investment and trade diversion effects due to the spread of regionalisation trends, in particular in Europe[3] and in the Western Hemisphere (NAFTA)[4].

The globalisation of competition, however, may also have opened new opportunities for DCs. One of these relates to the spread of increasingly dense networks for the exchange and the joint production of scientific knowledge, generic technologies, product design, production technology and market intelligence which have been identified as "the most ubiquitous mode" of current globalisation trends[5]. Access to such networks is widely perceived to be an essential prerequisite for international competitiveness[6].

Expectations are running high that the spread of international network transactions could open up new possibilities for technological co-operation among DCs. According to this view, DCs could avoid some of the earlier problems of technical co-operation among developing countries (TCDC) and technology transfer[7], if they could exploit some of the intrinsic advantages of network transactions. For instance during a workshop organised for the project on which this book is based[8], the following expectations were explicitly raised:

— network transactions are essentially "open systems" which allow reasonably easy access for industrial latecomers;

— they open up new possibilities for reducing the threshold barriers for production as much as for support services (procurement, finance, marketing and R&D);

— they make it easier to reconcile the conflicting requirements of cost reduction, customisation and speed-to-market;

— they broaden the scope for decentralised decision-making and thus could increase decision autonomy for SMEs (small- and medium-sized enterprises) and industrial districts;

— applied on a regional basis, they may also enable developing countries to reap new advantages of proximity and to reduce the enormous co-ordination costs involved in global sourcing and marketing networks;

— they represent a shift from "one way" to increasingly reciprocal technology exchange relationships, thus broadening the scope for technology diffusion and learning;

— they strengthen the position of subcontractors, in particular suppliers of parts and components;

— and, finally, they open up new possibilities for the selective internationalisation of a growing number of ancillary engineering, development and research activities which could also benefit some firms in developing countries.

In short, network transactions are believed to have a positive impact on market structure, acting as a countervailing force against powerful concentration and oligopolisation trends in the global economy. Access to international networks is expected to improve the position of DCs both in terms of market access and technology acquisition. This of course assumes that access to such networks is unproblematic and that different actors face similar entry conditions. Used as an instrument of south-south co-operation, networks, it is believed, could improve the diffusion and effective absorption of internationally available technological and organisational innovations[9]. In contrast to both trade- and investment-driven forms of south-south co-operation, with their predominant polarisation effects[10], the spread of more open technology-related networks might also help to improve the distribution of the costs and benefits among participants to such arrangements.

These are far-reaching expectations. If they were to materialise, they might help to contain, if not to reverse, the vast technology gap which separates most DCs from OECD countries[11]. But can such expectations be realised? And what changes in government policies and firm strategies are required so that technology-related networks can become a viable instrument of south-south co-operation? In order to identify the conditions under which these potential benefits can be realised, particularly for industrial latecomers, we need to separate out in a meaningful way different forms of network transactions and those factors which condition their impact on market structure and on international technology diffusion. Section two provides a conceptual framework for doing this. Section three analyses the impact of networks on market structures in the OECD countries, focusing on the electronics and automotive industries. Section four contains a detailed analysis of two types of north-south networking arrangements that have been observed in the electronics industry: subcontracting arrangements and technology co-operation agreements. It looks, in particular, at the extent to which DCs were able to use such arrangements to strengthen domestic technological capabilities. The chapter concludes with a few observations concerning the conflicting claims about how DCs would utilise network transactions as an instrument of south-south co-operation.

2.1 Networks

I use the term **network** because it highlights "...the mobility of alliances, the flexibility of arrangements, the volatility of configurations and the multiplicity of modes of coordination, e.g. the fact that in some parts of the network, the market is the instrument of co-ordination, while in others this involves non-market organisational mechanisms, confidence and recognition"[12]. Networks differ from both markets and hierarchies[13] and constitute a *sui generis* means of organising economic transactions.

Networks can exist within a firm (intra-firm networks) or between companies (inter-firm networks). Intra-firm networks link together, within a firm, different divisions and business functions, such as R&D, design, engineering, procurement, production, marketing, and sales and customer services. They enable firms to overcome the "Taylorist" separation of these different business functions and to pursue them concurrently. Empirical research has identified three main impacts of networking[14]: links between marketing, design and manufacturing become closer; throughput time and speed-to-market are shortened; and feedback information on user requirements is channelled more rapidly to product design and production planning.

Currently the world's biggest computer network is **Internet** which links several million people (mostly academics and researchers) around the world through more than 750 000 host computers (most of them mainframe or mini computers). Here, however, I will focus primarily on inter-firm networks which link together formally independent firms through a shared computer-based communication structure[15]. Most computer networks in the corporate sector can be found in the car and the electronics industry, where all the dominant market leaders have established their own worldwide computer networks[16]. As a result, both industries are currently experiencing a wave of inter-organisational change that includes arrangements to exchange and combine core assets and strategic capabilities and to collaborate in innovation, design and engineering, procurement, production and marketing.

Today, a company's performance depends increasingly not only on its internal organisation, but on its relationships with its suppliers, customers and competitors. The difference between the internal organisation of a firm and its outside relations becomes blurred, as external sourcing for parts and components as much as for product designs and production technology is gaining in importance, and as organised markets within firms are expanding. Inter-organisational networks thus empower companies to respond to the requirements of global competition, by offering them new ways to co-operate. They enable companies to join forces without merging and they provide a new basis for combining cost reduction and product differentiation strategies.

Increasingly, inter-organisational networks cut across national boundaries. For the purpose of this chapter four types of cross-border inter-organisational networks are distinguished:

— **supplier networks** which are defined to include subcontracting, OEM (original equipment manufacturing) and ODM (original design manufacturing) arrangements between foreign MNEs and domestic suppliers of intermediate production inputs, such as materials, parts and components, sub-assemblies and software;

— **customer networks** which are related to the MNE affiliate's forward linkages with distributors, marketing channels, value-added resellers and end users, either in the major export markets or in the domestic market;

— **production networks** which enable competing producers to pool their production capacities, financial and human resources in order to broaden their product portfolios and geographic coverage;

— and, finally, **technology networks** which are related to the acquisition of product design and production technology, to joint product and process development and to the sharing of generic scientific knowledge. This does not imply that each participant must contribute technology. Often such arrangements involve a broader *"quid pro quo"*, such as "technology versus cash", "technology versus manufacturing excellence", and "technology versus access to the domestic market or to the government procurement market".

Given the variety of actors involved in such networks, it is hardly surprising that there is no single driving force, but a cluster of basic motivations. Which of these motivations dominate depends on a number of factors, such as the type of firms involved (in terms of their market position, financial strength, technological capabilities and strategic focus), the specific market segments and product groups we are talking about, and some broader structural peculiarities of the home and host countries involved (in particular market size and demand structure; industry structure and firm organisation; the cost and availability of financial and human capital; the quality of the material and science and technology infrastructure; and the strength of supplier and related industries). Research in the electronics industry for instance has shown[17] that a cluster of seven basic motivations has been of particular importance for the spread of inter-organisational networks:

— First, electronics companies nearly everywhere are under increasing pressure to reduce the costs and risks involved in differentiation strategies, by sharing complementary technological capabilities and the huge investment outlays required for product development, technology acquisition, manufacturing and marketing.

— Second, confronted with unpredictable demand fluctuations and drastically shortened product life cycles, electronic companies perceive networks as an instrument for increasing their global market share at a relatively low cost. Finding the right partner can help to penetrate a new market much more quickly and at a lower cost than by going it alone. Networks can also help to bypass an increasingly severe protectionism surrounding the major growth markets of the electronics industry.

— Third, given the turmoil in international capital markets, the cost of and access to capital has become a major concern for electronic companies, first in the United States, but now also in Japan and Europe. As a result, networks are widely perceived to allow companies to pool their limited financial resources. Empirical research has shown that organisational innovations, like networking, may often be primarily a defensive reaction to short-term financial constraint rather than a sign of strategic foresight[18].

— A fourth motivation underlying the establishment of networks has been to ensure continuous and cost-effective access to key inputs of production such as materials, core components, sub-assemblies and software, but also to scarce human resources. As the costs of these intermediate inputs are responsible for an increasing share of overall production costs, the focus of cost reduction strategies is shifting from scale economics in manufacturing to a reduction of the cost of external sourcing[19].

In addition to these more short-term considerations, three somewhat longer-term goals have been observed:

— Fifth, as product life cycles have shortened and competitive rivalry has intensified, electronic companies are under increasing pressure to accelerate speed-to-market and to compress time in all stages of industrial production, from product development to manufacturing, right through to sales and distribution[20]. Inter-organisational networks are expected to reduce "transition costs", "...that is costs that organisations incur when they seek to undergo a drastic restructuring to meet new challenges and implement new strategies"[21]. Networks are thus expected to speed up decision-making and response time by reducing inventory-to-sales ratios and order cycles and by increasing the share of sales processed directly to order[22].

— Sixth, market leaders who are under threat from potential new competitors are increasingly relying on inter-organisational networks to shift from individual to more collective forces of market deterrence strategies. This applies in particular to generic technologies, product designs and "best practice" manufacturing technologies. Networks thus have been used to tighten "appropriability regimes", e.g. the degree to which firms can obtain economic returns to various kinds of innovation[23], and to exclude firms which are not parties to the network from acquiring these innovations[24]. While unintended technology leakages may occur[25], they are perceived to be of secondary importance relative to the afore-mentioned strategic benefits[26].

— Finally, electronics firms all over the world are forming loose coalitions to build support for industry standards and to influence the increasingly important regulatory framework. These coalitions are very heterogeneous and unstable, due to a great variety of trade-offs and conflicts of interest involved for the different participants. Yet, without any doubt, they play an important, and so far largely neglected role in reshaping the nature of global competition in this industry[27].

2.2 Impact on market structure

In order to understand the impact of networks on market structure, I propose to use two criteria:

— First, some measure of the costs and risks involved in setting up and maintaining networks. The same applies to the costs which participants face, if they want to withdraw from such arrangements, once they become a burden. I am referring to the barriers to entry and exit involved in network transactions.

— A second, somewhat more problematic criterion for assessing the impact of networks on market structures relates to the following questions: How is the control over strategic assets and capabilities (such as finance, technology, market intelligence and distribution) distributed among network participants and what does this imply for the distribution of costs and benefits? This raises complex theoretical and methodological issues which cannot be addressed here[28]. For our purpose, I propose to distinguish three cases:

Centred networks where a system company (i.e. a car or a computer company) is linked with its suppliers and subcontractors in a highly unequal relationship. In the computer industry, for instance, this applies to much of the more conventional peripheral equipment and sub-assemblies (such as monitors, printers, disk drives, and add-on cards) where computer firms predominantly rely on OEM arrangements with a great variety of small- and medium-sized enterprises. It also applies to a huge number of fairly "low tech" electronic components and dated vintages of standard semiconductors. Centred networks are predominantly shaped by the requirements of the system company: to rationalise its logistics, procurement and marketing by shifting costs and risks onto other shoulders; to improve the quality of the parts and components and services received; and to speed up "time-to-market".

Networks among leading oligopolists which are more or less equal in terms of financial clout, technological prowess, manufacturing capabilities and retaliation possibilities. In such networks, supplier firms often equal if not outdo system companies in terms of size and economic power. In the computer industry for instance, this applies in particular to memory chips, microprocessors and flat-panel displays where supply is dominated by a few powerful global oligopolies. The outcome of such networks is contingent in the sense that both their impact on market structure and the distribution of costs and benefits depend on specific features of competitive strategies.

Co-operative networks which are created and managed by a federation of more or less equal partners (mostly small- and medium-size enterprises) which mutually depend on each other's specialised capabilities and assets. In some parts of Europe (e.g. in South-West Germany; Northern Italy; in the Basque province of Spain; and in parts of Scandinavia), co-operative networks traditionally have been important instruments of regional policy and industrial district formation.

Section 4 contains a brief review of evidence available in OECD countries on barriers to entry and exit of network transactions and on how control over strategic assets and capabilities is distributed among network participants.

2.3 Networks and technology diffusion

In order to capture the impact of networks on technology diffusion, one can distinguish four types of international technology transactions[29]:

- the acquisition of the right to employ a technology which is protected by a patent;
- the acquisition of capital goods which embody a technology or a set of technologies;
- the provision of technology support services which enable the receiving firm to use the technology;
- and, finally, the transfer of knowledge about basic design features and specifications of the technology which, in principle, should enable the receiving firm to reproduce, adapt and further develop the imported technology.

In this chapter, I will focus primarily on this last aspect, i.e. the learning processes involved in foreign technology sourcing, right from the pre-investment phase to the effective start-up of a project. In Section 4, I will inquire how two different forms of network transactions, i.e. supplier and technology networks affect the extent to which domestic firms in DCs have learned to participate actively in all of the different stages of production and how they have been able to internalise the knowledge created through such participation.

Second, I consider the term **transfer** of technology to be somewhat misleading and prefer instead to talk about the **absorption** and **diffusion** of technology. While absorption takes place on the level of the firm and contributes to the formation of its **technological capabilities**, diffusion refers to broader impacts for the economy. Leading-edge foreign technologies will first be absorbed only by a few leading domestic companies. In the medium term what really matters, however, is the pace with which the technology becomes widely diffused among most firms operating in the same or related industries in the host country and how this interacts with the formation of domestic technology networks. What level of technology absorption a firm is able to achieve depends on the strengths and weaknesses of the firm's accumulated technological capabilities[30].

This also depends on the strength of the domestic technology linkages that improve a firm's capacity to "...internalise the relevant externalities that spill-over across industries and within industries from the R&D conducted by suppliers, customers and by competition"[31]. This brings us to an important difference between developing and developed countries. While the latter have been able to build up over many decades highly sophisticated domestic technology linkages, this has not been the case in most developing countries. Most technologies are not available from other domestic sources. Thus external technology sourcing in developing countries, first and foremost, relates to the effective acquisition of foreign technologies. As a DC progresses in its industrial transformation, the share of external technology sourcing within the domestic economy, however, may increase substantially. Consequently, an important criterion for the impact of networks on technology diffusion will be the creation and spread of domestic technology linkages.

It is also important to move beyond the limitations of earlier transfer of technology debates which focussed on "internalised" technology flows within a corporate group and on market-driven technology arrangements[32]. Here, therefore, a distinction is drawn between direct and indirect forms of technology diffusion through networks. Direct technology diffusion occurs when the foreign company makes conscious efforts and resource commitments to transfer certain product or process technologies or technical support services. Predominantly they relate to some basic production and quality assurance capabilities, and to the transfer of "good manufacturing practices".

Indirect technology diffusion in general does not result from any conscious effort by the foreign company, but occurs as a side effect of interactions with a foreign company. Due to the spread of international supplier networks, indirect mechanisms of technology diffusion are arguably today of at least equal, if not greater, importance than direct ones. This applies in particular to those DCs which have been heavily exposed to subcontracting and OEM relationships. For subcontracting arrangements in South East Asia for instance, three indirect forms of technology diffusion have been identified[33].

— **learning facilitation** which results from the exposure of the local subcontractor to the foreign buyer's qualification process and which includes testing and diagnostic feedback on quality and other dimensions of the performance of the supplier's products; the sourcing of technical experts to solve specific technical problems encountered by the supplier; and advanced indications on future quality/performance/feature requirements and targets.

— **knowledge spillover effects** which are a typical example of the "information disclosure" problem identified by Williamson (1986) and which include: product design specification and performance requirements; early supplier involvement in prototype development; access to technical and marketing information on competitors' products; informal sharing of technical information and ideas among the technical staff of both companies; and exposure to the foreign company's system of managing production and R&D.

— and **investment inducement effects** which relate to investments in the formation of technological capabilities which the local supplier can only undertake because the subcontracting relationship reduces the perceived risk of such investments through a procurement commitment by the foreign company; because it provides a stable source of income to finance the investment; and because it provides access to superior market information that may reduce the risks involved in the investment decision.

3. Networks and market structure — the experience of OECD countries

Empirical research on the economics of network formation in OECD countries indeed supports some healthy scepticism concerning the potential of network transactions to reduce inequality of access to strategic assets, such as product design and generic technologies, and to spread the diffusion of technological capabilities and organisational competence[34]. Three features of existing network transactions are of particular relevance which, if left unchanged, would clearly obstruct any attempt to use such arrangements as a vehicle for south-south co-operation:

— the prevalence of very high barriers to entry and exist;

— the dominance of leading oligopolists;

— and the increasingly stringent sourcing requirements imposed by large system companies on suppliers of parts and components.

3.1 Barriers to entry and exit

Establishing and maintaining inter-organisational networks requires substantial investments in hardware (in particular in computer networks and communication equipment) as well as in software, organisational restructuring and training. Empirical research has shown that intangible investments in fact are of increasing importance relative to tangible investments[35]. Overall system development costs for the required computer networks may range from tens to hundreds of million dollars, creating impenetrable entry barriers to smaller firms — unless they join forces and create co-operative networks[36]. Take the example of a customer network established in a fairly traditional industry like paper manufacturing. When 18 mid-size US paper companies jointly developed a global electronic information system to link themselves with hundreds of key customers and international sales offices, the total cost of developing such a system was roughly $50 million. To this needs to be added the often quite substantial costs of organisational adjustment and of retraining the workforce.

Network costs are likely to remain high in particular due to two reasons:

— First, international communication networks continue to remain segmented into national telephone carrier fiefdoms which keeps communication costs at very high levels. The leased lines that provide the long-distance backbone of computer networks "...are inflexible and expensive — particularly in Europe, whose lack of competition means that leased lines cost up to ten times more than they do in America. Worse, because data traffic is so "bursty" data networkers have to support leased lines that work, on average, at only 1-3 per cent of capacity"[37].

— Second, limited progress in standardisation makes switching from one network to another quite costly. In addition, it enables network operators to pursue aggressive "lock-in" strategies: "Users who have subscribed to a particular EDI (= electronic data interchange) network find it almost impossible to change to another because each one is unique and users' business procedures have been built around it. Lock-in will become even more of a problem as network operators add facilities to differentiate themselves..."[38].

There are hopes that network costs may decline in the future as a result of two new developments. First, states have now started to step in and subsidise existing computer networks such as Internet and BITNET and there are plans now to develop an EC-wide computer network[39]. At the same time, attempts are now under way to provide smaller firms with the possibility of using third party operated value-added network services. While such outsourcing of value-added networks seems to have become an established practice in the financial industry[40], this is certainly not the case for computer networks used by manufacturing companies. Leading oligopolists for instance both in the computer and in the car industry are setting up their own worldwide communications systems[41] and request their suppliers to participate in these proprietary networks.

As a result, most of the network arrangements that I have described in Section 2 continue to be characterised by very high economies of scale and exit barriers. Both features privilege large, vertically integrated corporations to the detriment of smaller network participants. Economies of scale result from the fact that "...the larger the network, the lower the operating costs, ...the larger per unit revenues, and the larger the opportunities to appropriate externalities generated by the circulation of information and the distribution of intangible assets[42].

Exit barriers in turn result from the substantial "sunk costs" required for setting up such networks, where intangible investments into the knowledge and competence base and complementary support services exceed the costs of hardware investment. A firm's knowledge and competence base includes such activities as R&D (including R&D required for software design), technology acquisition (patents and licenses), technology monitoring and search, design, adaptive engineering and training. Its complementary support services encompass organisational restructuring, the continuous upgrading of human resources, the implementation and upgrading of information systems, software maintenance, and system engineering. Barriers to exit are high because of the lack of interface standards which makes switching from one network to another very costly, if not prohibitive — the costs of exit are estimated to be as high as the original investment into the information network infrastructure[43]. These high exit costs are an important barrier for smaller parties, but a source of contractual power for the dominant network company.

High entry and exit barriers "...may slow progress when the expected benefits are not high or strong enough to encourage actors to continue building the network..."[44] — hence the necessity for the government to provide network externalities. In the absence of such countervailing policies, both features are likely to privilege large, vertically integrated corporations to the detriment of smaller network participants. If network formation is left to market forces alone, this may increase even further the already substantial inequalities between large and small companies as well as between industrialised and developing countries. Multinational corporations, which are able to afford the huge costs and risks involved in establishing inter-company networks, can use such arrangements to increase their size, without running into the substantial diseconomies of excessive vertical integration. Participation for instance in customer networks can make big companies look small and allows them to target customer needs and to improve customer services. Large companies can thus improve their differentiation capabilities without adding further to structural rigidity. In short, networks enable large companies to combine the advantages of centralised strategic decision-making with a decentralisation of specialised functional activities. They may thus be used by them as an instrument for protecting or amplifying a dominant market position.

3.2 The dominance of leading oligopolists

Large Multinational Corporations have played a dominant role in the formation of network transactions and have used them as an instrument of oligopolistic competition. Network transactions enable competitors to co-operate on basic support services (such as R&D and standardisation) and intermediate production inputs (such as materials and common components), while maintaining keen competition at the final product stage. They are part of the "strategic games" played among the leading oligopolists or coalitions of firms which try to position themselves, so as to discourage or dictate the actions and responses of their current and potential competitors. Such games are played on different levels, where co-operation often goes hand in hand with intense competition and where governments play an increasingly important role.

While we lack systematic empirical research, available evidence[45] indicates that, in terms of their impact on market structure, the networks of greatest importance are those which either link together the leading oligopolists or are centred networks. Co-operative networks among SMEs have played a relatively minor role. Leading oligopolists, for example, have played an important role in shaping the concept of customer networks. Attempts in the airline industry to rationalise reservation information networks have thus led to the confrontation of two powerful coalitions of airline companies, i.e. Amadeus and Galileo, which are now dominating the market. In the electronics industry, they have played a prominent role in forming both production and technology networks[46]. Typical examples include the broad strategic alliance between IBM and Apple which aims to create the dominant personal computer standard for the 1990s[47]; Apple's agreement with Sony for the joint development and production of notebook computers[48]; and the strategic alliance between IBM and Siemens in 64 Mb DRAMS[49]. As for supplier networks, most of them are characterised by a highly unequal distribution of control over strategic assets and decision-making power[50].

In short, the desire to consolidate established oligopolies probably has been the main driving force between the current wave of network transactions in OECD countries. In order to use such arrangements as an instrument of south-south co-operation, substantial changes are required in government policies as well as in firm strategies, some of which I will briefly discuss in the concluding section of this chapter.

3.3 Intensifying sourcing requirements

In a growing number of industries, the focus of technology development is shifting from the level of the final product to technologies related to materials and core components. This is particularly notable in the car and the computer industries[51]. In the car industry, for instance, the redeployment of materials research and component development to component suppliers has opened up vast possibilities for cost reduction. Car producers can thus focus on product and system innovation which enables them to shorten innovation and product cycles and to accelerate speed-to-market[52]. As a result, suppliers are under increasing pressure to upgrade their technological and organisational capabilities, with a clear shift from low-cost assembly to increasingly sophisticated product design, process technology and market development capabilities.

In principle, a strengthening of technological capabilities of suppliers could be viewed as a positive development as it may improve their competitiveness. It may also help to increase the specialisation and the efficiency of parts production, as much as the quality and performance features of the relevant components. The accumulation of specialised technological capabilities could substantially improve the overall position of the supplier industry which in turn could help to upgrade the competitiveness of the car industry. The problem however is under what conditions suppliers can realise these potential benefits. Only a few large and integrated suppliers may be able to mobilise on their own the substantial resources required to overcome the threshold barriers for investment in new equipment, and even more so for the intangible investments in R&D, technological capability formation, training and organisational restructuring. Policy interventions may thus be required in order to generate the necessary network externalities which would enable SMEs to participate in this upgrading of technological capabilities[53].

Detailed company interviews in the German automotive components industry have shown that a stricter subordination to the outsourcing requirements of the car company has often drastically reduced the subcontractor's decision autonomy[54]. This applies in particular to the suppliers of standard components which in any components industry, in terms of sheer numbers, constitute a great majority. Most of these firms are SMEs. While remaining formally independent, they have to integrate all stages of their production process into the planning and decision-making process of their main customers. This applies not only to production scheduling, quality assurance and sales and marketing but also to the R&D in which they are engaged. In most cases, the supplier's decision autonomy has been reduced to the extent that all substantial decisions depend on approval by the customer. Viewed from the perspective of the car company, this is perfectly rational behaviour. Outsourcing potentially implies a loss of control over key assets — the car company's profitability thus increasingly depends on the effectiveness and reliability of its external networks. At the same time, there is the constant threat of "opportunistic behaviour" of suppliers. Car companies thus must establish effective control over all stages of the outsourcing process by increasing the "transparency" of the supplier's production process.

Decreasing decision autonomy is no longer an exclusive concern of standard component suppliers. Increasingly, this also affects specialised sub-contractors and niche producers which have heavily invested in upgrading their technological capabilities but which lack the size and financial clout to withstand the increasingly demanding control requirements of car companies. Only one type of supplier has clearly remained unaffected by this decreasing decision autonomy — a few large and integrated suppliers of sophisticated core components and sub-assemblies such as, for instance, Bosch. Overall then the German automotive components industry has been transformed into a pyramid, where "...at the top of the pyramid the supplier's relations with the customer are shaped by autonomy and 'trust', while suppliers at the bottom of the pyramid are subordinated to direct control and command by their respective customers"[55].

Similar findings have been reported for other countries[56]. Expectations that the current restructuring of supplier networks will lead to a shift towards co-operative production[57] may thus have been somewhat exaggerated. Co-operative production does occur, but it is basically limited to a small club of large multinational component suppliers[58].

A majority of car component suppliers, and in particular SMEs, have thus experienced a substantial deterioration in their position. At the same time as their costs and risks are growing, the subcontractors become more vulnerable to decisions taken by the core company. A research project, jointly undertaken by the FAST Programme of the European Communities and OECD Secretariat concludes that "...the production process of independent subcontractors is governed and instructed by CAD/CAM centres owned and managed by larger firms responsible for research and development, product design, input selection, quality control, and incremental product and process innovation[59]. And a policy document, published by Ford Europe in the fall of 1989, on its new subcontracting policy, explicitly states: "In the long term we will consider that a supplier who has our (Ford Europe's CAD/CAM, DE) system, will have an advantage over one that does not, in sourcing decisions..."[60].

While there has been a shift from short-term to somewhat longer-term relations, contracts normally last only for a particular product generation. According to one German expert on networking strategies, "...while the previous daily fight for customers is a matter of the past, every five years the very existence of the subcontractor is at stake"[61]. Practically all the major car producers have drastically reduced the number of their suppliers and rely on a much smaller group of preferred subcontractors. Even the Japanese car industry with its supposedly more permanent and less adversarial relations, has not been immune to such developments. As a result of demand stagnation, over-capacity and profit squeeze, all major Japanese car producers have been forced to rationalise their sourcing networks and to shift risks and costs onto the shoulders of suppliers[62]. Unfortunately, most theoretical debates on the nature of Japanese industrial organisation have not yet addressed these new developments which hardly correspond to the earlier optimistic expectations that had influenced much of the debate on networking strategies in developing countries[63].

Vehicle makers today, moreover, regard themselves basically as assemblers of a great variety of components and sub-assemblies produced by formally independent external suppliers with whom however they have increasingly close interactions throughout all the stages of the development and manufacturing cycle of a particular car generation. Suppliers can no longer rely on component designs they receive from the car company, but are required to shoulder at least part of the costs and risks involved in component design, system engineering and market development. Suppliers thus are required to possess strong in-house R&D capabilities, highly efficient production processes and a global presence close to major growth markets.

Few SMEs can afford to make the huge investment outlays involved and this has led to an increasing concentration within the car parts industry[64]. In short, for car components, technology-related network transactions have hardly acted as an instrument for extending the diffusion of technologies beyond a rather limited group of fairly large-scale leading component suppliers. Similar developments in the electronics industry are probably proceeding at an even faster pace. Again, the focus will be on network transactions related to the supply of parts and components and OEM arrangements[65]. I will use the case of the US computer industry in order to demonstrate how more demanding sourcing requirements have led to the establishment of centred network transactions which, for all practical purposes, are closed to outsiders and which restrict technology diffusion to a limited number of preferred suppliers.

Fundamental changes in the economics of computer manufacturing are responsible for this development and it is thus unlikely to be only of a transitional nature. With the current "down-sizing" of computer systems, the importance of components has increased in a dual sense: their share in overall value has grown, while at the same time they have become the main vehicle for differentiation strategies. This applies in particular to core components, such as microprocessors, a few powerful logic and memory chips, floppy and hard disk drives, power supplies and flat-panel displays. For the next generations of PCs and workstations, currently being designed, semiconductors and displays alone are estimated to account for more than half of the total hardware cost, and this trend is likely to continue[66]. Thus, pricing strategies of computer firms, i.e. the final assemblers, crucially depend on the prices of core components. This is reflected in drastic changes in the cost structure of computer systems. As a share of overall (ex factory) production costs, the costs of components, software and services which a typical personal computer company has to purchase from outside has increased from less than 60 per cent to more than 80 per cent during the last decade[67]. At the same time, direct labour costs which have been the focus of earlier rationalisation strategies of US computer companies, today hardly surpass 3 per cent of total production costs. For all practical purposes, labour costs are no longer a major sourcing criterion for computer manufacturers.

As a result, the focus of rationalisation strategies is shifting from intra-firm value-added activities (particularly in manufacturing) to a reduction of the cost of external sourcing. Today, the share of co-ordination costs required for the management of external sourcing relations, in overall production costs, is nearly as high as the cost of in-house manufacturing activities, i.e. 10 per cent. In other words, US computer companies are currently under increasing pressure to identify and reduce the "hidden" costs of international sourcing networks. One way of doing this is to persuade component suppliers to reduce their price-per-part quotations. Another is to reshape the organisation and management of supply networks in such a way that co-ordination costs can be reduced.

But cost reduction is only one aspect. As in the car industry, mastery of low-cost production techniques is no longer sufficient for the survival of sub-contractors in the electronics industry. More than ever before, stringent requirements on quality, time-to-market and flexibility are decisive in determining whether a component firm can remain or become a member of a computer company's supplier network. This requires, first and foremost, that component suppliers must follow their customers in establishing production close to or in the major growth markets in the US, East Asia and Europe. Suppliers thus must engage in substantial FDI in order to globalise their production network. As a result, Japanese component suppliers, as much as their European and American counterparts, have substantially increased their outward foreign direct investments in all major international computer markets and mutual raiding of each other's markets has become the rule of the game[68]. As product life cycles for computers have been drastically shortened, computer firms prefer suppliers who provide assistance in reducing the time required to launch new products and who are capable of responding at short notice to changes in the marketplace. In order to ensure the rapid conversion of customer specifications into components, suppliers are required to have sophisticated CAD/CAM capabilities and to integrate themselves into the computer company's information network. In terms of technological capabilities, suppliers are requested not only to master the most sophisticated assembly technologies (including surface mount) but also to complement them with sound circuit design and system integration capabilities. At the same time, suppliers are required to be familiar with "state-of-the-art" materials and manufacturing processes and to provide a full range of engineering services, including design, prototyping, test, component qualification, and failure analysis. In short, the sourcing requirements imposed on the suppliers of electronic parts and components and of computer peripherals have drastically increased and suppliers are forced to substantially expand their investments in human resources development, technological capability formation and organisational restructuring. In the absence of corrective countervailing policies, the outcome may very well be an increasingly concentrated market structure rather than a decentralisation of decision-making power.

4. Networks and north-south technology diffusion — a preliminary assessment

Technological capability formation in developing countries, by definition, has to rely to a large degree on imported technology. This is so because most global R&D and technological resources are located in the US, Western Europe and Japan, with a large share concentrated in large TNCs in leading industries[69]. More than 90 per cent of world R&D expenditures are concentrated in OECD countries. The seven leading OECD countries account for about 75 to 80 per cent of total capital goods exports. At least 85 per cent if not 90 per cent of all technology licence transactions originate from just 5 ountries, the US, Japan, Germany, the UK and France. And all attempts to restructure and rationalise the organisation of firms and industries have originated in a few major OECD countries, in particular Western Europe, Japan and the US.

It is thus important to understand the changes that are currently taking place in international technology markets and how they are likely to affect the formation of technological capabilities in developing countries. In what follows, I will briefly discuss the degree to which DCs have been able to benefit from the spread of international network transactions and the impact this has had on north-south technology diffusion. More specifically, I will inquire into the validity of the following two expectations which have played an important role in the debate of this project on south-south co-operation[70]:

— The spread of north-south *supplier networks* "...has led to a more effective transfer of technology to local firms, thus strengthening their ability to innovate in the future".

— The emergence of at least some north-south *technology networks* has "...opened up new windows of opportunity for innovation in the developing countries and they are laying the basis for the kind of north-south linkages that could complement south-south ties".

Substantial empirical research is still required, in order to achieve a systematic assessment and the conclusions drawn here are thus of a preliminary nature. On the basis of existing research[71], however, it is fair to say that, while the experience with supplier networks, *cum grano salis*, has been fairly positive, in particular for countries at a relatively early stage of their technological capability formation, this is not the case for technology networks. This is hardly surprising for at least two reasons. First, the closer these East Asian companies are moving towards the "technology frontier", the more hesitant their OECD competitors become to share their advanced technologies with them. Second, "...[t]o take industrial advantage of generic knowledge or technology that is licensed from another company or more generally of understanding what another company has done and how now requires significant inputs of trained scientists and engineers, often involving research and development, aimed to tailor what has been learned to the specific relevant uses"[72]. Technology networks which thrive on continuous feedbacks among a great variety of economic actors have substantially increased the initial knowledge base required for each participant. While Korean and Taiwanese firms have excelled in production technology and quality assurance techniques, their knowledge base is still quite weak[73] and firms in most other developing countries cannot even match their level. In what follows I will look in more detail at each of these types of networks.

4.1 Supplier networks — an overview

Supplier networks have played an important role for north-south technology diffusion, particularly in the electronics industry[74]. Most of them are concentrated on the four leading East Asian Newly Industrialising Economies (EANIEs), i.e. South Korea, Taiwan, Hong Kong and Singapore. After 1985, Malaysia and Thailand also attracted a number of such arrangements[75]. In Section 4.2, I will review a few examples of subcontracting arrangements in the East Asian electronics industry and document the degree to which they have contributed to the formation of domestic technological capabilities and linkages. Due to a lack of empirical and firm-specific research it is not yet possible to provide an assessment of OEM relations[76].

Subcontracting refers to a fairly loose type of network where a foreign buyer firm procures supplies from domestic suppliers through arms' length market transactions. In the electronics industry, the foreign buyer normally is a large MNC which typically relies on multiple sources, sometimes located in different continents and whose main concern is to reduce the transaction costs involved in international sourcing and to accelerate its "speed-to-market". The status of domestic suppliers is somewhat more problematic to define. While some studies assume the domestic supplier to be an SME[77], there is sufficient empirical evidence to argue that the "domestic" supplier is often foreign, in particular a Japanese component producer, who has set up shop particularly in Malaysia and Thailand. The degree to which localisation of component sourcing may have benefited affiliates of Japanese electronic component producers may be gathered from the following figures: the number of affiliates of Japanese electronic components producers in ASEAN countries increased from 8 in 1980-1984 to 74 in 1985-1990. As a result, the share of ASEAN in the overall number of new affiliates in electronic components increased from 12.5 per cent in 1980-1984 to 36.4 per cent in 1985-1990[78]. When assessing the impact of subcontracting on the formation of **domestic** capabilities and linkages, one thus needs to be very careful not to overestimate such effects. Japanese subsidiaries in the electronics industry in Asia have indeed procured a relatively high share of their components and parts from local sources — a Japanese study published in 1988 reported a 40 per cent local sourcing share[79]. Yet probably a large part of these "domestic" sourcing requirements were provided by Japanese affiliates.

OEM arrangements differ from subcontracting arrangements in that they involve a broader scope and a higher degree of organisational integration. While this normally increases the effectiveness and impact of such arrangements, it may also increase co-ordination costs and reduce their flexibility[80]. As for their effectiveness and impact, OEM arrangements are probably one of the least costly ways for a firm to enter international electronics markets. In such arrangements the customer provides detailed technical "blueprints" to allow the contractor to produce according to specifications. Often, technical assistance in engineering and process technology is also provided, in order to ensure quality and cost efficiency. As the customer is responsible for marketing and distribution and for R&D, the OEM supplier can avoid the huge investment outlays required for these activities and thus can concentrate on the development of its core capabilities. In order to qualify as an OEM supplier a firm must already have developed considerable technological capabilities and organisational competence, particularly for production, investment and adaptive engineering. These capabilities need to be continuously upgraded in order to avoid losing OEM status. Such upgrading is even more necessary if the firm wants to move up to the higher value-added segment of the OEM market. This applies in particular if the supplier wants to be upgraded to the so-called ODM (original design manufacturer) status where, in addition to manufacturing services, detailed product design based on the fairly loosely defined requirements of the customer are also provided by the supplier. Obviously, the capacity to improve upon existing designs and to further develop them constitutes a "quantum jump" in the development of technological capabilities. All of this implies that there is a continuum between OEM and ODM arrangements which covers a great variety of degrees of technological sophistication and performance requirements. We need to keep in mind this plurality of OEM/ODM arrangements, when discussing their impact on technology diffusion.

As for the costs and risks involved in such arrangements, they can be quite substantial for both customers and suppliers. They are certainly higher than those involved in subcontracting arrangements. As both customers and suppliers have had to commit substantial resources, this may lead to "lock-in-effects". Customers may hesitate to shift suppliers, even if they lag behind in technological upgrading, due to the substantial "sunk costs" required for setting up such arrangements, in particular intangible investments in the suppliers' technological capabilities. To be able to produce a product of complex design to specifications at competitive costs normally requires a considerable transfer of engineering as well as managerial know-how. Such transfers cannot take place on short notice, but require relatively extended learning periods. A supplier, in turn, may become "locked in" an OEM relationship to the extent that it is hindered from developing its own independent brand name recognition and marketing channels. Profit margins are thinner in OEM sales than for own brand sales, which in turn makes it difficult to muster the capital needed to invest in R&D and market development required for an OBN (original brand name) strategy. This constraint would matter less if sales volumes could be large and fairly well predictable so that, despite low profit margins, total earnings may be substantial. While traditionally OEM relations in the electronics industry could rely on high and reasonably predictable production volumes, today this has become much more problematic[81]. This applies as much to the computer industry as to consumer electronics where growing constraints to rapid market growth have led to a transformation of sellers' into buyers' markets. As a result, for each product generation, sales volumes have declined and demand fluctuations intensified. This has had particularly negative implications for East Asian OEM producers of computer peripherals, colour TVs and Video cassette recorders.

4.2 Subcontracting arrangements

Subcontracting arrangements are a typical feature of the East Asian electronics industry. They cover a variety of activities, such as the assembly of printed circuit boards, the supply of electronic components other than integrated circuits (in particular capacitors, resistors, inductors, relays, coils and connectors), electro-mechanical components, metal stamping, mould and die making, plastic injection, precision tooling and machining services, automated equipment design and manufacturing, and electronics sub-assembly and prototyping services. Indirect forms of technology diffusion, such as learning facilitation, information spill-over and investment inducement[82], play a more important role than direct and deliberate transfer of technology activities by MNEs. Local suppliers in Singapore, for instance, have benefited most from customer feedback on quality testing and diagnostics, access to product design specifications and exposure to general "good manufacturing practices"[83]. In many cases, buyers have neither the incentives nor the expertise to transfer specific technological process know-how to their suppliers. This is hardly surprising as the main concern of foreign MNEs is the sharing of costs and risks while maintaining flexibility in the face of substantial uncertainties which are due to rapid technological change and abrupt demand fluctuations. As Wong thus argues, MNEs thus will "...only devote resources to transfer technological know-how to their suppliers if the expected returns from such efforts outweigh the costs (which include resource costs as well as potential rent dissipation)".

This observation is certainly true for standardized items where there is a great variety of alternative suppliers. For specialised items, where the supplier would need to engage in sizeable asset-specific investments, MNEs are however normally forced to provide an incentive to the supplier, mostly through a commitment to a long-term relationship. For specialised components, MNEs have also a strong interest to develop local talent. Take the case of Motorola. Through its international staffing offices in Schaumberg, Illinois and Phoenix, Arizona, Motorola has aggressively recruited American-educated Asian engineers and business executives for its subcontracting operations in their home countries[84], particularly in Malaysia and China.

In addition to a lack of incentives, MNEs may not transfer process technology simply because they lack a sufficiently strong expertise in this field. In many cases, MNEs rely on subcontracting in order to be able to "...specialize in product technology while tapping the specialist process know-how for various inputs to their products"[85]. Such know-how, in fact, is available today in some of the East Asian affiliates. In subcontracting arrangements related to the final assembly and testing of integrated circuits, US semiconductor firms (in particular Texas Instruments, Motorola and Intel) transferred early on substantial technological knowledge to their affiliates in East Asia[86]. As a result, local affiliates, for instance in Malaysia, have accumulated substantial first mover advantages in assembly and testing technologies. Take the case of Texas Instruments: "As far as assembly and testing are concerned we have more expertise here (i.e. in Malaysia, D.E.) than we have in the U.S. We sometimes have to send our Malaysian engineers to the States to solve their problems"[87]. In the case of Intel such expertise became particularly strong for automated equipment design and manufacturing. As a result, when Intel had to set up highly automated assembly plants in Chandler/Arizona (1983) and in Ireland, the company had to rely on senior Malaysian engineers from its Penang affiliate for plant lay-out, equipment design, as well as for sorting out technical teething problems[88]. Intel Penang even claims that the first manager of its Mechanisation and Automation group has now been seconded to automate Intel's wafer fabrication lines in the United States and that its current automation team makes substantial contributions to upgrade the level of automation in Intel's worldwide operations.

This localisation of technological knowledge has given rise to a number of domestic subcontracting arrangements which may act as a catalyst for the formation of domestic technology networks. Take again the case of Intel. In 1978, the company established a vendor development scheme, called "Executive Partnership Programme (EPP)", under which six local firms were selected to supply parts and automated equipment design, prototyping and manufacturing services. For these companies, Intel guarantees annual procurement volumes and provides process engineers and other support personnel to upgrade the skills of the supplier firms' engineers, designers and machinists. Today, five subcontractors provide 80 per cent of Intel's requirements for tool and die mould making and metalstamping, three companies provide 80 per cent of its plastic injection moulding inputs and two companies provide 85 per cent of the required printed circuit board assemblies.

As a result of these arrangements, local subcontractors were able to reap substantial benefits, particularly in terms of learning facilitation, information spill-over and investment inducement. Some of Intel's original subcontractors have also started to build their own domestic supplier networks and thus have contributed to the formation of domestic technology linkages. Lok Kim Teow Engineering (LKT) is a case in point[89]. When it was established in the 1950s, the company produced household fencing, window grills, metal doors and minor maintenance and parts replacement for vehicles and ship engines. Since 1978, participation in Intel's vendor development scheme has drastically changed the company's product mix and has led to a continuous upgrading of its technological capabilities. In 1991, out of a total sales volume of $6 million, automated equipment design and manufacturing (in particular precision tools for the semiconductor industry) accounted for 40 per cent, parts fabrication, jigs and fixtures for another 40 per cent, with the remaining 20 per cent covered by mould design and manufacturing. This product mix will change in the future, as automated equipment design has been farmed out to a sister company, Semiconductor Equipment Manufacturers (SEM), while LKT itself puts increasing emphasis on mould design and mould making due to its substantial future growth potential. To implement this diversification strategy, LKT has formed a joint venture with a Japanese mould designer who now works as an independent consultant, in order to take advantage of Japan's long experience in mould making, as well as to gain access to Japanese MNEs and the Japanese market. Finally, LKT has also set up a satellite company to which it subcontracts parts fabrication and a variety of metal jobbing activities.

Underlying LKTs diversification strategy have been three basic motivations:

— To overcome its considerable problems in the recruitment of engineers and skilled workers — the demand for skilled labour in mould making being less acute than for precision tooling and automation.

— To rationalise the increasingly demanding intangible investment requirements related to R&D, product design and marketing.

— And, probably of greatest importance, to reduce its excessive dependence on Intel's demand. In 1991 for instance, 80 per cent of LKT's output was sold to Intel with half of these sales being exports to Intel affiliates in the United States, Singapore and the Philippines where Intel has another major assembly plant for integrated circuits.

This last point brings us to some important constraints inherent in such subcontracting arrangements. These constraints, in fact, indicate why a reliance on purely market-driven forms of subcontracting arrangements is hardly sufficient for building a developing country's technological capabilities and that corrective policy interventions of one kind or another are clearly required. The most important constraint relates to the fact that most of these subcontracting arrangements have basically been shaped by the requirements of global corporate strategies where local effects are of only secondary concern.

Take again the case of Malaysia. Historically, FDI in this country has concentrated on the labour-intensive assembly of largely imported semi-finished items which have generated few opportunities for backward linkages in terms of a demand for local support services and the supply of parts and components. Only since around the mid-1980s has there been a substantial increase in local sourcing requirements. This has been due primarily to the following developments[90]:

— The upgrading of semiconductor assembly to include testing and technical support, as well as some front-end wafer fabrication and the increasing use of automated equipment, have generated a growing demand for a domestic precision engineering support industry.

— A huge inflow of FDI, particularly into consumer electronics and some computer peripherals, has substantially broadened the increasing demand for local support industries[91].

— The spread of International Procurement Office (IPO) activities in Singapore[92] have led to some spill-over of demand to Malaysian sources.

— Substantial currency realignments in Malaysia have made inputs imported from Japan, Singapore and Taiwan much more expensive and have thus induced firms from these countries to switch to local sourcing.

— Finally, and probably of greatest importance, has been the impact of regionalisation trends in the EC and North America which encourages intra-regional trade, sometimes at the cost of inter-regional trade[93]. In this context, new regulatory barriers have emerged which constrain traditional strategies and thus have forced foreign companies to localise their sourcing activities. For instance, the United States has started to impose much stricter requirements on ASEAN countries, in terms of their GSP status. In order for the exports of Japanese subsidiaries located in ASEAN countries to qualify for GSP status, certain minimum local content requirements need to be fulfilled. This has forced Japanese firms to increase local sourcing.

Although local sourcing requirements have increased, this has not necessarily led to a strengthening of domestic technology linkages. In many cases, MNEs, in particular Japanese firms, have increased their local value-added through the wholesale transfer of integrated production systems or the attraction of established component suppliers from Japan, pre-empting or at least slowing down the formation of domestic supplier and technology networks[94]. This obviously poses an important challenge for future policies to develop domestic technological capabilities and networks.

For a country like Malaysia, the challenges ahead are quite substantial. Important progress has been achieved in terms of backward linkages through purchases of local materials and components, and at least some manufacturing support services. Overall, however, Malaysia's electronics industry is still characterised by a very unbalanced product and sectoral structure and it lacks capital deepening and domestic linkages[95]. Existing subcontracting arrangements, for instance, have not led to any forward linkages where export-oriented MNE affiliates producing semiconductors would also sell to the local market: "All semiconductors ... are exported — providing no forward linkages in the domestic economy". This has led to "...the ridiculous situation whereby a company based near a factory producing integrated circuits places an order with the manufacturer's parent company or regional marketing office. Components that were made in and shipped from Malaysia a few days earlier are then shipped back"[96]. This is a major constraint since timely and cost-effective access to core components, like integrated circuits, is an essential prerequisite for building up a viable consumer and industrial electronics industry[97].

In short, subcontracting arrangements can make an important contribution to north-south technology diffusion, particularly in terms of manufacturing know-how, quality assurance and "best practice" management approaches. In some cases, they have laid the ground for strategies to become an international OEM supplier. Overall, however, the range of technological capabilities which DCs can acquire through such networks has been quite limited. Existing subcontracting arrangements have hardly been conducive to strengthening domestic product design and market development capabilities in the electronics industry[98]. In fact, one of their main objectives has been to strengthen the MNEs' product differentiation capabilities so that they can tighten their control over proprietary product designs. In addition, it has been quite difficult to integrate subcontracting arrangements into a DC's broader attempts to build domestic technology linkages. The localisation of component sourcing, in particular for higher value-added items, has mainly benefited the local affiliates of foreign suppliers. As a result, intra-regional procurement has been found to be much more important than local procurement in the East Asian electronics industry[99]. Primarily shaped by the international investment strategies of Japanese electronics companies, an intra-regional specialisation has emerged which, in countries like Malaysia and Thailand, may now prevent further progress in the formation of domestic linkages[100]. This raises an important issue for our debates on south-south co-operation, namely to what degree regional integration, left to the mere play of market forces, may sometimes hinder rather than strengthen the formation of domestic technological networks. I will come back to this in the concluding section.

Finally, existing subcontracting arrangements are today faced with some of the new challenges that I have identified earlier in the context of OECD countries[101]. Their capabilities, for example, need to be continuously upgraded which may require substantial investments and may force policy-makers to address some complex trade-off decisions. The supplier industry in Singapore today, for instance, is faced with increasing concentration and intensifying competitive pressures[102]. For standard parts, global sourcing from the cheapest location worldwide has become an established practice. And any attempt to move up into higher value-added items is immediately confronted with increasing competition from inward FDI by established foreign suppliers. According to one observer[103], survival necessitates some drastic improvements: Singaporean suppliers would have to increase their technological specialisation, to shift to longer-term co-operative relationships, to participate early on in (joint) product design and development, to enter some of the dominant buyer procurement information systems and to establish joint R&D projects with buyers, presumably by sharing some of the heavy financial outlays involved. While all of these recommendations make perfect sense, at least in principle, the question is how these firms are going to mobilise the substantial financial and human resource requirements for such an upgrading of subcontracting activities. In the case of Singapore, whose government has an established track record of providing externalities, if necessary, there is ground for some guarded optimism. Much less so, however, in countries like Malaysia and Thailand where existing production and trade structures would make this upgrading task even more demanding. Until quite recently, the integration of both countries into international trade flows in the electronics industry has been characterised by two basic features[104]:

— Vertical product specialisation (primarily for consumer electronics) where low-value items are exported primarily to the United States and the EC, while higher-value items and components are imported primarily from Japan.

— Vertical process specialisation where Japanese, American and European firms send mainly parts and components to both countries to be assembled into electronic systems for export to the United States and the EC.

Given such an unequal division of labour in foreign trade, it is hardly surprising that both countries find it difficult to upgrade their position as regional subcontractors, let alone to move up to the status of international OEM suppliers.

To conclude, subcontracting is one of the few proven instances where DCs have been able to benefit from international network transactions and to improve their technological capabilities. This applies in particular to countries at a relatively early stage of their technological development. Subcontracting arrangements could continue to make a valuable contribution to north-south technology diffusion, provided that they are not left exclusively to the free play of international market forces, and provided that governments step in, at least selectively, in order to provide some necessary externalities.

4.3 Technology networks

We now move on to a different type of network transaction whose impact on north-south technology diffusion presumably is of immediate importance only for those countries and companies which are reaching the limits of technological catching-up. I am referring to technology networks as defined in Section 2.1.

It would certainly be misleading to argue that developing countries could only qualify as participants in such networks if they have accumulated a number of patents which firms from the United States, Japan and Europe seek to exploit. As I have argued elsewhere, a developing country may also become an attractive partner if it possesses technological capabilities related to production, investment, adaptive engineering and organisational restructuring or has knowledge about user requirements[105]. In addition, it may also possess some complementary assets and capabilities required by the OECD partner such as: large cash reserves; control of domestic marketing and distribution networks; the capacity to influence national regulatory barriers and policies; a qualified workforce; and sophisticated support services and information management and co-ordination capabilities. At least in the larger developing countries, the government may be able to leverage the bargaining position of individual firms by trading market access for favourable technology arrangements with the foreign firm[106].

In what follows, I will review a few technology networks in the semiconductor industry between firms in Korea and Taiwan and industry leaders from the United States, Japan and Europe[107]. Once again it must be emphasized that these data are illustrative only since we still lack a systematic empirical analysis of the distribution of the costs and benefits involved in such arrangements and their impact on cross-border technology diffusion and effective technology absorption in NIEs[108].

The following examples may serve to highlight the need to differentiate between straightforward "second-sourcing" arrangements and more far-reaching forms of technology co-operation, where a shift from "one-way" to increasingly reciprocal technology exchange and co-development is possibly under way. Most of the networks that I am going to discuss belong to the first category. The following examples also show that the rationale for such arrangements vary across different product groups and market segments. At the same time, they show that market access invariably has been the major preoccupation of the foreign firm.

The most prominent cases relate to straightforward contract manufacturing arrangements for computer memories (DRAMs) which, however, are claimed to be intended for future upgrading. The following arrangements are of particular importance: Samsung's links with Intel (which date back to 1985) and IBM (since 1989); Hyundai's link to Texas Instruments (since 1986); Goldstar's link with Hitachi which started in 1989; and the agreement drawn between the Taiwanese computer company Acer and the US semiconductor firm Texas Instruments (also in 1989).

Of these five relationships, two have already been discontinued. Intel which originally had used Samsung as a "silicon foundry", in order to provide its microprocessor customers with a controlled source of DRAMs, meanwhile has established a joint venture with Japan's NMB Semiconductor Co. to build a highly automated DRAM foundry in Japan[109]. Intel will sell NMB's DRAMs under its own name and thus is unlikely to continue its relationship with Samsung. And Texas Instruments which, for a while, was trying to upgrade Hyundai into a reliable "second source" for its "one-generation-behind-the-leading-edge" DRAMs, seems to have withdrawn from this relationship in favour of its new link with Acer of Taiwan. This is hardly surprising, given the huge problems which Hyundai, a firm with a tradition in heavy mechanical and civil engineering, has had in entering the market for DRAMs and other advanced semiconductors without prior experience in electronics.

By far the most exciting of the apparently still existing arrangements is Samsung Electronics' technology agreement with IBM for a mutual semiconductor patent swop. Both companies are known for their secrecy, so there is no way of judging whether the transfer of technology involved in this arrangement really goes beyond the transfer of design specifications and production technology and whether it involves some forms of technology exchange and co-development. It is safe to say, however, that IBM has chosen this arrangement primarily as a strategic weapon against its Japanese competitors. In my view, the arrangement is a defensive move by IBM to stem the alarming decline in its leadership position in DRAMs. According to one of my interview sources: "In the mid-1970s, at the 64K level, IBM had a seven-year lead over the best of the merchant semiconductor suppliers. That lead has been narrowing with each generation of DRAMs, and now it is only about 6 months at the 16-Mb level". IBM wants to have reliable second sources and technology partners in East Asia as much as in Europe, where it has linked up with Siemens[110]. As all Japanese semiconductor producers are strong competitors for IBM in computers, linking up with any one of them would pose extreme risks. It is thus logical that IBM would choose the strongest non-Japanese firm in East Asia with lots of cash and at least sufficient technological capabilities which, however, is unlikely to become a serious competitor in the computer business. Samsung thus has not been chosen for its technological excellence, but rather because it was sitting on a pile of surplus cash and because it had a reputation for being a reliable low-cost and quality-conscious mass producer of standard semiconductor devices. It is due to these rather mundane capabilities that Samsung has been accepted into the IBM global technology network. In my view, this example nicely illustrates that a schematic analysis of co-operative agreements, without a sound knowledge of company and product specifics, is likely to lead to quite erroneous conclusions[111].

As for Goldstar Electronic Co.'s tie-up with Hitachi, one of the leading Japanese DRAM producers this, in my view, is a straightforward second-sourcing arrangement which enables Hitachi to expand market share at the lowest cost possible, once the demand for a particular DRAM takes off. To the best of my knowledge, no technology exchange, let alone joint technology development, is involved. Two phases need to be discerned. In 1989, Hitachi agreed to transfer production know-how for 1Mb DRAMs. Mass production started too late to reap the tremendous windfall profits which would have been possible during the 1989 supply crunch for 1Mb DRAMs. This phase thus basically served to gear up Goldstar's production capabilities to the current best practice.

In the Spring of 1990, Hitachi then agreed to transfer 4Mb DRAM production technology. However, Goldstar was not expected to start mass production before 1992. From the perspective of Hitachi this is a very clever timing, as demand for 4Mb DRAMs was not expected to take off before the first quarter of 1992. Hitachi would thus have a low-cost second source available right in time, when additional capacity is required.

In my view, this arrangement is basically driven by Hitachi's competition with Toshiba, the current market leader for 1Mb DRAMs. Having been defeated by Toshiba in the 1Mb DRAM generation, Hitachi intends to recapture market share in 4Mb DRAMs. From the agreement with Goldstar, Hitachi expects to have access, if need be, to additional low-cost production capacity, without being forced to undertake the huge investments required for an additional 4Mb DRAM wafer fabrication line which is totally funded by the cash-rich Lucky-Goldstar conglomerate[112]. Hitachi actually does not have much choice, as Toshiba has already secured a powerful second source, Tohoku Semiconductor Inc., its joint venture with Motorola, which had started to produce 4Mb DRAMs already in 1991.

This information, in my view, serves as a necessary reminder that easy and somewhat euphoric generalisations concerning the extent to which Korean *chaebol* have already qualified as equal partners in global technology network transactions are still quite premature. Goldstar's main concern, in fact, is how to catch up with the leading Korean semiconductor producer Samsung which, in 1989, had worldwide semiconductor sales of $1.4 billion, while Goldstar's turnover was a meagre $148 million[113]. As its own attempt to develop 4Mb DRAMs was not very successful, Goldstar desperately needed access to a foreign technology source. It was thus in a weak negotiating position relative to Hitachi, and is unlikely to have secured a far-reaching transfer of technology.

On the other hand, it is also possible to draw a somewhat less pessimistic conclusion. With higher levels of globalisation, even technology and market leaders are finding it increasingly difficult to restrict access to production technology. Hitachi's agreement with Goldstar is a case in point. According to one Hitachi executive, quoted in the *Japan Economic Journal*: "In this age of internationalisation, if we hadn't done it, someone else would have"[114]. In principle then, access to technology which is one generation behind the leading edge is always possible, if only the company has sufficient financial clout and if its technological capabilities and industrial competence enable it to effectively absorb the foreign technology. Obviously, in some cases, the State could play an important role by providing the necessary finance.

This brings me to my last example, the 1989 agreement between Texas Instruments and the leading Taiwanese computer company Acer to set up a huge wafer fabrication plant for 1Mb and 4Mb DRAMs in Taiwan's Hsinchu Science Park. The plant is estimated to cost possibly up to $500 million and thus ranks among the larger wafer fabrication lines[115]. TI gets a new memory chip factory at very little cost to itself[116] and no longer has to serve the increasingly important Taiwanese and Korean markets from its Japanese facility. Acer, in turn, not only gets an assured supply of core components that are critical to its computer business, but also can access TI's "state-of-the-art" semiconductor process technology. While Acer's main contributions are capital and management (and a captive market for a sizeable portion of the output), the company's technological capabilities must be strong for it to have been chosen as a partner in such a sophisticated endeavour.

It is still too early for a sound assessment of the success or failure of these examples. It can be safely concluded, however, that even for relatively mundane arrangements, related to second sourcing or contract manufacturing, barriers to entry are very high, both in terms of the financial resources required and the technological absorption capacity. As a result, such arrangements will remain the exception rather than the rule, and only a handful of large electronics companies in East Asian NIEs can aspire to benefit from them.

The great majority of electronics companies in developing countries are unlikely to qualify for participation in such co-operative agreements. They will have to continue to rely on the traditional mechanism of technology acquisition, i.e. FDI, technology licensing, capital goods imports, subcontracting arrangements and OEM relations. As I have argued elsewhere[117], restrictions to these traditional modes of international technology diffusion are substantially increasing. Chances are that most electronics firms in developing countries will become locked into outdated patterns of world market integration which would prevent them from gaining access to international technology networks.

4.4 Assessment

To conclude, developing countries today are confronted with conflicting tendencies with regard to access to international technology networks. On the one hand, there is sufficient evidence to show that in a variety of industrial sectors, market leaders have developed aggressive strategies to minimise "technology leakage" at nearly any cost. In the electronics industry, major firms have become increasingly reluctant to license core technologies to potential competitors and have increasingly prosecuted those alleged to have violated their intellectual property rights. A prominent example is Intel's refusal to allow second-sourcing for the current generation of its 486 micro-processors. In a number of cases, even access to pre-competitive research has been restricted by governments eager to strengthen the competitiveness of their electronics industries as, for instance, in the case of the US Sematech Program and Europe's JESSI programme.

This, however, does not preclude that there are cases where access to technology will continue to be relatively free. There are reasons after all for market leaders based in OECD countries not to be overly protective of their technological know-how. First, there is the issue of standards. Liberal licensing of a firm's product technology may be an effective means of gaining wide market acceptance and establishing the product as a *de facto* industry standard. In the computer industry, this strategy is currently pursued for instance, by Sun Microsystems in its attempt to establish its processor architecture as a standard for work stations. In addition, many firms, even the leading ones, are finding it increasingly difficult to bear all the development and commercialisation costs of new products on their own. With those costs rapidly escalating, firms are entering co-operative agreements which permit technology transfer and cost sharing, and provide access to marketing and distribution networks in foreign markets. For the most part, these alliances have been between American, Japanese and, to a lesser degree, European firms.

As I indicated before, there are however a few cases where an electronics firm based in an OECD country has chosen a Korean or Taiwanese firm as a strategic partner. I have argued that it is still too early to assess the success or failure of such arrangements.

This finding corresponds quite well to recent research on the global-isation of competition and its impact on international technology diffusion[118]. Current rounds of globalisation are shaped primarily by an increasing plurality of international investment flows, with technology-related network transactions emerging as the most prominent mode. In contrast to earlier rounds of trade-led internationalisation, the shift to investment-driven internationalisation patterns has led to an increase in international inequality. It has been shown[119] that international investment flows are much more concentrated than are international trade flows: the five leading OECD countries (the so-called G-5) account for over 75 per cent of foreign direct investment, but just over 40 per cent of world trade. With the exception of a few East Asian NIEs and China, the developing countries have been largely cut off from international investment flows. There has been a drastic fall in the share of FDI flowing into developing countries: from 24 per cent in 1983, this share declined to a little more than 17 per cent in 1988[120].

The spatial distribution of technology networks is even more concentrated than investment: over 90 per cent of such arrangements are made between companies with their home base in G-5 countries[121]. As a result, non-OECD Member countries are having increasing difficulties in gaining access to international capital and technology flows. During the 1990s, we will see a competitive bidding for investment and technology, as the former socialist countries and developing countries seek to overcome their shortage of domestic savings and technology[122]. But only very few countries will succeed — the rest will experience a further drastic decline in the inflow of foreign investment and technology. Without any doubt, the involuntary delinking from international capital and technology flows is likely to erode the international competitiveness of a great variety of developing countries and thus their access to international markets and corporate networks. To some degree, this may even apply to East Asian NIEs, despite all their impressive achievements.

What then can we say about the role of network transactions for south-south co-operation? Under what conditions could DCs utilise such concepts to develop some of the new, "innovation-driven" modes of south-south co-operation, described in the first chapter of this book? What constraints are involved? And how should firms and governments in DCs react to these constraints, in order to reap the potential benefits from such arrangements?

In this chapter I have shown that network transactions can help to broaden the diffusion of basic technological and organisational capabilities to DCs. This applies in particular to capabilities related to production, quality control and adaptive engineering. We have seen that subcontracting arrangements have played an important role in this respect, particularly for countries which are still at a relatively early stage of their technological development. For countries which have already progressed further, OEM and in some cases even ODM arrangements, have expanded the variety of learning effects. Finally, a few East Asian Newly Industrialising Economies which, for some products, may be getting close to the limits of technological catching-up, have started to get involved in somewhat more sophisticated network transactions, in particular customer and technology networks. For technology networks, I have shown that while substantial learning possibilities exist and probably also have been used by some of the participating East Asian firms, access to such networks cannot be assumed to occur automatically. As a matter of fact, barriers to entry to such networks are substantial and seem to have been growing over the last years. As a result, only a handful of large, cash-rich and vertically integrated companies normally can aspire to participate in such networks — unless the government steps in, as it has done in the case of Taiwan, and provides some of the necessary externalities[123].

This bring me to my **first** observation which deals with the role of governments in the formation of south-south networks. All types of network transactions that I have discussed in this chapter contain some potential for technology diffusion. Left on their own, firms have succeeded in reaping at least some basic learning effects, provided their structure and strategy was conducive to learning at all. Yet, sooner or later, constraints arise, in particular if developing countries' firms want to extend the scope of such arrangements beyond the sphere of production and broaden the technological learning effects. It is at this point that entry barriers become substantial and some network participants become more equal than others in terms of their access to such higher capabilities. This is hardly surprising since it reflects the fact that most inter-firm network transactions, rather than being "open systems", are basically an attempt to sustain existing market positions and to constrain entry possibilities for latecomers[124]. An important confusion in the debates on network transactions results from the assumption that findings concerning academic networks like BITNET, notably with regard to their "openness", apply with equal force to inter-firm networks. In Section 3 it has been documented that such an assumption is truely heroic. For different types of network transactions, important barriers to entry and exit exist. As a result, leading oligopolists have often shaped the goals of such arrangements. Under these conditions, it is clear that governments have an important role to play. In particular they could act as catalysts providing essential externalities, such as finance, human resources and infrastructure that would enable SMEs to participate in and benefit from network transactions. In other words, substantial yet selective policy interventions are required in order to use networks as an instrument for south-south co-operation.

For technology networks, I have already referred to the role of the state in Taiwan which has enabled smaller companies, that would normally lack the necessary financial means, to participate in such arrangements. Here, I will add a more general argument which I will demonstrate using the example of intra-ASEAN economic co-operation, in particular the planned transition to an ASEAN Free Trade Area (AFTA)[125]. Presumably, AFTA will enable its participants to reap "...potential dynamic gains from the change in production structure and more efficient resource allocation; economies of scale; scope for intra-industry trade; increased investments; and technological and innovative developments due to increased competition". While this potential is real, there are substantial problems along the way. For instance, Indonesian electronics companies today lag well behind their counterparts in Malaysia and Thailand, as well as in Singapore, in terms of their size, financial clout and the backing they can receive from foreign MNEs[126]. In general, their technological capabilities are very weak and they are involved in "screw driver" assembly. Yet, there are a few exceptions which have built up substantial technological capabilities. This applies in particular to one medium-sized national consumer electronics company producing colour TV sets. This company, which is not linked to a foreign principal, has developed its own designs and sells domestically under its own brand name. It has only just started to export and claims to have identified good future export potential. With a current production volume of around 100 000 units, it remains well below the minimum economic scale required to be profitable (around 500 000 units at the very least). TV production units in Malaysia and Thailand, most of which are subsidiaries of Japanese firms, have long since surpassed this critical threshold. In order to reach a competitive level of production, the company estimates that it will need "infant protection" for about five to seven years more. Yet, AFTA is scheduled to impose radical changes at very short notice: tariffs on electronic products were foreseen to come down to 20 per cent by January 1993. If that happens, the company claims that it would then have to close down. Irrespective of the merits of this particular claim, it clearly indicates the following important dilemma: south-south co-operation left to market forces alone may well lead to a premature exposure to international competition and may destroy existing technological capabilities. Clearly, a case can be made for selective policy interventions which would enable innovative SMEs to survive the exposure to international competition. This is one of the reasons why, in ASEAN countries, the pendulum is currently swinging from market-driven back to more policy-guided forms of economic co-operation[127].

My **second** observation relates to the notion of complementarity between north-south and south-south co-operation that was introduced in the first chapter of this book. In normative terms, i.e. as a guide for policy formulation, this statement is certainly correct. But one should be aware of some important limitations. As the work of Urata has indicated[128], south-south trade in the East Asian electronics industry today is predominantly shaped by globalisation strategies of foreign, in particular Japanese, firms. Future research should look into the extent to which this also applies to other industries, in particular to car components[129]. In any case, there is probably a lot of overlapping between north-south and south-south trade, investment and technology links. It is also problematic to assume, as Stewart (1989, pp. 93-94) does, that both would follow a different logic. It is probably fair to say that much of what is called today south-south co-operation may, in fact, be driven by the logic of globalisation strategies pursued by American, Japanese and European companies. For instance, when a MNE subsidiary based in Singapore engages in investment in Malaysia and Indonesia, it may not differ fundamentally from an investment made by the mother company. In any case, our discussion of technology-related network transactions in this chapter clearly supports Mytelka's suggestion that south-south co-operation should focus on "...the learning and dissemination of internationally available know-how"[130]. On its own, south-south co-operation, however, will face difficulties in reducing the inequality of access to strategic assets and capabilities, such as finance, human resources, product design, market intelligence and generic technologies. For these, DCs will continue to depend on access to north-south networks. In short, while south-south trade offers substantial learning possibilities, it cannot substitute for north-south trade, investment and technology links. It is necessary to spell out this uncomfortable truth: without improved access to international networks, dominated by leading OECD companies, chances for viable south-south technological co-operation may remain very limited[131].

My **third** and final observation relates to the role that technology can play in any attempt by developing countries to establish more viable forms of south-south co-operation. This chapter has shown that access to technology and its diffusion has been an important aspect of international network transactions. Both have also conditioned to a large degree the benefits and costs which different network participants can draw from such arrangements. Obviously, the same applies for networks in the context of south-south co-operation. There is every reason to argue that, in contrast to earlier debates which focused on trade and investment-related issues, technology should henceforth be given greater prominence.

Yet this should not induce us to fall into the trap of technological determinism. In the final analysis, technology cannot substitute for basic economic and social reforms without which sustainable development will not occur. This applies as much to domestic development as to development in the context of south-south co-operation. Technological change at best can act as a complement, albeit a powerful one, to such basic transformations of social institutions.

Technological capabilities, moreover, do not fall from heaven like manna. Their development requires a proper institutional and policy framework that encourages firms to invest in productivity-enhancing organisational and technological innovations as the primary means of competition. Yet, as Richard Nelson confesses, "...the conditions under which those needed investments ... are made, and the conditions under which they are not, remain ... the great mystery for development theory"[132]. Much emphasis should therefore be placed on these institutional and policy aspects in future research on the role of network transactions in south-south co-operation[133].

Notes

1. See Chapter 1 of this book.
2. For a detailed analysis of these challenges and opportunities, see Ernst and O'Connor (1989), Ernst and O'Connor (1992), and Chesnais (1992).
3. Trade and investment diversion effects resulting from higher forms of European integration are discussed in Wong (1991b) and in *The Economist Survey of the European Community*, 11th July 1992.
4. Possible implications of the North American Free Trade Agreement (NAFTA) are discussed in *The Financial Times*, 13th August 1992, p. 3.
5. OECD-TEP Tokyo Colloquium, Summary Record, 11 May 1990, p. 10.
6. For a comprehensive review of this debate, see OECD (1992), Chapters 3 and 4.
7. Ernst, ed., 1980, based on a joint international project directed by the author, examined many of these difficulties and sought to identify a number of concrete priority areas for TCDC.
8. Workshop of the OECD South-South Co-operation project, Paris, 1-3 November 1990.
9. Elsewhere, "innovation" has been defined as "...the processes by which firms master and implement the design and production of goods and services that are new to them, irrespective of whether they are new to their competitors — domestic or foreign" (Ernst, Mytelka and Ganiatsos, 1992, p. 9).
10. As discussed in Chapter 1 of this book.
11. The widening north-south technology gap has been documented in UNDP (1992), Chapter 3.
12. Callon *et al.* (1990), p. 13.
13. As defined in Williamson (1975) and (1985).
14. For a review, see OECD (1992), Chapter 4, "Technology and Corporate Organisation".
15. Individual computers are normally linked to a host computer by small "local-area networks" which use wires owned and operated by the respective universities or companies. Host computers are linked to each other via long-distance, high-capacity lines leased, often at high cost, from telephone companies. Another basically research-oriented computer network is **BITNET** that links local-area networks in universities so that scientists can share results.
16. For evidence, see *Business Week Special Report*, "A Scramble for Global Networks", 24 March 1988.
17. Ernst and O'Connor (1992).
18. An influential and highly critical review article of the concept of "just-in-time" (JIT) published in the *Harvard Business Review* of January/February 1991, concludes: "The turmoil in the financial markets over the past decade has certainly contributed to the appeal of the more radical versions of JIT ... [T]oo many companies have turned to JIT seeking fast, ostensibly painless financial surgery". The result has been an "...unfortunate trend of allowing short-term financial pressures to drive major operational decisions" (Zipkin, 1991, p. 44).
19. Ernst and O'Connor (1992), Chapter 1.
20. Two influential studies are Reinertsen and Smith (1991) and Stalk and Hout (1990).
21. Ciborra (1991), p. 51.
22. According to one recent World Bank survey, more than 60 per cent of production and sales is now processed directly to order (Peters, 1991).
23. Dosi (1988), p. 229-231.
24. Chenais (1992), p. 35.
25. As discussed in Antonelli and Foray (1991).
26. Bongardt (1991).
27. Flamm (1990), p. 24.
28. For a discussion of some of the issues involved, in particular with regard to the concept of "oligopolistic control", see Ernst (1992).
29. Based on Smith and Jordan (1990), pp. 8 and 9.
30. For a detailed classification of technological capabilities, see Ernst, Mytelka and Ganiatsos (1992).
31. Antonelli and Foray (1991), p. 2.
32. See the discussion of these earlier approaches in Lynn Mytelka's chapter in this volume.
33. Wong Poh Kam (1991), p. 15.
34. Ernst (1992).

35. For evidence, see "The Growth and Management of Intangible Investments", Chapter 5 of the OECD TEP Background Report (OECD, 1992).

36. Konsynski and McFarlan (1990), pp. 115-117, which also contains the following example of a co-operative network.

37. "The Fruitful, Tangled Trees of Knowledge. Survey on Computer Networks", *The Economist*, 20 June 1992, p. 132.

38. *Communicationsweek International*, 17 September 1990, p. 26.

39. An assessment of EC policy initiatives to develop an EC-wide computer network can be found in US Department of Commerce (1990).

40. *Financial Times Survey*, "Computer Networking", 20 November 1990, p. II.

41. See the *Business Week Special Report*, "A Scramble for Global Network", 21 March 1988, pp. 72-80.

42. Antonelli (1989), p. 92.

43. "Perspectives for Networking Strategies", *Communicationsweek International*, 9 April 1990, p. 10.

44. "Innovation-Related Networks and Technology Policy-Making", Chapter 5 of the OECD Background Report, (OECD, 1992), p. 79.

45. For some limited evidence, see Fornengo (1989a) and (1989b); Best (1990); and Chapters 3, 4, 10 and 11 of the OECD TEP Background Report (OECD, 1992).

46. Haklisch (1986); Haklisch and Vonortas (1988); Flamm (1990); Miyakawa (1990); and Hagedoorn (1990); Mytelka (1991).

47. Kehoe (1991), pp. 1 and 12.

48. *Financial Times*, 22 October 1991, p. 14.

49. *Electronic World News*, 8 July 1991, p. 6.

50. For evidence see the next section *Intensifying Sourcing Requirements*.

51. For the car industry, see Womack, Jones and Roos (1990). For the computer industry, see Ernst and O'Connor (1992), Chapters I and II.

52. The deputy chairman of Volkswagen AG, David Goeudevert, has given a vivid account of the rationale underlying these moves (Goeudevert, 1991, pp. 101 passim).

53. For a general debate, see Nelson (1991).

54. Bieber and Sauer (1991). For similar evidence on the German car components industry, see Doleschal (1991).

55. Bieber and Sauer (1991), p. 251 (translated from German, D. Ernst).

56. For an excellent review, see Jürgens, Malasch and Dohse (1989). Useful information can be found in Chanaron (1988), Ikeda (1987) and Lamming (1987).

57. For a typical example, see Sabel, Kern and Herrigel (1991).

58. For an excellent theoretical treatment, see Bieber (1992).

59. Antonelli (1989), p. 92.

60. Quoted in "The Advantages of Influence", *Financial Times*, 2 May 1990.

61. Prof. Horst Wildemann, cited in *Die Zeit*, 6 April 1990, p. 36.

62. For empirical evidence, see the *Economist Intelligence Unit*, Special Report, "Japan's Motor Industry — A Perspective on the Future", London, February 1992.

63. Two particularly influential examples are Aoki (1984), and Aoki (1988).

64. *US Industrial Outlook 1990*, Chapter 38, "Motor Vehicles and Parts"; and Griffiths (1990).

65. For details, see Ernst and O'Connor (1992), Chapters I and II.

66. Dataquest, "Proceedings of the 1989 Strategic Industry Focus Conference", Taipei, December 1989, as quoted in *Computer Eurotrade*, Taipei, January and February 1990.

67. Ernst and O'Connor (1992), Chapters I and II.

68. Examples can be found in the *Economist Intelligence Unit Special Report* "The International Electronics Industry", London, December 1990, in particular in Part II "Company Profiles", pp. 115-263. Additional evidence on outward FDI by Japanese electronic component companies can be found in Yannada (1990) and Urata (1991).

69. Vickery (1991). Additional information on the widening North-South technology gap can be found in UNDP (1992), Chapter 3, "The Widening Gap in Global Opportunities".

70. The following two quotations are taken from Lynn Mytelka's chapter in this volume.

71. The main sources are: Ernst and O'Connor (1989); Yamada (1990); Dörrenbächer and Wortmann (1991); Hou and San (1991); Kim Linsu (1991); Kim Ilyong and Chung (1991);

Petrella (1991); Lim and Pang (1991); Soete (1991); Urata (1991); Wong (1991a) and (1991b); Chesnais (1992); and Ernst and O'Connor (1992).

72. Nelson (1990a), p. 131.

73. For a review of evidence, see Ernst and O'Connor (1992), pp. 270 *passim*.

74. Similar developments can be discerned for textiles and clothing and for car components. For evidence on the former industry, see Anson and Simpson (1992), and Mytelka (1991). For car components, some evidence on north-south supplier networks can be found in Womack, Jones and Roos (1990).

75. Supplier networks have also played an important role in Mexico's northern border industries. For evidence, see Mercado and Giner (1988).

76. This issue will be addressed in a forthcoming research project on "Foreign Direct Investment and the Diffusion of Technology in East Asia", co-directed by Sylvia Ostry, Centre for International Studies, University of Toronto, and Laura Tyson, Berkeley Round Table on the International Economy, University of California at Berkeley.

77. See, for instance, Wong (1991a), p. 5.

78. Urata (1991), p. 39.

79. See Yonekura (1988) quoted in Chen and Wang (1991).

80. For a detailed analysis in the context of OECD countries, see "Innovation-Related Networks and Technology Policy Making", Chapter 3 of the OECD TEP Background Report, OECD (1992).

81. For detailed evidence, see Ernst and O'Connor (1992), Chapters I-IV. Current developments have more than confirmed our analysis made in 1991. See, for instance, the 1992 Midyear World Market forecasts in *Electronics World News*, 13 July 1992.

82. For the definition used, see Section 2.3, Networks and Technology Diffusion.

83. Based on Wong (1991a), p. 47 which also contains the following quotation.

84. See Crosly and Nakamori (1991), p. 66.

85. Wong (1991a), p. 48.

86. For details, see Ernst (1983).

87. See UNIDO (1987), p. 32.

88. This and the following information are based on an interview at Intel (April 1992), conducted by Ismail Salleh and the author.

89. Information on Lok Kim Teow Engineering is based on an interview (April 1992), conducted by Ismail Salleh and the author.

90. Based on author's interviews in the Malaysian electronics industry (April 1992).

91. Consumer and industrial electronics companies typically purchase much more local inputs than the semiconductor industry.

92. For evidence, see Lim and Pang (1991), Chapter 4.

93. For similar arguments, see the excellent study by Shujiro Urata on the Globalisation of the Japanese Electronics Industry (Urata, 1991, in particular pp. 44 *passim*).

94. For more evidence on this important issue, see Lim and Pang (1991).

95. Ample empirical evidence can be found in Salleh (1991). The following quotation is from p. 27.

96. *Electronics*, August 1987, p. 254.

97. For a detailed analysis, see Ernst and O'Connor (1992), Chapters I and II.

98. For Malaysia's electronics industry, the weakness of domestic design capabilities is documented in the *Malaysian Technology Masterplan Sector Study: Electronics Technology*, Ministry of Science, Technology and Energy, Kuala Lumpur, (1988), Chapter 4. The evidence for this is somewhat less conclusive for some of the larger clothing firms particularly in Hong Kong, Korea, Taiwan and Thailand (Mytelka, 1991b).

99. Urata (1991), p. 58.

100. This is also the case in the recent ASEAN Automobile Complementation Scheme. See Linda Lim's chapter in this volume.

101. See Section 4, "Networks and Market Structure — The Experience of OECD Countries".

102. For details, see "Singapore Country Focus", *Eurotrade Computer* (Taipei), March 1992, Vol. 4, No. 5, p. 16.

103. Wong (1991a), pp. 69 *passim*.

104. Economist Intelligence Unit Special Report, *The International Electronics Industry*, London, December 1990, Chapter 4, "International Trade and Overseas Investment in the Electronics Industry".

105." New Technology, Latecomer Industrialisation and Development Today", Chapter 12 of the OECD-TEP Background Report, OECD, 1992.

106. Ernst and O'Connor (1989), p. 108.

107. For details, see Ernst and O'Connor (1992), Chapter III.

108. This issue will be addressed in a forthcoming research project on "Foreign Direct Investment and the Diffusion of Technology in East Asia", co-directed by Sylvia Ostry, Centre for International Studies, University of Toronto and Laura Tyson, Berkeley Roundtable on the International Economy, University of California at Berkeley.

109. *Electronics Business Asia*, June 1990, p. 51.

110. In January 1990, IBM and Siemens signed an agreement to jointly develop 64Mb DRAMs by 1994, see *Electronics*, February 1990, p. 9.

111. This has been a weakness of the widely quoted work of the Hagedoorn-Schakenraad group which, based on sophisticated statistical analysis techniques, comes up with much too schematic conclusions. There are also certain factual errors. In Hagedoorn's paper prepared for the OECD experts meeting on "Globalisation in the Computer Industry" (Paris, 17 December 1990), he claims that Schlumberger had sold chip manufacturer Fairchild to Fujitsu (p. 19), while in fact Fairchild was sold to the US Company National Semiconductor. And on p. 22, it is claimed that NEC was a "dominant partner in arrangements with Siemens and BASF", while in reality this applies to Hitachi.

112. In 1990, the Lucky-Goldstar group had annual sales of $25 billion, nearly a third of them in consumer and industrial electronics, and net profits of $380 million (*Business Week*, 11 March 1991, p. 41).

113. Integrated Circuit Engineering Corp.'s Figures, quoted in *Electronic Business*, 25 June 1990, p. 35.

114. Quoted in *The Japan Economic Journal*, 7 July 1990, p. 15.

115. For details see *Electronic Business Asia*, June 1990, pp. 49-51.

116. Acer is financing most of the investment cost, much of it coming from a new share issue in Taipei's stock market.

117. Ernst and O'Connor (1989) and Ernst (1990).

118. Out of the rich literature see Chesnais (1988) and (1992); Ostry (1990a) and (1990b); Chapters 9 and 10 of the OECD TEP Background Report (OECD, 1992); Porter (1990); Cantwell (1989); Mytelka (1991); Julius (1990); and Ernst (1990).

119. Ostry (1990b), p. 1.

120. Ernst (1990), computed on the basis of IMF figures quoted in UN Commission on Transnational Corporations (E/C.10/1990/2), 1 March 1990, p. 9.

121. "International Development of Technology", Chapter 4 of an OECD-DSTI report to the Committee on Science and Technology Policy (DSTI/STP(91)12), March 1991.

122. Ostry (1990b), p. 8 and UNDP (1992), Chapter 4.

123. A thought-provoking analysis of the role of the State in Taiwan can be found in Wade (1990).

124. This is demonstrated, for example, in the case of the European ESPRIT Programme (Mytelka, 1992).

125. For details on AFTA, see Pangestu *et al.* (1992), pp. 16 *passim*. The following quotation is from p. 17 and Linda Lim in this volume.

126. The following is based on interviews conducted in the Indonesian electronics industry (March and June 1992) by Thee Kian Wie, Mari Pangestu and the author.

127. For similar conclusions, see the chapter by Linda Lim in this book and Pangestu (1992).

128. Urata (1991), in particular pp. 53 *passim*.

129. This would require an assessment of claims made by Nissan and Toyota on the effects of their respective regional supplier networks for car components in ASEAN countries, as reported in Linda Lim's chapter.

130. Chapter 1 of this book.

131. For a similar argument, see Sercovitch (1991), p. 4.

132. Nelson (1990), p. 46.

133. Some of the conceptual and methodological issues involved in a domestic context are discussed in Ernst, Mytelka and Ganiatsos (1992), pp. 28 *passim*.

Bibliography

ANSON, R. and P. SIMPSON (1992),"World Textile Trade and Production Trends", *EIU Textile Outlook International*, January.

ANTONELLI, C. (1989), "New Information Technology and Industrial Organisation", in *Information Technology and New Growth Opportunities*, OECD, Paris.

ANTONELLI, C., ed. (1989), *New Information Technology and Industrial Change — the Italian Case*, Dordrecht, Boston and London.

ANTONELLI, C. and D. FORAY (1991), "Technological Clubs: Cooperation and Competition", paper presented at the 7th Think Net Commission Meeting, "Scenarios Toward a Net World Order", Paris, June.

AOKI, M. (1984), *The Cooperative Game Theory of the Firm*, Stanford.

AOKI, M. (1988), "A New Paradigm of Work Organization: The Japanese Experience", Working Paper, WIDER, No. 36, February.

BEST, M. (1990), *The New Competition. Institutions of Industrial Restructuring*, Oxford.

BIEBER, D. (1992), "Systemische Rationalisierung und Produktionsnetzwerke", in Th. Malsch *et al.*, eds., *Arbyte. Modernisierung der Industriesoziologie?*, Berlin.

BIEBER, D. and D. SAUER (1991), "Autonomie und Beherrschung in Abnehmer-Zuliefererbeziehungen", in H.G. Mendius *et al.*, eds., *Zulieferer im Netz*, Cologne.

BONGARDT, A. (1991), "Global Competition by Innovation — The Case for R&D Cooperation in the Vertical Chain", mimeo, Brussels, European Research Institute.

CALLON, M. *et al.* (1990), "The Management and Evaluation of Technological Programs and the Dynamics of Techno-Economic Networks. The Case of The Agence Française de Maîtrise de l'Énergie (AFME)", manuscript, Centre de Sociologie de l'Innovation, École des Mines de Paris, Paris.

CANTWELL, J. (1989), *Technological Innovation and Multinational Corporations*, Oxford.

CHALMERS, I. (1991), "International and Regional Integration. The Political Economy of the Electronics Industry in ASEAN", in *ASEAN Economic Bulletin*, November.

CHANARON, J.J. (1988), "L'industrie des pièces automobiles des pays de l'OCDE : Situation et perspectives", a report prepared for the OECD Secretariat, OECD, Paris.

CHAPONNIÈRE, J.-R. (1992), "The NIEs Go International", paper prepared for INSEAD Conference, "Europe, U.S. and Japan in the Asia Pacific Region: Current Situation and Perspectives", Fontainebleau, February.

CHEN, E.K.Y. (1990), "The Electronics Industry", in Soesastro and Pangestu, eds., 1990.

CHEN, Tain-Jy and Wen-Thuen WANG (1991), "Globalization of Taiwan's Electronics Industry", manuscript, Chung-Hua Institution of Economic Research, Taipei, Taiwan.

CHESNAIS, F. (1988), "Multinational Enterprises and the International Diffusion of Technology", in G. Dosi *et al.*, eds., 1988.

CHESNAIS, F. (1992), "National Systems of Innovation, Foreign Direct Investment and the Operations of Multinational Enterprises", in S. Andersen *et al.*, eds., *National Systems of Innovation*, London.

CIBORRA, C. (1991), "Alliances as Learning Experiments — Cooperation, Competition and Change in Hightech Industries", in Mytelka, ed., 1991.

CROSLY, N. and Y. NAKAMORI (1991), "Motorola's Business Strategy in Southeast Asia", *Journal of Southeast Asia Business*, Vol. 7, No. 1, Winter.

DOLESCHAL, R. (1991), "Daten und Trends der bundesdeutschen Automobil-Zuliefererindustrie", in H.G. Mendius *et al.*, eds., *"Zulieferer im Netz"*, Cologne.

DÖRRENBÄCHER, C. and M. WORTMANN (1991), "The Internationalization of Corporate Research and Development", *Intereconomics*, May/June.

DOSI, G. (1988), "The Nature of the Innovation Process", in G. Dosi *et al.*, eds., 1988.

DOSI, G. *et al.*, eds. (1988), *Technical Change and Economic Theory*, London.

DUNNING, J.H. (1988), *Multinationals, Technology and Competitiveness*, London.

ECONOMIST INTELLIGENCE UNIT (1990), "The International Electronics Industry", Special Report, London, December.

ECONOMIST INTELLIGENCE UNIT (1992), "Japan's Motor Industry — A Perspective on the Future", Special Report, London, February.

ENOS, J.L. (1989), "Transfer of Technology", *Asia Pacific Economic Literatures*, Vol. 3, No. 1, pp. 3-37.

ERNST, D. (1983), *The Global Race in Microelectronics*, with a foreword by David Noble, MIT, Frankfurt am Main and New York, Campus.

ERNST, D. (1990), "Global Competition, New Information Technologies and International Technology Diffusion — Implications for Industrial Latecomers", paper prepared for the OECD Conference on "Technology and Competitiveness", Paris, June.

ERNST, D., ed. (1980), *The New International Division of Labour, Technology and Underdevelopment — Consequences for the Third World*, Frankfurt am Main and Campus, New York.

ERNST, D. and D. O'CONNOR (1989), *Technology and Global Competition. The Challenge for Newly Industrialising Economies*, Development Centre Studies, OECD, Paris.

ERNST, D. and D. O'CONNOR (1992), *Competing in the Electronics Industry. The Experience of Newly Industrialising Economies*, Development Centre Studies, OECD, Paris.

ERNST, D., T. GANIATSOS and L. MYTELKA, eds. (1993), *Technological Capabilities and Export Performance. Lessons from East Asia*, United Nations, New York.

ERNST, D., L. MYTELKA and T. GANIATSOS (1992) "Technological Capabilities and Export Performance. A Conceptual Framework", to be published as Chapter I in Ernst, Ganiatsos and Mytelka, eds.

FLAMM, K. (1990), "Cooperation and Competition in the Global Computer Industry", paper prepared for the seminar on "Globalisation in the Computer Industry", OECD, Paris.

FORNENGO, G. (1989a), "Manufacturing Networks: Telematics in the Automotive Industry", in C. Antonelli, ed., 1989.

FORNENGO, G. (1989b), "Interorganisational Networks and Market Structure", in C. Antonelli, ed., 1989.

FREEMAN, C. (1982), *Economics of Industrial Innovation*, Frances Pinter, London.

GRIFFITHS, J. (1990), "Europe's Motor Components Makers Braced for Japanese Onslaught", *Financial Times*, 10 September.

GOEUDEVERT, D. (1991), "Die Rolle der Zuliefererindustrie angesichts der weltweiten Wettbewerbsverschärfung", in H.G. Mendius, eds., "Zuleiferer im Netz", Cologne.

HAGEDOORN, J. (1990), "Globalisation in the Computer Industry: Inter-Firm Technology Cooperation", paper presented to the seminar on "Globalisation in the Computer Industry", OECD, Paris, December.

HAKLISCH, C. (1986), "Technical Alliances in the Semiconductor Industry", Centre for Science and Technology Policy, Graduate School of Business Administration, New York University, New York.

HAKLISCH, C. and N.S. VONORTAS (1988), "Export Controls and the International Technology System: The U.S. Semiconductor Industry", Centre for Science and Technology Policy, Rensselaer Polytechnic Institute, New York.

HOU, Chi-Ming and Gee SAN (1991), "National Systems Supporting Technical Advance in Industry — The Case of Taiwan", manuscript, Chung-Hua Institution of Economic Research, Taipei.

IKEDA, M. (1987), "An International Comparison of Subcontracting Systems in the Automotive Component Manufacturing Industry, report prepared for the MIT International Motor Vehicle Program, Cambridge, Mass, MIT.

IMAI, K. and Y. BABA (1991), "Systemic Innovation and Cross-Border Networks", in *Technology and Productivity. The Challenge for Economic Policy*, OECD, Paris.

ITOH, M. *et al.* (1988), "Industrial Policy as a Corrective to Market Failures", in R. Komiya *et al.*, eds., *Industrial Policy in Japan*, Tokyo, New York, etc.

JULIUS, D. (1990), *Global Companies and Public Policy. The Growing Challenge of Foreign Direct Investment*, The Royal Institute of International Affairs, London.

JÜRGENS, U., Th. MALSCH and K. DOHSE (1989), *Moderne Zeiten in der Automobilfabrik*, Berlin, Heidelberg, etc.

KIM, Linsu (1991), "National System of Industrial Innovation: Dynamics of Capability Building in Korea", Working Paper 91-1, Business Management Research Centre, Korea University, Seoul.

KIM, Ilyong and Sunyang CHUNG (1991), "R&D Cooperation Between Large Manufacturing Companies and Suppliers", mimeo, Centre for Science and Technology Policy, Korea Advanced Institute of Science and Technology, Seoul.

KEHOE, L. (1991), "IBM, Apple to Emphasize Fast Product Development", *Financial Times*, 2 October, pp. 1 and 12.

KONSYNSKI and McFARLAN (1990), "Information Partnerships — Shared Data, Shared Scale", *Harvard Business Review*, September-October.

LAMMING, R. (1987), "The International Automotive Components Industry", a report prepared for the MIT International Motor Vehicle Program, MIT, Cambridge, Mass.

LECRAW, D.J. (1991), "Trading Blocs in Southeast Asia and the Pacific Rim: Implications for Business Operations", *Journal of Southeast Asia Business*, Vol. 7, No. 2, Spring.

LIM, L.Y.C. and Eng Fong PANG (1991), *Foreign Direct Investment and Industrialisation in Malaysia, Singapore, Taiwan and Thailand*, Development Centre Studies, OECD, Paris.

MERCADO, A. and F. GINER (1988), "The Electrical Equipment and Electronics Industry", in V. Urquidi *et al.*, eds., *Export Promotion of Manufacturers in Mexico*, Institute of Developing Economies, Tokyo.

MIYAKAWA, T. (1990), "The Computer Industry in the Globalisation Age: A Japanese Viewpoint", paper presented to seminar on "Globalisation in the Computer Industry", OECD, Paris, December.

MURAKAMI, J. (1987), "The Japanese Model of Political Economy", in K. Yamamura *et al.*, eds., *The Political Economy of Japan. Vol. 1. The Domestic Transformation*, Stanford University Press, Stanford, Ca.

MYTELKA, L. (1992), "Dancing with Wolves: Global Oligopolies and Strategic Partnerships", paper presented to the Conference on Convergence and Divergence in Economic Growth, Merit, Maastricht.

MYTELKA, L. (1991a), "States, Strategic Alliances and International Oligopolies: The European ESPRIT Programme", in Mytelka, ed.

MYTELKA, L. (1991b), "Technological Change and the Global Relocation of Production in Textiles and Clothing", *Studies in Political Economy*, No. 36, Fall.

MYTELKA, L., ed. (1991), *Strategic Partnerships and the World Economy*, London.

NELSON, R. (1990), "Acquiring Technology" in Soesastro and Pangestu, eds.

NELSON, R. (1990a), "U.S. Technological Leadership: Where Did it Come From and Where Did it Go?", *Research Policy*, April.

NELSON, R. (1991), "National Innovation Systems: A Retrospective on a Study", manuscript, Columbia University, New York.

OECD (1992), *Technology and the Economy: The Key Relationships*, Paris.

OSTRY, S. (1990a), *Governments and Corporations in a Shrinking World: Trade and Innovation Policies in the United States, Europe and Japan*, Council on Foreign Relations Press, New York.

OSTRY, S. (1990b), "Exploring the Policy Options for the 1990s", paper presented at the OECD conference "Support Policies for Strategic Industries: Systemic Risks and Emerging Issues", OECD, Paris, October.

PANGESTU, M. *et al.* (1992), "Intra ASEAN Economic Cooperation: A New Perspective", *ASEAN Economic Bulletin*, March.

PETERS, H. (1991), "Trade and Industry Logistics in Developing Countries. A Strategy for Improving Competitiveness in Changing International Markets", mimeo, Infrastructure and Urban Development Department, World Bank, Washington, D.C.

PETRELLA, R. (1991), "Internationalisation, Multinationalisation and Globalisation of R&D", mimeo, FAST, Commission of the European Communities.

PORTER, M. (1990), *The Competitive Advantage of Nations*, London.

REINERTSEN, D. and P. SMITH (1991), *Developing Products in Half the Time*, London and New York.

SABEL, Ch.F., H. KERN and G. HERRIGEL (1991), "Kooperative Produktion", in H.G. Mendius *et al.*, eds., *Zulieferer im Netz*, Cologne.

SALLEH, I. (1991), "Sector Report: Electronic/Electrical Machinery", manuscript, Institute for Strategic and International Studies, Kuala Lumpur, Malaysia.

SERCOVITCH, F. (1991), "Industrial Policy in the Field of Biotechnology — Guidelines for Newly Industrialising Economies", UNIDO, Vienna, April.

SMITH, B. and H. JORDAN (1990), "Transformation and Technology Transfer", in Soesastro and Pangestu, eds.

SOESASTRO, H. and M. PANGESTU, eds. (1990), *Technological Challenge in the Asia-Pacific Economy*, Allen and Unwin, Sydney, London, etc.

SOETE, L. (1991), "The Search for a New Theory of Innovation and Diffusion — The Policy Implications", manuscript, Merit, Maastricht, September.

STALK, G. and T.M. HOUT (1990), *Competing Against Time. How Time-Based Competition is Reshaping Global Markets*, New York.

STEWART, F. (1984), "Recent Theories of International Trade: Some Implications for the South", in H. Kierzkowski, ed., *Monopolistic Competition and International Trade*, Oxford.

UNDP (1992), *Human Development Report 1992*, Oxford University Press, New York and Oxford.

UNIDO (1987), *Microelectronics Monitor*, Vienna, No. 2, p. 32.

UNITED NATIONS (1978), "Report of the United Nations Conference on Technical Cooperation among Developing Countries", New York.

UNITED NATIONS (1979), "Report on the United Nations Conference on Science and Technology for Development (UNCSTED)", Vienna and New York.

URATA, S. (1991), "The Globalisation of the Japanese Electronics Industry and its Impact on International Trade in Electronics Products", manuscript, Development Centre, OECD, Paris.

US Department of Commerce (1990), "U.S. Telecommunications in a Global Economy", Washington, D.C., Chapter VI.

VICKERY, G. (1991), *Globalisation — Developments and Industrial Policy Issues for the Nineties*, OECD, Paris.

WADE, R. (1990), *Governing the Market. Economic Theory and the Role of Government in East Asian Industrialisation*, Princeton University Press, Princeton.

WILLIAMSON, O.E. (1975), *Markets and Hierarchies: Analysis and Antitrust Implications*, New York.

WILLIAMSON, O.E. (1985), *The Economic Institutions of Capitalism*, New York.

WILLIAMSON, O.E. (1986), *Economic Organization: Firms, Markets and Policy Control*, New York.

WOMACK, J.P., D.T. JONES, and D. ROOS (1990), *The Machine that Changed the World*, New York.

WONG, Poh Kam (1991a), "Technological Development Through Subcontracting Linkages", Asia Productivity Organization, Tokyo, p. 15.

WONG, Poh Kam (1991b), "The EC Internal Market and the ASEAN Electronics Industry", manuscript, Centre for Management and Technology (CMT), National University of Singapore, Singapore.

YAMADA, B. (1990), *Internationalization Strategies of Japanese Electronics Companies — Implications for Asian Newly Industrializing Economies*, Technical Paper No. 28, Development Centre, OECD, Paris.

YONEKURA, M. (1988), "Chukan, Chuso Denki Kigyo No Kaigai Shinshutsu", (Overseas Operations of Medium and Small Electronics Firms), *Sekai Keizai Hyoron*, Vol. 32, No. 4, in Chen and Wang (1991).

ZIPKIN, P.H. (1991), "Does Manufacturing Need a JIT Revolution?", *Harvard Business Review*, January-February.

Chapter 4

THE ROLE OF THE PRIVATE SECTOR IN ASEAN REGIONAL ECONOMIC CO-OPERATION

Linda Y.C. Lim

Les projets classiques de co-opération économique fondée sur les échanges sont peu nombreux dans le groupement régional que constitue l'ANASE. La réussite économique des pays de l'ANASE est plutôt fondée sur les échanges ainsi que sur les investissements étrangers. Ce chapitre étudie le rôle qu'a joué le secteur privé dans l'intégration économique de l'ANASE, notamment par le biais des investissements directs intra-régionaux. Il suggère que les formes de coopération sud-sud les plus prometteuses sont principalement celles menées par le secteur privé, fondées sur les mécanismes de marché et sur les avantages comparatifs. Pour soutenir ces initiatives, les pouvoirs publics peuvent : supprimer les obstacles politiques aux projets transfrontaliers du secteur privé ; mettre en place un ensemble coordonné de mesures nationales d'incitation à l'investissement ; participer à certains projets régionaux menés par le secteur privé, en tant que partenaires partageant les coûts, les risques et les bénéfices ; enfin, coopérer avec ce secteur dans des projets communs de développement des infrastructures et des ressources humaines, afin de permettre l'acquisition ou l'amélioration des avantages comparatifs des pays membres et des avantages compétitifs des entreprises privées de la région.

Formal trade-based economic co-operation schemes within the ASEAN regional grouping have been minimal. Rather, the ASEAN countries' economic success has been largely based on trade and investment from non-member countries. This chapter examines the role of the private sector from both within and outside the region in integrating these economies through intra-regional direct investments. It suggests that the most promising forms of South-South co-operation are primarily private-sector-led, market-based and comparative-advantage-driven. Governments can support such initiatives by removing political hurdles to cross-border private sector ventures, co-ordinating supportive national investment incentives, participating in some regional private-sector-led ventures as cost-, risk- and profit-sharing partners and co-operating with the private sector in joint infrastructure and human resource development projects that can shape or enhance the comparative advantage of member nations and the competitive advantages of regional private firms.

Introduction

The Association of South East Asian Nations (ASEAN) was founded in 1967 with five members — Indonesia, Malaysia, the Philippines, Singapore and Thailand — who were joined in 1984 by the tiny oil-rich sultanate of Brunei (Appendix 1). Since that time, the ASEAN countries have prospered economically, their 330 million citizens enjoying real GDP growth rates averaging over 6 per cent per year, and (with the exception of the Philippines) real per capita GNP growth rates of over 4 per cent per year for well over two decades (World Bank, various years; see also Appendix 2). Since the late

1980s, ASEAN economic growth rates have surpassed those of the East Asian newly-industrialised economies (NIEs) of South Korea, Taiwan and Hong Kong to become the fastest in the world, and ASEAN member nations are now considered to be the most likely "next", "near" or "new" NIEs to emerge in the world economy by the end of the 1990s.

At the same time, the ASEAN regional organisation which binds these six countries together in a network of co-operative relations is the most long-lived, and considered the most successful, such arrangement in the developing world. This inevitably raises the question of the extent to which regional co-operation has been a factor in the economic success of ASEAN member nations. The answer is "very little". Unlike most other regional groupings, ASEAN to date has not been a trade-driven organisation, and intra-regional trade has actually **declined** as a proportion of member nations' total trade over the past quarter-century. Intra-regional investment also accounts for only a very small proportion of total foreign investment in ASEAN member nations.

There are three major reasons for this low level of intra-ASEAN economic interaction. First, individual ASEAN countries' external economic relations remain dominated by trade with and investment from advanced industrial and, more recently, newly-industrialised Asian countries. Very rapid growth in trade and investment with non-ASEAN partners over the past two decades have thus dwarfed in relative terms the absolute increases in intra-ASEAN trade and investment which have occurred. Second, the principal objective of the ASEAN organisation has always been to promote regional peace and prosperity, and not economic integration *per se* (Appendix 3). Thus regional economic integration schemes have been very limited in scope and progress. Third, ASEAN governments have always accorded priority to economic growth and development on the national level, at which they have individually been very successful. National-level economic success reduces the perceived need for regional co-operation, especially where the two may conflict.

While the economic success of the ASEAN countries to date owes very little to regional economic co-operation, ASEAN as a **political** bloc has contributed to regional political stability, without which national economic development would have been more difficult. At the same time, the internal political stability and economic prosperity of individual ASEAN member nations has contributed to the viability of the regional grouping itself. Indeed, the ASEAN experience suggests that it is successful national economic development which promotes regional integration, rather than vice versa. It is only now, in the 1990s, after two decades of successful national-based economic growth, that the development of ASEAN regional economic linkages is beginning to accelerate. While government-to-government policies are important to this process — particularly with respect to trade liberalisation — private sector linkages and private-public sector co-operation appear to be assuming a more dominant role. They are the focus of this chapter.

The private sector in ASEAN

Considerable diversity exists among the ASEAN member nations in size, resource endowment, ethnic and cultural background, colonial history, economic structure, income level and stage of development. At one extreme, Singapore is a high-income, heavily-industrialised, predominantly ethnic Chinese island city-state of 3 million people, while at the other extreme Indonesia is a low-income, predominantly rural and resource-rich nation of 190 million people and over 300 ethno-linguistic groups inhabiting an archipelago of more than 17 000 islands.

Despite these differences, in all the ASEAN countries the state has been a major player in economic development, beyond the minimal "free-market" roles of promoting macroeconomic stability and providing basic infrastructure and public services. All the governments except Brunei — even Singapore for a while — followed trade-restricting import-substitution industrialisation policies to diversify their economies away from previous colonial-era dependence on commodity exports. But beginning with Singapore in the late 1960s, all also ventured into labour-intensive manufacturing for world markets. This required at least partial trade liberalisation, most notably in segregated free-trade export processing zones or "bonded factories" which permitted the development of export-oriented industry without necessitating the dismantling of import-substitution trade barriers (Ariff and Hill, 1985). Foreign investment was allowed into export industries virtually without restriction, while raw material- and domestic market-based industries remained protected. By the early 1980s, Singapore, Indonesia and Malaysia ranked third, fourth and fifth respectively among developing countries in terms of the cumulative stock of foreign direct investment they had received (World Bank, 1987, p. 17), and by the mid-1980s, manufactures accounted for more than half of the foreign exchange earnings of Malaysia, Thailand and the Philippines.

Despite the importance of foreign investment and export markets, since the 1950s the goal of the "ASEAN-4" (Indonesia, Malaysia, Philippines, Thailand) governments has been to promote national industrialisation, through various nationalist and indigenist policies (Golay et al., 1969). These have included import protection of domestic industries, restrictions on foreign investment and on local ethnic Chinese business, the establishment of state enterprises, and discriminatory industrial licensing, regulation and credit allocation schemes.

The basic goal of these policies, which varied in detail and in extent from country to country and from time to time, was to carve out a protected sphere of operations in the economy for indigenous Southeast Asian ethnic groups, who during the colonial era had tended to occupy the lowest rungs of the economic hierarchy while foreigners and Chinese immigrants controlled trade and the private sector. The growth of a state sector and state protection and privileges for a nascent indigenous private sector were aimed at shifting economic resources and control to the indigenous non-immigrant population.

The *pribumi* policy in Indonesia sought to protect and nurture indigenous private entrepreneurs at the same time as a huge state sector was being built up. The *bumiputra* policy in Malaysia imposed ethnic ownership and employment quotas to increase indigenous Malay (as opposed to foreign and Chinese) participation in private business while simultaneously developing Malay-controlled state enterprises and using state funds to make market acquisitions of foreign-owned companies. By the 1980s, when an indigenous business class had begun to take root — benefiting from political patronage, state policy, strategic business alliances and rapid economic growth — privatisation offered it yet more privileged opportunities to take over previously state-owned enterprises.

In Thailand and the Philippines, governments have been weaker and less stable, and have not similarly sought to promote indigenous private enterprise or to curtail the business activities of the ethnic Chinese. In Thailand, the Chinese are much more dominant in the private sector than in the Philippines, where indigenous Filipinos, especially members of the mestizo agrarian landed elite, have a strong presence in business despite the still disproportionate role of the Chinese. Political democratisation and the ensuing economic liberalisation in the Philippines (after 1986) and in Thailand (1988-1991), by creating a more *laissez-faire* policy environment, have more recently favoured Chinese business (Lim, 1991).

Given the large amounts of foreign investment that the ASEAN countries have received over the past twenty years, foreign capital continues to play an important role in these economies. Without the technology, management expertise and foreign market access brought by multinationals, the ASEAN countries would not have been able to industrialise as efficiently and as rapidly, to create as many jobs (especially in labour-intensive export manufacturing) for the indigenous working class, and as many opportunities for joint-venture partnerships and technology transfer for the nascent indigenous private sector, as they did. Foreign capital provided a counterweight to Chinese dominance of the local modern sector, as well as access to more sophisticated technologies and markets than the local Chinese could provide. Indigenous control of the state and state economic policy provided the incentive for foreign corporations and local Chinese business to cultivate and nurture indigenous partners from both the state and private sectors.

Today, the ASEAN private sector consists of a dynamic mix of local and foreign, Chinese and indigenous enterprises involved in complex complementary as well as competitive relationships with each other and with state enterprises. While the specific interests of all these different groups sometimes conflict, they are resolved through "flexible" adaptive strategies of alliance- and coalition-building, consultation, negotiation, bargaining and compromise (Doner, 1991). Thus for all the "statist" character of much of Southeast Asian development to date, the private sector has, together with the state, played an active and important role in national development. This is reflected in its growing role in ASEAN regional economic co-operation.

ASEAN regional economic co-operation

ASEAN was formed at a meeting of ASEAN Foreign Ministers in Bangkok in 1967, during a time of revolution and war in neighbouring Indochina which threatened the stability of the non-communist countries of the region. Their banding together was motivated largely by political and security considerations, since in the economic sphere all were focused on following their own individual national development strategies. But little happened to promote co-operation until the United States, with whom the ASEAN countries had been firmly aligned, was defeated in the Vietnam War and a communist government took over control of a reunified Vietnam in 1975.

Unlike the summitry that has characterised the integration process in Africa and Latin America, the ASEAN Heads of Government did not hold their first meeting until February 1976, in Bali, where it was decided to accelerate the pace of regional co-operation in the economic, social, cultural, technical, scientific and administrative fields, and to co-operate politically on international and regional matters. It was also decided that ASEAN Economic Ministers should meet regularly to develop and implement economic co-operation proposals. A second summit was held in Kuala Lumpur in August 1977, when ASEAN "dialogues" were begun with ASEAN's major international economic partners, and a third summit took place in Manila in 1987, focusing heavily on economic co-operation measures and relations with Japan. The fourth and most recent summit held in Singapore in January 1992 — twenty-five years after ASEAN's inception — resulted in an agreement to establish an ASEAN Free Trade Area (AFTA) over a 15-year period[1].

Since 1979, ASEAN's highest profile has been in the international political arena, where it has taken the lead in the United Nations in opposing Vietnam's 1979 invasion and occupation of Cambodia, and in settlement of the Cambodian problem. Regional economic co-operation is directed by the ASEAN Economic Ministers through five permanent committees, on Finance and Banking; Food, Agriculture and Forestry; Industry, Minerals and Energy; Trade and Communications; and Trade and Tourism. The committees meet at least twice a year, and are in turn served by various sub-committees and ad hoc working groups[2].

Trade liberalisation

ASEAN does not represent an exchange-driven form of regional co-operation. Regional trade liberalisation has never been high on the association's agenda, and not until the Singapore summit in 1992 did it seek to become a free trade area. Prior to that point, opposition to the creation of a regional free trade area came at one extreme from Indonesia — which had and still has the largest, most heavily-protected domestic market and most inefficient industrial sector, and thus the most to lose from import liberalisation — and at the other extreme from Singapore, which would not accept a common external tariff because of its heavy dependence on free trade with the rest of the world. A further consideration has been that, except for trade with Singapore, an important trading intermediary for the region, the ASEAN members' major trade partners are not each other but rather the major industrialised nations, especially Japan and the United States. The ASEAN-4 have all unilaterally reduced tariffs and other trade barriers as part of liberal national economic reform packages in the 1980s and early 1990s, but these liberalisations have been applied to all trading partners, not only to fellow ASEAN members.

These factors explain the lack of progress in trade liberalisation under the ASEAN Preferential Trading Arrangements (PTA) approved in 1977, and suggest that the AFTA agreement of January 1992 may also be limited in its progress and impact. ASEAN members agreed to exchange tariff preferences on approved imports from each other under the PTA, which by 1987 covered more than 20 000 items. But it did not boost intra-ASEAN trade significantly because most member countries excluded their most important traded items from the PTA list (Devan, 1987). PTA products currently account for less than 1 per cent of total intra-ASEAN trade, which has fallen from 21 per cent of total ASEAN trade in the mid-1980s to around 18 per cent today — much of it accounted for by Singapore's role as a trading intermediary for the region[3]. The 1987 Manila summit announced a five-year plan to extend PTA coverage to 90 per cent of total goods traded within the region and at least 50 per cent of the value of total ASEAN-sourced imports. This target has not been achieved, and the PTA itself as a mechanism for trade liberalisation appears now to be superseded by the AFTA proposal.

Approved at the ASEAN summit in Singapore in January 1992, AFTA involves implementation of a Common Effective Preferential Tariff (CEPT) Scheme for manufactured products with at least 40 per cent ASEAN-wide content. Unprocessed agricultural goods and service industries are not included. The goal is to reduce current tariffs on manufactures to no more than 20 per cent in five to eight years, and to no more than 5 per cent by January 1, 2008. Currently, overall average tariff levels are close to zero for Brunei and Singapore, 15.64 per cent for Malaysia, 21.68 per cent for Indonesia, 25.96 per cent for the Philippines, and 43.83 per cent for Thailand (Stone, 1992, p. 26)[4]. Fifteen product categories[5] have been selected for the first round of tariff reductions, but countries will be allowed to temporarily exclude specific products as required to protect "sensitive" domestic industries. These exclusions, together with the relatively long timetable, suggest that progress toward a regional free trade area under AFTA may be less smooth, less speedy and less complete than promised. While on the one hand, the ASEAN countries have come a long distance in favouring free trade among themselves, on the other, there remain many serious obstacles to the realisation of this goal.

Originally, national government priorities in ASEAN did not favour free trade because they focused on protecting and nurturing an indigenous entrepreneurial class — which, however, needed capital, technical and managerial support from Chinese and foreign business partners. Being the dominant established local business group, including in manufacturing for domestic markets, the Chinese were the most threatened by import competition. Where the Chinese business class has had more political influence over government economic policy, as in Indonesia and Thailand, the level of import protection and resistance to free trade has been much higher than where Chinese political influence has been weaker, as in Malaysia. In Singapore, where multinationals overwhelmingly dominate the manufacturing sector and the local Chinese business class has been politically weak (Lim, 1987), free trade has never been seriously opposed.

On the other hand, multinationals throughout ASEAN have generally favoured freer trade, as they would benefit from this in local markets, given their superior competitive strengths, scale economies, and the high cost of serving small individual markets. Before the advent of import-substituting industrialisation (ISI), multinationals in the area were engaged in commodity production for export and in import-export activities, both of which were undermined by ISI policies which forced multinationals to substitute local manufacturing for previous direct exports from their home countries. The local Chinese and indigenous businesses that they were required to take on as joint-venture partners then emerged as the main beneficiaries of ISI[6].

When the ASEAN-4 countries moved from ISI to export manufacturing — beginning with Malaysia in 1970 — they introduced selective free trade in export processing zones and bonded factories and allowed 100 per cent foreign ownership for export-oriented industries. Multinationals in these industries naturally favoured free trade, as did their local employees and suppliers drawn from the ranks of Chinese and indigenous local business, thereby expanding over time the political constituency supportive of trade liberalisation[7]. The benefits of export manufacturing based on selective free trade (i.e. free trade zones) — rapid industrial growth, mass employment creation, rising incomes, technology transfer and skill acquisition — also created a positive "demonstration effect" supporting free trade. For the local business community previously engaged in ISI, increased exports of manufactures promised faster growth and larger markets, both directly by producing for export to foreign countries, and indirectly by supplying locally-based export industries and their newly-prosperous employees.

As the local business community in ASEAN countries has become more established, more efficient, and more confident — in part because of import-substituting as well as export manufacturing successes — its greater ability to compete and its desire to expand beyond the domestic market have begun to reduce resistance to trade liberalisation. At the same time, national-level economic reforms of the 1980s, including selective deregulation, privatisation and unilateral trade and investment liberalisation, have borne fruit in the accelerated economic growth experienced in the late 1980s and early 1990s, strengthening the case for further liberalisation[8]. Privatisation, in particular, is reducing the stable of state-owned enterprises whose need for protection was a major obstacle to regional free trade.

According to private sector spokespersons I interviewed, not only local business communities, but also ASEAN governments which previously "lacked the political will" to implement free trade, are now willing to do so because of the greater confidence engendered by the economic successes of the past five years. But according to government statements, the impetus for the recent push for regional free trade in ASEAN is largely external. The emergence of regional economic blocs in Europe (EC-92 single market integration together with the prospect of EFTA and some Eastern European countries eventually becoming EC members) and North America (the North America Free Trade Area encompassing Canada, Mexico and the United States) has led to fears that Asian countries including those in ASEAN might face exclusionary trade practices that would threaten their thriving export industries. In that event the regional market would be a necessary substitute for current world markets for ASEAN manufactures and commodities[9]. It is also felt that a unified regional market would help ASEAN to compete with other emerging regions — particularly Latin America — in attracting more foreign direct investment. Certainly a lack of an integrated regional market to date has been a perennial complaint of multinational investors and potential investors in ASEAN, and has deterred investments that would serve the regional as opposed to the world market.

Thus the growing regional constituency in favour of ASEAN free trade is the result of both external pressures — potential competition with other regional economic blocs — and internal developments — increasing government and industry confidence in the ability of national firms to compete without import protection, based on decades of successful economic growth. In the latter regard, the ASEAN countries resemble present-day industrialised countries (North America, Western Europe and Japan) whose willingness to accept free trade on a global or regional basis increased as they became richer and more competitive. This falls in line with expectations that the need for infant industry protection in late-industrialising counties declines as their industrial experience grows and their industries become more world-competitive. In other words, support for free trade is the outcome of successful industrial development.

But in ASEAN as in the developed countries, this move toward free trade is not universally accepted — there remain deep differences by country, sector, industry and company according to the degree of entrenched dependence on import protection and the likelihood of achieving international competitiveness without it. Thus on the country level, AFTA's long timetable is partly designed to accommodate the slower pace of regional integration preferred by the two least-developed ASEAN members, Indonesia and the Philippines. Even in more-developed Malaysia and Thailand, however, there have been vacillations reflecting divided private sector interests.

Thailand in particular provides a good example of the political complexities of support for free trade. AFTA was first proposed by Anand Panyarachun, a retired career civil servant and former head of both a large private business group and an influential Thai business association. Anand was appointed Prime Minister by the King in February 1991 after a military coup which deposed the allegedly corrupt elected Prime Minister. After the AFTA proposal was approved at the ASEAN summit in Singapore in January 1992, Thailand declared that it would lower its tariffs ahead of the AFTA schedule. When elections in late March 1992 led to the appointment of former military general Suchinda Krapayoon as Prime Minister, however, members of his government sought to adopt a slower pace of trade liberalisation, apparently in response to pressures from a segment of the local private business sector. (Recall that Thailand has the highest average level of protection among the ASEAN nations.) But following violent street unrest in May 1992, Suchinda was forced to resign, Anand was reappointed by the King (temporarily, pending new elections scheduled for September 1992), and Thailand once again officially reaffirmed its strong support for AFTA and accelerated tariff cuts. This was also the position taken by the Thai business delegation at the ASEAN-CCI (Chambers of Commerce and Industry) general meeting in Jakarta in July 1992.

Commitment to AFTA and interest in accelerating its tariff-reduction schedule was strongly affirmed as well by all parties at the ASEAN Foreign Ministers' Meeting in Manila in July 1992, with the need to attract external (non-ASEAN) investments being cited as the major motivating force. Despite this, there remain divisions and obstacles to free trade within the region (as indeed, there are to NAFTA in North America, and to the Maastricht agreement and full monetary union in the EC).

In ASEAN, governments, or parts of the state sector, may be reluctant to give up protection of the domestic market — including of state-owned enterprises — from which they derive some power and revenues. (Similar considerations have already slowed down the privatisation of state enterprises.) Parts of the private sector which are dependent on national protective barriers also remain opposed to increased competition from within the region. Stone (1992) presents a quick calculation of which ASEAN business groups are likely to benefit and which to lose from free trade in the fifteen fast-track sectors, and this table is reproduced in Appendix 4. Most ASEAN companies compete in the same industrial sectors and product segments with each other, and thus some might be expected to object to increased competition from their neighbours who might be more competitive. For example, Thailand's heavily-protected palm oil industry is expected to be very vulnerable to Malaysian and Indonesian competition and will likely disappear with regional free trade[10]. Local Thai businessmen in other sectors (e.g. glass) have also been lobbying their governments to exempt their products and industries from the CEPT scheme. As a marginal factor, throughout ASEAN some indigenous enterprises may oppose a regional free trade area because they fear it would only increase linkages between ethnic Chinese businesses in the different ASEAN member countries, enhancing their dominance of the private sector.

Multinationals in general support regional free trade, but have not been active in AFTA deliberations, and are less likely to be affected by the outcomes than local firms, given their greater global competitiveness and representation in free trade zones[11]. It is possible that some multinationals which have sunk heavy investments into particular countries expecting long-term protected local markets may object to a change in the terms on which their investment decisions were made, but these objections are more likely to be made by their local partners. Overall, companies' policy positions on regional free trade are much more a function of individual company-, industry- and country-specific factors than they are of national ownership characteristics.

While there remains interest-group opposition to regional trade liberalisation, the argument in favour of a regional free trade area may be additionally weakened by ongoing unilateral and universal trade liberalisation at the national level. The ASEAN countries were already staunch supporters of the GATT Uruguay Round, which is arguably the "first-best" trade policy alternative for them, given their closer integration with the world than with their own regional economy. (By the same token, lack of progress on GATT would have strengthened the case for AFTA as a "second-best" alternative.) Indeed, it is possible that the gains from regional free trade will only be marginal. A recent study (Imada, Montes and Naya, 1991) suggests that a 50 per cent preferential tariff reduction will enlarge the share of intra-ASEAN trade to total trade by about 10 percent or less; since intra-ASEAN trade is only 18 per cent of ASEAN's total trade, the gains in terms of total trade and income are likely to be small. These figures do not take into account possible dynamic effects of free trade, but in the ASEAN case these are likely to have already been partially realised by low tariffs or free trade especially between Malaysia and Singapore — the two largest ASEAN trading nations — and between free trade zones in different member countries[12].

Regional free trade in ASEAN is therefore a highly complex affair, currently pushed largely by external developments and restricted mainly by national political economy considerations. Economically, the gains from free trade may be modest, while institutionally, ASEAN's vaunted "flexibility" —

allowing individual countries to opt out of particular co-operation schemes as they choose — and its willingness to proceed on a lowest-common-denominator basis to achieve group-wide consensus — e.g. by allowing exclusions — are likely to continue slowing the progress towards trade-based integration. In any event, reducing tariff barriers alone will not remove other, arguably greater, non-tariff barriers to intra-ASEAN trade arising from different national taxes, regulations and standards (as shown by the European Community's 35-year experience), as well as by the continued importance of political connections in doing business in the ASEAN countries (i.e. locally-domiciled firms will always have better connections in their own home market than competitors from other countries). Thus despite the recent progress represented by the AFTA agreement, a truly integrated ASEAN regional market based on regional free trade is probably still a long way off.

Regional industrial co-operation

While ASEAN has not been an exchange-driven regional grouping, it has adopted a few of the features common to production specialisation models of regional integration. These include the ASEAN Industrial Projects (AIPs), the ASEAN Industrial Complementation (AIC) and the ASEAN Industrial Joint Ventures (AIJV) schemes (e.g. Suriyamongkol, 1987; Appendix 5). AIPs are large-scale, capital-intensive public-private sector projects in which all the ASEAN member governments hold equity stakes; their output enjoys tariff preferences in ASEAN member markets. The projects have been beset with difficulties and currently only two have been established, both urea plants in Indonesia and Malaysia established with the assistance of Japanese financing and technology.

The AIC scheme aims to promote complementary (tariff-favoured) trade exchanges of specified manufactured products among private industry in ASEAN member countries. So far it has been implemented only for automotive parts and components under a brand-to-brand complementation scheme approved in 1988 (Smith, 1989; Goldstein, 1990), which Malaysia, Thailand and the Philippines have joined. The scheme benefits mainly Japanese multinational auto companies (and their ASEAN joint venture partners)[13] with plants in these different ASEAN countries, allowing them to exchange parts between different local subsidiaries at a preferential tariff rate (see Appendix 6).

AIJVs were introduced in 1983 to promote relatively small-scale private sector projects, which receive tariff preferences if they have partners from two or more ASEAN countries (Low, 1990). AIJV projects currently enjoy preferential tariff margins of 90 per cent and are guaranteed against government expropriation or nationalisation. Foreign investors are allowed to hold up to 60 per cent of the equity in these ventures, and an even higher proportion under certain conditions[14]. As with the AIP and AIC schemes, the results so far are meagre. As of July 1991, only 18 AIJV projects had been approved, with a concentration in the production of auto components; four of the projects were processed foods projects by a single multinational, Nestlé (see Appendix 7). Only five projects were in commercial operation, and three had been dropped[15].

Both the AIC and AIJV programmes owe a great deal to the leadership and participation of the ASEAN Chambers of Commerce and Industry (ASEAN-CCI), a regional private sector organisation that was established with ASEAN government support in 1972. The ASEAN-CCI is a voluntary association of the national chambers of commerce and industry from the six ASEAN countries. The membership of national chambers consists overwhelmingly of local firms, though there is some marginal representation of foreign firms[16]. The ASEAN-CCI's four-tier structure comprises: an administrative Council; four active Working Groupings (on Industrial Co-operation; Trade; Food, Agriculture and Forestry; and Transport and Communications); Regional Industry and Commodity Clubs; and National Industry and Commodity Clubs (Appendices 8 and 9). In addition, the ASEAN-CCI established joint Business Councils with the private sector in ASEAN's major trading partners — the same dialogue partners represented in public sector co-operation (see below) — such as the US-ASEAN Business Council, etc. The ASEAN-CCI does not have a permanent secretariat but rotates among national chambers in different ASEAN countries, with a research institute recently established in temporary premises at the Institute of Southeast Asian Studies in Singapore.

The ASEAN-CCI President reports formally on the membership's views to the annual meeting of ASEAN Economic Ministers, and the organisation has taken the initiative and been actively involved in the formulation of co-operation programmes involving the private sector, especially in the areas of trade and industry. Suriyamongkol (1987) has outlined the role of ASEAN Regional Industry Clubs[17] in developing the ASEAN Industrial Complementation scheme. The ASEAN-CCI and the ASEAN Automotive Federation worked with the ASEAN Committee on Industry, Minerals and Energy (COIME) to realise an AIC scheme for the automotive industry. This remains the only operational AIC programme to date, though several other Regional Industry Clubs are working on product packages for possible AICs in their industries. The time frame for this process was very long; the ASEAN Automotive Federation was founded in 1976 but it was not until 1981 that the AIC Basic Agreement was signed and not until 1988 that the automotive AIC brand-to-brand complementation scheme was approved and implemented; still, Indonesia, potentially the largest automotive manufacturer and market in the region, has not joined the scheme. The ASEAN-CCI also initiated the slightly more successful — though still very limited — AIJV scheme.

Despite these apparent successes in private-public sector co-operation to establish regional industrial co-operation schemes, ASEAN Deputy Director-General Chng Meng Kng notes that:

> ASEAN governments have generally been reluctant to directly involve the ASEAN-CCI in their decision-making at the regional level, and official ASEAN organs have generally kept the ASEAN-CCI at arm's length.....As an interest group (the ASEAN-CCI) may present its views but clearly cannot engage directly in the decision-making processes of official ASEAN bodies.....with six private sectors and six governments, the problems of coordinating the relationship at national level with that at regional level is very complex.....getting governmental consensus at regional level to ASEAN-CCI initiatives is extremely difficult. (Chng, 1990, p. 276)[18].

Besides inevitable coordination problems and conflicting interests within the ASEAN-CCI, between the ASEAN-CCI and ASEAN national governments and regional inter-governmental bodies, and among ASEAN governments which have different attitudes toward private enterprise, state intervention and the market economy, Chng further notes that the ASEAN-CCI itself does not necessarily represent the interests of the entire private sector, but could on occasion represent only the self-interest of an organised industrial elite. He quotes Singapore's then Minister for Trade and Industry, Goh Chok Tong, who said in a 1980 speech that:

> Private enterprise generally disdains governmental intervention in business; but when they dream up complementation schemes, they want governments to intervene and protect them from competition. In the end, it was the governments which resisted iron-clad protection for those so fortunate as to be allocated the products under the AICs. (Chng, 1990, p. 277)[19].

In short, while the ASEAN private sector as represented by the ASEAN-CCI has played an active, and in some cases even leading role in regional economic co-operation, this has in the past not always been effective, efficient or equitable. Most past regional co-operation schemes were based on the general principle of regional import substitution, so it is not surprising that conflicts of interest arose within and among nations, their private sectors and governments. It is arguable that the greatest promise for more intra-regional private and private-public sector co-operation lies outside these formal ASEAN-wide schemes. But the ASEAN-CCI and its Regional Industry Clubs retain a potentially important role as business associations through which the ASEAN private sector can interact and develop the business contacts, shared expertise and resources which can result in cross-national private sector joint ventures within the region[20].

It is likely that active members of the ASEAN-CCI and its Regional Industry Clubs are a self-selected group of those with the greatest interest in such intra-regional private joint ventures, and now, also in intra-regional free trade — in line with the evolution through time of private sector policy positions discussed above. The ASEAN-CCI has responded enthusiastically to the AFTA proposal, and has made recommendations to the ASEAN member governments on how this should be implemented, including: that there not be an exclusion list, that tariff reduction take place on a sectoral and gradual basis, that tariff and non-tariff barriers be wholly eliminated, and that capital goods and services not be excepted (ASEAN-CCI, 1992). Its members clearly favour an accelerated move to a Free Trade Area with the broadest possible coverage, arguing, for example, that "the ASEAN content requirement (for CEPT qualification) be reduced by all members to 40 per cent for the first five years and that at the end of this five-year period.....lower origin requirements be allowed to some industrial sectors" (*ibid.*, p. 9). The organisation also advocates the quick admission of Vietnam, Cambodia, Laos and Myanmar (ASEAN's socialist neighbours) into ASEAN, the promotion of sub-regional co-operation zones (see below), and links with other Free Trade Areas.

With respect to AFTA, the ASEAN-CCI sees its role as one of disseminating more information about ASEAN, its industrial and commercial enterprises, and its products throughout the member nations. In order to do this effectively, it will bring together more manufacturers into the fold, i.e. small and medium enterprises, MNCs and state-owned enterprise (SOEs), and improve cross-marketing of intra-ASEAN products and services. (ASEAN-CCI, 1992, p. 15)

With respect to links with Indochina and Myanmar, it says that

ASEAN-CCI members are in a unique position to seek out investment opportunities, arrange for training, seek offshore funding and take the first steps in channelling direct investments into these promising economies (ASEAN-CCI, 1992, p. 16)

With respect to links with NAFTA and the EC, it says that

The private sector can spearhead much of this development, given that existing links are already being forged through the MNCs. The possibility of greater franchising, licensing, joint ventures, and acquisitions and mergers amongst ASEAN, EC and NAFTA companies seems alluring enough from a distance. The opportunities for acquisition of new technology and skills must be the foremost drivers of much of this development, in addition to the larger market which then becomes accessible. (ASEAN-CCI, 1992, p. 21)

These comments clearly suggest the global and inclusive rather than national/regional and exclusive orientation of the organised ASEAN private sector elite as represented in the ASEAN-CCI, and the total absence of a "zero-sum" or protectionist mentality amongst this industrial elite. Despite Goh Chok Tong's (possibly dated) criticism, and some apparent disagreement at the national level in some countries at some points of time, the official ASEAN-CCI policy position has always been in favour of regional free trade — most recently confirmed at its meeting in Jakarta in July 1992 — and ASEAN-CCI activists tend to blame national governments for the slow progress to date in this area. Indeed, this discussion suggests that attempts at regional industrial co-operation involving the ASEAN private sector may have come full circle — as priorities shift from industrial co-operation as an alternative to regional free trade, to the new (though — as in NAFTA and the EC — by no means unanimous or unambiguous) current enthusiasm for progress in AFTA.

Though it is an organisation which unambiguously represents the interests of the local, rather than the multinational, private sector in ASEAN, the ASEAN-CCI's recent policy positions with regard to regional free trade and industrial co-operation — particularly the preference for relatively low local content — do not appear to differ from those that multinationals in the region might be expected to favour. There are several reasons for this. First, to a considerable extent, the interests of the local private sector and of multinationals merge rather than conflict. Even in import-substitution, and definitely in export manufacturing, the competitiveness, profitability, indeed the very existence of local private businesses depend on their relations with multinationals as their investors, joint-venture partners, customers and suppliers. For example, ASEAN firms' best hopes for penetrating the NAFTA, EC and Japan markets, and for competing with other multinationals in their own home and regional markets, are through linkages with multinationals from those countries.

Second, even where local firms are competitive rather than complementary with multinationals, they also benefit from similarly liberal trade policies. For example, the relatively low (40 per cent) local content requirement proposed for AFTA/CEPT qualification will enable ASEAN firms to qualify even if they have to import a sizeable proportion of components. Non-ASEAN imports are likely for more technologically-sophisticated equipment and components that ASEAN firms are less able than multinationals to make internally or source locally or regionally themselves. Non-ASEAN imports are also likely for very labour-intensive items that many ASEAN firms (from Thailand, Malaysia and Singapore especially) are looking to source from Indochina and China to maintain their competitive edge as local wage costs rise and labour shortages intensify.

Third, enlargement of markets through regional free trade will facilitate technological upgrading, increased R and D, and new product introduction by ASEAN firms, by giving them access to the scale economies that multinationals can already obtain on a global if not a regional basis. So long as they remain limited to supplying small, relatively unsophisticated, heavily protected and segmented national markets, ASEAN firms will find it difficult if not impossible to compete with multinationals regionally as well as internationally and in world export markets. Thus as more ASEAN firms grow to a certain size, experience, sophistication and ambition, they naturally seek to compete more directly with multinationals outside of their own home markets, and thus are more likely to favour regional trade liberalisation as a necessary step in their own internationalisation. In short, just as the ASEAN countries are following in the path of previously industrialised countries by increasingly favouring free trade as they become more economically successful, so too ASEAN companies are following the trade policy preferences of multinationals as they become more competitive and global in their orientation, capabilities and ambition.

Co-operation in non-industrial sectors

Outside of the industrial sector, many other sector-specific co-operation schemes have been launched or identified (ASEAN-CCI, 1990). In finance and banking, an ASEAN Swap Arrangement has been in existence since 1977, making available to member countries a standby credit facility of up to $200 million that could be used to alleviate temporary balance-of-payments problems. Other measures in this sector include an intra-ASEAN Double Taxation Convention, the "liberalised use of ASEAN currencies for intra-regional trade and investment activities", and establishment of an ASEAN Reinsurance Corporation. In food, agriculture and forestry, there is an ASEAN Food Security Reserve and an ASEAN Food Handling Bureau, as well as projects in afforestation, forest and watershed management, and timber technology, implemented with financial and technical assistance from ASEAN's "dialogue" partners. In minerals and energy, an ASEAN Emergency Petroleum Scheme has been in existence since 1977, and the ASEAN Minerals Co-operation Plan has identified many joint projects in areas such as kaolin and barite beneficiation and marketing, mine safety, mining technology exchanges, and joint explorations for mineral and energy resources. In transportation and communications, over a hundred projects have been identified for joint development; those currently under way are the Pan Borneo Highway project to link Brunei with the East Malaysian states of Sabah and Sarawak, and ferry services between Penang (Malaysia) and Belawan (Sumatra, Indonesia). In tourism, 1992 has been designated "Visit ASEAN Year" with joint promotion and the establishment of an ASEAN Tourist Information Office in Kuala Lumpur. Co-operative projects also exist in the non-economic areas of science and technology, culture and information, and social development.

Despite the existence of these and many other regional co-operation schemes, the lack of significant progress in trade liberalisation and industrial co-operation has led many writers to seek to explain the slow pace and limited extent of ASEAN economic co-operation to date (e.g. Kuntjoro-Jakti, 1987; Villegas, 1987; Chng, 1990). This has been attributed to several factors, some of which I have noted above, including: (a) the competitive rather than complementary structure of ASEAN members' economies, particularly their dependence on exporting the same primary commodities and manufactured goods to the world market; (b) the outward-orientation to the world market of the ASEAN economies, particularly the much greater importance to them of trade with industrialised countries than with their neighbours; (c) the priority given to national rather than regional economic development, reflecting the dominance of nationalist over regionalist development philosophies; (d) the success of existing strategies of world market-oriented, national-focused development, and thus the absence of any perceived need to generate faster growth through regional economic integration; (e) the (deliberately?) weak institutional structure of the ASEAN regional organisation, and its reliance on decentralised, consensus-based, ad hoc decision-making.

These and other factors may have limited "traditional" regional economic co-operation of the type characterised by trade liberalisation and sector-specific industrial co-operation as practised by the European Community. But it is arguable that ASEAN has developed and is developing other "non-traditional" forms of regional economic co-operation which are better suited to its particular needs and circumstances, and which more directly involve the private sector. These are discussed below.

External economic relations

Co-operating in external economic relations with major non-ASEAN trade and investment partners is an important aspect of ASEAN regional co-operation. Indeed, "Third country relations have emerged as a central area of ASEAN's regional co-operation from the early 1970s" (Chng, 1990, p. 277). The formal mechanism for this is provided by the ASEAN "dialogues" with "dialogue partners" which take place after the annual ASEAN post-ministerial conference. The six ASEAN Foreign Ministers meet with their counterparts from the US, Japan, Australia, New Zealand, the European Community and Canada. South Korea was accepted as an ASEAN dialogue partner in 1991, and requests by Russia and China for similar status are being considered. These new dialogue partners are expected to change the nature of the bilateral dialogues from their past "donor-recipient" character to one of "equal partners". So far the ASEAN dialogues have focused on issues of market access, trade and tourism promotion, aid and investments, industrial development, transfer of technology, human resources development, and dialogue partners' support for ASEAN positions in international fora. ASEAN members bargain as a group with their individual dialogue partners on specific trade and investment policy issues, and co-operate on schemes which can increase their bargaining power in international trade[21].

The ASEAN countries also frequently take "bloc" positions in international fora on both political (e.g. Vietnam/Cambodia) and economic issues. For example, in the GATT Uruguay Round of multilateral trade negotiations, the ASEAN countries were united (and allied with several of their dialogue partners) in favouring the liberalisation of agricultural trade and of trade in services, despite the fact that some ASEAN members had reservations that the latter would hurt their domestic services industries. The ASEAN countries also took a very prominent role at the UN Conference on Environment and Development in Brazil in June 1992. Singapore — which presents itself as a model of successful environmental management — chaired the committee which set the agenda for the conference, while Malaysia emerged as the leading spokesperson for the developing world in insisting that developed countries be held responsible — including financially — for environmental degradation in developing countries resulting from their over-consumption of natural resources. Other examples of "anti-Western" positions held in common by the ASEAN countries and frequently propounded by them in international fora include: opposition to economic sanctions against China and Myanmar on grounds of their domestic human rights violations (in contrast to the long and successful ASEAN-led UN campaign for an international economic blockade against Vietnam for its invasion of Cambodia); and opposition to the perennially proposed linking of developing country trade privileges (GSP) to their observance of intellectual property rights, human rights, labour rights and environmental conservation.

Several factors explain why the ASEAN — unlike Latin American — countries have been able to take common positions and bargain collectively (and often successfully) for them in the international arena. First, these common positions usually reflect members' shared interests, e.g. in restraining Vietnamese territorial expansionism, in obtaining better terms of trade for commodity exports, in freeing world agricultural trade, in holding on to GSP privileges for manufactured exports, in retaining rights to exploit their own natural resources (including the tropical rainforest) against the opposition of Western environmental activists, in developing lucrative trade and investment relations with China and Myanmar, and in forestalling possible Western trade restrictions based on non-observance of human and labour rights.

Second, the ASEAN countries are well-known for their "flexibility", rarely insisting on unanimity among themselves in regional or international fora. This is the famous "x+y=6" formula articulated by former Singapore Prime Minister Lee Kuan Yew, which allows for a common ASEAN policy or position to be established even when not all six member countries accept or participate in it, so long as the others do not object. Thus, for example, not all ASEAN members have participated in the ASEAN Industrial Projects; only three members are participating in the automotive complementation scheme; Thailand broke ranks on relations with Vietnam; Indonesia did not join its neighbours in supporting the Gulf War effort against Iraq; and so on. Currently, Thailand is seeking ASEAN support in opposing the extension of the MFA which regulates textile trade, but it may not get unanimous support (since some member countries are comfortable with their MFA quotas, and may not wish to face increased competition from Thailand in this industry). More seriously, several ASEAN countries have competing claims with each other and with China and Vietnam over the oil-rich Spratly Islands in the South China Sea, and other territorial disputes among members exist. But so far, these and other national policy differences have never been allowed to jeopardise the organisation's integrity and collective interests. The ASEAN countries remain ruled by pragmatism rather than by principle in their regional as well as national and international dealings.

Third, because of their long-established relative openness (compared with other developing countries) to international trade and investment, and their active participation in the world economy, the ASEAN countries have close and sympathetic ties with both private and public sectors in the developed world. They are sufficiently important to the economic interests of the West and Japan that they have some leverage in collective bargaining with these countries, within which they also have lobbying support from their multinational partners. Thus they are able to at once criticise the developed countries and obtain favourable policy concessions from them. The ASEAN countries are also very adept diplomatically, particularly at exploiting shifting alliances with different parts of the Northern "Triad" against other parts, e.g. with the US and Japan against Europe, or with the US and Europe against Japan, or with Japan against the US and Europe, depending on the specific issue at hand.

In November 1989, ASEAN joined in an Australian initiative which established an Asia-Pacific Economic Community (APEC) including, besides the ASEAN countries, Canada, the US, Australia, New Zealand, Japan and South Korea; the Chinese territories of China, Taiwan and Hong Kong joined in 1991 under a loose "compromise" arrangement accommodating the ambivalent sovereignty of the latter two members. APEC itself is a loose regional forum in which ASEAN was supposed to "take the lead" in exploring closer economic relations among APEC members. In December 1990, Malaysia proposed yet another, more structured regional grouping, the East Asia Economic Grouping (EAEG) which would exclude Australia, New Zealand, Canada and the US, and function as a counterweight to the EC and NAFTA. Opposition to the concept from other APEC members, particularly the US,[22] resulted in the grouping being "downgraded" to a East Asia Economic Caucus (EAEC) following the ASEAN summit in January 1992 (among ASEAN members, Indonesia was especially opposed to the EAEG).

The EAEG/C was unpopular with many of its proposed members mainly because it would exclude the US — the first or second largest trading partner of all the countries in the group — and secondarily because — with the US out — the regional grouping would be economically dominated by Japan. At the same time, the Malaysian proposal simply recognised and sought to formalise the fact that intra-Asian economic relations have expanded much more rapidly in the past decade than Asian economic relations with the US. In particular, the huge influx of Northeast Asian industrial investment to the ASEAN countries in the late 1980s following the worldwide currency realignment both provided a tremendous boost to economic and industrial growth in ASEAN and made Japan and the East Asian NIEs the region's major trade and investment partners, supplanting the US. There are some indications that in recent months the Japanese, especially, are softening their attitude toward an EAEG — support for which may be boosted by the August 1992 signing of the NAFTA agreement. Nevertheless, the ASEAN countries are discussing an ASEAN-EC agreement and an ASEAN-NAFTA agreement, both of which would help to ensure continued trade and investment linkages with these important non-Asian external economic partners as they form and deepen their own regional blocs.

Sub-regional co-operation zones: the "Growth Triangle"

With domestic economic liberalisation in the 1980s, the ASEAN economies' outward-orientation to world markets increased and their growth accelerated, leading some to see the association as "in danger of declining into irrelevancy" (Vatikiotis, 1991). But in addition to the recent external stimulus to closer regional co-operation, Singapore Prime Minister Goh Chok Tong has hailed what he calls ASEAN's new phase of "outward-looking, competitive co-operation" — based on co-operation to develop each nation's own competitive advantage as decided by the market, rather than "zero-sum co-operation" decided by bureaucrats insisting on "an equal spread of benefits" among members. According to Goh, such co-operation should enhance the competitiveness of the regional grouping and of its members so that international investments will continue to flow into the region and ASEAN products can compete in the world market despite the emergence of other regional blocs in Europe and North America. To quote him,

> ...economic co-operation is more permanent and effective if it results in the greater competitiveness of the participating nations than in merely increasing intra-regional trade or getting a few investments which would not come unless they receive some financial incentives or protection (*Straits Times Weekly Overseas Edition* 9 March 1991, p. 1).

In line with this new philosophy, Goh in December 1989 articulated the concept of a "Growth Triangle" to promote the integrated development of Batam Island in the Indonesian province of Riau, the neighbouring Malaysian state of Johor, and Singapore (Appendix 1). Under this form of co-operation, the governments of contiguous territories work together to attract investments into the "triangle" — for example, through joint investment promotion missions to third countries, joint infrastructure development, and coordination of national investment policies — leaving it to the private sector to decide where the investments should go, according to the competitive advantage of different areas. Thus in the Johor-Singapore-Riau triangle, Johor's and Riau's cheaper land and labour are combined with Singapore's human skills, managerial expertise, technology, transportation and communications infrastructure to attract ASEAN and non-ASEAN investment to all three locations[23]. The Batam Free Trade Zone, located within this triangle, was first developed by the Indonesian government in 1978 to compete with Singapore as an oil services and transshipment port, export manufacturing location and tourism centre. But progress was limited until co-operation was established in 1989 with Singapore, which persuaded Indonesia to allow 100 per cent foreign ownership of enterprises in the Batam Economic Zone, which includes Batam and five surrounding islands. The Batam Industrial Park was established as a commercial joint venture between Indonesian-owned PT Batamindo Investment Corp. (a subsidiary of the powerful Salim and Bimantara Groups[24]) and Singapore-owned Batamindo Management (formed by two state-controlled companies in Singapore — Singapore Technologies Industrial Corp. and Jurong Environmental Engineering). This technically private sector venture is supported by public sector infrastructural projects in transportation, utilities and communications, which also extend to include Johor[25]. Johor already has extensive industrial parks of its own, but Singapore is designing a high-tech industrial park for Johor and will be staffing an industrial training institute there. Each of the three governments operates its own tax incentive programme for investors, but they co-operate in joint investment promotion. The Singapore Economic Development Board also provides technical and financial assistance to encourage Singapore businesses to relocate to neighbouring Malaysia and Indonesia.

Most of the economic activity in the Growth Triangle areas has been generated by the private sector — in manufacturing, processing, property development and tourism. **Tourism** activities have developed most rapidly, with weekend condominiums, beach resort hotels, country clubs and golf courses being developed on the Riau islands and Johor largely for land-hungry Singaporeans and other ASEAN and Asian tourists. For example, tourism and real estate projects accounted for more than half of the over $500 million in foreign investments in Batam between 1980 and 1990, and nearly all of this originated in Singapore (Pangestu, 1991, pp. 92-93).

Currently, a $2 billion "mega-beach resort" is being built on the Indonesian Riau island of Bintan, to be jointly marketed with Singapore as one common tourist destination. The resort will have more than 20 hotels, 10 condominium complexes, 30 villa clusters and 10 golf courses, with a 45-minute direct ferry service from Singapore and a mini-airport. The project is a joint venture between two consortia of six Singapore and five Indonesian companies, including both state-owned and private sector enterprises. The consortia are playing a key role in the Bintan Integrated Development Project which is expected to create at least 750 000 jobs for Indonesians in the next 10 to 15 years, 100 000 of them in the beach resort. There will also be a 500-hectare industrial estate on the island with light industries such as souvenirs, crafts, textiles, woodworking and food processing.

Tourism is already an important source of foreign exchange for the ASEAN countries and it is expected to become even more important with continued rapid income growth in the Asia-Pacific region at large, which is the source of the vast majority (over 80 per cent) of tourist arrivals in the region. For example, Singaporeans account for about 75 per cent of Malaysia's tourists, ASEAN citizens account for about one-third of Singapore's 5 million tourists a year, and Singaporeans account for over 75 per cent of foreign tourists in Batam, constituting by far the largest group of foreign tourists in Indonesia at large, where Malaysians are in second place. Domestic value-added in the tourist industry is high due to its labour-intensity and the rich food, handicraft and cultural resources of the ASEAN countries, which are already major world producers and exporters of agricultural and manufactured products. Most tourist facilities — hotels, regional airlines, recreational attractions — are locally-owned, so that the bulk of revenues remain in the region. Regional co-operation in tourism thus yields potentially large mutual benefits, since it serves ASEAN citizens as the industry's major owners, consumers, workers and suppliers, and provides for economies of scale and other efficiencies in the sharing of infrastructural and promotional costs.

Besides tourism, the Growth Triangle is focused on developing **manufacturing** linkages between Singapore and the other two members of the triangle. The Singapore government and market forces have been encouraging the relocation out of Singapore of both multinational and locally-owned labour-intensive manufacturing industries which cannot maintain their export competitiveness in Singapore's high-cost, land- and labour-scarce, strong-currency business environment. Even before the articulation of the Growth Triangle, Johor was the favoured host location for labour-intensive manufacturing investments from Singapore, given its close proximity, land-bridge connection, good infrastructure, and long-established close historical, cultural and business ties. But Johor itself was "running out of labour" and cheap land, and the Riau group, the closest alternative in Indonesia, was very underdeveloped. The Growth Triangle provided a rationale for Indonesian and Singaporean joint development of Riau without excluding Malaysia.

Singapore was the largest cumulative foreign investor in manufacturing in Malaysia at the end of 1989, with a 30.3 per cent share of total investment, ahead of Japan which had a 25.7 per cent share[26]. The Singapore share of approved investments in Johor between 1981 and 1990 was actually lower, at 22.7 per cent, second to Japan's 27 per cent share. In contrast, cumulative manufacturing investments in Batam at the end of 1990 were dominated by the US, with a 71 per cent share, followed by Singapore's 15.6 per cent share. This reflects heavy investments by US petroleum companies in oil-mining equipment and equipment servicing which the Indonesian government required of companies involved in Indonesian oil-exploration; there are similar (though smaller) investments by the Netherlands (Shell Oil Corp.) and Singapore. Iron and steel, a heavy land-using industry, was the second largest in Batam, with investments by companies from Japan, Singapore, the US and Netherlands. Among labour-intensive light manufacturing industries, food and agriculture projects by Singapore companies accounted for the largest category, followed by electronics (Singapore and Hong Kong) and toys (Singapore and US) (Pangestu, 1991, pp. 92-93).

Although more labour-intensive manufacturing investments have been made in Batam since the end of 1990, the investors appear to be mainly larger Singapore companies (including government-linked companies), Hong Kong and Taiwan companies, and some multinationals with long-established operations in Singapore. According to my interviews conducted in July 1992, Singapore small and medium-sized enterprises (SMEs) appear to have suffered from or been discouraged by the lack of indigenous labour on Batam, which has a native population of only 100 000. The need to import labour from elsewhere in Indonesia significantly raises labour costs — including recruitment, administrative and housing costs. This deters SME investment, which tends to prefer other locations in Malaysia, Indonesia and other countries. However, the Singapore Manufacturers' Association, whose members are mostly SMEs, was planning an investors' fact-finding mission to the larger Riau island of Bintan in late 1992.

The most dramatic recent development in Batam is the announcement in July 1992 of a plan by the government of Taiwan to invest $10 billion in Batam over the next decade "to turn it into a global manufacturing, financial shipping and re-export centre" (Straits Times, 21 July 1992). The $10 billion investment will be put up by Taiwan state-owned companies like the Taiwan Development and Trust Corporation (TDTC), China Steel and China Petroleum, and an "unnamed giant Taiwan airline and shipping company" (probably the Evergreen group). They will develop a 340-hectare industrial park, the Kuang Hwa Industrial Park, which will be 75 per cent owned by the TDTC and 25 per cent by the private Indonesian Kayu Lapis Group. The park will include a processing centre for Taiwan's deep-sea fisheries industry, a high-tech electronics park making semiconductors and telecommunications products, and a raw material processing centre for commodities like palm oil, silica for the glass industry and iron ore. The project is an attempt by the Taiwan government to swing Taiwan private investment away from its currently preferred location, China, and to create "a bargaining chip in the signing of investment guarantee agreements with other ASEAN countries" — which is important to Taiwan because of the risk that China, with whom all the ASEAN countries have diplomatic relations, might claim rights to the billions of dollars of investments that Taiwan companies have already made in the region. With strong government encouragement, Taiwan is also putting together a consortium of private companies that will compete with

Singapore's established Keppel Corporation to undertake similar developments in Subic Bay in the Philippines, to be converted into a commercial free trade zone following the withdrawal of US military forces (*Straits Times*, 6 August 1992).

As this discussion suggests, the idea behind the Singapore-Johor-Riau triangle and possible other ASEAN Growth Triangles is pure comparative advantage:

> Three factors are required to establish an economic-growth triangle: first, a highly developed city that has run out of land and labour; second, a surrounding area plentiful in both land and labour; third, the political will to reduce the visible and invisible barriers separating city from hinterland. (Holloway, 1991, p. 34)

Besides Singapore, where all three elements are present, at least one other possible sub-regional Growth Triangle within ASEAN has been proposed, based on the northern Malaysian port-city and industrial centre of Penang and its northwestern Malaysian hinterland, Medan and north Sumatra across the Straits of Malacca, and southern Thailand up to the city of Phuket (see Appendix 1). Progress is slowly being made on this triangle, mainly in tourism co-operation. A third triangle has been proposed for the Southern Philippines, Sabah in Malaysia, and northeastern Kalimantan, Sulawesi and Maluku in Indonesia, the easternmost territories of the ASEAN group. Outside of ASEAN, the Hong Kong-Taiwan-Southeastern coastal China triangle is already well-established.

As the Singapore-Johor-Riau Growth Triangle experience suggests, intergovernmental co-operation may be necessary for the joint exploitation of comparative advantage by contiguous territories. Joint infrastructure development, some (limited) coordination of investment incentive policies and promotion missions, and lots of high-profile official exchanges and publicity appear to have been successful in provoking private sector investor response where (at least in Riau) market forces alone did not do so. Increased investor interest in the three areas is seen as the major goal and success of the triangle, which was achievable because the three governments were willing to "not be concerned with who benefits more, so long as each benefits" (*Straits Times Weekly Overseas Edition*, 9 March 1991, p. 24, paraphrased). The result has been "fewer meetings, faster development and no haggling over the spread of benefits because of the recognition that this would depend on the competitive and comparative advantages of the participating parties". This is an instance where regional co-operation has been necessary for the realisation of national-level economic gains which would not have occurred without it.

As one commentator has noted:

> The triangle is important for Asean because it illustrates an obvious point: small plans are much more likely to succeed than big ones. Pipe dreams to integrate the economies of all six members of the grouping...are doomed to failure because they are too ambitious. (Holloway, 1991, p. 34)

In addition to encouraging the exploitation of comparative advantage, the Growth Triangle enables the partners to pool and share scarce resources — including managerial skills, technical expertise, and capital for both public infrastructure development and private commercial ventures — and to exploit economies of scale. Bureaucratic coordination problems are minimised since most of the activity is undertaken by private firms; in other words, regional co-operation in this case boils down to managing the private joint venture partnership. It is also possible that,

> The creation of different sub-regional co-operation zones within ASEAN will allow greater transparency of policies and bring forth the means to overcome difficulties in trans-border issues. As the sub-regions coalesce

into one regional unit, the basis for greater intra-ASEAN trade will be set. The pressures for this to happen would be evident well before the investment zones become more homogeneous. In fact, for the different sub-regions to become complementary to one another, there has to be free movement of goods and services, including labour, across the boundaries of the zones. These will sow the seeds for freer trade within ASEAN. (ASEAN-CCI, 1992, pp. 18-19).

This analysis, if correct, suggests that sub-regional co-operation may be viewed as both a "second-best" alternative to, and a stepping-stone toward, regional free trade, the ultimately most favoured goal.

Despite these rosy assessments, sub-regional co-operation zones can pose some potential problems, although in the ASEAN case these have so far been muted. Most of the concerns have to do with distributional issues. One concern is that the Singapore-Johor-Riau "triangle" currently only has Singapore-Johor and Singapore-Riau links, with the Johor-Riau connection being virtually non-existent. Singapore is seen as the main beneficiary of this arrangement, while Johor and Riau may be left to compete with each other to attract Singapore investment and tourism[27]. A second concern is with distribution within Malaysia and Indonesia, where concentration of development on Johor and Riau might divert resources and investor interest away from other parts of these countries, particularly poorer remote locations like northeastern Peninsular Malaysia and the islands of eastern Indonesia. There may also be conflicts between national/federal and state/provincial governments over aspects of Growth Triangle policy which could raise questions of sovereignty — for example, the state government of Johor might grant Singapore investors concessions that are at odds with federal government policy and with the interests of other states in Malaysia. Sub-regional co-operation might then widen regional disparities within member nations and reduce national economic integration while causing national political friction. In Indonesia there are additional concerns about the monopolisation of Growth Triangle economic opportunities by politically favoured business groups close to President Suharto, such as Salim and Bimantara.

> With the possible exception of B.J. Habibie, Indonesia's research and technology minister, nobody has done more than the chief executive of the Salim Group to push the economic alliance...On Batam Island, Salim manages and partly owns the Batamindo industrial estate. Other partners in the project include...Suharto's second son Bambang Trihatmodjo and Habibie's brother Timmy (Schwartz, 1991, p. 48).

In Singapore, former Prime Minister Lee Kuan Yew has stated that there is a "risk" that the Growth Triangle might, by increasing the efficiency and attractiveness to investors of Johor/Malaysia and Riau/Indonesia, create new competition for Singapore and threaten its current economic pre-eminence in the region. But he also contends that more prosperous and peaceful neighbours will make Singapore stronger, not to mention that there are potential political-security payoffs for Singapore in making its neighbours dependent on its own stability and prosperity. Indeed, even without the Growth Triangle, the development of its neighbours is bound to reduce their demand for many of Singapore's services. For example, the development of the Indonesian ports of Semarang and Surabaya is expected to reduce Singapore's re-export of Indonesian products, 80 per cent of which now find their way to the world market via Singapore (*Straits Times* 10 August 1992). Clearly, Singapore benefits from the triangle by being able to attract and retain on its own territory high-value, capital- and human-capital-intensive services and manufacturing related to the land- and labour-intensive manufacturing activities being located in Johor and Riau, and from the resulting increased demand for its transportation, communications, utilities and financial and business services sectors. Linking its economy with those of neighbouring territories helps Singapore to overcome its intrinsic disadvantages of small market size and resource scarcity.

Intra-ASEAN private investment

Like intra-ASEAN trade, intra-ASEAN investment has generally taken a back seat to investment from non-ASEAN countries and remains a small proportion, though a growing total, of the huge amounts of foreign investment that individual ASEAN countries have received in recent years[28]. Except for Malaysia, where investments originating in other ASEAN countries accounted for nearly a third of cumulative foreign investments in manufacturing at the end of 1989, intra-ASEAN investments typically account for less than 10 per cent of total foreign investments in individual ASEAN countries, with over 90 per cent of this coming from Singapore alone (as is the case in Malaysia).

The investments from Singapore parallel those from the other Asian NIEs and in recent years have been, like theirs, motivated by the need to escape high costs, land scarcity, labour shortages, strong currencies, and loss of US GSP privileges for export industries at home. But among the NIEs, Taiwan and Hong Kong, and in some cases also South Korea, have typically been larger investors in other ASEAN countries than Singapore, which is the smallest of the four. This may change, with expected continuation of the 1991 decline in Taiwan, Hong Kong and South Korean investment in ASEAN, and continued appreciation of the Singapore dollar against the US dollar. Already a "second wave" of smaller Singapore manufacturing firms have begun relocating to Malaysia to support earlier, bigger investors (*Straits Times*, 11 August, 1992).

Non-ASEAN, including Asian NIE, dominance of foreign investment inflows into the ASEAN countries is not surprising, given that the ASEAN countries have long been large host countries for foreign capital, have abundant and growing domestic investment opportunities, relatively open trade and investment policies, and an absence of special incentives for ASEAN-domiciled investors (O'Brien and Muegge, 1987). Most ASEAN-based companies lack a particular firm-specific advantage in investing in their neighbours, especially in competition with protected local firms and non-ASEAN multinationals which enjoy locational/home market and techno-logical/world market advantages respectively. In the manufacturing sector, most home-grown ASEAN companies have invested in production for their individual protected national markets or for non-ASEAN world markets in labour-intensive manufactures also exported by their ASEAN neighbours.

Exceptions to this generalisation are found mostly in the agricultural and agribusiness sectors, where some ASEAN-domiciled firms enjoy firm-specific advantages that they may seek to exploit by investing in neighbouring countries which offer complementary location-specific advantages. The Malaysian company Sime Darby, for example, has invested in rubber, palm oil and cacao production in the Philippines where it can take advantage of its pioneering technology, experience and world market networks while escaping Malaysia's higher land costs and acute shortage of plantation labour[29]. However, most recently, Malaysian natural-resource companies including Petronas, the national oil company, have looked to invest in Vietnam and other non-ASEAN Asian countries rather than in their ASEAN neighbours. According to business persons and academics I interviewed in Malaysia, this is because Malaysian companies see Thailand and Indonesia in particular as competitors on the world market for such commodities as rubber and palm oil. Vietnam, on the other hand, is "virgin territory" with plenty of land and labour that can be combined in contract farming or joint-venture plantation arrangements with Malaysian capital, technical expertise and international marketing networks to serve the world market. In other words, Malaysian companies are investing in non-ASEAN countries to help them compete with their ASEAN partners[30].

Among other ASEAN companies with firm-specific advantages in agribusiness is Charoen Pokphand, a Thai multinational agribusiness conglomerate which has operations in the other ASEAN countries as well as in Taiwan, China and Turkey in feedgrains and poultry. Thai companies involved in aquaculture of freshwater shrimp have also established similar operations in Indonesia as they have run out of suitable land in Thailand itself. Thailand is one of the world's largest exporters of shrimp.

Outside of agribusiness, most intra-ASEAN investments are in the services sector. One example is the Bangkok Bank, Southeast Asia's largest private commercial bank, which developed to serve the pre-eminent Chinese business community in Thailand and early on established branches in neighbouring ASEAN countries. Most ASEAN banks now have branches in other ASEAN member countries. Investments in property, real-estate and tourism are also popular.

In both manufacturing and services, the dominance of Singapore firms in intra-ASEAN investments reflects the advantage that many of them have over local firms in technology, managerial expertise, finance and international marketing. Some of these investments are made by Singapore government-owned or government-linked companies, including some in the process of privatisation. Most notable are various publicly-listed Singapore-owned shipyards which have been relocating shipbuilding and repair operations to ASEAN and non-ASEAN developing countries[31], and several joint ventures recently announced by newly-privatised Singapore Telecommunications with private and state-owned firms in Thailand and Indonesia. In the private sector, Singapore hotel chains, retail chains (supermarkets, department stores), restaurant chains, travel and resort companies, and computer skills training centres — facing mature, saturated markets at home — have been investing in takeovers, branches, joint ventures and franchises in neighbouring ASEAN as well as non-ASEAN countries, often with funding assistance from Singapore government agencies.

In short, foreign investments by ASEAN firms in other ASEAN countries are motivated by (1) differential country comparative advantages (based on resource endowments of land, labour, capital, skills, etc.), and (2) firm competitive advantages, particularly technology-based advantages, which tend to have some location-specific aspects (e.g. in agribusiness for Thai and Malaysian companies, in services for Singapore companies). In addition, (3) government policies (particularly those of Singapore), can play a role in encouraging or facilitating intra-ASEAN investments. ASEAN membership *per se* appears to be incidental to the vast majority of intra-ASEAN investments[32]. Rather, companies make their investment decisions based on their own competitive needs and strategies and the comparative advantages of different potential host countries, whether or not the latter belong to ASEAN. Any advantage that fellow ASEAN countries have as host locations arise from geographical proximity, cultural familiarity and institutional similarity, rather than from ASEAN membership *per se*.

Indeed, ASEAN companies and governments have recently shown an equal if not greater interest in investments in non-ASEAN, than in ASEAN countries. A content analysis of the major English-language newspapers in Malaysia, Indonesia and Singapore in July 1992 revealed that announcements of ASEAN-country investments, government and private sector investment missions, and trade missions in non-ASEAN developing countries outnumbered those in ASEAN countries by about three to one[33]. Among the non-ASEAN developing countries, by far the greatest amount of investment activity and interest was focused on Vietnam, but ventures in China, Cambodia, Laos, Myanmar, Sri Lanka and Mexico were also featured. For example, it was announced that Singapore investments in Sri Lanka now amount to $160 million, mostly in tourism and manufacturing, while its cumulative investments in China total $900 million. During this month, Singapore hosted trade and investment missions from Swaziland, Ghana and Peru, while Malaysia hosted similar missions from Mauritius and Kazahkstan, and Singapore and Brunei were planning to team up for trade missions and joint ventures in Vietnam and other Asian countries.

The Malaysian government has particularly been promoting South-South trade and investment linkages, in line with Prime Minister Mahathir Mohammed's third-world-nationalist positions in international fora. Mahathir led large (over 200 businessmen and government officials) Malaysian trade and investment delegations to Brazil and Mexico in 1991, and to Vietnam in 1992 (the latter shortly after Singapore Prime Minister Lee Kuan Yew led a similar Singapore mission). Following these visits, private as well as public sector linkages have proliferated. For example, Malaysia and Vietnam have extended Most Favoured Nation (MFN) trading status to each other; Malaysia is the largest ASEAN investor in Vietnam (with the national oil company Petronas being the largest single Malaysian investor); Vietnam has "reserved" three areas within the country for manufacturing and tourism projects by Malaysian investors; and Malaysia has proposed that Vietnam and Laos be admitted to ASEAN soon[34]. Malaysia is also actively exploring co-operation with South Africa, which sees Malaysia as a possible model of democratic, multi-racial, market-based development.

Despite their small share of total foreign investments in ASEAN, it may still be useful to take a closer look at the intra-ASEAN private sector investments which are taking place. Given recent declines in external investments into the ASEAN countries[35], it is likely that intra-ASEAN investments will soon account for a larger share of total foreign investments in the region, particularly if the AIJV and AFTA schemes mature and materialise. Here I will briefly examine two cases of different types of intra-ASEAN investments which serve to integrate the private sectors of the ASEAN economies.

Southeast Asian Chinese investors

Large conglomerates owned and run by ethnic Chinese business families domiciled in the ASEAN countries are particularly active in intra-ASEAN investments. A prominent example is the Indonesian Salim Group, headed by President Suharto's close associate Liem Sioe Liong, which has played such an active role in the Growth Triangle:

> Liem can claim the widest regional business presence of any Overseas-Chinese entrepreneur. Through Hongkong-based First Pacific, Liem's interests extend to the Philippines, Thailand, Australia, Malaysia and China as well as to the US and Europe. First Pacific has assets of $1.18 billion. Liem-controlled offshore companies are as diverse as the businessman's Indonesian interests. They are involved in everything from manufacturing soap and shampoo in the Philippines to selling cars in the Netherlands, from making mortgage loans in San Francisco to providing portable phones to Malaysian consumers. First Pacific, which has 75 operating companies in 24 countries, is the holding company for most of Liem's offshore real estate, banking, marketing, distribution and telecommunications businesses (Friedland, 1991b, pp. 49-50).

In December 1990, Liem took over Singapore's United Industrial Corp. (UIC) and its 75 per cent-owned subsidiary, Singapore Land, giving his Salim group control of the ninth- and tenth-largest companies in Singapore by market capitalisation, worth a combined total of $1.6 billion. In so doing, Salim joins other prominent Chinese-Indonesian companies which have taken control of Singapore public companies, including the Astra Group, Raja Garuda Mas, Sinar Mas and the Masagung family.

For these and other Chinese-Indonesian businesses, intra-ASEAN investments reflect the influence of several factors: a commercially prudent diversification of their Indonesian home-based empires; record earnings made in the booming Indonesian home economy; a more liberal Indonesian government outlook toward outward investment; and security-motivated investments to hedge against the possibility that highly visible commercial success at home might lead to a revival of anti-Chinese ethnic tensions and discriminatory policies in Indonesia, especially after the rule of President Suharto ends. Despite this recent outward orientation, however, the Chinese-Indonesian conglomerates' core businesses remain firmly anchored in their own large and fast-growing home market, where their competitive advantage and returns are greatest (Lim, 1991).

For ASEAN host countries, the chief contribution made by these ethnic Chinese investors is their capital and regional and international market networks, since in manufacturing, in particular, they are unlikely to have firm-specific global competitive advantages. But this varies by individual company. The Robert Kuok group, for example, arguably has firm competitive advantages in commodity production, trading and processing, and in hotels and resorts (through the Shangrila group). These activities may be seen to have contributed to the efficient development and operation and international competitiveness of the important commodity and tourism sectors in ASEAN countries.

Southeast Asian Chinese investments in other ASEAN countries are less likely to impose a cost on their hosts in terms of reduced market competition than in the conglomerates' home countries, where politically-ensured monopolistic market positions (particularly in Indonesia) create inefficiencies and inequities in the domestic economy. Indeed it is arguable that investments overseas are distributionally desirable since they reduce ownership concentration in the home markets of these family companies. Regional investment opportunities also discourage capital flight out of the region. At the same time, regionalisation may force Chinese companies which are protected monopolies at home to develop competitive advantages abroad. This in turn will help them to become global companies that can compete in at least some sectors and locations with multinationals from the developed countries. The existence of such large companies with international networks may also enhance the bargaining power of the ASEAN private sector vis-a-vis multinational competitors, partners, suppliers and customers.

Publicly-listed Singapore companies

Singapore has a well-developed capital market, one of the highest national savings rates in the world, and the highest per capita foreign exchange reserves in the world. Many of its large, cash-rich, publicly-listed corporations — some of them partly government-owned — have fully exploited the mature, stagnant home market and are now venturing overseas in search of new sources of growth. Besides abundant capital ("deep pockets"), these companies often have firm-specific advantages in technology or management which they developed in a home market where most sectors have always been open to foreign competition[36].

One such company, Natsteel, now a selectively diversified, vertically-integrated, steel-based conglomerate that was once state-owned, has chosen geographical diversification as a strategy to overcome the resource and market-size constraints of the (very open) domestic Singapore market (Lim, 1992). To penetrate the neighbouring ASEAN markets, which are all heavily regulated and protected, Natsteel is establishing joint ventures with local steel companies in these markets. It has a ten-year-old joint venture in Penang, Malaysia, is setting up one in Bangkok, Thailand, and is discussing a venture in Indonesia. Joint venture partners were located through ASEAN-CCI Regional Industry Club linkages, in which Natsteel has participated actively.

Natsteel makes itself attractive to its partners by providing them with financing, access to state-of-the-art technology, global information networks, low-cost training, and export market outlets. At the same time, it relocates its low-end production to them (buying back the output), and brings new high-end products to Singapore. Natsteel's core steel business is also used to facilitate the later entry into neighbouring countries of its profitable steel-related businesses like engineering, chemicals, construction and services which were first developed in the Singapore market. Thus besides its Penang manufacturing joint venture plant, Natsteel has invested in Malaysia in the manufacture of wire ropes, steel pipes, steel containers, steel services, a lime-kiln, a pre-cast concrete plant, and a plastics company — all of whose products are related to its core construction business.

Eventually, Natsteel expects that ASEAN steel markets will be liberalised, though this had not yet been negotiated at the time of writing. In that event, Natsteel's holdings in several different countries will position it well as a pan-regional company. In the meantime, with a regional grouping, it foresees economies for sister companies with joint procurement of raw materials, the sharing of spares and equipment for standardised plants, economies of scale, shared research and development, and eventual product specialisation by country according to different comparative advantages.

Natsteel's corporate strategy also includes industry diversification out of steel into related businesses. Being a large internal user of sophisticated information systems itself, with a subsidiary specialising in developing software for steel companies, Natsteel has branched out into electronics, to capitalise on the established strengths of Singapore and neighbouring ASEAN countries in this sector. It now operates electronics plants in Batam and in Penang. From construction, Natsteel has diversified into the development of leisure properties, including a joint venture resort in Bintan island and possible other Asia-Pacific locations. The Batam and Bintan investments were facilitated by Growth Triangle co-operation.

Natsteel's investments in its ASEAN neighbours will clearly have the effect of integrating the region through intra-regional flows of goods, capital, services and (skilled) labour. At the same time they enable Natsteel to exploit, maintain and enhance its own firm competitive advantages even as its home country comparative advantages shift. Host countries, meanwhile, acquire capital, technology and market outlets which should help them to develop more competitive steel and steel-related industries.

Non-ASEAN private investment

Private investments originating from non-ASEAN companies also play a role in ASEAN regional integration. Here, two different types of investors are considered.

Asian NIE investors

Singapore aside, most of the investments to date from the other Asian NIEs (Taiwan, Hong Kong, South Korea) have been in labour-intensive export manufacturing projects for the world rather than the ASEAN regional market — in low-value industries such as textiles, garments, footwear, toys, household appliances and consumer electronics. Parts and raw materials are imported from the parent country and elsewhere, processed or assembled in the ASEAN countries, and then re-exported, mostly to Western markets. In some cases, Taiwan companies in particular have brought their experienced home-country suppliers with them as secondary investors in the ASEAN locations. This pattern of investment resembles that of developed-country multinationals in the region twenty years ago (which has since changed)[37]. There are some exceptions to this general pattern, especially in resource-intensive industries. Besides the Taiwan Batam project mentioned above, China Steel (Taiwan) is considering building a major integrated steel mill in Johor[38].

In the private sector, Taiwan's giant computer multinational Acer is restructuring its worldwide operations in a way which will have implications for ASEAN countries which are part of its global network. Specifically, Acer plans to set up manufacturing franchises where its markets are, and to supply these locally-owned or joint-venture assembly plants with components shipped from "mother plants" located mainly in Asia — currently in Taiwan and Penang, Malaysia. Technology and marketing would be shared on a global basis. The company is relocating its headquarters for Asia, Latin America and the Pacific (ALAP) from Taiwan to Singapore, where it has applied for Operational Headquarters (OHQ) tax status. The OHQ will provide technical support to Acer's distributors in Asia and Latin America, and be responsible for procuring parts and components in the region. Acer is also looking for local partners in Indonesia and Thailand to manufacture and market its products in those countries under its new franchise scheme. It already has a software facility in the Philippines.

Acer is not a "typical" investor from the Asian NIEs, but it is an example of an Asian company which aims to become a "borderless" global company, including in ownership, and to function as a multinational worldwide, including in the ASEAN countries, where its activities will increase economic interchanges among member countries. If the manufacturing franchise system works, the Acer system will include ASEAN manufacturers as part owners of the global corporation, and as marketers of its products in their home countries — in contrast to the OEM subcontracting practised by many Western and Japanese multinationals.

Japanese multinationals

Japanese multinationals have long invested in the ASEAN countries in a wide range of industries including resource extraction, heavy industries and consumer durables for the local market, and labour-intensive and high-tech manufacturing for export to world markets, including Japan. Until recently when foreign investment rules were liberalised, most Japanese investments were in joint ventures with local (mostly ethnic Chinese or state-owned) enterprises, including in minority Japanese-owned ventures. The late 1980s saw a massive relocation of export-oriented industry from Japan to ASEAN, but in the 1990s new investments are increasingly geared to the booming ASEAN market, the fastest-growing in the world.

For example, Mitsubishi Electric is building an elevator plant in Thailand to supply that country, Malaysia, Singapore and other Southeast Asian nations because "We can't keep up with growing demand in the Asian market any more with exports from Japan". Matsushita Electric is increasing its investments in Southeast Asia producing refrigerators, washing machines, audio sets, video recorders, colour televisions and other consumer products, because "Asia is the highest-growth area in the world of electronics products.....our basic policy (is) to produce at the place where there is demand." Daikin Industries has begun local production of airconditioners in Thailand "to meet a rise in local demand and to set up a stronghold near the market." (All quotes are from Pura, 1991.)

Compared to its Japanese rivals, consumer electronics giant Sony Corp. is a relative latecomer to Southeast Asia, but its investments in the region since the late 1980s are typical of the increasingly regionally-integrated investments of Japanese multinationals here (Pang 1992). They were motivated both by rising production costs in Japan and by rapid growth in demand for consumer electronics products in the Asian region.

Sony's regional operational headquarters in Singapore serves as the company's international procurement office, sourcing parts and components for Sony companies the world over from a network of suppliers in Southeast Asia. It also tests components and designs products for manufacture in Southeast Asia, provides engineering support for Sony plants in the region, undertakes international logistics planning, provides financial services to Sony companies in the region, and recruits and trains personnel for Sony subsidiaries. Other Sony operations in Singapore include a robotised, high-precision component plant engaged in capital-intensive production, a warehousing and distribution facility, a software company which develops and designs computer systems for Sony subsidiaries in ASEAN, Taiwan and South Korea, a sales office, and a colour picture tube plant which is integrated with the production of colour televisions in other ASEAN plants.

Sony's five manufacturing facilities in Malaysia produce a full range of audio and video products for export, as well as micro floppy disk drives for computer makers in Asia. There is a local audio equipment design centre, and more research- and design-intensive activities are being brought to the company's Penang site. In Thailand, Sony has plants producing audio and video products, and bipolar integrated circuits which are exported to other Sony factories in the region. An $82 million audio equipment manufacturing plant has been built in Indonesia, and Malaysian technicians and supervisors have been sent to train its workers. Throughout Southeast Asia and the world, Sony practises its well-known "global localisation" philosophy, which includes the training of local managers (often in Japan) for the global corporation.

Clearly, Sony's investments and operations in any single ASEAN country are dictated not just by that country's local comparative advantages and by the global corporation's firm competitive advantages, but also by what the company chooses to and can do in neighbouring ASEAN countries. Sony's ASEAN facilities are integrated with one another — or at least with the regional OHQ in Singapore — with respect to component sourcing, product distribution, training and technical support. Though it is not yet an integrated regional market, to Sony and companies like it, ASEAN already functions as a single investment and production location. Besides exports to foreign final consumers and to sister companies within the region and worldwide, host countries benefit from the skills learned from rapid technological diffusion and constant upgrading within the firm, and from the company's global policy of promoting localisation of management, R&D and parts procurement[39].

Conclusions

Regional economic co-operation in ASEAN has been extremely limited, with virtually negligible results over a very long period of time. ASEAN is clearly not a trade-driven regional grouping, and it is not clear if the recent agreement to pursue a regional free trade area will deliver significant results by the end of the prescribed 15-year phase-in period. But individually, the ASEAN economies' success has been based on international trade, and particularly on exports of commodities, manufactures and services to the world rather than the regional market. Foreign investment has played a key role in providing the capital, technology and market access required to successfully pursue these export-oriented national development strategies. Because of this history, the ASEAN countries have been understandably reluctant to promote or favour intra-regional trade and investment over extra-regional trade and investment with non-ASEAN partners. Since the 1980s they have unilaterally been pursuing nondiscriminatory trade and investment liberalisation to expand trade with, and to attract more investment from, non-ASEAN partners, including the Asian NIEs as well as Japan and Western industrial nations.

Indeed, most of the regional co-operation schemes proposed to date also seem primarily motivated by the desire to make the region more attractive to foreign investment from outside the region. The AIJV scheme, for example, allows for a non-ASEAN investment share of 60 per cent or more, while AFTA preferential tariffs will be allowed on goods with as much as 60 per cent non-ASEAN content. The AFTA agreement itself was precipitated by the emergence of regional economic blocs elsewhere which were seen to threaten ASEAN exports to those markets and to compete with ASEAN for international investments. Sub-regional co-operation zones like the Singapore-Johor-Riau Growth Triangle also have as their objective the attraction of more foreign investment, by promoting several linked ASEAN territories as a joint investment location.

ASEAN countries have been very successful in attracting large amounts of foreign investment from non-ASEAN — especially other Asian — countries, particularly in the manufacturing sector. But this has been based mainly on their individual national attractions rather than on the attractions of an elusive regional market. Some multinationals — particularly in the electronics industry — have practised a regional division of labour among plants sited in neighbouring ASEAN countries, but mainly in production for the world market from free trade zones. The ASEAN complementation scheme for the automotive industry remains limited in its scope and impact due to the continued dominance of national automobile industrialisation strategies.

Besides the regional linkages created by multinationals, which are based on the exploitation of differential country comparative advantages, there is a growing volume — though not a growing share — of intra-ASEAN investments. These consist overwhelmingly of investments by Singapore in its less-developed neighbours, which resemble the investments made by the other Asian NIEs and are also based on exploitation of comparative advantage, and in the case of service sector investments, also on geographical proximity. Intra-ASEAN investments among the ASEAN-4 of Malaysia, Indonesia, Thailand and the Philippines, are extremely low — less than 2 per cent of total foreign investment flows for the individual host countries. These investments are based on the exploitation of firm competitive advantages as well as of country comparative advantages, and are concentrated in agribusiness and services. Such advantages apply equally, if not more so, to ASEAN-4 investments in non-ASEAN countries at a lower level of development, primarily in China, Indochina and South Asia.

In short, intra-ASEAN investments to date appear to have little to do with ASEAN's existence as a regional grouping[40], but rather reflect patterns dictated by market forces — specifically, the match between individual firms' competitive advantages and corporate strategies, and host countries' differential comparative cost advantages — the same considerations that extend to investments in non-ASEAN countries. For example, Ghana and Singapore have recently agreed to co-operate in areas which will combine Ghana's rich resources with Singapore's technology and know-how. Geographical proximity, and political, cultural and ethnic factors also play a role in firms' investment decisions. For example, Singapore companies have flocked disproportionately to invest in the Xiamen industrial zone of Fujian province in China, "mainly because of the pull of ancestral ties" (*Straits Times*, 8 March 1992).

Besides trade and investment, intra-regional labour flows and the skill and remittance flows they generate also play a role in linking the ASEAN economies. Brunei, Singapore and Malaysia rely heavily on foreign labour imported from neighbouring ASEAN countries. This includes Malaysian engineers, Filipina maids and Thai construction workers in Singapore, Indonesian plantation and construction workers in Malaysia, and skilled and unskilled labour from Singapore, Malaysia and the Philippines in Brunei. As with investments, these labour flows are not limited to intra-ASEAN flows; on the contrary there are and have been larger flows of ASEAN skilled and unskilled labour to non-ASEAN countries, especially the Middle East and Northeast Asia (Hong Kong, Taiwan and Japan), while many unskilled foreign workers in Singapore, for example, come from South Asia.

In ASEAN, then, regional economic integration is likely to evolve as the result rather than the cause of increased intra-regional investment and trade linked to such investment. The regional production strategies of non-ASEAN multinationals, and the diversification strategies of Singapore-based firms and ethnic Chinese business conglomerates from the ASEAN-4, all produce intra-ASEAN flows of capital, goods, services, technology and personnel which over time will knit these economies more closely together than any formal regional integration schemes. In particular, intra-ASEAN investments and a regional division of labour may encourage more technological innovation in the region by both ASEAN companies and non-ASEAN multinationals. This is because larger production bases both will require more regionally-based R and D activity, and can support it with shared capital and human skill resources.

For example, parallel national development strategies favouring the electronics industry in individual ASEAN countries have already created a large regional production base which has attracted technological widening and deepening by both multinational and regional firms. As multinationals have located more investments in the ASEAN countries, they have had to increase investments in local technology development and skills training in order to support higher-value production activities, and to exploit synergies between production, process engineering and design activities. Some of the skills training programmes established by multinationals are undertaken co-operatively among firms, or with national agencies (universities, technology institutes, investment promotion agencies) in individual host countries. But there is also an increasing regional component to these activities. For example, companies like Intel and Motorola have established in-house engineering training centres in Penang which share courses, resources and facilities with other companies, and are used to train engineers from other ASEAN countries as well. Given ever-changing new technologies, manufacturing arguably cannot take place without constant training and upgrading, which must be provided locally or, increasingly, regionally. Singapore's role as a regional technology and training centre for multinationals is well-established, but Malaysia is also increasingly taking on this role. Intel, Motorola, Sony and other multinationals based in Malaysia now send their Malaysian engineers and supervisors to other countries in the region to help train their staff.

The creation of a large regional production base in electronics has also stimulated the emergence of entrepreneurial local firms in various niches of the industry. Many of these firms are started by local employees of multinationals and serve as subcontractors or suppliers of parts and services to them. The global trend of vertical de-integration in branches of the computer industry (as represented in different ways by Sun Microsystems,

IBM and Acer) has supported many of these firms. But some local firms are also independent competitors of the multinationals, particularly in low-end personal computers.

But despite the rapid growth and internationalisation of local firms, ASEAN is now and for the foreseeable future likely to remain more dependent on its non-ASEAN trade and investment partners. This may eventually decline relative to growing dependence on its ASEAN neighbours. Such a shift, if it occurs, will reflect a combination of the withdrawal of other regional economic blocs from trade and investment relations with ASEAN, the growing importance to both ASEAN and non-ASEAN firms alike of the ASEAN regional market itself relative to exports to the rest of the world, and the developing competitive advantages of ASEAN firms as they mature and become more outward-looking as domestic protection recedes even further.

In the meantime, ASEAN continues to harness regional co-operation to facilitate its continued integration into the world and Asia-Pacific economies. Overall, the ASEAN experience suggests that South-South economic co-operation in this region is an ancillary and not an alternative to North-South economic relations, and further that it is likely to be patterned after North-South relations in terms of asymmetrical exchanges between more-developed and less-developed countries. Both the relationship between the Asian NIEs (including Singapore) and the ASEAN-4, and the evolving relationship between ASEAN and Indochina, repeat this pattern of capital and technology flows from the more- to the less-developed countries of the South[41]. The very limited economic relations among the ASEAN-4 themselves suggest that competitive resource bases and production structures are a deterrent to closer economic relations, as compared with complementary relationships between both more and less developed countries.

The ASEAN experience also suggests that, where a dynamic private sector exists, the most promising forms of South-South co-operation are primarily private-sector-led, market-based and comparative-advantage-driven. Governments can help by removing political hurdles to cross-border private sector ventures and to regional free trade, by providing and coordinating supportive national investment incentives, by co-operating with the private sector in joint infrastructure and human resource development projects which can shape or enhance the comparative advantage of member nations and the competitive advantages of regional private firms, and by participating directly in some regional private-sector-led ventures as cost-, risk- and profit-sharing partners. (The Growth Triangle is a good example of all these activities in action.) Governments might also be called upon to design programmemes to support less favoured regions as potential investment sites.

Finally, the ASEAN experience suggests that a formal regional organisation such as ASEAN and the geographical contiguity upon which it is based are not necessary for the development of South-South co-operation. The ASEAN countries are already involved in private and public sector projects in many non-ASEAN developing countries both in the immediate region and further afield, driven largely by a desire to exploit country comparative advantages and firm competitive advantages, and encouraged and assisted by their governments in doing so.

1. The ASEAN organisation and its activities are extensively documented. See, for example, such periodical publications as the *ASEAN Newsletter*, published by the ASEAN Secretariat, the *ASEAN Economic Bulletin*, published by the ASEAN Economic Research Unit of the Institute of Southeast Asian Studies in Singapore, the *ASEAN Handbook* published in Singapore by the ASEAN Chambers of Commerce and Industry. A useful recent compendium is Rieger (1991).

2. Chng (1990) discusses ASEAN's institutional structure and its impact on economic co-operation. Currently, discussions are under way on how to restructure this to facilitate progress on AFTA, the ASEAN Free Trade Area agreement.

3. The share of intra-ASEAN trade (18 per cent) is about double the average share of intra-group trade in other developing country regional groupings, due largely to Singapore's entrepôt role in the region. If Singapore is excluded, intra-ASEAN trade declines to about 5 per cent of total ASEAN trade (Imada, Montes and Naya, 1991, p. 4).

4. These differential tariff levels reflect several decades of differing economic policies among the ASEAN member countries. In particular, the smaller countries (Brunei, Singapore, Malaysia) have been much more export-oriented and thus favoured relatively free trade, while the larger countries until very recently gave higher priority to import substitution for their domestic markets (Thailand, Philippines, Indonesia). The relatively strong political position of the urban-based (predominantly ethnic Chinese and Sino-Thai) local industrial entrepreneurial class in Thailand relative to the state, foreign capital, domestic workers and consumers explains that country's particularly high tariff levels. See, for example, Doner (1989).

5. The categories are: vegetable oils, cement, chemicals, pharmaceuticals, fertilizer, plastics, rubber and leather products, pulp, textiles, ceramic and glass products, gems and jewellery, copper cathodes, electronics and wooden furniture.

6. In Latin America, by contrast, multinationals pressed for market protection in small countries where they readily practised inefficient ISI. The reasons for this difference with ASEAN are a matter for historical conjecture. One explanation might be that in Latin America, a stronger, more concentrated and more unified nationalist elite made ISI an unambiguous and unavoidable policy favourite. Under these circumstances, the "second best" solution (to free trade) for multinationals was to partner with local elites and demand high tariff protection (against other multinationals). In ASEAN, on the other hand, the national industrial elite was fragmented (between state, indigenous and Chinese capital), and populist nationalism also accorded greater political weight to the interests of "the masses", including indigenous consumers. This helped to restrain ISI relative to the multinationals' "first best" ideal of free trade. The highest levels of protection developed where local (Chinese) capital was the strongest, and Western multinationals the weakest — i.e. in Thailand, which was never colonised. Multinationals have shown their preference for free trade by investing disproportionately much more in the ASEAN countries with more liberal trade regimes — Malaysia and Singapore — than in those with high levels of import protection.

7. See Lim and Pang (1991) and references therein for evidence of the many linkages with local firms created by multinationals. As local businesses develop the required expertise and experience, often under the tutelage of multinational customers and mentors, supplier linkages increase. While multinationals may still source a majority of their inputs from outside a given host country, both the proportion and the volume of their local purchases has grown over time, generating ever-increasing business for growing numbers of local suppliers. An increasing proportion of foreign-sourced inputs also comes from neighbouring ASEAN countries (e.g. inputs for Malaysian electronics factories come from Singapore and vice versa), thereby stimulating their local supplier industries. Over time this creates in each country a local business community supportive of regional free trade.

8. The reforms themselves were a response to the commodity price slump, regional recession and external debt problems of the early and mid-1980s, and in some cases (Philippines, Thailand) creeping political democratisation in the late 1980s which included demands for increased competition in the economy.

9. This regional market would encompass other Asian-Pacific countries besides those of ASEAN, but no attempt at a wider pan-Asian regional free trade area (incorporating China, Hong Kong, Taiwan, Korea and Japan) is presently considered likely, for reasons of history, geography, politics and economics. See the discussion below on Malaysian Prime Minister Mahathir's unsupported proposal for an East Asian Economic Grouping (EAEG) that would extend beyond ASEAN.

10. Indonesia's comparative advantage in oil palm is based on much cheaper labour, much more abundant land and longer experience in the industry than Thailand has. Malaysia's labour cost advantage has disappeared but its industry's competitiveness remains sustained by massive imports of cheap Indonesian labour, still-abundant (though more costly) land, the world's most advanced technology and research capability in the industry, and extensive established world marketing networks — all of which make it still the world's largest exporter in this industry.

11. Stone (1992), p. 26, quotes the Japanese managing director of Matsushita Electric (Malaysia) as saying, "If AFTA takes off, fine. If not, (also) fine".

12. Trade between industry located in a free trade zone or bonded factory site in, say, Thailand or Indonesia with similarly-located industry in Malaysia, or with free-trading Singapore, takes place without import or export duties. Most of this trade is intra-industry, much of it taking place between multinational subsidiaries. Together with the dominant trading position of Singapore (which accounts for 40 per cent of ASEAN's total trade), free trade zones arguably constitute a *de facto* "shadow free trade area" which already exists within the ASEAN region.

13. Since the complementation scheme includes only large, high-value branded parts whose production involves scale economies (e.g. engines), it is not relevant for the many small local parts suppliers concentrated in the more competitive sectors of the industry, who supply mainly labour-intensive, low-value, low-technology, non-company-specific parts (e.g. wire harnesses).

14. The conditions allowing for more than 60 per cent foreign ownership of an AIJV are: where the governments agree to a lower ASEAN equity in a particular case; where a minimum of 50 per cent of the production is exported to non-ASEAN markets; where the product is already being produced by an entity in a participating country prior to its inclusion in the final list; or where an entity has already been approved by a participating country to produce that product prior to the inclusion of the product in the AIJV final list. (Federation of Malaysian Manufacturers, 1991).

15. The ASEAN-CCI's *ASEAN Handbook 1991/92*, pp. 245-266, presents a report on the progress of the AIJV scheme, including an analysis of problems faced by the projects in Thailand.

16. As examples, the national chambers of commerce in Malaysia and Singapore consist of the various ethnic chambers — Malay Chamber, Indian Chamber, Chinese Chamber — together with local manufacturers' associations and international chambers which mostly represent long-established expatriate European firms in the service sector (former British agency houses, banks and insurance companies). Associations of Japanese, American and other foreign manufacturers (e.g. the American Business Council, etc.) are not included. Some multinationals do belong to constituent members of national chambers, e.g. local manufacturers' associations, while the Thai joint chambers also include bilateral associations such as the Thai-US, Thai-Sweden chambers of commerce, etc. However, my interviews confirm that multinationals generally reserve most of their efforts for their own home-country business associations and do not play an active part in the ASEAN national or regional chambers. Thus the ASEAN-CCI and its national constituent members are primarily representatives of the local, not multinational, private sectors in the ASEAN countries.

17. See Appendix 8 for the list of ASEAN Regional Industry Clubs. They function largely as the regional counterpart of national industry associations involved in information gathering and sharing, policy proposal preparation, and lobbying of their respective governments.

18. Chng (1990) cites two examples of (in one case, temporary) failure to achieve the private sector's policy goals. Proposals worked out by the ASEAN-CCI for liberalising intra-ASEAN trade proved unacceptable to the inter-governmental Committee on Trade and Tourism despite close government-private sector consultations at national levels. And the Basic Agreement on AIJVs promoted by the ASEAN-CCI and agreed to by the ASEAN Economic Ministers was delayed at the last minute when Malaysian businessmen at the national level got their government to change certain provisions of the Agreement.

19. Note, however, the date of the quote from Minister Goh, and the fact that AICs have since dwindled in importance relative to both AIJVs and, now, AFTA. Note also the change over time in the ASEAN private sector's views on trade liberalisation discussed in the previous section.

20. See, for example, the case of Natsteel discussed below. Besides the ASEAN-CCI, the ASEAN Institute (Institute of South East Asian Business) was established in November 1991 with a membership of "100 leading ASEAN companies". According to the Indonesian President of the Institute, its existence has already been "advantageous to the development of trade and business relations among the member companies in the Institute.....because member companies/businessmen can negotiate directly with each other". As a result, a number of joint venture companies had been formed since the establishment of the Institute (*Indonesian Times*, 21 July, 1992).

21. For example, an ASEAN common contract for vegetable oil is being formulated "to stop edible oil contracts terms from being dictated by the European Rotterdam market and American Chicago Board of Trade" (*Indonesia Times*, 21 July, 1992). The ASEAN region accounts for 20 per cent of global production and 43 per cent of global exports of edible oils, mainly palm and coconut oil.

22. In 1990, proposed EAEG countries accounted for one-third of total US trade (compared with 23 per cent in the case of the EC); the share of other East Asian countries was nearly twice the share of Japan (Lim, 1992).

23. For a comprehensive review of the Growth Triangle to date, see Lee Tsao, ed., 1991.

24. The Salim Group is an Indonesian Chinese-owned conglomerate which has very close ties with President Suharto, and accounts for 8 per cent of Indonesia's GDP with a global turnover of $8 billion (making it the largest Overseas Chinese conglomerate in the world). The Bimantara Group is an indigenous Indonesian conglomerate whose largest owner is a son of President Suharto. President Suharto negotiated the change in Batam's status and its special co-operation with Singapore with then Prime Minister Lee Kuan Yew of Singapore in October 1989, two months before new Singapore Prime Minister Goh Chok Tong announced the Growth Triangle concept.

25. It is difficult to define many Growth Triangle projects as either "private" or "public". Many are joint ventures between private and state-owned enterprises, and many of the state-owned enterprises have been or are being at least partially privatised, while many of the private enterprises are closely politically connected with the state.

26. Kamil, Pangestu and Fredericks (1991), pp. 48-49. According to the Malaysian Industrial Development Authority (MIDA), investment figures for Singapore do not include investments from multinational companies based in Singapore. Note that Singapore's share has probably fallen since 1989 due to huge new investments from Taiwan and Hong Kong companies in 1990 and 1991.

27. Competition between Johor and Riau for Singapore investment and tourism does not appear to me to be intentional on the part of Singapore who, by initiating Growth Triangle co-operation, actually sought to increase Singapore investment in **both** neighbouring territories. Singapore is the largest ASEAN source of trade, investment and tourists for all its ASEAN partners, and despite the Growth Triangle, Johor and Riau must still compete with other, non-Triangle, locations for them.

28. For an overview and two industry studies (electronics, automobiles) of foreign investment in three of the ASEAN countries, see Lim and Pang (1991). See also Soon, ed., 1990.

29. Malaysian companies' world leadership, if not monopoly, of cultivation and processing technology in palm oil and rubber arise from their long-established dominance of the world market in these industries. Besides heavy investments in R and D by Malaysian state agencies such as the Federal Land Development Authority (FELDA) which support smallholders, in-house research is conducted by plantation-based companies like Sime Darby — one of many former British colonial companies which were bought over by the Malaysian government and private stockholders in the 1970s and are now publicly-listed on the Kuala Lumpur Stock Exchange.

30. There are also locally-specific reasons for the lack of interest by ASEAN resource-based companies in investing in their ASEAN neighbours. For example, in 1991 Sime Darby began selling off its Philippine rubber, cocoa and coconut plantations because of "difficulties in complying with the agrarian reform law" (Tiglao, 1991).

31. For example, government-linked Keppel Co. is the top candidate to undertake commercial conversion of military naval bases in Subic Bay, the Philippines, and Cam Ranh Bay, Vietnam. Now a diversified business group, it already has $40 million worth of projects lined up in Vietnam, including a bank, a business services centre, a project to upgrade airport and air cargo facilities, the development of service apartments in Ho Chi Minh City, and development of a sea port in southern Vietnam. The group is also teaming up with Indonesian businessman Liem Sioe Liong (Salim Group) to invest in a $75 million office-cum-hotel project in Ho Chi Minh City, and has set up a $50 million country fund "to tap growth opportunities arising from Vietnam's economic reforms" (*Straits Times*, 28 July, 1992).

32. Possible exceptions would be the handful of AIJVs, and joint-ventures which may have arisen from contacts developed through membership of the ASEAN-CCI and ASEAN Institute.

33. July 1992 was selected for in-depth content analysis because it was the most recent month, showing the latest trends. The results appear to be representative of news reports over the past year, which may be biased because non-ASEAN developing countries constitute newer and therefore more newsworthy terrain for outward investments. The extent to which these news events eventually translate into realised investments can only be ascertained at a much later date.

34. My interviews in Malaysia in July 1992 suggested that there were "very close" government-to-government relations between Malaysia and Vietnam, that Malaysian government agencies and enterprises were preferentially selected to undertake various infrastructural projects in Vietnam, that Malaysia was particularly interested in natural resource development in Vietnam to exploit its own technological advantages while coping with extreme labour shortages in Malaysia in this sector and in labour-intensive export manufacturing, and that Malaysia preferred Vietnam to Thailand and Indonesia as an investment location because it was "very open", "virgin territory" and "not a competitor". Note that the US economic embargo on Vietnam has limited the involvement of US, some other Western, and Japanese companies, thereby arguably creating an at least temporary

investment niche for countries like Malaysia. However the largest foreign investors in Vietnam presently are the East Asian NIEs.

35. The reasons for this decline include: completion of labour-intensive export-oriented industrial relocations from Northeast to Southeast Asia in response to the currency realignments and changing international competitiveness of the late 1980s; appearance of supply-side absorptive capacity constraints especially in human skills and infrastructure in ASEAN host countries; increased attractiveness of China as an alternative investment location especially for Taiwan, Hong Kong and Overseas Chinese business; economic downturn and a credit crunch in Japan; and a worsening current-account deficit situation and depreciation of the won in South Korea combined with the potential attractiveness of North Korea and Northeastern China as investment locations for Korean firms. Japanese investment in ASEAN is expected to resume strongly with that nation's economic recovery, but investment from the NIEs will be continue to be tempered by the China/Korea factors.

36. For more on outward investments from Singapore, see Pang and Komaran, 1985; Pang and Hill, 1991; and Pang, 1991. On Singapore's increasingly strategic economic role in ASEAN, see Wu, 1991.

37. Over time, export-oriented developed country multinational subsidiaries in the region have engaged in product and technology upgrading, including shifting into higher-value product lines, more sophisticated manufacturing processes, local design and development activities, and increased local content. See, for example, Lim and Pang (1991).

38. While the Growth Triangle is a factor in the Taiwan Batam project, it is not a factor in the similar Taiwan Subic (Philippines) project, and is not a factor in the China Steel Johor project. While many foreign investment projects in Riau would not occur without the Growth Triangle, Johor on its own has always attracted foreign investment. Many of these projects have much more to do with Malaysia-based than with Singapore-based considerations, and this is true of the proposed China Steel project, which is aimed at supplying the Malaysian market.

39. It should be noted that Japanese multinationals in the ASEAN countries have been frequently criticised for lagging behind American and European companies in management localisation, even in a highly-skilled location like Singapore. The Japanese attribute this to the "language problem".

40. Some intra-ASEAN investments have been attracted by the Growth Triangle, but this would exist even without ASEAN (note the similar, if also different, Hong Kong-Taiwan-China triangle), and has no formal connection with it.

41. For example, Singapore has established a US$10 million Indochina Assistance Fund to help with the reconstruction and rehabilitation of Vietnam, Cambodia and Laos through the provision of technical assistance projects and training, beginning with areas in which Singapore's expertise is among the world's best, such as civil aviation, port management, telecommunications, public housing, health care, and urban planning and management. To quote Singapore's Foreign Minister, "Singapore is better off today because other countries helped us upgrade the skills of our people. We will now play our part in sharing our experience with other countries." (*Straits Times* 23 June 1992).

ARIFF, Mohamed and Hal HILL (1985), *Export-Oriented Industrialisation: The ASEAN Experience*, Allen and Unwin, Sydney/London/Boston.

ASEAN-CCI (Chambers of Commerce and Industry) (1990), *ASEAN Handbook 1990*, ASEAN-CCI, Singapore.

ASEAN-CCI (Chambers of Commerce and Industry) (1991), *ASEAN Handbook 1991/92*, ASEAN-CCI, Singapore.

ASEAN-CCI (Chambers of Commerce and Industry) (1992), *ASEAN Economic Development and the Private Sector: Partners in Progress*, ASEAN-CCI, Singapore.

CHNG, Meng Kng (1990), "ASEAN's Institutional Structural and Economic Co-operation", *ASEAN Economic Bulletin* Vol. 6, No. 3, March 1990, pp. 268-282.

DEVAN, Janamitra (1987), "The ASEAN Preferential Trading Arrangement: Some Problems, Ex Ante Results, and a Multipronged Approach to Future Intra-ASEAN Trade Development", *ASEAN Economic Bulletin* Vol. 4, No. 2, November 1987, pp. 197-209.

DONER, Richard F. (1991), *Driving A Bargain: Automobile Industrialisation and Japanese Firms in Southeast Asia*, University of California Press, Berkeley, California.

FEDERATION OF MALAYSIAN MANUFACTURERS (FMM) (1991), *Guide to ASEAN Industrial Joint Ventures*, FMM, Kuala Lumpur.

FRIEDLAND, Jonathan (1991a), "Kuok the kingpin" and other articles, *Far Eastern Economic Review*, 7 February, 1991, pp. 46-50.

FRIEDLAND, Jonathan (1991b), "Island shopping", *Far Eastern Economic Review*, 21 February, 1991 p. 45.

GOLAY, Frank, Ralph ANSPACH, Ruth PFANNER and Eliezer AYAL (1969), *Underdevelopment and Economic Nationalism in Southeast Asia*, Cornell University Press, Ithaca, NY.

GOLDSTEIN, Carl (1990), "Steering committee", *Far Eastern Economic Review*, 15 February, 1990, p. 67.

HOLLOWAY, Nigel (1991), "Southeast Asia's golden triangles", *Far Eastern Economic Review*, 3 January, 1991, p. 34.

IMADA, Pearl, Manual MONTES and Seiji NAYA (1991), *A Free Trade Area: Implications for ASEAN*, Institute of Southeast Asian Studies, Singapore.

INDONESIAN TIMES (1992), various issues.

KAMIL, Yuhanis, Mari PANGESTU and Christina FREDERICKS (1991), "A Malaysian Perspective", in Lee Tsao, ed., pp. 37-74.

KUNTJORO-JAKTI, Dorodjatun (1987), "ASEAN's External Trade Relations in 1987: Entering a Growing Environmental Turbulence", *Contemporary Southeast Asia*, Vol. 9, No. 2, September 1987, pp. 113-119.

LEE TSAO, Yuan, ed. (1991), *Growth Triangle: The Johor-Singapore-Riau Experience*, Institute of Southeast Asian Studies and Institute of Policy Studies, Singapore.

LIM, Linda Y.C. (1987), "The State and Private Capital in Singapore's Economic Development", *Political Economy, Studies in the Surplus Approach*, Vol. 3, No. 2, pp. 201-222.

LIM, Linda Y.C. (1991), "The New Ascendancy of Chinese Business in Southeast Asia". Paper presented at the Panel on Chinese Business in Southeast Asia: the Changing Dynamics of Dominance, 43rd annual meeting of the Association for Asian Studies, New Orleans, Louisiana, April 14, 1991 (mimeo).

LIM, Linda Y.C. (1992), "Natsteel: A Case Study", Southeast Asia Business Programme, University of Michigan (mimeo).

LIM, Linda Y.C. and PANG Eng Fong (1991), *Foreign Investment and Industrial Restructuring in Malaysia, Thailand, Singapore and Taiwan*, OECD Development Centre, Paris.

LOW Peng Lum (1990), "ASEAN Industrial Joint Ventures", *Forum 1990*, Journal of the Federation of Malaysian Manufacturers, Kuala Lumpur, Malaysia, pp. 52-59.

References

NEW STRAITS TIMES (1992), Malaysia, various issues.

O'BRIEN, Peter and Herman MUEGGE (1987), "Prospects for Intra-ASEAN Investment", *ASEAN Economic Bulletin* Vol. 4, No. 2, November 1987, pp. 190-196.

PANG, Eng Fong (1991), "Chinese Business in Singapore: Adjusting to Challenges at Home and Abroad". Paper presented at the Panel on Chinese Business in Southeast Asia: the Changing Dynamics of Dominance, 43rd annual meeting of the Association for Asian Studies, New Orleans, Louisiana, April 14, 1991.

PANG, Eng Fong (1992), "Sony in Singapore and Southeast Asia: A Case Study", Southeast Asia Business Programme, University of Michigan (mimeo).

PANG, Eng Fong and Hal HILL (1991), "Technology Exports from Singapore", *World Development* Vol. 19, No. 4 April, 1991.

PANG, Eng Fong and Rajah KOMARAN (1985), "Singapore Multinationals", *Columbia Journal of World Business* Vol. 2, No. 2, Summer 1985, pp. 35-43.

PANGESTU, Mari (1991), "An Indonesian Perspective", in Lee Tsao, ed., 1991, pp. 75-115.

PURA, Raphael (1991), "Consumer outlays in Asia expected to remain brisk", *Asian Wall Street Journal Weekly*, 14 January, 1991, pp. 1-2.

RIEGER, Hans Christoph (1991), *ASEAN Economic Co-operation Handbook*, Institute of Southeast Asian Studies, Singapore.

SCHWARZ, Adam (1991), "Empire of the son" and other articles, *Far Eastern Economic Review*, 14 March 1991, pp. 46-49.

SMITH, Charles (1989), "Part exchange", *Far Eastern Economic Review*, 21 September, 1989, p. 73.

SOON Lee Ying (1990), *Foreign Direct Investment in ASEAN*, Malaysian Economic Association, Kuala Lumpur.

STONE, Eric (1992), "Trading on ASEAN's Future", *Asian Business*, July 1992, pp. 20-27.

STRAITS TIMES and *STRAITS TIMES WEEKLY OVERSEAS EDITION* (1991 and 1992), various issues.

SURIYAMONGKOL, M.L. (1987), "The Role of US Foreign Investment in ASEAN Industrial Co-operation", *ASEAN Economic Bulletin* Vol. 4, No. 2, November 1987, pp. 133-160.

TIGLAO, Rigoberto (1991), "Planters uprooted", *Far Eastern Economic Review*, 16 May, 1991, p. 74.

VATIKIOTIS, Michael (1991), "Time to rethink", *Far Eastern Economic Review*, 21 March, 1991, pp. 18-19.

VILLEGAS, Bernardo M. (1987), "The Challenge to ASEAN Economic Co-operation", *Contemporary Southeast Asia* Vol. 9, No. 2, September 1987, pp. 120-128.

WORLD BANK (1987, 1990), *World Development Report 1987, 1990*.

WU, Frederich (1991), "The ASEAN Economies in the 1990s and Singapore's Regional Role", *California Management Review* Fall 1991, pp. 103-114.

Appendix 1. Map of the ASEAN countries

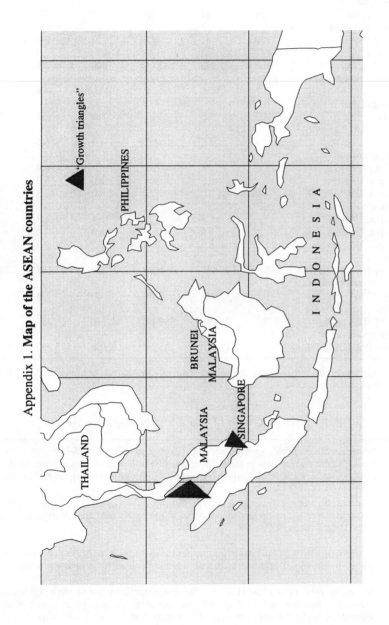

Appendix 2. **ASEAN economic indicators**

	Brunei	Indonesia	Malaysia	Philippines	Singapore	Thailand
Population						
1990 (millions)	0.3	189.4	17.9	66.1	3.0	55.7
Life expectancy						
1990 (years)	76	62	70	64	74	66
Urban population						
1990 (%)	60	31	43	43	100	23
Land area						
'000 sq. km.	5.8	1 948	330.4	300	0.625	514
GDP @ market prices						
1990 (US$ billion)	3.7	107.3	42.4	43.9	34.6	80.2
Per capita GNP						
1990 (US$)	15 200	570	2 320	730	11 160	1 420
Per capita GNP growth						
% p.a. 1965-90	-	4.5	4.0	1.3	6.5	4.4
GDP real growth						
% p.a. 1980-91	-	5.6	5.5	0.8	6.4	7.6
% p.a. 1992 est.	-	6.5	8.5	2.0	5.0	7.0
% p.a. 1993 est.	-	7.0	7.5	4.0	5.5	7.5
Inflation						
% p.a. 1980-91	-	8.5	1.8	15.1	1.8	3.6
% p.a. 1992 est.	-	8.5	4.5	9.5	2.0	4.0
% p.a. 1993 est.	-	8.0	4.5	7.5	2.0	4.5
Exports						
1991 (US$ million)	2 597	29 142	34 405	8 840	59 188	27 562
Manufactured exports						
1990 (%)	0.5	46	49	69	78	70
Imports						
1991 (US$ million)	1 781	25 869	36 749	12 945	66 257	37 518
Foreign reserves (excl. gold)						
mid 1992 (US$ billion)	-	10 710	12 790	3 180	35 750	18 980

*Sources:*World Bank, *World Development Report 1992*. IMF, *Direction of Trade Statistics Yearbook 1992*. Merrill Lynch, Singapore, August 1992.

Appendix 3. **Goals of the ASEAN Organisation**

- To accelerate economic growth, social progress and cultural development in the region through joint endeavours in the spirit of equality and partnership in order to strengthen the foundation for a prosperous and peaceful community of South East Asian nations.

- To promote regional peace and stability through abiding respect for justice and the rule of law in the relationship among countries in the region and adherence to the principles of the United Nations Charter.

- To promote active collaboration and mutual assistance on matters of common interest in the economic, social, cultural, technical, scientific and administrative spheres.

- To collaborate more effectively for the greater utilisation of their agriculture and industries, the expansion of their trade, including the study of problems of international commodity trade, the improvement of their transportation and communication facilities, and the raising of the living standards of their peoples.

- To promote South East Asian studies.

- To maintain close co-operation and beneficial co-operation with existing international and regional organisations with similar aims and purposes, and explore all avenues for even closer co-operation among themselves.

Source: Bangkok Declaration (1987), as represented in ASEAN-CCI, *ASEAN Handbook 1990*, p. 2.

Appendix 4. AFTA winners and losers

Winners and losers
Selected major ASEAN companies affected by CEPT fast-track sectors
(I=Indonesia, M=Malaysia, P=Philippines, T=Thailand)

Sector	Likely to gain	Likely to lose
Cement	Indocement (I) Siam Cement (T)	Cement Ind (M) Bacnotan Cons Ind (P)
Ceramic & glass products	MCB Holdings (M)	Thai Glass Ind (T) Indonesian and Philippine glass companies
Chemicals	Salim Group * (I) Chemical Co (M)	
Copper cathodes	Atlas Cons Mining (P) Indonesian mining companies	Malaysian and Thai mining companies
Electronics	Matsushita Electric (M) Precision Electronics (P)	Sanyo Universal (T) Indonesian electronics firms
Fertilizer	Pacific Chem (M) Atlas Fertilizer (P) Charoen Pokphand Feedmill (T)	Indonesian fertilizer companies
Gems & jewellery	Pranda Jewelry (T)	Malaysian and Indonesian jewellery makers
Leather goods	Indonesian and Thai leather manufacturers	
Pharmaceuticals	Kalbe Farma (I) Metro Drug (P)	
Plastics	Bimantara Group * (I) Malaysian Pacific Ind (M)	Thai Plastic & Chem (T)
Pulp	Sinar Mas * (I) Paper Ind Corp (P) Malaysian paper companies	Siam Pulp & Paper (T)
Rubber products	Gadjah Tunggal (I) Kumpulan Guthrie (M) Philtread Tire & Rubber (P) Bangkok Rubber (T)	
Textiles	Argo Pantes (I) Saha Union (T)	MWE Holdings (M) Filsyn Corp (P)
Vegetable oil	Salim Group * (I) Sime Darby (M)	NDC-Guthrie Plantations (P) Thai plantation firms
Wood & rattan furniture	Indonesian and Malaysian furniture makers	Philippine furniture makers

Notes:
1. Advantage and disadvantage are determined by the extent to which companies in the sector are currently protected within their domestic market and an estimate of the company's current export capability.
2. Brunei and Singapore companies are not included as they are all likely to gain from the fast-track CEPT sectors.
3. In countries where there is little domestic activity in a sector, the country is likely to benefit from lower tariffs as a consumer. In such cases there is neither a company or country notation on the chart.
* Unlisted group, although some individual companies within the group may be listed.
Source: Asian Business research.

Appendix 5. **Four Techniques for Industrial Co-operation**

	Preferential trade arrangements	Industrial projects	Industrial complementation	Industrial joint venture
Objective	production specialisation	planned specialisation of new industries	planned rationalisation of existing industries	planned specialisation and possibly rationalisation for a minimum time period, existing and new products
Focus	broad spectrum of market commodities	specific large-scale heterogeneous industries	inter-related industries or industry group, e.g. auto components	manufactured products, generally identified by private sector
Prerequisites	government commitment to adjust tariff policies	commitment to co-ordinate related policies, incentives (if assigned location at "not naturally favoured site")	existing body of manufacturers to agree and to negotiate between nations	consensus agreement by all governments to allow joint venture among private investors from at least 2 member countries and possibly non-ASEAN investors.
Mechanism	market forces, after eliminating distortions caused by tariff policies	agree to rationalise then use tariffs and other policies to deal with disparities	agree to rationalise, then adjust tariffs and other policy instruments	agree to rationalise by pooling markets, use of directional tariff policies, treat investors no less favourably than nationals
Implementing agent	government commitment to an automatic mechanism specifying negotiating timetable and rates of concession	governments agree to assign specific industries within the package. Government closely monitoring costs and financing; carefully planned implementation procedures	private sector initiative to identify and make technical study of appropriate industries followed by government policy adjustments	private sector identifies products for possible allocation and makes technical feasibility studies
Equity and efficiency	polarisation effects unless special measures taken to promote equity; prediction of specific effects is difficult	costs of one product can offset benefits from another; more accuracy in assessing gains and losses	specific trade adjustments facilitate equity in distribution, but assume all producers agree to rationalise in an industry group	focus on reciprocity with minimum of 2 countries, total ASEAN ownership not required, price should be competitive, reasonable assurance of supply continuity

Source: Suriyamongkol, 1987.

Appendix 6. **ASEAN automobile complementation scheme**

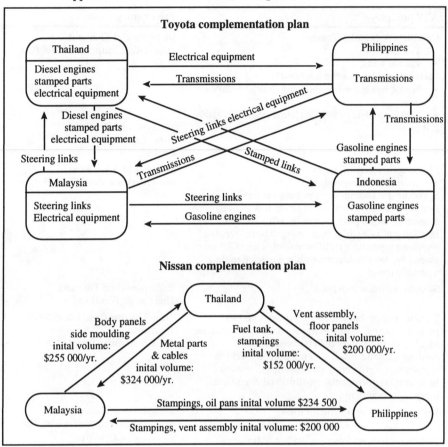

Toyota complementation plan

Thailand
Diesel engines
stamped parts
electrical equipment

Philippines
Transmissions

Electrical equipment →
← Transmissions

Diesel engines
stamped parts
electrical equipment

Steering links electrical equipment

Transmissions

Gasoline engines
stamped parts

Steering links

Transmissions

Stamped links

Malaysia
Steering links
Electrical equipment

Indonesia
Gasoline engines
stamped parts

Steering links →
← Gasoline engines

Nissan complementation plan

Thailand

Body panels
side moulding
inital volume:
$255 000/yr.

Metal parts
& cables
inital volume:
$324 000/yr.

Fuel tank,
stampings
inital volume:
$152 000/yr.

Vent assembly,
floor panels
inital volume:
$200 000/yr.

Malaysia

Stampings, oil pans inital volume $234 500 →
← Stampings, vent assembly inital volume: $200 000

Philippines

Source: Kevin Rushton, " Auto Parts Complementation in ASEAN" *Southeast Asia Business* No. 23 (spring/summer 1990), pp. 14, 15.

Appendix 7. Final list of AIJV products

	AIJV products	Participating countries
1.	Complete Assemblies (new) • Tie-rods • Tie-rod ends Parts of complete assemblies (new) • For tie-rod assembly; housing studs; bellows; bearings • For tie-rod end/outer ball joints assembly; studs	Malaysia and Thailand AAE-TRW Components Sdn. Bhd.
2.	Frit (new)	Malaysia and Thailand Asian Cerachem Manufacturing Co. Ltd.
3.	Motor cycle electrical parts • main switch assembly Speedometer assembly; pilot lamps assembly; stop switch; head light assembly; horn; flasher; relay assembly; audio pilot assembly; wire harness; ignition coil assembly; fuel; guague hose; rectifier regulator assembly; rectifier assembly and CDI unit assembly; liner holder assembly; switch handle assembly (new)	Malaysia and Thailand Siam Electrical Parts Co. Ltd.
4.	Slaughered meat (existing)	Philippines and Thailand Thai Pacific Foods Ltd.
5.	Security paper; banknotes; passport; cheques; postage stamps; postage/money orders; tax stamps; identity cards; lottery tickets; bonds/share certificates; land titles; driving licenses; vehicle registration certificates; road tax discs; licenses; immigration documents; institutional documents; insurance documents	Brunei Darussalam, Malaysia and Thailand ASEAN Security Paper Mills Sdn. Bhd.
6.	Ball joints for motor vehicles (new)	Malaysia and Thailand AAE-TRW Components Sdn. Bhd.
7.	Steering columns including shafts and linkages (columns include conventional, collapsible and adjustable columns) (new)	Malaysia and Thailand AAE-TRW Components Sdn. Bhd.
8.	Ethoxylates, i.e. fatty alcohol Ethocylates and nonyl Phenol ethoxylates (new)	Indonesia, Singapore and Thailand Ethoxylates Manufacturing Pte. Ltd. of Singapore
9.	Multi-stage, high powered, centrifugal pumps (new)	Singapore and Indonesia Grundfors Pumps Pte. Ltd.
10.	Titanium dioxide pigments	Malaysia and Indonesia c/o TAPL (Malaysia) Sdn. Bhd.
11.	DAF steering columns/box, DAF steering pumps, DAF fuel pumps	Thailand, Philippines and Malaysia H.J. Malal Maskhor
	DAF rear axles	Thailand, Philippines, Brunei Darussalam and Malaysia DAF-Tan Chong Autoparts
	DAF front axles	Thailand, Philippines, Brunei Darussalam and Malaysia Columbia Motor Corp.
	DAF Diesel Engines 50 - 99 KWH-HP 115 WP 100 - 199 KWY-HP 135-272 >200 KWH-HP >272	Thailand, Philippines, Brunei Darussalam and Malaysia Thai Rung Union Car
12.	Enamel	Malaysia and Indonesia P.T. Ridjadson
13.	Track-tyre tractors (bulldozers) wheel loaders; motor graders; hydraulic excavators; diesel engines; gensets and components of these products	Malaysia and Indonesia P.T. Natra Raya

Appendix 7 (cont.). **Final list of AIJV products**

AIJV products	Participating countries
14. Aluminium Hydroxide	Indonesia and Thailand P.T. Alhydro Bintan
15. Breakfast cereals	Indonesia, Malaysia, Philippines and Thailand Nestlé
16. Soya based milk; Soyex meat analogue	Indonesia, Malaysia, Philippines and Thailand Nestlé
17. Chocolate wafer; bouillon tablets	Indonesia, Malaysia, Philippines and Thailand Nestlé
18. Non-dairy coffee creamer	Indonesia, Malaysia, Philippines and Thailand Nestlé

Source: Extracted from COIME Report presented at the Executive Committee Meeting of the ASEAN-CCI Working Group on Industrial Co-operation (WGIC) on July 26, 1991, in Manila, Philippines.

Appendix 8. **ASEAN regional industry clubs**

ASEAN Agricultural Machinery Federation
ASEAN Aluminium Industry Club
ASEAN Automotive Federation
ASEAN Chemical Industries Club
ASEAN Federation of Cement Manufacturers
ASEAN Federation of Electrical, Electronics and Allied Industries
ASEAN Federation of Food Processing Industries
ASEAN Federation of Furniture Manufacturers
ASEAN Federation of Glass Manufacturers
ASEAN Federation of Plastic Industries
ASEAN Federation of Textile Industries
ASEAN Panel Products Federation
ASEAN Iron and Steel Industry Federation
ASEAN Pharmaceutical INdustry CLub
ASSEAN Pulp and Paper Industry Club
Ceramic Industry Club of ASEAN
Rubber Industries Association of Southeast Asian Nations

ASEAN regional commodity clubs

Coffee
Handicraft
Livestock
Pepper
Sugar

Source: ASEAN-CCI, *ASEAN Handbook 1990*, pp. 6-7.

Appendix 9. ASEAN government/ASEAN CCI interaction chart

ASEAN GOVERNMENTS

- ASEAN Economic Ministers
  - (1G) Committee on industry minerals & energy (COIME)
    - (1P) Working group on industrial cooperation (WGIC)
      - Regional industry clubs
      - National industry clubs
  - (2G) Committee on food, agriculture & forestry (COFAF)
    - (2P) Working group on food, agriculture & forestry (WGFAF)
  - (4G) Committee on transportation & communications (COTAC)
    - (4P) Working group on transportation & communications (WGTAC)
  - (3G) Committee on trade & tourism (COTT)
    - Trade preferences negotiating group
    - (3P) Working group on trade (WGT)
      - Regional commodity clubs
      - National commodity clubs

- Executive Committee
  - ASEAN CCI Council
    - ASEAN Australia Business Council
    - ASEAN EEC Business Council
    - ASEAN Japan Economic Council
    - ASEAN New Zealand Business Council
    - ASEAN US Business Council
    - ASEAN Canada Business Council

ASEAN CCI

- NCCI NBD Brunei Darussalam
- Kadin Indonesia
- NCCIM Malaysia
- PCCI Philippines
- SFCCI Singapore
- JSCCIB Thailand

Soource: ASEAN-CCI Handbook 1991/92.

Chapter 5

REVIVING SOUTH-SOUTH CO-OPERATION: ARGENTINA, BRAZIL AND THE MERCOSUR[1]

Daniel Chudnovsky

Bien que le processus d'intégration argentino-brésilien lancé en 1986 se soit heurté au départ à certaines difficultés, des progrès ont pu être accomplis tant du point de vue du volume que de la structure des échanges. Parallèlement, un mouvement d'intégration fondé sur l'innovation s'est engagé dans certains secteurs industriels : les machines-outils, les biotechnologies et l'équipement automobile. Certaines de ces initiatives ont toutefois été entravées, d'une part, par les problèmes financiers constants des pays membres et, d'autre part, par la décision prise de mettre en place le Mercosur d'ici 1995 (Traité d'Asunción — 1991). Ce chapitre évoque les principales questions soulevées par la seconde phase du processus d'intégration en cours, et qui résultent de la déréglementation et de la libéralisation unilatérale des échanges. Il propose des scénarios pour l'avenir de la coopération sud-sud dans cette région.

Despite the difficulties experienced in the initial phase of the Argentine-Brazilian integration process launched in 1986, some progress in terms of trade expansion and changes in the composition of trade were made. At the same time, movement towards an innovation-driven integration process began at the sector level in machine tools, biotechnology and auto parts. Some of these initiatives, however, were weakened by the continued financial difficulties of the member-states and the decision taken in the Asunción Treaty of 1991 to create a Mercosur by 1995. The main issues raised in this second phase of the integration process resulting from the unilateral trade liberalisation and deregulation that is being undertaken are discussed and possible scenarios for the future of South-South co-operation in the region are suggested.

1. Introduction

One of the few initiatives to promote south-south co-operation undertaken in the 1980s was the set of agreements signed by Argentina and Brazil in 1986 that revived the moribund process of economic integration in Latin America. In its initial phase the new process of co-operation was based on the negotiation of a number of "protocols" in such areas as agriculture, biotechnology and capital goods. Though the focus appeared narrow it had the general aim of increasing bilateral trade and changing its composition. With the signature of the Asunción Treaty in March 1991, a second phase in the integration process began. It involves the implementation of general trade preferences aimed at the creation of a southern cone common market (Mercosur) by 1995. In March 1991 Uruguay and Paraguay formally joined the process of sub-regional integration. The focus of this chapter, however, will remain on the two initial countries, Argentina and Brazil.

In contrast to the Asunción Treaty, the text of the first set of agreements made it clear that trade expansion was conceived as an instrument for industrial restructuring and technological upgrading. In practice, however, most of the subsequent bilateral negotiations focused almost exclusively on trade matters. Despite the inclusion of some innovative elements in the protocols, the agreements signed in the initial phase were thus mainly variations of the old exchange driven model of regional integration[2]. By emphasizing and generalising the trade aspects of the economic integration process, the features of the old integration model were accentuated in the new phase, though in a context of much reduced external protection and without a heavy formal organisational structure. The main purpose of this chapter is to analyse the specific way in which traditional integration models have been applied in this new case. It does so by examining the rationale for both the initial and the current phase and identifying the main factors which constrain the process of economic integration in each of these phases looking at both macroeconomic factors and at the reaction of some important actors to it.

Section 2 sketches out the main political and economic expectations as well as the structural and policy differences between the two partners. Section 3 then argues that the difficulties experienced in the initial phase were not solely due to the way in which the integration project was conceived. The adverse macroeconomic picture and other factors also militated against the programme. As Section 4 shows, however, some progress in terms of trade expansion and changes in the composition of trade were made in this period and some interesting developments at the sectoral level started to take place, notably in the machine tool sector, in autoparts and in biotechnology. The discussion highlights not only the specific advances and limitations in each area but also gives an idea of how key actors — domestic and foreign firms and the research community — have started to react to the ongoing integration process. Although these three case studies suggest that some elements of an innovation driven model are, thus, present at the micro level, these elements are not significant enough to generate sizable externalities and modify the generally negative evaluation of the initial phase.

The current phase was not built upon the previous one. Rather, it was launched in the middle of unilateral trade liberalisation and other structural reforms that were being applied by both partners though with different timing and policies. Section 5 thus argues that given the type of integration model chosen, the macroeconomic difficulties confronting both countries, and policy divergences between them, the current phase may end in yet another failure. However, on the assumption that the macroeconomic situation improves and a number of policy modifications are implemented, an attempt to speculate on a more optimistic scenario is also undertaken here.

2. The rationale and the models used

The establishment of the various protocols of integration between Argentina and Brazil in 1986 constituted, above all, a far-reaching political decision that put an end to a history of rivalries and discord in bilateral political and trade relations. Integration was spurred by the need to strengthen the infant democratic regimes in both countries and eliminate potential sources of conflict between neighbouring countries, thus turning traditional military rivalry[3] into fruitful political and economic co-operation (Jaguaribe, 1987; Hirst, 1987; Camilion, 1987; van Klaveren, 1990).

The public announcement of the agreements, however, came as a surprise, and their signature was not preceded by a broad debate in either country. On the contrary, it was the debate's starting point. The initial decision to enter into a process of co-operation and eventually integration, however, can be explained by a number of external and internal factors that emerged in the course of the public debate.

Both Argentina and Brazil, for example, faced serious difficulties in coping with the external and fiscal imbalances that derived from the debt crisis of the 1980s. Both were led to introduce, almost simultaneously, heterodox anti-inflationary policies (known respectively as the Plan Austral and the Plan Cruzado). The profound crisis of the 1980s also unleashed, in both countries, a debate on the options to resume growth and industrialisation. These adverse external economic conditions created the need for new alliances in both countries.

In addition to the common problem of a huge external debt, both countries faced other external problems for which collaboration appeared to be a solution. Bilateral conflicts with the United States in a number of trade and technology issues and divergence with the United States and other developed countries on some of the new issues raised in the GATT Uruguay Round, for example, encouraged Brazil to search for a revival in its relations with Latin America, and within the region, with its most important neighbour, Argentina[4]. Although its conflicts with the United States were less severe, Argentina's manufactured exports had been affected by protectionist trends in the North and its agriculture exports had been hit by subsidies from Europe and the United States in third countries, thus stimulating a search for new markets.

From the Argentine perspective Brazil represents an enormous consumer market, capable of generating prospects for increased agricultural and manufacturing exports, that would help to ease the problem of scale afflicting many branches of production. At the same time it is a partner endowed with an appreciable industrial and technological capacity and with a very diversified export apparatus. Access to the Brazilian market, by stimulating new investments, could thus function as a new frontier for a re-industrialisation strategy.

For Brazil, Argentina, despite its economic problems, looks like a natural partner. Although the consumer market is much smaller, it has a relatively high (for developing countries) income per capita. Furthermore, Argentina has other attributes that suggest an initial complementarity for the integration process. Its agricultural and agro-industrial production is highly competitive and would help to bring down the prices of some key items in the Brazilian family basket and facilitate joint efforts in other markets. Likewise, Argentina still has a greater relative abundance of skilled labour, including engineering and scientific personnel, a factor that would favour development efforts in production branches which make intensive use of this type of labour. Thus, even in a context in which manufacturing capacities have seriously deteriorated, there are some skill-intensive branches with short production runs that are currently competitive in international markets. This base would make it possible to complement the advantages already acquired by Brazilian industry in large scale production and make possible the intensive use of common inputs.

Theoretically, therefore, if the assumptions of unaltered terms of trade and constant costs are eliminated, then the advantages of an Argentine-Brazilian customs union will be greater not only than protection but also than unilateral trade liberalisation because, given these complementarities, a customs union would facilitate trade creation in an expanded market protected against third countries. In turn, if industrialisation is introduced as a strategic goal or a collective good which warrants a certain amount of protection, a custom union reduces the relevant costs without sacrificing the collective good[5].

In the case of Argentina and Brazil renewed industrialisation will require both a restructuring of existing branches and an increase in output in branches where technological progress is rapid. Within the context of common protection for some activities, these changes would be stimulated by preferential imports from Argentina that would compete with domestic production instead of being complementary to it, as had previously been the case in Brazil (Tavares de Araujo Jr, 1990). For Argentina this approach looked very attractive not only in view of the access to a larger market but also as an alternative to the unilateral deregulation already attempted in 1979-1981 with clearly negative results.

The search for dynamic effects of production restructuring associated with economies of scale and specialisation, and with the capacity to introduce technical progress, against a background of greater competition, leads to the exploration of potential intra-sectoral advantages. In this hypothesis the possibilities for trade creation depend directly on the dynamic production of new comparative advantages. As one Brazilian economist argued: "the point of departure of this discussion is the common challenge for the growth prospects of both economies: the challenge of training to be able to keep pace with shifts in the world technological frontier and, at the same time, to ensure conditions for international competitiveness for each country's industrial capacity" (Tavares de Araujo Jr, 1988, own translation).

Recognition of the existence of political will and potential complementarities, common needs and theoretical justifications cannot, however, disguise the structural differences between the two economies and their current built-in macroeconomic instabilities. The Brazilian GDP is four times larger than that of Argentina. Manufacturing GDP is not only five times bigger in Brazil than Argentina but Brazilian production is more diversified and its growth record has been better, even in the hard times of the 1980s. Productive investment has been reduced in both countries since the debt crisis, but the fall was far more pronounced in Argentina where, in the 1980s, hardly any new net fixed investment took place.

Although the Brazilian market is very attractive to Argentine exporters, the share of Argentine exports directed towards Brazil amounted to 6 per cent in the early 1980s. In this period imports from Brazil were about 8-18 per cent of Argentine imports, while Argentine goods accounted for 2-3 per cent of Brazilian imports. The Argentine market was hardly significant for Brazilian exports (only 3 per cent of total exports) (Table 1). The debt crisis, which led to a decrease in imports and a preference for export markets which paid in hard currencies, reduced bilateral trade.

Table 1. **Argentina-Brazil: share of bilateral trade in total trade**
(%)

Year	Argentina		Brazil	
	Xb/X	Mb/M	Xa/X	Ma/M
1981	6.5	9.3	3.8	2.5
1982	7.4	12.5	3.3	2.7
1983	4.3	14.5	3.0	2.0
1984	5.9	18.6	3.2	3.1
1985	5.8	14.5	2.1	3.4
1986	10.2	14.6	3.1	4.9
1987	8.7	14.4	3.1	3.6
1988	8.7	18.3	2.9	4.2
1989	11.4	18.2	2.1	6.1
1990	11.6	17.6	2.3	7.0

X = exports, M = imports
a = with origin or destination in Argentina
b = with origin or destination in Brazil
Source: Own calculations on information from Industry and Trade Secretariat, Argentina.

As former Brazilian finance Minister Bresser Pereira pointed out, these structural differences implied that "Integration is more important for Argentina than for Brazil. This is an objective fact and Brazilians should not be blamed for that. The fact is that the market open for Brazil inside Argentina is much smaller than that open for Argentina inside Brazil. Therefore, a big effort is necessary to convince Brazilian entrepreneurs that this integration process is really important. It is also necessary to convince Argentine entrepreneurs since many of them have great doubts. But if it is important to convince the Argentinians it is even more important to convince the Brazilians" (Bresser Pereira, 1990, p. 200, own translation).

For many Brazilians, therefore, integration was looked upon as an affair pushed by Itamaraty[6] mainly for political reasons.

On the Argentine side, the composition of trade — Brazilian exports of manufactured goods in exchange for Argentinian agricultural commodities and agro-based manufactures — coupled with the permanent trade surplus in Brazil's favour were major preoccupations. Competition from the more advanced Brazilian industrial sector, it was feared, might exacerbate this pattern of inter-sectoral specialisation and decrease further the level of industrial activity in Argentina. For Argentina, therefore, a major objective of the programme initiated in 1986 was to increase bilateral trade and change its composition so as to promote intra-industry trade. To this end protocols were signed covering a variety of subjects. These included a sectoral focus in the approach to integration in the manufacturing sector, notably in capital goods, food processing and automobiles, joint technological programmes in biotechnology, aerospace and nuclear energy and provisions for the expansion of trade and investment through the creation of an Investment Fund of $200 million, an account currency (the gaucho) to cancel trade between both countries not involving hard currency, and a Statute of Bi-national Enterprises.

The sectoral approach adopted in this first phase was useful to start the integration process but it became very difficult to negotiate, sequence and manage later on. For example, it was not clear how to proceed from capital goods to intermediate products or to consumer goods. Furthermore, many of the key protocols, involving the generation of new comparative advantages through technological modernisation, were never implemented because of a lack of commitment by the member governments.

Although some elements aimed at production specialisation are mentioned in the protocols, an exchange driven model with a light formal structure prevailed in the initial phase. Initiative was and remained the preserve of the Ministries of Foreign Affairs in both countries. Although the integration programme was thus clearly top-down in conception and led in its development by some segments of the national bureaucracies, more recently other agents, especially domestic and foreign firms, some sections of the scientific community and provincial governments, have begun to participate in the process. After the initial surprise and given the gradual and flexible manner in which the government conducted the negotiations through protocols, Argentine entrepreneurs, for example, started to take more interest in the programme, especially when Brazilian trade barriers were actually lifted. In this way the credibility of the programme was enhanced. However, while in some branches negotiations were initiated by the private sector (automobiles) in other branches (steel, electrical machinery) Argentine entrepreneurs took a defensive position.

Some advances towards unilateral trade liberalisation were also made in 1987-1989 but the main thrust of the integration process in this period was to open small segments of the economy to neighbouring products while keeping it well protected vis-à-vis the rest of the world.

In November 1988, a significant change in the approach to integration was made when both governments signed a Treaty of Integration, Co-operation and Development aimed at the establishment of a free trade area between the two countries in ten years. The Treaty was approved by both Parliaments in August 1989. The integration process was further accelerated when President Menem, who took office in Argentina in 1989, and President Collor, who was elected in Brazil in 1990, not only ratified the ongoing integration process, but decided to move towards a common market instead of a free trade area and to bring forward the date for its establishment from 1999 to the end of 1994. In January 1991 a 40 per cent cut in tariffs on bilateral trade was implemented, pending further automatic reductions each six months until a zero tariff is achieved on December 31 1994. Both Brazil and Argentina agreed to a specific number of exceptions to the tariff reduction programme and to reduce that number by 20 per cent each calendar year. Uruguay and Paraguay have a separate timetable[7]. Non-tariffs barriers are also to be eliminated by the end of 1994. However, sectoral agreements are envisaged for a number of sensitive branches. A joint working group to co-ordinate macroeconomic, tax, trade and industrial policies has also been established.

In contrast to the initial phase, in the new phase of the integration process preferential tariff reductions are being implemented at the same time as both countries are unilaterally opening their economies, pursuing structural adjustment measures and moving towards a reduction in the role of the State in the economy. The pace of these changes, however, is uneven and they have not been co-ordinated between the two countries. In Argentina unilateral trade liberalisation is taking place rapidly[8]. Tariff rates have already been reduced to a maximum of 22 per cent (and a weighted average of 10 per cent) except for automobiles and consumer electronics where a maximum of 35 per cent is in force for the time being. In Brazil the process is more gradual and is aimed at achieving average tariff rates of 20 per cent in 1994 with a 40 per cent rate for certain goods to be especially protected. Furthermore, whereas in Argentina no industrial and technological policy is envisaged, in Brazil the government has announced guidelines for industrial and technology policy aimed at increasing the quality and competitiveness of manufactured goods and fostering the entry into high tech branches.

The new integration programme is far more ambitious and generalised than that implemented in the previous phase and it relies even more heavily on trade liberalisation as the agent of change. It thus depends crucially upon the ability and interest of key economic actors in the region to take advantage of the rapid pace of intra-regional tariff reduction to restructure trade. Yet the parallel process of more generalised trade liberalisation appears to be undermining the rationale for bilateral integration, particularly for Brazil, since unilateral trade liberalisation in Argentina has left less room for trade diversion, and has reduced the impact of tariff preferences on the industrial restructuring process and hence on trade creation. Given the fact that the Brazilian market is not only bigger but also more protected vis-à-vis third parties, Argentina has still significant incentives for trade creation. Counterbalancing this are pressures to form a southern trading bloc that flow from Mexico's decision to sign a North America Free Trade Agreement (NAFTA), the establishment of a single market in Europe and the uncertainty which so long surrounded the outcome of the Uruguay Round of GATT. In this connection, the support President Bush gave to the creation of a hemispheric free trade zone and to sub-regional trade liberalisation arrangements in his "Enterprise for the Americas" proposal, came as a welcome surprise. With this initiative not only was the suspicion that Southern Cone co-operation was promoted as an alternative to north-south co-operation dispelled, but the possibility of joint negotiations with the United States over the difficult agenda of trade, investment, technology and debt issues could now also be envisaged. Some even hoped that they would have greater bargaining power than in the past, thus giving substance to one of the arguments favouring south-south co-operation. However, a clear trend towards accepting many US demands is already visible in Argentina, making future negotiations easier but, at the same time, reducing the relative need for more collective bargaining in each case[9].

The Argentine government, for example, has taken significant steps to improve relations with the United States. It was the only Latin American country to commit warships to the Gulf blockade, it has unilaterally reduced tariffs and removed non-tariff barriers. It resumed interest payments to creditor banks, submitted a project to Parliament to modify existing laws to allow pharmaceutical products to be patented in two years' time, and shared a common position with the United States in the GATT negotiations in opposing the EC's Common Agricultural Policy.

Although the Brazilian government has also taken steps to reduce tensions with the United States, liberalising trade, making concessions in long-running disputes over patents in the pharmaceutical industry, over prohibitions on computer imports and over software copyrights, it has made less progress than Argentina in implementing the structural reforms that the "Washington Consensus" strongly recommends for developing countries (Williamson, 1990). Furthermore, given the trade diversion effects on Brazilian exports and the likely impact of US imports on non competitive industrial branches, the Bush Initiative was cautiously received in Brazil (Azambuja, 1991).

On the whole, therefore, despite the political will and US support, the economic rationale for bilateral integration appears less compelling than previously, especially for Brazil.

a) The adverse macroeconomic picture

It is impossible to understand the difficulties faced during the initial phase of the integration process without recognising the consequences for policy making that resulted from the dramatic shift in the macroeconomic situation that took place a year after initial negotiations began in 1986. Indeed 1986 was an exceptional year. The main macroeconomic variables behaved favourably in both countries; growth of the economy in general and the manufacturing sector in particular, relative price stability and an upturn, although a weak one, in the investment rate. Since 1987 little if any growth took place in Brazil (with the exception of 1989, when the GDP grew 3.6 per cent) and the Argentine economy registered negative rates of growth between 1988 and 1990. Restrictive monetary policies proved incapable of halting the runaway inflation and both countries entered into hyperinflation in 1989. In early 1987 Brazil was forced to declare a moratorium on the payment of its external debt service and Argentina observed a *de facto* but undeclared moratorium from April 1988 to the middle of 1990. In a context of inflation and balance of payments disequilibrium in both countries, the fluctuations in the two exchange rates and in their relative parities have been spectacular.

During 1990 economic policy was directed at stabilizing the economies, deepening recession in both economies. Fiscal reforms were begun, efforts were made to re-define the direction and financing of government spending, while suspension or reduction of subsidies and privatisation of state owned companies took place.

b) The lack of co-ordination in economic policy making

What is particularly important, insofar as the co-operation and integration programme is concerned, is not only the problems engendered by

3. Difficulties and advances in the initial phase

the adverse macroeconomic situation, notably the growing difficulties faced by each government in controlling the fiscal and external disequilibrium, but the unco-ordinated way in which key economic policy decisions were being made. It is the latter which severely weakened the integration process in this first phase.

Regarding the external debt, for example, although apparently there was an attempt to act together vis-à-vis creditor banks[10], in practice each country followed separate policies. In fact, it seems that Argentina benefited from the Brazilian moratorium on the debt to reach an agreement with the IMF in 1987.

Even more important for the purpose of the integration process, when in 1988 both countries started to deregulate their trade regime, they did so without any co-ordination. In May 1988 the Brazilian Government announced a New Industrial and Tariff Policy to rationalise the protection enjoyed by many branches of the manufacturing sector. Nominal tariffs were reduced and several special import regimes were eliminated, though most non-tariff barriers remained in force. In the same year, the Argentine government following pressures from the World Bank and as part of a trade policy loan, sharply reduced the number of goods to be imported with the approval of local producers and fixed specific duties on 300 of these items and made changes in the general tariff level and nominal tariffs. Although these measures were designed to make existing protection more rational and they did not constitute as deep a unilateral opening as that started in 1990, they were announced without any consultation between the partners.

The absence of co-ordination in the area where bilateral negotiations were the key to progress, suggests that not only on the more difficult issues of short term economic policy and debt negotiations but also in crucial aspects of the trade regime, no serious commitment from either government to the ongoing programme was actually made. Moreover, when important modifications to domestic economic policies were needed in order to implement the various protocols of the integration programme, little if any progress was made. A good example is trade in wheat negotiated under protocol number two. The aim of this protocol was to increase Argentine exports to Brazil with prices lower than imports from third parties. Even though bilateral trade expanded, the Brazilian government and more specifically the Ministry of Agriculture continued giving enormous subsidies ($2 billion annually) to domestic wheat producers (Tavares de Araujo Jr, 1990).

This example reveals that the different policy priorities in the various government agencies have been the main factor behind the lack of bilateral co-ordination. In the Brazilian case, the organisation dealing with import control and export promotion measures (CACEX) was far more cautious than the Tariff Policy Commission and the Ministry of Foreign Affairs. Far more important was the low profile taken by the Finance Ministry (except on a few occasions) showing very clearly that for Brazil integration was considered a low priority issue, more a diplomatic than an economic policy exercise.

In the Argentine case, though there was an unusual degree of co-operation between the Ministry of Foreign Affairs and the just created Secretary for International Trade and Industry (under the Ministry of Economics) when the programme was first initiated, since mid-1987 only the Ministry of Foreign Affairs, which has no power to implement the international economic agreements that it negotiates, has become the main agency pushing for the programme's effective implementation. The Ministry of Economics not only played a low profile role in the negotiations but it did not provide the finance needed for the establishment of the Investment Fund, nor did it supply the funds for relatively minor commitments like the Biotechnological Programme as we shall see below.

c) Trends in bilateral trade

With the previous picture in mind, it is rather surprising that bilateral trade increased significantly (Table 2) from the very low levels reached before the integration process began. In 1989 and 1990 bilateral trade was not only a bit higher in nominal dollars than the maximum achieved in 1980, but these were also the first years in the decade in which Argentina had a significant surplus. This surplus is explained by the sharp increase in Argentine exports and a small reduction in imports from Brazil. By 1990 Brazil was absorbing 11.6 per cent of Argentina's exports.

Table 2. **Argentina-Brazil trade**
(in current $ million)

Year	Argentina exports	Argentina imports	Balance	Total trade
1980	765.0	1072.3	-307.3	1837.3
1981	595.1	893.3	-298.2	1488.4
1982	567.7	687.7	-120.0	1255.4
1983	358.3	666.8	-308.5	1025.1
1984	478.2	831.2	-353.0	1309.4
1985	496.3	611.5	-115.2	1107.8
1986	698.1	691.3	6.8	1389.4
1987	539.3	819.2	-279.9	1358.5
1988	607.9	971.4	-363.5	1579.3
1989	1124.0	721.4	402.6	1845.4
1990	1421.6	717.9	703.7	2139.5

Source: As in Table 1 on p. 172, above.

Although the sharp depreciation of the Argentine currency in 1989 explained the growth in exports to Brazil in that year, the situation in 1990 and generally the new trends in bilateral trade are not only due to foreign exchange fluctuations. In fact in the last decade bilateral trade flows have been largely unaffected by such fluctuations (Iglesias, 1991). The sectoral negotiations, the more pronounced recessionary conditions in the Argentine market, and steps taken in Brazil to liberalise imports, were also important explanatory factors, though to assess the relative weight of each would require a more detailed investigation.

Nevertheless it is important to note that in mid-1989, 90 per cent of the Argentine exports to Brazil were negotiated items whereas only 50 per cent of the Brazilian exports to Argentina entered under similar conditions. While many of the items traded were negotiated through bilateral agreements in ALADI in which reciprocal preferences were given in the tariff rates, in the case of capital goods and processed food, special protocols were in force.

In addition to trade expansion, what is very significant in the period under analysis is the growing participation of manufactures of industrial origin in Argentine exports. Such manufactures gradually rose from $109 million in 1985 to $560 million in 1990. Whereas for all Argentine exports the share of manufactures of industrial origin (excluding oil products) increased from 18.4 per cent in 1985 to 33 per cent in 1989, in exports to Brazil, such manufactures increased from 21 to 44 per cent over the same period.

In 1990 the deficit in trade in manufactures of industrial origin was transformed into a small surplus, suggesting that a pattern of intra-industry trade had started to emerge in some manufacturing items[11]. Nonetheless, it is important to point out that manufactures of agricultural origin (as well as primary goods) reached record levels in Argentine exports in 1990 (Table 3)[12].

Table 3. Argentina-Brazil: composition of bilateral trade
(in current $ million)

	Primary	Maunfactures of agricultural origin	Oil	Manufactures of industrial origin	Total
Exports					
1985	176.7	146.9	63.5	109.0	496.0
1986	315.4	206.7	23.4	150.4	698.0
1987	218.2	113.1	0.1	207.8	539.0
1988	210.3	93.6	4.3	298.9	607.6
1989	346.2	259.6	18.0	499.1	1 124.0
1990	560.4	305.8	5.7	550.8	1 422.7
Imports					
1985	144.1	14.5	17.7	435.3	611.6
1986	166.4	26.3	0.3	497.8	690.2
1987	158.6	26.3	30.6	603.8	819.3
1988	135.7	58.6	50.4	726.6	971.3
1989	163.5	38.9	1.7	516.7	721.3
1990	155.9	45.0	9.3	506.4	717.9
Balance (for Argentina)					
1985	32.6	132.4	45.8	-326.3	-115.6
1986	149.0	180.4	23.1	-346.8	7.8
1987	59.6	86.8	-30.5	-396.0	-280.3
1988	74.6	35.0	-46.1	-427.7	-363.7
1989	182.7	220.7	16.3	-17.6	402.7
1990	99.5	260.8	-3.6	44.4	575.2

Source: As in Table 1 on p. 172, above.

d) Capital goods

Protocol number one was intended to create a customs union in selected capital goods by the addition, every six months, of new products to a common list. However, since a common tariff on these goods vis-à-vis third countries was never negotiated, the products included in the common list remained more protected in Brazil than in Argentina. Moreover, due to the Brazilian market reserve policy in informatics and electronics these items were excluded from this protocol[13].

Trade was to be balanced with specific clauses and the choice of the specific capital goods to include in trade was to be balanced through the choice of the specific capital goods to include in each successive common list. From the Argentine viewpoint this provision was extremely important because the country had been a net importer of capital goods not only from Brazil but also from the industrialised countries. Protocol number one thus gave Argentina an incentive to reduce capital goods imports from third countries (i.e. trade diversion) with whom no mechanism existed to ensure an opening of their markets and to import them form Brazil while, at the same time, expanding in a significant manner exports to Brazil, a market almost closed to imports of capital goods from Argentina. This incentive was less important for Brazil because its overall trade deficit in capital goods was very small compared with that in Argentina. Furthermore, relatively few of the capital goods items made in Argentina were not also produced in Brazil.

In addition to the trade promoting features of protocol number one, other measures included in the text were intended to transform this protocol into an industrial policy instrument. These included explicit statements regarding the gradual harmonisation of policies related to production, trade and technological development in the capital goods sector in both countries and the implicit expectation that the agreement would provide the two industries with a wider market, allowing for economies of scope and specialisation and leading to greater technological development and increased productivity.

In order to fulfil such expectations, complementarities would have to be established both at the horizontal level across finished goods and, at the vertical level, in the supply of parts and components. This would be a significant departure from the pattern of national import substitution which had previously characterised the development of these two industries (Porta, 1989; Erber, 1989).

In practice the common list was defined on the basis of offers from the producers in each of the two countries. Since the producers had to approve the inclusion of products in the common list, for the most part they could avoid major competitive threats from firms in the other country. Even so, in a few cases, governments did exert pressure for the inclusion of a product (e.g. harvesters in the Argentine case). Over time a change in the defensive attitude of the producers became visible as governments adopted a more offensive attitude in 1990 in the wake of the decision to get the new phase in the general integration programme underway.

Thus from a universe of more than 600 items covering mostly non electrical machinery, electrical machinery, railway equipment and ships, a common list was negotiated to launch protocol number one in January 1987. A further four negotiations (the last, in July 1990) added new products or generalisations of some tariff positions to this list. The list thus contained more than 300 items of which 162 were included in a generic manner. Once products were included in the common list they could not be taken off.

During the two and a half years of negotiations, however, a number of modifications to the original proposals in the protocol were made. These would reduce the impact of this protocol on technological development and industrial structure in this sector. The two most important changes, in addition to abandoning the proposal for a common external tariff, were the decisions to defer the inclusion of parts and components until the last negotiation in 1990, and the exclusion of custom made capital goods mainly purchased by the public sector. The former was due to the resistance of Brazil's highly integrated manufacturers; the latter to the difficulties faced in harmonizing public sector procurement policies and to the idle capacity facing this segment of the industry (Porta, 1989).

Despite these problems and the adverse macroeconomic conditions and especially limited amount of new investment taking place in both economies, trade in negotiated items increased from $17 million in 1986 to $95 million in 1989 and the balance moved from $-12.5 to +7.5 million in favour of Argentina. Whereas in capital goods not belonging to the common list (but negotiated with partial tariff preferences within ALADI) trade also expanded, its increase was lower and the balance was slightly in Brazil's favour.

Although the volume of trade was far less important than that originally envisaged in the protocol[14], the steady expansion in bilateral trade (especially for Argentine exports) was mostly due to the implementation of the agreement.

Argentine exports within the common list consisted mainly of machine tools to which we will return below, food machinery, pumps, agricultural machinery and machines for the glass and plastic industries. Brazilian exports were more diversified and included electrical furnaces, construction machinery and elevating equipment. However, the increase in Brazilian exports within the common list was far less significant than in the Argentine case and, more importantly, total exports within the universe of the protocol remained at the same level from 1987 to 1989.

It is also important to note that, at least from the Argentine side, the firms generating these exports were mainly nationally owned small and medium size enterprises, specialised in mechanical engineering products made in small batches and with skilled labour (see below the example of machine tools). In the Brazilian case, the products incorporated in the common list are made in long batches where economies of scale are more relevant. In this way, traded goods represented to some extent the previous factor and technical endowment of each economy.

e) Technology items

In addition to the failed attempt to use the capital goods protocol as an instrument for technological development, the first phase of the Argentine-Brazilian integration process included a number of other innovation-driven initiatives. The most significant were in biotechnology (to be discussed below), informatics, nuclear matters and aerospace.

Since the capital goods protocol eliminated the whole electronics industry, attempts have been made to enhance co-operation in informatics, centred around human resources and research and development (Correa, 1989; Erber, 1989). In this connection, the two Governments sponsored yearly teaching meetings called the Argentinian-Brazilian School of Informatics[15], at which courses at different levels of complexity were taught using specifically prepared text-books. Scientific and technological workshops were held at the same time. About 500 students from Argentina and Brazil and 50 from other Latin American countries have gone to each School.

Partly as a result of the School, a common research programme was established through the workshops attended by scientists from both countries. The programme was focused especially on software engineering, design and production of integrated circuits, non-conventional architectures and artificial intelligence. Among the research projects the most significant was the ETHOS project aimed at developing a heuristic workstation oriented to software engineering, involving not only academic institutions but also national manufacturing firms.

Beyond this, however, little if any progress has been made in this programme due to the lack of funds and to domestic policy changes, notably in Brazil where priority has shifted away from ensuring technological autonomy in selected segments of the informatics industry to measures which facilitate the diffusion of informatics. In a number of cases, moreover, Argentine scientists connected to the bilateral research programmes, ultimately migrated to Brazil where working conditions seemed more favourable than in Argentina.

Without denying the importance of the School as a novel and practical attempt for bilateral co-operation particularly in research, it is important to note that no serious attempt was made to promote industrial co-operation or complementation in the various areas of the electronics complex. The main reasons for the lack of co-operation on this crucial front are well explained by a leading Brazilian expert on the subject:

"Economic and technological factors, such as scale economies and size of the markets, as well as common policy objectives present a strong case for furthering electronics co-operation into industrial activities. However, there are considerable obstacles on this path. As in non-electronic capital goods, the local production of electronics goods has evolved following parallel lines, although covering a much narrower range in Argentina than in Brazil. Therefore, the same defensive attitude seen in capital goods is likely to arise among national producers of the two countries. It is also probable that greater integration between the two industries will require adjustments in the licensing and production strategies of multinational companies. Finally, a major obstacle is the criteria by which firms are considered 'national' under the two policies, which are much stricter in Brazil than in Argentina. In fact, as they are now, the acceptance of Argentinian products as 'nationally' produced by Brazil would mean the complete overhaul of the latter's electronics policy, but for Argentina to change its rule of 'national' enterprise would mean a reversal of its present liberal policy towards foreign investment and a major political conflict with the forces which support the regime" (Erber, 1989, p. 36)[16].

With current moves to liberalise the Brazilian informatics policy and eliminate the excess tariff that protected Argentine electronic production, it is not clear to what extent some of the above mentioned obstacles are still valid. It is even less clear what the impact of these changes will be on local production of electronic products in both countries.

In contrast to the difficulties faced in informatics, and despite the problems that both countries face due to budget constraints, some advances have been made in unifying international positions on nuclear issues and in scientific and technological co-operation. A number of common projects have been initiated, for example, and a free trade agreement for nuclear equipment was recently signed (Hirst, 1990).

In the aeronautics sector, the major project was the co-production of a joint plane for civilian use between EMBRAER (Brazil) and FAMA (Argentina), for the utilisation for both Air Forces and for export to third markets. While some advances were made in the design phase, the production stage has been delayed due to Argentine budget constraints that limited FAMA's contribution to the common project to close to zero.

To better understand the extent to which the initial phase of the Argentine-Brazilian integration approach involved a few small steps towards an innovation-driven integration process, this section examines the response of significant actors to the integration momentum in three sectors: machine tools, biotechnology and automobiles and auto parts. It is important to bear in mind that developments in machine tools and biotechnology are direct consequences of the implementation of the respective protocols since 1987. This is not the case in auto parts and automobiles where a protocol was under negotiation from 1987 to July 1990 and has only been in force since 1991. However, some important decisions were taken by the firms during the long period of negotiation leading to the conclusion of the automobile protocol.

4. Micro developments in machine tools, automobiles and biotechnology

a) Machine tools

Machine tools accounted for half of Argentina's exports of capital goods under protocol number one. They are made using skilled labour in small batches by indigenous small and medium size enterprises in Argentina and, although the electronic control unit was not included in the agreement, a relatively advanced technology, numerically controlled lathes constituted an important part of the increase in trade.

Argentina and Brazil are among the small number of developing countries that have an indigenous production of machine tools, including computerised numerically controlled machine tools (NCMTs)[17]. In both countries, production evolved from repair shops established mostly by immigrants of Italian origin and the industry developed rapidly since the 1950s and 1960s.

While Argentine machine tool production rose steadily until 1977, the set of policies put into practice by the government from that date to 1981 completely reversed its previous development. Initially the machine tool producers were able to compensate for the fall in the domestic market by increasing exports. But the contraction of the Latin American market, its main market, and the crisis that followed the introduction of these government policies led to a dramatic decline in production capacity, employment and number of establishments. Within this difficult context, a few firms attempted to keep up with developments at the international level and began to design and produce limited numbers of NCMTs.

In comparison with Argentina, the Brazilian machine tool industry expanded throughout the 1970s. However, the crisis of the 1980s has seriously affected its growth and only in 1988 did it regain the production and employment levels of 1980 only to see production fall again in 1989 to the level of 1981 (Laplane, 1990).

Although Brazilian machine tool output fell over the 1980s, production in 1987-1988 was nonetheless ten times larger in value and nearly six times higher in number of units, than in Argentina. In addition to many small and medium size enterprises, several large domestic and foreign firms account for most of the production in this branch in Brazil. The leading domestic firms are very large enterprises with a diversified product mix and a high level of vertical integration. Foreign subsidiaries make sophisticated machine tools with technology supplied by parent companies, most of which are German. Brazilian global exports of machine tools have been relatively poor in the 1980s and imports very limited. Hence, export and import coefficients are much lower than in Argentina where import coefficients in machine tools have been high despite the low level of investments and non tariff barriers. Export coefficients became very significant with the opening of the Brazilian market.

Despite the reservations of some machine tool firms in Argentina, due to the bigger size and potentially higher competitiveness of Brazilian production, the incorporation of several machine tools in the first common list was well received by the most competitive firms in Argentina. Brazilian machine tool exports to Argentina rose to near $2 million in 1987 but decreased in the following years. In contrast, Argentine exports increased to $11.2 million in 1987, to $22.2 million and $23.5 million in 1988 and 1989, respectively. The share of Argentina in Brazilian imports of machine tools increased from 14 per cent in 1987 to near 20 per cent in 1988. However, Argentine imports were only 5 per cent of Brazilian apparent consumption in that year.

Argentine machine tools in the Brazilian market thus turned out to be more competitive than originally expected[18]. Prices were 20 to 50 per cent lower than those charged for comparable Brazilian machine tools and the quality was similar or slightly better. Although price differentials were subsequently reduced because of the competition between Argentine and Brazilian machinery makers, the gap was not due solely to foreign exchange fluctuations or to short term market considerations but must be explained by a number of structural differences as well.

The lack of competition among the numerous Brazilian machinery makers operating in a market closed to competitive imports, favoured high mark ups which in some cases were used to finance capacity expansion. Despite the economies of scale that can be achieved in such a large market, however, the excessive degree of national (and in some cases of vertical) integration of production in Brazil combined with a high degree of product diversification led to higher production costs there than in Argentina. Not only electronic components (due to the market reserve policy in informatics) but also electrical and some mechanical components had prices well above international ones[19] and suffered from quality problems.

In comparison, Argentine machinery producers enjoyed the advantage of a less expensive skilled labour force, lower prices for some inputs such as foundry parts and some mechanical components, and the possibility of importing some key electrical and electronic components from third countries[20]. When the price differential started to narrow, Argentine machinery makers, moreover, began to compete in an innovative way by customising their products to the special needs of their clients and by offering before and after sales services that were not very common in Brazil. In the case of NCMTs, for example, an engineer from the Argentine company was sent to the Brazilian customer to examine in detail their machining operation requirements with a view to adapting the machine in question to them. In addition, training courses for operating NCMTs are offered free of charge. In offering such services Argentine firms have not only the advantage of their smaller size and hence greater flexibility but they also pay lower salaries to the technicians and engineers who are based in Argentina.

In addition to these innovative steps, in some of the more successful Argentine exporters, the new market has led to a substantial increase in production, though a smaller increase in employment.

Some machine tool producers have incorporated new capital equipment (especially NCMTs) and have started to increase installed physical and technological capacity. In this way a small virtuous circle of higher exports and production and growing capacity expansion began to take place in some of the leading Argentine machine tool makers despite the uncertain domestic economic situation. However, for most Argentine exporters the Brazilian market has been a way to compensate for the tremendous reduction in the domestic market and hence little capacity expansion or technological development has taken place.

Given the importance that the Brazilian market has for leading Argentine machine tool makers, it is surprising that, in this capacity expansion process, no joint ventures with Brazilian partners have yet materialised. Four main reasons were given in interviews with Argentine machine tool makers for this negative development. They were the uncertain Brazilian macroeconomic situation, the unequal size between leading Argentine and Brazilian firms, the lower costs of production in Argentina and the individualistic attitude of machinery producers.

As to the Brazilian machine tool makers, while they have accepted the presence of Argentine products in their market, it is more difficult to imagine that they would take the initiative in establishing joint ventures with Argentine producers. However, and although the pending restructuring of the Brazilian machine tool industry may lead to the search for more advanced technological partners, under the second phase of the integration process it is possible that Argentine firms may be motivated to form strategic partnerships in order to complement existing production lines.

In summary, Argentine firms were able to take advantage of the niches available in the huge Brazilian market. This reduced the prices of some machines, introduced a more customised type of competition and led in a few instances to capacity expansion. In this way some elements of an innovation driven model have appeared in this case. Though important, these elements, however, have not been significant enough to induce Argentine machine tool makers to search for more substantive forms of technology or production co-operation with their Brazilian counterparts.

b) Automobiles and autoparts

In 1991, as part of the protocol governing trade in automobiles and auto parts, 10 000 (later 18 000) finished cars were authorised to be exported by each country to its neighbour for a total of $200 million in finished cars and $600 million in auto parts. Unlike the small and medium-sized machine tool makers in Argentina who were reluctant to enter into complementary activities with their Brazilian counterparts, the same cannot be said for the leading TNCs operating in this branch.

Thus in 1987, as negotiations for an auto protocol got underway, Ford and Volkswagen decided to merge their operations in Argentina and Brazil and constitute a new company called Autolatina. At the same time, both Sevel (the Argentine company in which Fiat hold's a minority share and provides the management and technology) and the Argentine affiliate of Mercedes Benz have established complementation agreements with their Brazilian counterparts, to increase bilateral trade in auto parts. In 1991 the Argentine affiliate of Renault which had been reluctant to enter into the agreement, finally concluded a complementation deal with Volvo of Brazil, as part of the accords celebrated by both companies at the international level. These developments are surprising in view of the parallel development paths pursued by firms in this industry since their establishment in the 1950s and hence the established interests which the integration process confronts. How the present situation differs from the past thus needs to be explained.

Created with the participation of American and European TNCs, the Brazilian auto industry grew over the 1960s and 1970s reaching a maximum production of nearly 1.2 million vehicles in 1980. As the recession deepened, production fell to about 800 000 units, rising to one million vehicles in 1986, 1988 and 1989, and declining to a bit more than 900 000 units in 1990. Over the same period the number of firms contracted and with only three major automobile producers left, Autolatina, General Motors and Fiat, the industry easily achieved the scale requirements of mass production.

Brazilian exports started in the early 1970s through export promotion schemes negotiated by the Government with the leading firms. Since 1975 the trade balance in this branch has been positive and in the 1980s exports compensated for the abrupt reduction in the internal market and by contributing 25-35 per cent of the volume produced helped to keep production levels high. Exports not only comprised finished cars, trucks and buses exported mainly to developing countries and accounting for more than half of total exports, but also engines and autoparts, exported primarily to developed countries. In 1990, however, exports fell and the prospects of both car and autoparts exports do not seem favourable for the 1990s (Ferro, 1990).

Despite the significant growth in exports, the Brazilian automobile industry has serious competitive problems. Four major Brazilian plants were systematically studied as part of an MIT automobile project and the findings can be summarised as follows (Womack, 1990; Womack, Jones and Roos, 1990; Ferro, 1990).

The Brazilian plants lag far behind world average practice, regarding productivity (48 hours per vehicle in comparison with 16 hours in Japan), quality (even in vehicles made for export to the United States), level of automation and product age (11. 4 years, the oldest of the sample). Brazilian plants were behind not only producers from industrialised countries but also those from Mexico and East Asia. However, in some plants elements of lean production[21] had already been introduced, though without changing the basic manufacturing approach followed in mass production.

Contrary to most explanations, the Brazilian productivity gap was not due to the two more obvious factors: the low levels of automation and the complexity of the product mix. Rather management practices, such as poor factory organisation, work systems and human resources policies, were key to explaining the competitive position of Brazilian plants. Additional problems were created by the poor relations between parent companies and subcontractors and by the old design of products and hence their poor manufacturability. According to this study a strategy based on long product lives, highly standardized design and competition in world markets on the basis of price (as was the case with exports of cheap cars in the mid 1980s) is no longer valid in the 1990s.

A more promising path for Brazil in the 1990s would consist of three elements according to the MIT authors. First is the introduction of lean production systems, mainly by inviting Japanese firms into the industry. In this connection, they found that Honda's motorcycle plant at Manaus, far up in the Amazon, demonstrated that lean production can work in Brazil under the most demanding conditions and hence should also work in Sao Paulo. Second, is to increase competition by allowing imports of whole vehicles and parts. Third, taking into account a world trend in the automotive industry towards operating on a regional basis, Brazil will need to integrate its production system with its neighbours, beginning with Argentina.

Output in Argentina peaked in 1974 when more than 320 000 units, made with a high level of local integration, were produced. In the late 1970s the industry underwent major changes in the wake of the Argentine government's decision to permit imports of motor cars and higher import content allowances. Several TNCs, GM, Chrysler, Citroen and Peugeot chose to leave the country. Only Ford, Renault, Sevel (a local company that took over the Fiat and Peugeot facilities in 1982) and Volkswagen which acquired Chrysler's assets in 1979-1980 remained.

With the crisis, production levels fell to about 150 000 units per year in the early 1980s, rose to 193 000 units in 1987, dropped to only 100 000 units in 1990 and as economic conditions improved in 1991, rose again to 150 000 units. With the fall in production levels, reduced local integration requirements and very small exports not only did the industry's contribution to total GDP decrease from 5.2 per cent to 3.9 per cent, but employment fell from 55 000 to 19 000 people and the annual trade deficit in this sector increased from \$53 million in 1965-1975, to \$124 million in 1976-1983 and to \$183 million current dollars in 1984-1987 (Cardozo, 1989).

Following a methodology similar to that employed in the MIT study, it was found that Argentine plants had even lower productivity levels than their Brazilian counterparts (on average 55.6 working hours per vehicle) while both product age (10. 9 years) and level of automation were similar in Brazilian and Argentine plants. Using rough indicators, it was also found that production is run by probably one of the most robust/buffered set of management practices, despite the labour force multiskilling features (Cardozo, 1989).

In this context and without any specific inducements from government, other than exhortations to increase exports and reduce the trade deficit, it is possible to understand the rationale of the current process of complementing Argentine and Brazilian automotive plants.

For the Argentine subsidiaries, integration with Brazil is vital as a means to increase exports of parts and components and thus reverse the traditional negative trade balance. In the medium term there is also the possibility that specialisation in final vehicles will enable plants in both countries to complement production and thereby reduce production costs.

The model these firms have in mind is that followed by Scania (Sweden) which has heavy truck and bus assembly plants in both Brazil and Argentina. In addition to its assembly operations, the plant Scania built in the Northern Argentine city of Tucuman in 1976 specialises in the production of steering gears and paliers which are exported to the company's Brazilian and Swedish plants. Engines and other components for the trucks and buses assembled in Tucuman are mostly imported from plants in Sao Paulo and Sweden. Whereas the Argentine plant has a production capacity of 1750 final units, the Brazilian plant assembles 5 500 units and the Swedish one 20 000. However, it is important to note that in heavy trucks and buses, scale economies are far less important than in automobiles. Production in Argentina and Brazil involves relatively low levels of local integration (42 per cent in the Argentine case).

So far, Scania's operations generated a systematic trade surplus in favour of Argentina, mainly because sales of finished trucks and buses in the internal market have been less significant than originally expected. In contrast to the Brazilian subsidiary hardly any exports were made and thus imports for these units were lower than planned. At the same time, production of gearboxes has expanded from 4 000 to 14 000 units and now accounts for 40 per cent of total sales, instead of 25 per cent as originally planned.

Gearboxes are manufactured in Argentina with advanced machinery mostly imported (though some machines were provided by a leading Argentine machinery maker) using total quality principles (transferred by Swedish engineers) and with a labour productivity not too different from that obtained in Sweden. Just-in-time methods for keeping inventories, however, are hardly applied given the customs and foreign exchange problems for the imported parts and components and the lack of reliability in domestic suppliers. However, stocks have been reduced as far as possible due to the high financial costs of keeping them[22].

The main rationale behind the merger of Ford and VW to create Autolatina is to achieve large scale and thus to be able to specialise Argentine and Brazilian plants in the production of parts and components thereby obtaining lower unit costs. Assembly of the final vehicle will be continued in each country, though in theory it would be better to also specialise the assembly process, for example, of cars in Brazil and trucks in Argentina. Some minor specialisation in car production is, however, expected.

In addition to bilateral trade in final vehicles which in the case of Autolatina amounts to one third of Argentine exports and more than half of the Brazilian exports[23], and growing trade in parts of components[24], the company is building a new plant in Argentina to produce 200 000 gearboxes per year, using state of the art manufacturing technology. Production will be mostly for export to Brazil. With the export of gearboxes, Autolatina aims at compensating in 1993 the foreign exchange costs of importing parts and components from Brazil and other countries for its vehicle assembly operations in Argentina[25].

A similar strategy of compensating component imports from Brazil, Italy and France has been followed by Sevel which is expanding its facilities to manufacture engines for export to Brazil and Italy. Sevel is also producing a GM pick up vehicle under the Chevrolet name with engines and other parts imported from Brazil. Regarding trade in finished cars, Sevel is exporting a 5-door Fiat UNO to Brazil and importing the 3-door Fiat UNO and other more sophisticated models of this car from Brazil. The Argentine subsidiary of Mercedes Benz, which used to have a high trade deficit, is following the same approach by bringing, from Brazil, a plant to make 50 000 gearboxes in Argentina. The gearboxes will then be exported to Brazil and other countries.

The Renault subsidiary in Argentina, currently in serious financial difficulty and now offered for sale, had built a plant specialised in dies whose production is mostly for export. With the export of dies and other items such as castings, the Renault subsidiary also expects to reverse the trade deficit incurred by its operations in Argentina.

From the above examples it is evident that low skilled labour costs and a good mechanical tradition are facilitating the specialisation of Argentine plants in the manufacture of complex parts for both the Argentine and Brazilian market. However, in contrast to machine tools, these products are made in capital intensive facilities using sophisticated machinery that has mainly been imported, so many of the technological and economic benefits of backward linkage are lost here. Nonetheless, the overall impact on trade and production costs is positive.

For the subsidiaries operating in Brazil, imports of auto parts from Argentina are, for the time being, a means of reducing some of the costs associated with high domestic integration and reliance on local parts producers. It is thus understandable that the delays in putting into practice the automobile protocol were mostly due to the opposition of independent Brazilian autoparts makers who did not want competition from Argentina.

Developments over the past several years suggest that TNC subsidiaries operating in Argentina are mainly transforming themselves into autoparts makers while continuing to assemble cars with a relatively low degree of local integration and poor production management. Of course, if production reaches more reasonable levels than has been the case over the 1980s, it would be possible to justify the necessary investments in automation, management and product design to approach world standards (Cardozo, 1989).

In view of recent trends that show a decline in interest by automobile and autoparts producers to source in developing countries (see Hoffman & Kaplinsky, 1988), it appears that the specialisation followed by Argentine subsidiaries only makes sense as part of a regional strategy.

The emerging pattern of specialisation in the Argentine-Brazil case, however, seems quite different from that implemented by Toyota and Nissan within ASEAN. In contrast to ASEAN, a very important and integrated automobile production within South America already exists in Brazil. Hence any regional strategy depends basically on the restructuring of the auto industry in that country where, as previously noted, very traditional non Japanese subsidiaries operate and this, in turn, depends not only on the policies adopted by the Brazilian government particularly with regard to new entrants and to a continuation of the trade liberalisation process but also upon the strategies that will be pursued by both existing firms and potential newcomers.

c) Biotechnology

In protocol number nine, an Argentine-Brazilian Biotechnological Centre, *Centro Argentino Brasileño de Biotecnología* (CABBIO), was created to foster collaborative research projects to be undertaken by universities, public research institutions and private firms in topics of common interest for both countries. Human resources were also to be developed through an Argentine-Brazilian School in Biotechnology.

It was initially expected that each country would provide a total of $10 million over a five year period to finance CABBIO. However, in the 1987-1990 period Argentina allocated only $760 000 and Brazil $1.5 million. For the 1991 budget, Brazil allocated $600 000 and Argentina promised $450 000[26].

Not only have the actual resources available to CABBIO fallen far below original expectations, but it has become clear that the Argentine government has given a lower priority to this joint venture. Thus, despite a higher contribution of $478 000 as compared with $396 000 from Brazil in 1987-1988, the Argentine grant in 1989 fell to $42 000 and the Centre was virtually closed. With great effort, the new Argentine Director of the Centre obtained additional resources in 1990 and 1991 but still the Argentine contribution lags far behind that of Brazil. This has had negative consequences for the activities CABBIO was designed to stimulate and financially support.

With regard to human resource development, in addition to a meeting organised in April 1988 in Curitiba where more than a hundred students from both countries attended lectures by Argentine and Brazilian experts on a variety of topics, the activities of the Biotechnology School are organised through courses offered by Brazilian and Argentine research and teaching institutions each year. In 1988, two such courses were organised in each country. In 1989 four courses were offered in Brazilian institutions but only one in the National Institute of Agricultural Technology in Argentina and in 1990-1991 seven courses were offered in Brazil and four in Argentina.

From ten to twenty graduate students received scholarships from the joint School to attend the two to four week courses in each other's country. Despite their short duration, these courses have apparently been useful not only in providing graduate training but also in facilitating further co-operation between institutions not only in Buenos Aires, Sao Paulo and Rio de Janeiro but also in centres located elsewhere in Argentina and Brazil.

The main purpose of CABBIO, however, was to finance joint research projects on selected topics[27] as submitted by research centres or universities of both countries with the participation in principle of a private firm. Of the nineteen joint projects originally approved, eight have actually started and a few are nearly completed. The average cost of each research project has been low and ranged from a high of $200 000 for a project to develop diagnostic tests for hepatitis to a low of $25 000 in the case of a project involving the cultivation of a type of crustacean. As of 1991, 80 per cent of the budget for these eight projects had been provided, but with significant delays. With its current budget, the Centre aims to provide the remaining 20 per cent and to finance two new research projects, among which is the most expensive of all.

Evaluations undertaken by the research steering committee have been positive and the findings of one project (on crustaceans) are ready to be transferred to the private sector. However, in this particular case there are legal problems regarding the proprietary technology that need to be resolved.

The research communities of both countries seem to be pleased by the actual and especially by the potential opportunities offered by the ongoing co-operation[28], although they are critical of the limited financial support coming from government, especially in Argentina.

At the level of private firms, these research projects seem to be received with scepticism. It is interesting to mention, in this connection, that the Centre is not supporting the only binational R&D joint venture currently in operation[29]. In this undertaking Biotica, an Argentine firm, and Agroceres, the leading Brazilian seed company, have established a company, Biocedes, to develop high quality potato seeds for both markets. Initially the project was supported by the Centre. When this funding was discontinued, the project was fortunate in being able to secure other funding. Much of the development process, for example, takes place in the South of Argentina where there are good ecological conditions. The work is done by Argentine scientists from a leading biotechnology company, Polychaco, with the help of the National Institute of Agricultural Technology.

The Brazilian company supports part of the development costs of this project, but is not currently doing any major biotechnological research of its own, as was the case after 1985, when it took majority control of Biomatrix, a company formed the previous year by researchers at the Federal University of Rio de Janeiro to produce and sell tissue culture products, especially vegetables and ornamental plants[30]. Despite some initial success, the products developed by Biomatrix were too expensive for the Brazilian market and lacked the legal protection to export to developed countries (like Holland). At the same time, Agroceres' main seed business was not generating sufficient resources to enable it to invest further in Biomatrix and in late 1989 the company was closed[31]. Similar difficulties have affected a number of other Brazilian biotech companies that started operations at the end of the 1970s. Bioplanta, a company created by British American Tobacco, and set up in

Campinas with a large number of researchers, specialising in fruit and forestry plants, is a case in point[32].

Whereas agricultural biotechnological companies in Brazil have been facing difficulties in their recent growth, the government has allocated important resources to finance research at the university level and to provide new equipment for university laboratories, especially in Sao Paulo and Campinas Universities. In 1987, for example, Brazil spent $150 million on biotechnology (Sorj and Wilkinson, 1990). From the current World Bank supported programme for the Development of Science and Technology, $68 million (out of a total of $300 million) have been allocated to biotechnology research projects.

Argentina has a solid base in biochemistry and molecular biology (especially in the Campomar Institute led by Nobel Prize winner Leloir). It is also one of the few developing countries with an important segment of the pharmaceutical industry in domestic hands and with some of those companies successfully entering into health biotechnology. In addition, the interest shown in biotechnology by some food producers, the good research record of the National Institute of Agriculture Technology in maize hybrid seeds and generally in plant genetics are certainly important factors in encouraging research co-operation in this promising new technology. However, in contrast to Brazil the public funds allocated to R&D in biotechnology in 1988 were insignificant, less than $2 million, if the commitment to CABBIO is excluded. Privately financed R&D was estimated to be about $2.2 million in the same year (Bercovich and Katz, 1990). Though the significant participation of private firms in R&D is an interesting development, still the low level of resources allocated in Argentina to biotechnology is shocking.

The Brazilian situation is a complete contrast. Despite the setbacks of some private biotechnological companies and the fact that the pharmaceutical industry in Brazil is almost completely in the hands of TNCs with almost no R&D activities in the country, public institutions have played an important research role. In health biotechnology, the Oswaldo Cruz and Butanta Institutes have done research on and produced vaccines and serums for many years. In industrial biotechnology, IPT in Sao Paulo, and EMBRAPA for plant genetics, the several university research centres, the new university-industry biotechnology complex in Rio de Janeiro, Biorio, and the significant number of private companies operating in this emerging industry (Sorj and Wilkinson, 1990) all give a clear indication of the importance that biotechnology has been receiving in Brazil.

As a result of their contrasting situations, interests of both researchers and firms in the two countries differ. For Argentine researchers co-operation with Brazil in biotechnology is a means to access funds and research facilities that are not available at home. Whereas the scarce funds assigned to CABBIO are thus a major source of financing for Argentine research groups, for Brazilian researchers they constitute only a small addition to other resources. For Brazilian researchers, however, co-operation with Argentina could complement their ambitious programmes by drawing on the weak but still active Argentine research groups with their good scientific tradition in biochemistry and molecular biology. Further co-operation in research, however, implies a commitment from the Argentine government that has not thus far been forthcoming.

Insofar as private firms are concerned, the fact that biotechnology is mainly an emerging industry should imply that the defensive attitudes found in other more established sectors would not exist here. However, despite efforts made by CABBIO and by some private fora, the recent financial difficulties faced by some of the larger private firms in Brazil and in Argentina have operated against any further moves towards co-operation. Moreover, although the very small size of many of the enterprises formed by university researchers might create an interest in joint efforts to exploit technologies for both markets, this very factor makes such collaborative ventures more difficult, particularly in the current economic situation and given a policy framework that is far from conducive.

5. Issues raised by the new phase

The new phase of economic integration is characterised by the decision to reach a very ambitious target, the creation of a common market, in a short period of time. Although the joint working groups that are to tackle the difficult issues of policy co-ordination and harmonization have already had several meetings, so far the most tangible effect of the decision to create a Mercosur has been the automatic across the board reduction in tariff rates on goods traded among the member countries that began in January 1991.

Although the Asunción Treaty explicitly mandates the holding of sectoral negotiations with a view to the signing of complementation agreements in steel, petrochemicals and chemicals, textiles, shoes, paper, electronics, agroindustries and automobiles, several of these branches are on the exclusion list. Negotiations, however, have already begun to take place at the private sector level without any government guidelines. The stimulus in the new model thus rests almost exclusively on trade preferences.

Yet in contrast to the previous phase in which the integration process was conceived as a way to reduce the levels of protection accorded to many activities that no longer needed it in a more gradual and negotiated manner than in schemes for unilateral import liberalisation, in the new phase the impact of trade preferences seems far more limited and uncertain, especially for Brazil. Whereas trade preferences in a context of unilateral opening are expected to lead to less trade diversion, the possibilities of trade creation in value added activities will depend very much on the way the restructuring process is carried out in each economy and the seriousness with which Brazil and Argentina take the Mercosur in their growth strategies.

a) Trade and industrial policies in Brazil and Argentina

The main policy objective of the General Guidelines on Industrial and Trade Policy announced by the Brazilian government in June 1990, is to increase efficiency in the production of goods and services through the modernisation and restructuring of the manufacturing sector. The principal instruments to achieve this objective are trade and competition policy, the Industrial Competitiveness Programme and the Brazilian Programme on Quality and Productivity.

Existing tariffs with an average of 35 per cent and extreme rates of 0 and 105 per cent are being reduced in a gradual manner since 1991, with a view to reaching a range of from 0 to 40 per cent with a modal tariff rate of 20 per cent and an average of 14.2 per cent in 1994. A 40 per cent rate is only reserved for products to be especially protected for the purpose of technological learning or to meet other criteria fixed by the government. At the same time, non-tariff measures are also being sharply reduced.

Both the Programmes on Industrial Competitiveness and on Quality and Productivity are aimed at increasing the competitiveness of Brazilian goods and services. The former does so by focusing on the development of high tech branches and the restructuring of existing sectors. The latter, launched in November 1990, is to encourage the Brazilian modernisation effort by promoting quality and productivity.

On paper, the trade and industrial policy regulations that the Brazilian government has formulated are a significant departure from the traditional protectionist policies followed thus far. At the same time, to the extent that trade liberalisation is conceived as a gradual process in which explicit industrial and technological policies are supposed to operate, the Brazilian approach also differs from the neoliberalism applied in Argentina and other Latin American countries.

In practice, however, the deep recession that is affecting Brazilian industry, the lack of compensation through exports that took place in the early 1980s because of the exchange policy and other factors, the unsuccessful attempts to reduce inflation through heterodox and orthodox measures, and the difficult external debt situation, are all factors contributing to a climate of pessimism and uncertainty. Moreover, whereas trade liberalisation measures are being applied more or less on schedule, the incentives for restructuring and modernising the manufacturing sector for the most part have not been implemented. Key decisions concerning industrial restructuring thus appear to have simply been postponed.

Meanwhile, the Argentine government has taken significant steps towards unilateral trade liberalisation in 1990 and 1991. As of November 1991 five levels of tariffs are in force: 35 per cent for automobiles and electronic products, 22 per cent for all final goods, 13 per cent for inputs 5 per cent for non-produced inputs and 0 per cent for non-produced capital goods. The average tariff was 11.2 per cent and the mode 5 per cent. Although specific duties have been eliminated, excise taxes are higher for imported than for locally produced goods and quotas exist for automobile imports.

In the second half of 1990, the overvalued Argentine currency, coupled with a deep recession, reduced the impact of rapid trade liberalisation on imports. In 1991 imports grew significantly. However, it is still too early to assess how local producers have been affected by the new situation.

Unlike Brazil, only two industrial policy instruments were used in Argentina — the public procurement law and subsidies under the Industrial Promotion law. When the Menem government took office in July 1989 these measures were partially suspended for two years and then abolished. Something similar happened with export promotion subsidies and financing that, in any case, have partially lost their importance in recent years. At the same time, the government launched a privatisation programme in public services such as telephones and airlines, railways, and some intermediate industries like petrochemicals, steel and defense production.

Until early 1991, therefore, the Argentine government had no policies in the industrial area except trade liberalisation and privatisation. Since Mr Cavallo was appointed Ministry of Economics in January 1991, attempts have been made to reach agreements with firms in important branches to reduce prices in the domestic market and increase production levels. In addition, though no clear indication of any industrial or technological policy has yet emerged, in the new regime for automobile production announced in January 1992, tariff rates and quotas are used as part of a scheme to restructure the industry.

b) Likely scenarios

Given the macroeconomic problems that both countries are facing, it is reasonable to assume that, despite the political will, the deadline of 1995 for achieving a common market will have to be postponed. This is all the more likely if the current unilateral liberalisation programme cannot be sustained in the medium term in Argentina for balance of payments or other reasons and/ or the Brazilian tariff reduction programme is not applied as envisaged. Under these conditions, although in theory bilateral trade liberalisation may still be applied, and hence trade preferences become more important, this is unlikely to occur. This should not, however, be taken to mean that the integration process will end in total failure.

If it is assumed that Argentina is able to keep inflation under control and Brazil has some success in reducing inflation, exchange rate fluctuations will be reduced and hence agreed trade preferences should become more significant. In this context, the likely impact of the integration process would depend to a large degree upon the reactions of key economic actors to the general incentives provided by the evolving macroeconomic environment, upon the trade and industrial policies in Brazil and Argentina, and upon the way pending issues such as the sectoral agreements, common external tariff and foreign exchange policies are approached[33].

For firms based in Argentina, a larger market, greater protection vis-à-vis third countries in Brazil than in Argentina at least for the time being, trade preferences and favourable transport costs[34] are opportunities opened by the ongoing process. At the same time, competitive imports entering with lower tariffs and enjoying lower transportation costs are a threat to several branches in Argentina.

For Brazil, the more drastic unilateral opening reduces the size of trade preferences, nonetheless Brazilian firms might benefit from reduced transportation costs in their exports to Argentina and from sourcing inputs at lower prices (and transportation costs) from Argentina.

Overall, greater imports from Argentina should not be a serious threat to Brazilian firms. However, for some agroindustrial activities, mostly in the Southern States and/or for some sensitive products in specific branches, imports from Argentina are certainly a problem. Furthermore, the way the rules of origin are negotiated is a critical issue for Brazilian enterprises in order to avoid the entry of third country products via Argentina or Uruguay.

For existing TNC subsidiaries, an expanded market will require a significant restructuring process by which affiliates located in Argentina (and in some cases in Brazil) will become more specialised in certain product lines; production may eventually be discontinued in one location and subsidiaries may become more integrated with other offshore plants. In this way rationalised investments would reduce transaction costs and improve resource allocation.

An expanded market may also attract fresh foreign direct investment, and TNCs (or eventually binational enterprises) may be able to increase their internalisation advantages by allocating value-adding activities in view of the new configuration of locational advantages among members of the subregion.

In this scenario whereas industrial restructuring is certainly going to be the name of the game, depending on how trade liberalisation is combined with industrial and technology policies and how sectoral agreements are negotiated and applied, two different variants can be imagined.

In the first variant, trade would expand but inter-sectoral specialisation and some cartelised intra-industry trade would mainly prevail. In the second variant, trade would also expand but the industrial restructuring process would mostly favour intra-industry specialisation with a view to creating dynamic comparative advantages. Given the present orientation of public policies in both countries, the first variant seems far more likely than the second. Of course, a range of combinations are possible, but it is easier to think in terms of two broad pictures.

Assuming that Brazilian trade and industrial policies are ineffective in stimulating the modernisation and technological upgrading of the many currently non competitive branches in the manufacturing sector, it is likely that mainly firms engaged in low value added resource-based and low wage labour-intensive branches would be successful in the medium term.

If a similar situation takes place in Argentina, a different set of resource-based firms, and eventually a few skill- and capital-intensive firms in sectors in which private sectoral agreements are likely to be negotiated, would succeed as well.

In this variant, given the reduced transportation costs and the existence of tariff preferences, the expansion of bilateral trade would mainly take the form of intersectoral trade, primarily based on relatively low value added activities. Argentine industry would continue the chaotic restructuring process that has been taking place since the mid 1970s and become mostly a supplier of agricultural and agroindustrial goods, and perhaps some energy intensive commodities[35], to the Brazilian market. In exchange, Argentina would probably import many intermediate goods and some scale intensive capital and consumer goods from Brazil. Most high tech goods would continue to be imported by both countries from suppliers in the industrialised countries.

Whereas in terms of existing factor endowments this variant certainly leads to trade creation and minimises trade diversion, the dynamic effects associated with a furthering of the industrialisation process are limited. Insofar as intra-industry trade would take place through private arrangements defending established positions, and intersectoral specialisation is based largely on static comparative advantages, the negotiation of a common external tariff, however, will be easier than in the second variant.

The second variant assumes that the existence of a more stable and conducive environment will provide incentives for physical and technological investments. This, coupled with the eventual application of industrial and technology policies in Brazil, will help to foster an industrial revival through technological change and, at the same time, facilitate the restructuring of skill-intensive branches using means other than traditional market reserve policies. Under these assumptions, Brazilian industry would eventually act as a locomotive for the sub-regional integration process not only because of its size but also because of the opportunities it might open for trade creation and for technological co-operation with the other partners.

The gradual opening of the Brazilian market and the industrial and technological policies to be applied there provide an opportunity to orient domestic industrial restructuring in Argentina via proactive policies that foster externalities and dynamic comparative advantages. For Argentine skill-intensive branches, in particular, the most advantageous situation would be the eventual adoption of a pro-active policy in Argentina closely co-ordinated with Brazilian industrial and technological policies. If this does not occur, in view of Argentina's unilateral market opening, skill intensive branches may continue their historic deterioration, missing yet another opportunity.

For those branches like textiles, steel, petrochemicals and paper where Argentina does not seem to be generally competitive with Brazil, Argentine firms may survive either by defending their current market positions through cartelised agreements with their Brazilian counterparts, or by specialising in certain product lines through rationalised investments to be able to develop a more dynamic intra-industry trade. Unless governments are prepared to issue precise guidelines to the private sector actors to ensure that sectoral agreements conform to domestic policy objectives and enhance social net benefits and externalities, it is likely that some form of cartelisation would prevail in such agreements. This would tend to reduce the dynamic effects of the integration process.

For the branches in which the competitiveness of Argentine production is mostly based on the availability of natural resources (like agroindustries and to some extent petrochemicals), the integration process with Brazil should in principle not create major problems. Even more, the possibilities of operating in a larger market would certainly facilitate scale economies and capacity expansion jointly with Brazilian partners.

While in principle the intra-industry specialisation of the second variant may facilitate the creation of dynamic comparative advantages it is by no means assured. Active industrial and technological policies pursued in both countries and specific guidelines for sectoral agreements, if well managed and implemented, should increase the developmental possibilities of this process. At the same time, the complexity of the issues will make the negotiation of an external common tariff and policy co-ordination in this field an extremely difficult but very challenging task.

6. Concluding remarks

The cases studied in Section 4 clearly indicate that, at least from the Argentine side, significant advantages in terms of trade expansion can be obtained from the integration process. It is also possible that some industrial complementation may take place where actors like TNCs or large domestic groups are involved. Unfortunately, in the case of technological efforts in which small and medium size firms or the research community are the principal actors, the lack of government support and specific policies have thus far limited the development of greater co-operation.

Though significant at microeconomic or at very specific industry levels, the small changes noted in the machine tool, automobile and autoparts and biotechnology case studies are not important enough to modify the overall negative evaluation of the initial phase of the integration process. Even more importantly, they do not support the orthodox view that all governments need to do is liberalise trade (and eventually co-ordinate exchange rate policy), and industrial restructuring and technological co-operation will follow.

No attempt to build on the failures of the initial phase, however, has been made in the current phase. Integration is now proceeding through generalised trade preferences, and technology and industrial issues are hardly on the agenda. Bilateral trade deregulation, moreover, is being undertaken in a context of unilateral trade opening thus giving less room for both trade diversion and creation. Under these conditions, the likelihood of making progress in industrial and technological co-operation seems rather limited.

The future of this sub-regional integration attempt, however, will largely depend on how key economic actors react to the general incentives provided by the evolving macroeconomic environment, the trade and industrial policies in Brazil and Argentina and the sectoral agreements, common external tariff and foreign exchange policies that will be negotiated in the context of the Mercosur itself. Two scenarios are sketched out in this paper. In the first variant it is assumed that Brazilian trade and industrial policies are unsuccessful in stimulating the technological upgrading of non-competitive manufacturing branches and Argentine industry restructuring accentuates the bias in favour of agroindustrial and eventually energy intensive goods. Under these circumstances trade expansion would mainly follow the lines of intersectoral specialisation, on the basis of relatively low value added activities. However, some intra-industry trade may take place in this variant through cartelisation agreements negotiated by the private sector operating in Argentine and Brazilian non competitive branches.

If Brazilian policies are effective in restructuring the manufacturing sector through technological modernisation and foster an efficient entry into the production of high tech goods, and Argentina takes advantage of this opportunity to restructure its own non-competitive branches and foster skilled intensive production, a second variant can be imagined. In this variant, trade expansion would mainly take the form of intra-industry specialisation on the basis of dynamic comparative advantages. To prevent defensive actions from established producers, sectoral agreements would have to be negotiated with clear guidelines and participation from the two governments. At the same time, the external common tariff and rules of origin would become crucial points in the negotiation agenda along with policy co-ordination in the trade, industrial and technology fields.

Despite the fact that the general orientation in Argentina and Brazil does not provide many grounds for expecting the emergence of the second variant, in which innovation driven forms of south-south co-operation may flourish, it is also true that changing conditions at both the domestic and international levels pose a challenge to the imagination of all relevant private and public actors. This alone makes a strong case for the need to develop newer and more effective policy lines and actions that go beyond the narrow confines of the Washington consensus in Latin American policy-making.

Notes

1. Comments and suggestions by Lynn Mytelka and Vivianne Ventura Dias on an earlier draft are gratefully acknowledged. The usual caveats apply. The Collor impeachment process and other developments that took place in 1992 such as the huge bilateral trade surplus in Brazil's favour which complicated the Mercosur project, have not be taken into account since the research for this paper was done in 1991 and the last version written in March 1992.

2. See Chapter 1 by Lynn Mytelka in this volume for a discussion of this and other models of regional integration and co-operation.

3. Despite the traditional rivalry between the Argentine and Brazilian armed forces for geopolitical reasons, in 1979 a tripartite agreement (with Paraguay) was signed by both military governments to take advantage of the latter's hydroelectric resources.

4. Both countries are members of the Cairns Group within GATT; however, the outcome of the agricultural negotiations in that forum is far more important for Argentina than for Brazil. Moreover, on most of the new issues, both countries were far apart throughout the 1980s.

5. For a fuller discussion and review of the literature, see Chudnovsky and Porta (1989).

6. The name of the Ministry of Foreign Affairs.

7. Argentina started with 394 excepted items, Brazil 324, Paraguay 439 and Uruguay 960. After the first reduction in the number of exceptions that Argentina and Brazil negotiated in December 1990, they have to reduce the absolute number of exceptions by 20 per cent each calendar year (it means no exceptions by 31 December 1994). In the case of Paraguay and Uruguay the reduction is planned at a lower percentage at the beginning and the aim is to have no exceptions by 31 December 1995.

8. As of November 1991.

9. A good example of the Argentine position towards the US and to Brazil is a recent episode in which the US decided in late April 1991 to export 700 000 tons of subsidised wheat to Brazil, to which Argentina will export 2 million tons in the current year. Besides breaking the gentlemen's agreement of not selling subsidised wheat to Argentina's main partner, the US move has immediately reduced the price of Argentine wheat. The Argentine government has strongly protested. The US explanation is that the export will compete with a subsidised offer from the EEC and it would not affect Argentine exports since the delivery is made in different months and Brazil needs 4 to 4.5 million tons, an amount that Argentine is in no condition to supply. Brazil was in a difficult position. On the one hand, the US offer is a way to reduce cost of wheat imports in a year in which domestic production has fallen. On the other hand, importing subsidised wheat from the US will affect its relationship with Argentina. Eventually a compromise arrangement was accepted under which any private Brazilian purchases after July 10 would have to pay a 29.7 per cent countervailing duty.

10. According to the former Brazilian Minister of Finance an attempt to have a common moratorium was made in late 1988 but failed (Bresser Pereira, 1990).

11. It seems that within manufactures of industrial origin, more significant intra-industrial trade flows started to emerge in items like non electrical machinery, foundry, some chemicals and autoparts. More detailed research and with a longer time perspective would be needed to assess these changes in bilateral trade.

12. The main growth items in Argentine exports to Brazil were dairy products, foundry, non electrical machinery, motor vehicles (mostly auto parts), prepared vegetables and fruits and plastic materials. The composition of imports from Brazil has not changed very much. The main items are iron, organic chemicals, foundry, non electrical machinery, motor vehicles and electrical machinery.

13. Trucks, buses and auto parts were also excluded because they were negotiated in the automobiles agreement.

14. In the text of protocol number one the following figures (in millions of US dollars) are mentioned for expected bilateral trade in capital goods: in 1987, 300; in 1988, 400; in 1989, 500 and in 1990, 750. In practice total trade of the goods included in the universe of the protocol were 124 in 1987, 134 in 1988 and 166 in 1989.

15. Taking place one year in an Argentine city and the other in a Brazilian city.

16. In addition to the points made by Erber, it was evident that Argentina was not eager to support Brazil in its dispute with the US regarding informatics policy, suggesting that also in this case, common cause with the North avoided crucial issues.

17. Studies by made Fleury (1988), Erber (1989) and Laplane (1990) give a good account of the Brazilian machine tool industry. Our own studies (Chudnovsky and Groissman, 1987; Chudnovsky 1988 and 1990) examine the evolution of the Argentine machine tool sector and the impact of the agreement with Brazil. In addition, interviews with Brazilian and Argentine machine tool producers undertaken in 1990 were used to prepare this section.

18. In a study of price differentials between European, Asian and comparable Argentine machine tools, we found that Argentine prices were a bit higher than Taiwan and South Korean prices, similar to the Spanish prices and lower than the prices of Japanese and other

European countries. In NCMTs Argentine prices were much higher than those machines coming from Asian developing countries but similar to the Japanese ones (Chudnovsky and Groisman, 1987). It is important to take into account that very few NCMTs were made in Argentina before the agreement with Brazil. With the agreement production increased and reached 100 units in 1988 (of which most are lathes). Brazilian production of these machines was 1041 units in 1988.

19. The electronic unit for the NCMTs was sold in Brazil at prices two or three times higher than the international ones, except in the very simple units.

20. Only 20 per cent of the value of products included in the common list can be imported from third countries. In Argentina, the degree of local integration is somewhat lower than in Brazil where it is about 90-95 per cent. Basically Argentine machinery makers import the electronic control unit from Germany or Japan and some hydraulic and electrical parts. They have benefited not only from the technological advances made in electronic units but also from the continuous reduction in their prices at the international level. In Brazil machinery makers are required to use domestically made NC units and almost all hydraulic, electrical and mechanical components.

21. Lean production (or toyotism) is "lean" because "it uses less of everything compared with mass production — half the human effort in the factory, half the manufacturing space, half the investment in tools, half the engineering hours to develop a new product in half the time. Also, it requires keeping far less than half the needed inventory on site, results in many fewer defects, and produces a greater and ever growing variety of products" (Womack, Jones and Roos, 1990, p. 13).

22. Interview with a Senior Manager at Scania in Argentina.

23. So far they mostly import the 2 door Escort from Brazil and export 4 door Escorts from Argentina.

24. VW's subsidiaries in Argentina and Brazil complement their production of parts and components but thus far compensated trade has been negative for Argentina.

25. Interview with Senior Managers of Autolatina both in Sao Paulo and Buenos Aires.

26. All information regarding CABBIO was given to us by the Argentine and Brazilian Directors of the Centre.

27. Common topics for both countries were triple vaccines, diagnostic tests and vaccines for hepatitis B, antibiotics via fermentation monoclonal antibodies in health biotechnology; improving plant and animal agriculture through biotechnological methods, vaccines and tests for animal use in agricultural biotechnology, and complementary activities such as enzyme production and scaling up for the production of monoclonal antibodies and protein purification.

28. In the interviews undertaken in both Brazil and Argentina, researchers pointed out that the Centre has facilitated co-operation in research which in the past had been very limited.

29. In addition to the joint venture between Biotica and Agroceres, there was an unsuccessful attempt to develop interferon between Biobras (the major Brazilian biotechnology firm in the health sector) and Biosidus (the leading health biotechnology firm in Argentina, owned by the powerful domestic pharmaceutical company Sidus).

30. The following information was obtained in an interview with the Director of Agroceres in Sao Paulo.

31. Agroceres currently employs only a few biotechnology technicians to improve conventional techniques and has a small laboratory to develop new technologies. From the Biomatrix techniques to generate disease-free potato seeds, Agroceres has kept a stock that allows it to participate in the development process with the Argentine firm.

32. See Sorj and Wilkinson, 1990, for a good account of biotechnology development in Brazil.

33. The rigidity of some policy instruments, such as the Argentine foreign exchange convertibility law, in force since April 1991, is itself a problem for economic policy co-ordination.

34. Transportation costs that used to be high between Argentina and Brazil have been reduced in a significant manner over the last few years. The deregulation of the trucking system and modifications in customs procedures have facilitated trade. Maritime transport costs (important only for wheat and iron ore) are still high but it is likely that they will be reduced in the near future.

35. This assumes that the planned privatisation process of the energy sector, in contrast to that of telephone and air services, leads to reasonable prices for the users.

Bibliography

AZAMBUJA, M.C. de (1991), "Initiativa para as Américas e integracao latino-americana: convergencia e divergencia de intereses entre EUA e America Latina", Forum Nacional O Brazil e o Plano Bush, Nobel, Sao Paulo.

BERCOVICH, N. and J. KATZ (1990), *Biotecnología y economía política: estudios del caso argentino*, CEAL-CEPAL, Buenos Aires.

BRESSER PEREIRA, L.C. (1990), "Presupuestos y obstáculos de la integración Argentina-Brazil" in M. Hirst, ed., *Argentina-Brazil: Perspectivas comparativas y ejes de integración*, FLACSO, Ed. Tesis, Buenos Aires.

CAMILIÓN , O. (1987), "Integración Argentina-Brazil: realidades y proyecciones" *Integración Latinoamericana*, Buenos Aires, abril.

CARDOZO, J. (1989), "The Argentine automobile industry: international comparative performance, technological gap and policy issues for the 1990s", M. Phil. thesis, SPRU, Sussex University, England.

CORREA, C. (1989), *Tecnología y desarrollo de la informática en el contexto Norte-Sur*, EUDEBA, Buenos Aires.

CHUDNOVSKY, D. y S. GROISMAN (1987), "La industria argentina de maquinas herramientas para el trabajo de los metales: Situacion actual, contexto internacional y recomendaciones de politica", Proyecto Banco Mundial-Secretaria de Industria y Comercio Exterior, Buenos Aires.

CHUDNOVSKY, D. (1988), "The diffusion and production of new technologies. The case of numerically controlled machine tools", *World Development*, Oxford, Vol. 16, No. 6.

CHUDNOVSKY, D. and F. PORTA (1989), "On Argentine-Brazilian economic integration" *CEPAL Review* No. 39, December.

CHUDNOVSKY, D. (1990), "La competitividad de la industria argentina de maquinas herramientas y el acuerdo de integración con Brazil", Universidade Estadual de Campinas, (mimeo).

ERBER, F. (1989), "The electronic complex and industrial automation: a comparison between Argentina and Brazil", Rio de Janeiro (mimeo).

FERRO, J.R. (1990), "Para sair da estagnacao e disminuir o atraso tecnológico da industria automobilística brasileira", Universidade Estadual de Campinas (mimeo).

FLEURY, A. (1988), "The impact of microelectronics on employment and income in the Brazilian metal-engineering industry", World Employment Programme Research Working Paper 2-22, ILO, Geneva.

HIRST, M. (1987), "Las relaciones Argentina-Brazil: de la asimetría al equilibrio", *Integración Latinoamericana*, Buenos Aires, abril.

HIRST, M. (1990), "Continuidad y cambio del programa de integración Argentina-Brazil", FLACSO, diciembre.

HOFFMAN, K. and R. KAPLINSKY (1988), *Driving Force: The Global Restructuring of Technology, Labour, and Investment in the Automobile and Components Industries*, An UNCTC Study, Westview Press, Boulder, San Francisco.

IGLESIAS, R. (1991), "A política cambial da Argentina e do Brazil no período 1970-1989", in P. Motta Veiga, ed., *Cone Sul: a economia política da integracao*, FUNCEX, Rio de Janeiro.

JAGUARIBE, H. (1987), "La integración Argentina-Brazil", *Integración Latinoamericana*, Buenos Aires, noviembre.

LAPLANE, M. (1990), "Diagnóstico da industria brasileira de máquinas-ferramenta", Universidade Estadual de Campinas (mimeo).

PORTA, F. (1989). "El acuerdo de integración argentino-brasileño en bienes de capital: características y evolución reciente", Centro de Economía Internacional DT 08/89, Buenos Aires.

SORJ, B. and J. WILKINSON (1990), "Biotechnology and developing country agriculture: Maize in Brazil", OECD Development Centre Technical Paper No. 17, Paris.

TAVARES DE ARAUJO, Jr. J. (1988), "Os fundamentos económicos de programa de integracao Argentina-Brazil", *Revista de Economía Política* Sao Paulo, June.

TAVARES DE ARAUJO, Jr. J. (1990), "El programa de integración Argentina-Brazil y las tendencias actuales de la economía mundial", en M. Hirst, ed., *op. cit.*

VAN KLAVEREN, A. (1990). "Democratización y política exterior: el acercamiento entre Argentina y Brazil", *Affers Internacionals*, Barcelona, No. 18.

WILLIAMSON, J. (1990), "What Washington means by policy reform", in J. Williamson ed., *Latin American Adjustment: How much has happened?*, Institute for International Economics, Washington, D.C.

WOMACK, J.P., D.T. JONES, and D. ROOS (1990), *The Machine that Changed the World*, Rawson Associates, New York.

WOMACK, J.P. (1990), "Development strategies for the Brazilian Motor Industry: A global perspective", Universidade Estadual de Campinas (mimeo).

Chapter 6

SOUTH-SOUTH CO-OPERATION: OPPORTUNITIES IN MINERALS DEVELOPMENT

Alyson Warhurst[1]

Le secteur minier est aujourd'hui dans une phase de transition marquée par une libéralisation des procédures d'investissement, par le passage d'une structure d'entreprises publiques à une structure de co-entreprises à capitaux nationaux et internationaux, par la montée en force de l'innovation technologique dans le domaine du traitement des minerais et par un renforcement des réglementations pour la protection de l'environnement. Le chapitre étudie les perspectives qui s'offrent aux pays en développement producteurs de pétrole et de minerais ainsi que les défis qu'ils doivent relever. Ces perspectives et ces défis résultent de la présence de vastes gisements de ressources naturelles et d'une longue expérience dans l'exploration et la transformation de ces ressources. Le chapitre passe en revue quelques exemples récents de coopération sud-sud qui illustrent le rôle que la collaboration dans le domaine technique et les projets communs d'investissement peuvent jouer dans le développement.

The mineral industry is currently undergoing a transition characterised by a liberalisation of investment regimes, a move from state ownership to joint ventures involving both national and international capital, increasing technological innovation in mineral processing and a strengthening of regulatory regimes to improve environmental management. Against this exciting backdrop, this chapter explores the common technological opportunities and challenges faced by mineral and petroleum producing developing countries that result from their rich natural resource base and long histories of accumulated expertise in mining and in mineral processing. It reviews some recent examples of South-South co-operation which illustrate the contribution to development that collaboration in technology development and investment projects may bring.

1. Introduction

The mineral industry is currently undergoing a transition characterised by a liberalisation of investment regimes, a move from state ownership to joint ventures involving both national and international capital, increasing technological innovation in mineral processing and a strengthening of regulatory regimes to improve environmental management. Against this exciting backdrop, this chapter explores the common technological opportunities and challenges faced by mineral producing developing countries (DCs) that result from their rich natural resource base and long histories of accumulated expertise in mining. It reviews some recent examples of south-south co-operation which illustrate the contribution to development that collaboration in technology development and investment projects may bring. It argues that mineral deposits are not confined by political boundaries and therefore pose similar metallurgical and engineering problems for neighbouring countries in their exploitation and management. These in turn require similar solutions, and thus could benefit from shared responses and joint technological efforts. The list of potential areas for such collaboration is quite extensive, for example, Andean mining of the sulphide minerals — copper, gold, silver, zinc, lead and tin — by Chile, Peru, Bolivia, Ecuador and Colombia; Amazonian mining of gold in similar environments by Colombia, Ecuador, Bolivia, Peru and Brazil; salt-flat mining which involves Bolivia, Argentina and Chile in the exploitation of valuable minerals such as lithium; Pacific basin mining of copper and gold by island states like Indonesia, Papua New Guinea and Fiji; African rift valley mining of copper and cobalt by neighbouring countries such as Zambia, Zaire and Uganda; and Caribbean mining which involves Jamaica and Venezuela in the exploitation of bauxite.

There are also common problems faced by petroleum producing DCs, not least with respect to the geologically and geographically specific conditions influencing the location of petroleum reserves and the ways in which they can be optimally exploited. For example, Brazil and China have deep water reserves; Ecuador, Peru and Chile have petroleum reserves in the same long Pacific basin stretching down the west coast of South America; Venezuela and the Caribbean have shallow water petroleum reserves while countries such as Egypt, Nigeria and China also have substantial on-shore reserves with different sets of technology requirements.

Collaboration in technological development and investment projects is particularly important for the many DCs in Africa, Asia and South America which remain dependent on mineral exports for employment, income generation and foreign exchange, after a period of failed industrialisation based on import substitution in the manufacturing sector. In cases like Zambia, Bolivia, Peru and Chile, more than 50 per cent of their foreign exchange earnings have come from mineral exports in recent years, while in other countries including Zimbabwe, Botswana, Papua New Guinea, and to a lesser extent Brazil, mineral production accounts for significant portions of GNP. The extent of these dependencies is shown in Table 1. In spite of their capacity to earn scarce foreign exchange, these countries tend to experience common problems in their economic development. Relative to other DCs they exhibit lower incremental savings rates, greater "technological dualism" (extremes of capital or labour intensity in production), wider inter-sectoral wage differentials, higher unemployment and lower school enrolment ratios. Inflation tends to be higher, agriculture grows more slowly, food constitutes a large share of imports and they experience a number of problems associated with the high instability of export earnings (Nankini, 1979; Daniel, 1986).

Despite their economic difficulties, many of these mineral producing DCs have built up considerable local expertise over time. In part this is due to the gradual professionalisation of mining elites in countries as diverse as Chile, Bolivia, Peru, Brazil, Papua New Guinea, India and Indonesia over the last 50 years. This trend has been the result of two phenomena. First, the tendency for mine ownership to pass down through families, particularly in South America. Second, the move by these elites to send their sons abroad for training in engineering or business management, who then return to take over the family firm. This training, combined with the long build up of hands-on skills in mine management, and local knowledge of the geology and metallurgy of their mineral deposits has led to the development of a new professional class of mine-owners and managers who are fast learning to commercialise their expertise as consultants or industrial partners in mineral projects in their own and other developing countries. Indeed private national mining groups such as these are playing a growing role in the minerals sector of DCs and account for about 25 per cent of mining production in the case of Latin American producers[2].

Table 1. Share of ores and metals in total exports

Region/Country	Total Export Value (US$ mn)		Ores and Metals Share (%)	
	1970	1987	1970	1987
Latin America				
Bolivia	225.4	569.8	88.0	36.4
Jamaica	334.9	705.2	28.0	42.5
Peru	1 044.4	2 576.7	48.4	48.6
Chile	1 233.6	5 101.9	88.1	49.1
Mexico	1 205.4	19 353.8	15.5	6.0
Brazil[a]	2 738.7	26 228.6	10.1	10.2
Cuba	1 046.3	5 401.0	16.7	5.9
Guyana[a]	130.2	218.0	53.4	21.0
Haiti[a]	40.5	170.0	16.9	1.2
Africa				
Zaire[a]	735.4	1 092.0	77.8	50.4
Zambia[a]	994.5	425.0	99.1	92.2
Niger[b]	31.6	454.8	0.2	79.8
Rwanda	24.5	113.8	35.0	1.4
Ghana[c]	425.9	570.6	12.9	5.0
Mauritania	88.8	427.8	88.3	31.2
Liberia[a]	212.6	404.4	73.6	59.7
Sierra Leone[a]	101.5	148.0	18.9	35.9
Senegal[a]	160.6	411.0	9.3	13.2
Zimbabwe[a,d]	844.8	1 018.8	26.0	15.4
Cameroon	225.9	829.4	9.8	8.6
South Africa[e]	2 146.7	17 791.6	22.0	7.7
Gabon[a]	121.0	1 311.5	13.7	7.8
Togo[a]	54.6	182.0	24.9	35.5
Tanzania[a]	236.1	346.0	0.8	5.5
Asia and Oceania				
Laos[f]	7.2	11.3	36.1	11.9
India	2 012.6	11 593.0	11.9	6.7
Indonesia	1 055.1	16 860.9	11.4	4.4
Papua N.G.[g]	85.9	1 172.2	0.8	46.1
Philippines[a]	1 059.7	4 730.0	21.0	10.0
Malaysia	1 686.6	17 920.9	22.6	3.1
Thailand	685.2	11 629.5	14.6	1.6
Australia	4 482.4	24 165.0	22.6	17.8
N. Africa & M. East				
Egypt	761.7	4 351.5	0.6	13.1
Jordan	26.1	730.3	24.3	36.5
Morocco	487.9	2 806.9	32.6	19.0
Tunisia	182.5	2 152.4	19.0	2.1

Notes:
a. Final year: 1986
b. Final year: 1981
c. Final year: 1984
d. Initial year: 1976
e. Final year: 1982
f. Final year: 1974
g. Initial year: 1971

Prepared by D. O'Connor and reproduced in Warhust (1993).

Source: UNCTAD, *Handbook of International Trade and Development Statistics*, 1989.

These enterprises, moreover, are now emerging as the source of a number of exciting innovations in mining production and mineral processing, as will be discussed later in this chapter. In addition professionals who own such enterprises have frequently received governmental appointments to manage or advise the running of state mining corporations. This again has provided important learning opportunities. Considerable engineering, research and operating expertise has been built up in this way, reinforced through training abroad in leading international companies. Research institutions and educational establishments, geared to solving local problems, have also emerged in countries such as Peru, Bolivia and particularly Chile; and they have developed comparative advantages through their crucial knowledge of local geology and engineering conditions. Local consultancy companies, such as URZAM in Bolivia, and professional societies, such as the Society of Mining Engineers of Peru, are also poised to play major roles in the economic development of these countries.

This chapter analyses the relationship between south-south co-operation and the development of technological learning in this sector from two perspectives. First, it investigates changing patterns of technological collaboration between countries and firms over time. The predominance in the 1960s and 1970s of one-way technology transfer from industrialised country-based firms to developing country state corporations, it argues, has given way to more complex and collaborative arrangements. These involve joint R&D, project development and production, between partners in developing countries. Regional technology transfer has become more important and consultants from developing countries are playing a greater role in the design of investment projects in neighbouring economies. Several reasons for these new trends are suggested in the chapter but they all point towards an increase in south-south co-operation through technological collaboration and learning.

Second, the chapter examines the way in which new economic challenges faced by regions in the South, and the growing environmental degradation of their natural resource base, have created new opportunities for south-south collaboration in R&D and in technological innovation to improve environmental management practices. Again the chapter suggests that south-south co-operation, in the forms of joint-ventures, consultancies, training and scientific and technological interchanges, have led to a growth in technological learning over time within developing country institutions and enterprises.

2. Changing patterns of technological collaboration

Technological collaboration involving actors from the South has changed over time as a reflection of the nature of mining investment in their economies. In general terms, three 'eras' can now be identified in their history. First, there was a period of direct foreign investment mainly by multinational mining companies. Second, was the era of state-mining ventures, during which large debts were often accumulated and endemic inefficiencies contributed towards declining levels of productivity and an absence of innovativeness. Third, is the current era of joint ventures, privatisation schemes and dynamic national entrepreneurship. It has been during this third era of mining activities that south-south collaboration has developed to provide a springboard for successful investment projects in minerals development in the South.

Historical investment trends

Historically, the pattern of foreign investment by DC firms, most of which has gone to other DCs, does not appear to have matched their comparative advantages and production profiles at home. It moreover differed substantially from investments by OECD firms abroad. Thus an analysis by Svetlicic (1986) showed that the largest number of affiliates originating in DCs are in manufacturing. In contrast, despite substantial inter-country differences, it is the extractive industry that has traditionally accounted for the largest part of foreign investment by industrialised country firms. Manufacturing, for example, accounted for a relatively small share of investment by American firms abroad, much smaller in proportion than in the case of investment by DC firms. Of the flow of direct foreign investment undertaken by American firms in the period 1977-81, 23.4 per cent was directed to manufacturing. In other OECD countries, the share of manufacturing investment was 28.5 per cent. Primary industry accounted for over 50 per cent of American direct investments abroad[3]. The primary sector which includes agriculture, forestry, fishing, metal mining, oil and gas extraction and non-metallic minerals, however, accounted for only 5.1 per cent of the total number of subsidiaries established by DC firms in other DCs; with mining alone accounting for merely 3.3 per cent (Svetlicic, 1986, p. 70).

This phenomenon introduces into the discussion the possibility of a "mis-match" between the skills, technological knowledge and experience of mining firms in DCs, and DC investment activities abroad in other mineral-producing economies during the first two periods noted above. A number of factors, however, explain this anomaly. In addition to the high capital cost where investments in mining are concerned, the relative abundance of primary commodities in DCs and the historically important role that north-south investments have played in their development have certainly played a role in limiting the extent to which DC investment abroad concentrated in the extractive sector[4].

The growing role of DC participation in their own mineral economies was highlighted by a recent survey of the majority of mining and metals projects undertaken since 1970 (Oman, 1989). This showed that two-thirds of these projects could be categorised as "New Forms of Investment (NFI)". These, Oman defines as: the set of methods (generally, a range of joint venture agreements), by which a foreign company has been able to undertake, and even in certain cases to stimulate, the creation of production capacity in a host country without having to rely on equity ownership to assert partial or total control over the investment project. However, the increased instability of metal markets over the period and the debt burden associated with these projects, meant that these new forms of investment have not yet resulted in the expected flow of commercial returns for DC partners — which in many cases were the state in the host country (Bomsel, 1990).

New partnerships

Following the new trend of liberalisation in many of the mineral producing economies, there has been a tendency for foreign capital to seek local entrepreneurs to form partnerships. In Bolivia, for example, RTZ formed a partnership with COMSUR and Battle Mountain Gold with Inti Raymis. In Chile a new bioleaching plant, to be located at Andacollo, will be a joint venture between Placer Dome (USA) and Empressa Nacional de Minería (ENAMI); the Lince copper project of acid leaching followed by solvent-extraction/electro-winning is a joint venture between Michilla (Chile), Offshore Equities of the Chemical Bank of New York, and Outokumpu Oy of Finland. The Quebrada Blanca project is interesting in that it will use a proprietary copper recovery technology developed by the innovative local company Pudahuel. This constitutes the 10 per cent equity contribution to the project of that company which has formed a joint-venture to exploit the deposit with ENAMI, COMINCO (Canada), and the Teck Corporation (USA).

All these projects are very new and have just reached the initial investment or early operating stages of their cycles. The interesting issue with regard to south-south co-operation is whether the learning experience of these new north-south partnerships prompts the DC partners to look for new collaborative arrangements with other mining companies abroad.

Already, it is possible to identify a growing number of individual cases of south-south technological collaboration. These include:

— the commercialisation of "disembodied technology";
— joint ventures in mining, mineral and oil exploration;
— collaboration between engineering consultancy firms;
— university-industry linkages;

— consortia involving technology transfer, innovation and training.

In the following sections, we will look at a number of examples of these new south-south technology partnerships.

South-south investment

Examples of the successful south-south commercialisation of 'disembodied' technology include: Petrobras of Brazil, with its deep water drilling expertise in China and the North Sea (Noroil, June, 1988) which will be discussed in more detail below; CODELCO and Pudahuel of Chile in Africa and India; Peruvian mining consultants working in Africa and Bolivian tin mining engineers working in Malaysia. There have also been reports recently in the industry press about Brazilian technology being used by a gold refinery, Mineras de Corales, in Rivera Province in Uruguay (*Mining Magazine*, November 1990, p. 392) and a joint agreement signed between the Cuban and Indian governments for collaborative efforts in the exploitation of their respective deposits of nickel (*Mining Magazine*, May 1991, p. 332).

Examples of joint-venture projects amongst DC consultants and suppliers to the mining industry are also growing, in part as a direct reflection of increasing south-south collaboration on the project level. Selected cases are summarised in Table 2. For example the local Chilean engineering firm NCL Ltd. has increased its innovative activities through active collaboration with the Michilla Company and Outokumpu at Lince, as has the small-scale equipment supplier Macmin. Reicotex Ltd. has grown to be a key supplier of filter fabric to the mining industry in Chile as well as in Peru, Bolivia, Ecuador and Paraguay. Sabinco, the Chilean firm which built the modular mining camp at Escondida, has also been collaborating with firms in Iraq, Peru, Bolivia, Mexico, Brazil and Australia (*Mining Magazine*, April 1992).

Table 2. **Selected South-South joint ventures in minerals development**

Countries	Project	Minerals	Companies	Capital	Notes	Reference
Peru Chile	Quellaveco Southern Peru	Copper	Empresa Minera de Mantos Blancos (Chilean subsidiary of Anglo American of South America)	$12m initially; $562m planned investment in bioleaching process	SPPC (52.3 % Asarco) held concession but lost rights when Peruvian government passed a retroactive law limiting time companies could hold concessions without production. 10 000 t/d min. output. Potential for 40 000 t/d. Reserves of 388 Mt grading 0.85 Cu.	*Mining Journal*, Jan. 8, 1993; *Mining Journal*, Dec. 18/25, 1992
China Peru	Purchase of Hierro Peru (state iron producer)	Iron and Steel	Shougang Corporation	$312m ($120m cash + $150m investment and $42m to cover accumulated debts)	Investment to include steel mill and associated industrial complex. Other bidders include Chilean consortium.	*Financial Times*, Jan. 14, 1993; *Mining Journal*, Nov. 27, 1992
US Ukraine Jamaica	Lydford mine, Jamaica	Bauxite	Nikolaev Alumina, Ukraine; Global Interholding Corp., US	$50	Refurbishment and reopening of mine closed since 1984. Production expected to reach 1.5 Mt/y within 18 months, 2.5 Mt/y within 5 years. Majority of production will go to Ukraine.	*Mining Magazine*, December 1992

Countries	Project	Minerals	Companies	Capital	Notes	Reference
Bolivia Brazil US	Tasna/ Catavi		Comibol; Cominesa (subsid. Speciality Metals, US), Mineraçao Taboca (subsid. Paranapaneme, Brazil)			*Mining Journal*, Oct. 30, 1992
China Pakistan	Saindak Baluchistan Pakistan	Copper, Gold, Silver	Chinese government (Metallurgical Construction Corp. of China)	$110-448m	19 year life; 15 500 t. blister Cu, 1.47 t. Au, 2.76 t Ag. Turnkey development.	*Mining Journal*, Dec. 11, 1992
Nigeria Bulgaria	Owulpa and Okaba	Coal	NNC EC Henstroy		Joint venture to develop opencast mines. Estimated annual production 0.9Mt	*Mining Journal*, Aug. 28, 1992
Bolivia Chile Canada	Western Bolivia (exploration)	Gold Coppper	Orvana Minerals Corp., Vancouver (14%); Merwin Bernstein, Santiago (6%); Empresa Minera Unificada SA (Emusa)	$400 000 (Emusa, 80%).		*Mining Journal*, July 31, 1992
Brazil Bolivia	Catavi-Siglo Viente, Bolivia	Tin	Paranapanema (Mineracao Taboca) Comibol		Proposal to retreat tin tailings dumps from the closed mine (60Mt)	*Mining Journal*, July 10, 1992
Mauritania Kuwait Iraq Morocco	Tiris, Mauritania	Iron ore	SNIM (Société Nationale Industrielle et Minière): Islamic Republic of Mauritania (76.99%); Kuwait Real Estate Consortium (7.62%); Arab Mining Co. (6.02%); Iraq Fund for External Development; Bureau Marocain des Recherches et des Participations Minières; Islamic Bank for Development		Ongoing exploration and exploitation of many deposits and proven reserves of iron-ore	*Mining Magazine*, April 1992
Brazil Peru	Izcay Cruz, Peru	Zinc Lead Silver	Paraibuna Matais (45%); Constructora Odebrecht (15%); Companhia Norberto de Minas Buenaventura (15%); Minero Peru (25%). (Consortium: Empresa Minera Especial Izcay Cruz)	$50m	Full production expected 1996. Est. 720 000 t Zinc, 180 000 t Lead reserves. 3.3 Mt deposit; 19% Zinc, 2% Lead, 52 g/t Silver	*Mining Journal*, May 17, 1991
Morocco Algeria	Touissit border region	Lead Zinc			Mining engineers and geologists meeting to exchange information and technical expertise	*Mining Magazine*, January 1991

Perhaps the most interesting and recent illustration of a significant south-south partnership involving both investment and technological collaboration is the recent establishment of the joint Brazilian-Peruvian enterprise: Empressa Minera Especial Izcay Cruz, in Peru (*Mining Journal*, May 1991, Vol. 316, No. 8122, p. 369). It is formed by two Brazilian companies: Paraibuna Metais (45 per cent) and Constructora Norberto Odebrecht (15 per cent); and two Peruvian companies: Compañía de Minas Buenaventura (15 per cent) and MINEROPERU (25 per cent) which, unlike the others, is State-owned. The venture has required an investment of $50 million over 4 years to mine 720 000 tons of zinc and 180 000 tons of lead with still to be determined reserves of silver. The 3.3 million tons reserves of 19 per cent zinc,

2 per cent lead and 52 grams per ton of silver will make it the world's largest mixed-sulphide mine. Besides the precedent that this investment sets for the effective combining of resources and capabilities of mineral producing DCs, there are two other interesting issues regarding south-south collaboration. First, the Peruvian participation is to be financed in part by converting debts owed to Brazil and in part through credit provided by the International Finance Corporation (IFC) of the World Bank. Second, the zinc production is planned to ensure security of supply for Brazil's zinc refineries which are currently suffering an under-utilisation of capacity due to its low domestic reserves of zinc ore.

Other recent examples of technological collaboration between Southern partners mentioned in the professional literature include: a copper project in the Saindak region of Pakistan which involves the China Metallurgical Construction Corporation. This large investment, which will produce 15 000-16 000 tons of blister copper annually, will cost $205 million, to be underpinned by the European Investment Bank (*Mining Journal*, Vol. 317, No. 8147, p. 345). Compañía de Minas Buenaventura of Peru is also actively seeking investment partners in both Bolivia and Chile, building upon a successful innovation strategy.

Joint ventures such as these do not automatically imply that technology transfer takes place, especially where one partner is technologically and economically more dominant. However in the Latin American cases the evidence so far indicates that common language and 'engineering cultural traditions', combined with the economic necessity to pool resources and engage in joint problem solving, are resulting in significant learning opportunities for all actors concerned. While south-south co-operation is not *a priori* a "better thing", the particular advantage of these partnerships has been their ability to contribute to the building of technological and managerial capabilities within DC enterprises. These in turn have enabled the local enterprise to innovate, to make technical changes and to improve its economic performance in subsequent operations, whether these are wholly owned or run as joint ventures with other DC firms or with multinational enterprises.

Scientific and technological infrastructure

Education and research establishments also play important roles in developing the knowledge base of mineral producing countries. In so doing they provide a "springboard" for the development of professionals who are well positioned to facilitate future south-south technological collaboration. This has clearly been the case with regard to the collaboration between Chilean and Peruvian chemical engineers in leaching projects in mines in Southern Peru and Northern Chile[5] and the process of creating a centre for mineral expertise is now underway in Africa. Notwithstanding these developments, links between industry and R&D institutions do not take place automatically. Evidence suggests these needs to be a building of technological capabilities within industry and then industrial engineers and scientists draw on expertise within external R&D institutions, involving them at different stages in applied technology projects (Bell, 1990; Warhurst, 1986). Thus in February 1992 a new laboratory complex was founded in Tanzania. The Eastern and Southern African Mineral Resources Development Centre (ESAMRDC), built at a cost of $1.5 million, is an intergovernmental organisation providing assistance in the field of mineral resource development to the region through consultancy, laboratory and training services (*Mining Magazine*, February 1992, p. 113).

Of crucial importance in the development of such capabilities, however, is the inclusion of personnel from these consultancy and engineering companies in DC industrial investment projects. Indeed, the evidence suggests that the origin of the consultancy and engineering companies responsible for undertaking the pre-feasibility studies for large mineral projects often determines the nature and source of the technology selected in the investment phase (Warhurst, 1986). Where local consultancy companies and engineers have played major roles, as in Chile, the result has been a greater utilisation of Chilean R&D resources, personnel and equipment suppliers. Once the local company gets into the 'loop', the scope for future participation increases due to the obvious advantages of greater local knowledge of geological and metallurgical characteristics, of local suppliers' capabilities and of price.

Technological collaboration and innovation

As technological capabilities developed over the 1970s and 1980s they have become the basis for a process of innovation in the mining industries of several countries in the south. Recently, two of the most significant innovations in Andean minerals development have originated from the local private sector. The Buenaventura company in Peru is in the process of commercialising a pressure-vat oxidation process for silver recovery (*Financial Times*, March 22, 1990), while the Pudahuel Mining Company of Chile developed a thin-layer leach process for copper extraction. Due to local geological similarities which give rise to comparable mineral profiles, and therefore similar metallurgical problems, the former innovation is being commercialised for application in the Potosi mine in Bolivia and the latter at the Cerro Verde project in Peru, which is currently being privatised. In both cases the R&D was funded through revenue generated and loans raised from the mines' own metal production. Table 3 summarises selected examples of south-south technological collaboration stemming from the commercialisation of innovative capabilities in developing country firms. The challenge is finding the appropriate new mechanisms required for such south-south technology diffusion. These mechanisms would involve, as a first priority, opening new lines of credit and the provision of incentives to select local engineering consultants to undertake feasibility studies and technological search activities.

A further issue is the advantages offered by technological collaboration over marketing co-operation and joint trade agreements. The successive failure of CIPEC, the International Tin Agreement and the Bauxite Common Agreement attest to the difficulties involved in implementing joint action regarding cutting back or increasing mineral supplies where very different economic implications are at stake for member countries. On the other hand, technological collaboration may be politically easier and less demanding of scarce resources. It can involve fewer countries and is more flexible in scale, starting with a joint research project funded by a donor agency leading to pilot plant experimentation, as in the case of the Andean Pact Copper Project; or commercial exploitation, as in the case of the Chilean mining company Pudahuel and its consultancy activities and technology transfer of proprietary leaching techniques to the Hindustan Mining Company of India. Technological collaboration can also involve joint training activities and taking advantages of the benefits of sharing consultant visits. Again the Andean Pact has been pioneering in organising the development of technological capabilities in this collaborative way. Table 4 summarises a range of different co-operation agreements in minerals development between developing country governments.

Table 3. Selected examples of South-South technology collaboration in metals production

Source of technology	Collaborating countries	Details	Reference
Brazil	Uruguay	Gold refinery at Minas de Corales uses Brazilian refining technology	*Mining Magazine*, November 1990
Reicotex Ltd, Chile	Peru, Bolivia, Ecuador, Paraguay	Suppliers of filter materials	*Mining Magazine, April 1992*
Sabinco - Manufacturas La Forja SA, Chile	Iraq	Mine camp construction	*Mining Magazine*, April 1992
Shell Chile SACI, Chile	Peru, Bolivia, Mexico, Brazil, Australia	Flotation chemicals	*Mining Magazine*, April 1992
Tec-Harseim SAIC, Chile	Peru, Bolivia, Argentina, Uruguay, Ecuador, Venezuela, Turkey, Pakistan, Australia, USA	Blasting accessories	*Mining Magazine*, April 1992
Vulco SA, Chile	Company represented in Bolivia, Ecuador, Colombia, Argentina, Venezuela, Brazil	Market leader in the protection of equipment from abrasion and corrosion	*Mining Magazine*, April 1992
Buenaventura, Peru	Bolivia	Proprietary pressure vat oxidation process for silver recovery	*Financial Times*, March 22, 1990
Pudahuel, Chile	Hindustan Mining Company, India; Cerroverde, Peru	Proprietary thin-layer leach process	J. Gana, Resources Policy, March 1992

Table 4. Recent co-operative agreements between developing country governments in minerals development

Countries	Minerals	Details	Reference
Myanmar (Burma), China	Tin, Coal	Contract signed for tin mining in East Myanmar. Separate agreement for coal mining within Myanmar.	*Mining Journal*, Nov. 20, 1992
Hungary, Russia	Aluminium, Alumina	Agreement to exchange aluminium ingots from Russia with Hungarian alumina.	*Mining Journal*, Nov. 20, 1992
Iran, Malaysia, Guinea	Bauxite, Gold	Agreement signed on joint investment in bauxite mining. Discussions on agreements on bauxite and gold mining in Guinea. Malaysia and Iran have also signed a barter agreement to exchange palm oil and iron/steel.	*Mining Journal*, Oct. 23, 1992
Egypt, Zambia	Copper	Egyptian government to present proposals for the establishment of a copper mining joint venture in Zambia.	*Mining Journal*, Sept. 4, 1992
Argentina, Romania	Aluminium	Discussions on the possibilities of Argentinean companies modernising the aluminium smelter at Slatina, Romania. Romanian payment will be in the form of surplus aluminium.	*Mining Journal*, Aug. 14, 1992
Jordan, China		Letter of understanding concluded in which China provides technical know-how on the development and utilisation of Jordan's mineral resources.	*Mining Journal*, July 24, 1992
Vietnam, Russia	Gold	The Russian foreign ministry and the Vietnam Precious Metals Corp. have signed an agreement to establish gold exploration and mining in Bac Thai province, Northern Vietnam — total capital of $1.9 million.	*Mining Journal*, July 10, 1992
Mongolia, Russia	Copper	Trade agreement for 1992 for Mongolian export of copper concentrate — trade turnover of $400 million. Also discussions on joint venture for production of cathode copper and copper wire.	*Mining Journal*, Jan. 8, 1993 *Mining Journal*, July 3, 1992

Table 4 (cont). **Recent co-operative agreements between developing country governments in minerals development**

Countries	Minerals	Details	Reference
Vietnam, Indonesia	Coal	$27 million Indonesian investment in anthracite mining project in Vietnam.	*Mining Journal*, May 22, 1992
Malaysia, Vietnam	Steel	Consideration of joint venture to market steel billets in Vietnam.	*Mining Journal*, Mar. 13, 1992
Russia, Estonia	Ferrous and non-ferrous metals	$150 million trade agreement to exchange ferrous and non-ferrous metals as well as chemicals and petrochemicals.	*Mining Journal*, Mar. 6, 1992
Romania, Yemen		Discussions about joint geological prospecting.	*Mining Journal*, Mar. 6, 1992
Iran, Armenia	Cooper, Gold, Silver, Molybdenum	Prospects being investigated for co-operation in areas of non-ferrous and precious metals, particularly copper.	*Mining Journal*, Feb. 21, 1992
Malaysia, Vietnam	Tin, Gold	Plan to set up tin and gold mining joint ventures.	*Mining Journal*, Feb. 15, 1992
Nigeria, Czech Republic, Slovakia	Titanium oxide	$160 million joint venture agreement to extract titanium dioxide from limestone deposits in Nigeria, to be used in Nigerian paint plants and enable Nigeria to stop imports.	*Mining Journal*, Jan. 3, 1992
Brazil, Morocco		Agreement signed between Moroccan Mining Board and Brazil's state service company (CPRM) covering geological and mining research co-operation.	*Mining Journal*, Oct. 11, 1991
Mauritania, Algeria	Gold	Agreement for joint exploration of gold deposits in Yetti region of northern Mauritania.	*Mining Journal*, Sept. 6, 1991
Angola, Namibia	Ornamental stones	Joint venture formed for prospecting, mining and domestic and international marketing.	*Mining Magazine*, Aug. 1991
Chile, Peru		Agreement to increase co-operation in the mining industry.	*Mining Magazine*, July 1991
Algeria, Burkina Faso	Gold and base metals	Joint research in mining in Burkino Faso.	*Mining Magazine*, June 1991
Indonesia, Algeria	Phosphates	Agreement to increase bilateral trade. Indonesia is said to re-export some Algerian phosphates to Brazil and Europe.	*Mining Magazine*, June 1991
China, Papua New Guinea	Copper	China has granted PNG a $10 million interest-free loan for development projects. The agreement is to enhance trade and investment in primary and secondary products including copper concentrates.	*Mining Magazine*, June 1991
Cuba, India	Nickel	Agreement to co-operate in exploitation of nickel and other metals in both countries.	*Mining Magazine*, May 1991
Albania, Egypt	Ferrochrome Phosphates	Barter agreement signed in February 1991. Albania to export ferrochrome, Egypt to export phosphates.	*Mining Magazine*, Apr. 1991
India, Poland	Coal	Joint commission looking at development of a deep coking coal mine in India and supply of longwall equipment.	*Mining Magazine*, Mar. 1991
Bulgaria, Turkey		Discussions on co-operation in mining and metallurgical industries.	*Mining Magazine*, Mar. 15, 1991
India, China	Coal	Joint venture set up to develop coking coal deposits in India.	*Mining Magazine*, Mar. 15, 1991
Iran, Brazil		Protocol signed to expand co-operation in mining, among other industries.	*Mining Magazine*, Jan. 1991
Albania, Yugoslavia		Talks on co-operation in the exploitation and processing of minerals.	*Mining Magazine*, Jan 1991
Myanmar (Burma), Thailand	Tin	Tin-production-sharing contract signed. Four tin production-sharing ventures signed in 1990.	*Mining Journal*, Jan. 18, 1991

The Andean Pact copper project

The technological collaboration undertaken within the Andean copper project provides an interesting example of how innovations can be promoted through sharing the costs and efforts involved in risky R&D. Moreover, since the costs of the long-term training programme were met through technological assistance agreements with German and Canadian donor agencies and coordinated by the Andean Pact, this created a positive sum situation for the countries concerned.

The Andean Pact copper project (1974-85) was designed to solve the region's problem of the recovery of copper from low grade ore in new mines and waste dumps. It had the aim of developing local R&D facilities and skills and a more efficient system of technology transfer both from the industrialised countries and from within the region. The project was financed through the Andean Pact and a donor agency — GTZ — of the Federal Republic of Germany. Its estimated cost was $2 million. Since metals biotechnology is principally knowledge intensive and dependent on building up empirical experience, training is an important mechanism for technology acquisition. This training involved personnel from CENTROMIN and MINEROPERU, the national mining companies of Peru; COMIBOL, the national mining company of Bolivia; and the state research institutions of Peru and Bolivia, INGEMMET and IIMM. The project was successful in that it resulted in the development and consolidation of important capabilities in metals biotechnology in Peru, and to a lesser extent in Bolivia, and the successful running of a pilot plant programme in Peru which indicated the viability of the technique for Peruvian ores (Warhurst, 1985 and 1990). The training programme involved formal seminar courses, on site training by international experts, and field visits undertaken by the trainees with these experts to commercial leaching operations in the USA. The planning phase of the copper project involved a consultancy by a Canadian bacterial leaching expert, a chemical engineer, and a German research scientist in electrochemistry who had quite different backgrounds and were in touch with advances on the North American and European fronts respectively. Training was to involve evaluating ore in the field and laboratory, research and development and scale-up to industrial operation. However, fieldwork revealed many weaknesses as the training programme developed, relating to the skill composition of the trainers and trainees and the nature of the training material (Warhurst, 1990).

Important benefits arose from the combination of expertise in the training programme. The technical literature and research programmes generated during the copper project are unique in terms of the present state of the art of the technology, since emphasis was placed on the theory of the relationship between the electro-chemistry of semiconductors and bacterial leaching. Building on this theoretical knowledge the teams independently devised innovative research programmes to solve country specific problems. The Bolivian team developed a new technique for leaching zinc sulphide concentrates and the Peruvian team adapted the technology to leach pollutant arsenic from copper concentrates. The success of the first series of seminars in Peru in 1976 led to another series in Bolivia, which focused on tin, silver, bismuth and antimony as well as copper. Engineers from Colombia and Ecuador were also invited. Although the training was to involve using newly donated electrochemical and laboratory equipment, its late arrival reduced the impact. (This yields an important lesson on the importance of coordinating training with equipment availability).

Disembodied knowledge without physical technology is not a sufficient base for innovation. Disembodied technology is none the less paramount in metals biotechnology. So, finding the appropriate mechanism to transfer it is important. In this respect the training courses of the copper project were illuminating. They revealed the importance of foreign language capabilities, the utility of creating a good learning environment by hosting the seminars in hotels far away from the demands of everyday work, and the importance of informal discussions during fieldwork visits to their mines. A series of visits undertaken by the teams and international experts to bacterial leaching operations and conferences in Mexico, the USA and southern Peru were also an integral part of the training and contributed to its success.

In a long-term project like the copper project, and especially in one where developing knowledge based technology is central, personnel turnover becomes a key factor. In the case of the Bolivian team there was a high rate of personnel turnover and a tendency for knowledge to be personalised and subsequently lost in the absence of any institutionalised information storage and retrieval systems. In contrast, in the case of Peru, in addition to the greater stability of personnel one of the main factors explaining the strong capabilities in metals biotechnology exhibited by several of the mining companies and the state research institution was a well organised information system. This enabled trainees to draw upon a broader knowledge of the technology and its potential than they might otherwise have been able to do as individuals.

These observations point towards the minimal requirements of organisation, informed and determined technology search and language capabilities on the part of technology recipients to absorb efficiently knowledge imparted in training programmes. It also implies a need for a strategy to maximise the benefits of training and to accelerate learning. The quality of training will also depend upon what is being asked of the trainers. Lastly, where a technology requires particularly integrated work to be undertaken by researchers, engineering and production personnel, combined involvement is required from the outset of training.

Chinese National Offshore Oil Corporation

The training and human resource development potential of joint venture arrangements is illustrated by the strategy of the Chinese National Offshore Oil Corporation (CNOOC) in China. When in the early 1980s China opened up its offshore basins for oil exploration, it formed joint ventures with consortia of the major international oil companies. This included a joint-venture with a developing country partner — PETROBRAS of Brazil — which has developed proprietary technology in deep-sea drilling, an area of special interest for China. One of China's primary objectives in forming these partnerships was to achieve a transfer of best-practice technology and working methods and build up a capacity to innovate in all areas of exploration, development and production. Each foreign company was targeted for a particular technological strength, additional fees were paid to cover the cost of learning and a variety of arrangements were formed which included working together on-the-job to solve production problems, joint research projects in the oil companies' R&D centres, working in the partner's overseas operations, and training courses.

Considerable success has now been achieved with this strategy of technological learning through clearly-defined joint-venture arrangements. Case-studies of CNOOC's efforts to develop capabilities in offshore oil technology strengthen some of the findings of recent research on technology transfer and technological learning (Warhurst, 1991). Three of these findings merit particular mention:

  i) The governments and enterprises involved had formulated explicit objectives about acquiring and developing technology. They had designed strategies to achieve them. They had also made concerted efforts to develop their decision-making skills and had introduced procedural mechanisms and organisational changes for technology management which frequently stretched beyond the individual 'firm' to include the broader science and technology infrastructure.

ii) An international technology search played a crucial role in the planning period; and the selection of suppliers involved criteria such as willingness to transfer technology and capacity to contribute to the building up of the recipient's capabilities.

iii) The agreement reached between the local and foreign enterprises involved the contractual separation of technology supply and technology transfer. That is, it involved the separate negotiation of and payment for training and disembodied technology transfer outside the usual contractual framework for equipment supply and consultancy. This separation apparently contributed to the efficiency of both processes.

3. South-south co-operation in environmental management

After a period of relatively little change the mining industry is currently facing two major challenges which are likely to restructure the international minerals industry and the role of developing countries within it.

First, there is a new economic imperative that is stimulating innovation in the industry. Many mining operations have simply reached a threshold of incremental technical change to achieve economic efficiency and are now experiencing rising production costs. This is forcing companies in the North, like INCO and Noranda, to invest substantial resources in R&D and to generate new technology in order to remain competitive.

Second, there is a growing environmental imperative, reinforced by credit conditionality, to improve the environmental management of existing mining operations and to ensure the control of pollution from new mines and processing plants, as well as their reclamation on closure. Sound environmental management does not always require radical new technology but may be a combination of incremental changes, adaptation to existing technology and a reorganisation of the 'house-keeping' of the mineral operation. Local expertise and knowledge is crucial for the fine-tuning of the operation and cheaper than bringing in expensive foreign consulting engineers. Furthermore, it is a hypothesis of this chapter that such incremental changes — new smelter scrubbers, new water treatment plants, dust precipitators, the leaching and recovery of metals from waste waters — can also lead to economic benefits for the enterprise, improving its overall efficiency through raising productivity levels, for example by enhancing metal recovery or generating a saleable by-product.

Such initiatives need to be considered in the context of new trends which are poised to re-structure the international minerals industries (Warhurst, 1991).

First, the current trend towards developing new less-pollutant hydro-metallurgical (leaching) alternatives to smelting, given increased air emission regulations in metal-consuming countries, could lead to more processing taking place at the mine site in DCs, which would then benefit from the increased value-added of selling final copper cathodes in end-metal markets. This is because hydrometallurgical processing must take place at the mine site, unlike smelting and refining, since liquid products cannot easily be transported. Moreover, the firms commercialising some of these hydrometallurgical options are "new entrants" from Japan and Germany, seizing the market opportunities offered by environmental concerns.

Second, public and governmental pressure in mineral-rich industrialised countries such as Canada, is forcing international companies to adopt environmentally best-practice techniques in their overseas operations as well as at home, even in the absence of regulation, so as to appease shareholders, improve public image, commercialise technologies they have already been forced to develop and to reduce the risk of retrospective expropriation if new regulations are introduced in DCs.

Third, lobby organisations such as Eurometaux (for the European metal producers) and the Mining Association of Canada, are pushing DC governments to introduce environmental regulation since they claim their comparative lack of regulation is giving DC producers increasingly unfair cost advantages in metals markets.

Fourth, introducing new environmentally-efficient technology into third world mineral production is unlikely to achieve the pollution control aims desired, unless production efficiency is also improved and the appropriate skills for improved environmental management are also developed within industry.

Finally, environmental regulation, however detailed, is unlikely to achieve success in DCs unless training programmes are also developed to enable technicians in industry and regulatory authorities to interpret and enforce controls well-adapted to the mining environment under consideration.

It is this set of economic factors that is encouraging joint south-south investment, and providing a framework within which to foster south-south technological collaboration. The environmental imperative thus provides the real stimulus or *raison-d'être* for south-south co-operation. Currently most of these mineral exporting countries depend upon the use of imported mining and smelting technologies, developed in the industrialised countries in accordance with specifications that were designed before the damaging environmental effects of associated waste-products and pollutant emissions were fully documented (Warhurst, 1990). In spite of important country-specific differences there are a common set of strategic and policy issues which mineral exporters face. Technological collaboration could ease the economic burden of response and, in so doing, enhance the economic competitiveness of developing country firms.

The nature of environmental degradation

Mining and mineral processing are one of the principal causes of industrial and rural pollution in the developing countries (UNEP, 1984). Mining, for example, can be a major cause of land degradation, forest clearance and ecosystem disruption (Figure 1). Mineral dumps and tailings are a major source of solid waste pollution. Mining, concentration and smelting processes contribute effluents, toxic chemicals and metals to groundwater and rivers. And smelting and refining are a major source of the planet's air pollutants — including compounds of carbon, sulphur and nitrogen, as well as heavy metals like cadmium, copper, mercury, lead and zinc. Most of these metals are found in complex sulphide ores (the principal source of the world's major metals). The sulphur content is transformed to harmful sulphur dioxide by the oxidation process involved in heating. There are also indirect emission effects related to the burning of fossil fuels to generate the power required for mineral processing activities. In addition, excess copper, nickel, mercury, cyanide, zinc, lead and cadmium all have negative biological effects on the body and in the food chain, while the dust and water in the mine environment make mines a potentially hazardous workplace. Furthermore, economic inefficiency related to under- utilised capacity, equipment malfunctions, lack of reagent controls, irregular operating regimes and the use of high-sulphur fuels, which are endemic problems in many mineral-producing DCs, contribute significantly to worsen

Figure 1. The mining process and the environment

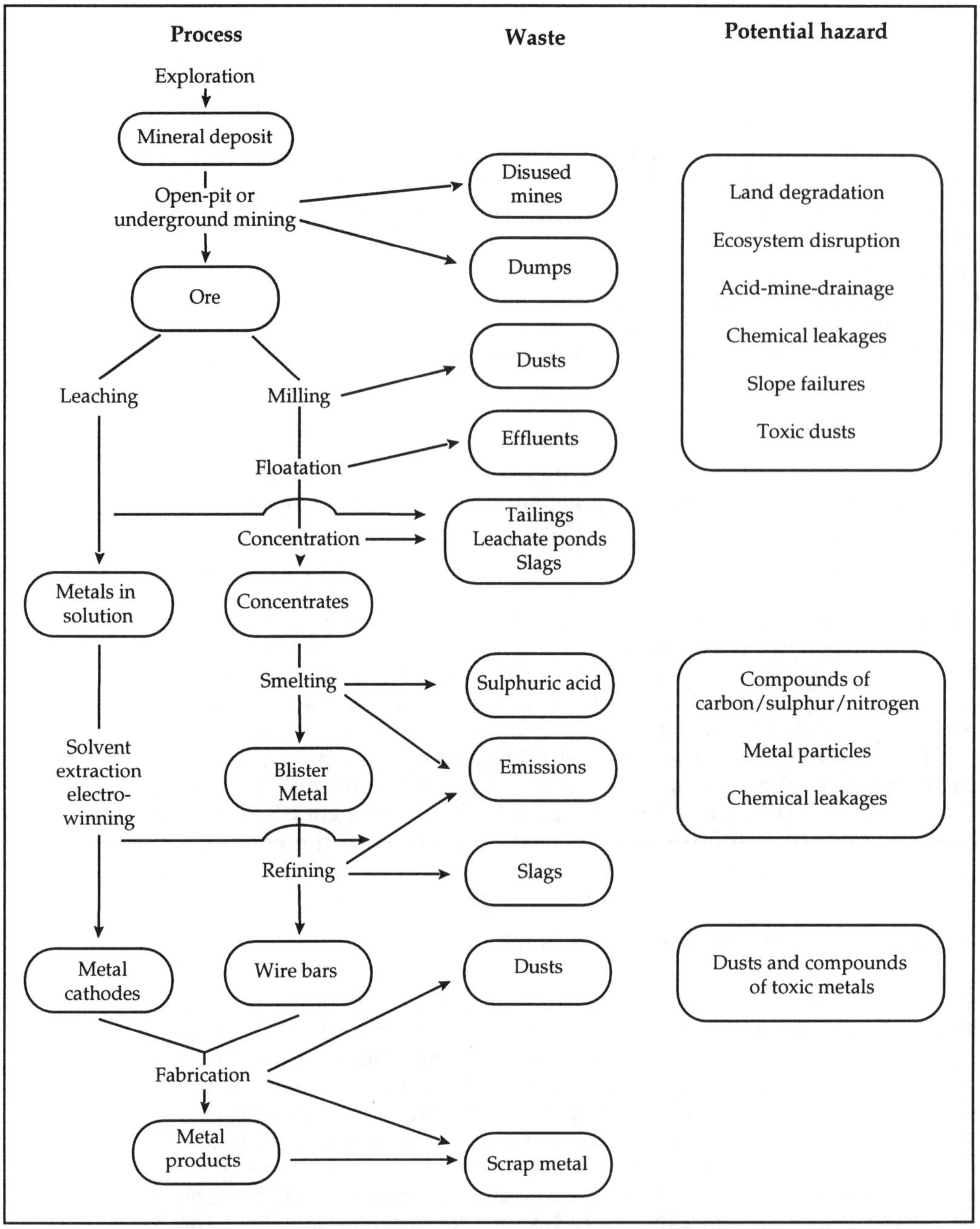

Process	Waste	Potential hazard

Process

Exploration
↓
Mineral deposit
↓
Open-pit or underground mining
↓
Ore

Leaching ← Ore → Milling

Floatation

Concentration

Metals in solution ← Leaching

Concentrates ← Concentration

Smelting

Blister Metal

Refining

Solvent extraction electro-winning

Metal cathodes

Wire bars

Fabrication

Metal products

Waste

Disused mines

Dumps

Dusts

Effluents

Tailings / Leachate ponds / Slags

Sulphuric acid

Emissions

Slags

Dusts

Scrap metal

Potential hazard

Land degradation
Ecosystem disruption
Acid-mine-drainage
Chemical leakages
Slope failures
Toxic dusts

Compounds of carbon/sulphur/nitrogen
Metal particles
Chemical leakages

Dusts and compounds of toxic metals

Source: A. Warhurst, *Environmental Degradation from Mining and Mineral processing in Developing Countries*, (OECD), 1993.

pollution effects. Therein lies the challenge for south-south co-operation — to lead both to an improvement in environmental management as well as a parallel enhancement of economic efficiency. The two tend to go hand-in-hand.

The environmental hazards of mining and mineral processing are evident on both the micro- and macro-scale in DCs. For example, dust and toxic gases in the mine environment of some of the poorer mineral-dependent DCs like Zaire, Zambia, Peru and Bolivia are a major factor in explaining miners' premature deaths. Large-scale mineral projects in, for example, Papua New Guinea, India, Peru, Brazil and Bolivia have also been responsible for detrimental health effects on local communities, and associated water- and air-borne pollution have been linked to the destruction of neighbouring farmland, forests and fisheries. The poorest of the poor in those countries isolated rural peasant communities or miners' families — are those most affected and least in a position to respond. Moreover, in these countries there are also large groups of 'informally' organised miners working as individuals or in co-operatives, extracting metals such as gold, tin and copper from alluvial deposits or from the 'waste' products of larger scale mining operations. They tend to work in remote and precarious conditions, have no training in the use of reagents such as mercury and cyanide, and have limited access to technology. This situation is also creating growing problems of water pollution and contamination of the regional food chain.

South-south co-operation in innovation to meet the environmental imperative

There are potential benefits to be gained from addressing south-south co-operation on a number of fronts relating to environmental degradation from mining and mineral processing, including: sharing information about the design of functional and appropriate regulations for ground, water and air pollution; training of professionals to monitor mining activities, implement regulations and work with companies on pollution abatement; the joint development of pollution control and environmental management programmes; and the sharing of information regarding the improved environmental practices of mining companies in different countries. Already limited moves in this direction are underway under the auspices of several UN development and technical assistance programmes. However, a major issue common to many mineral producing DCs remains to be addressed. That is the endemic inefficiency which underlies most State sector and small-scale mining enterprises, which needs to be resolved as a first step towards achieving environmental efficiency. This inefficiency is a direct result of the economic history of mining in developing countries.

State-run operations are mainly nationalised properties which previously belonged to multinational companies. When the latter withdrew they took with them their specialised human resources and lines of access to modern technology and of course capital. State-run companies, since then, in countries such as Zambia, Zaire, Peru and Bolivia, have tended to provide their respective governments with foreign exchange and revenue for ill-fated industrial diversification schemes and debt-repayment, receiving little back themselves for re-investment in new technology, training, exploration, or for that matter environmental management. The pressure on these enterprises has been directed towards raising output to bring in revenue rather than raising productivity and ensuring the longer term sustainability of the mining operation. High grade ores were extracted and exhausted quickly to improve output rather than ensuing the carefully planned exploitation of even grades over time. This meant that in periods of unstable metal prices, as, for example, during the tin price crash of 1985, state enterprises were unable to respond and in turn became a drain on their governments' resources leading to a vicious circle of further indebtedness that only foreign exchange from metal sales could service (Jordan and Warhurst, 1992). This situation has been a major factor constraining Bolivian economic development.

Small scale enterprises have similarly suffered from growing inefficiency. They cannot achieve economies of scale in extraction techniques, reagent use, in metal processing or in marketing. They have limited access to the capital required for investment to raise their productivity, and the lack of education and training on the part of the miners themselves inhibits changing their situation for the better. Indeed, it is the medium-sized national and private enterprises and the large scale international enterprises which for the most part are the most economically efficient mineral producers.

There is growing evidence that there is great scope to improve the environmental efficiency of existing mining operations in DCs through 'good housekeeping' and incremental improvements. Moreover, some environmental control innovations, although initially developed reluctantly, have ended up providing a cost-saving or economic benefit for the production enterprise (Warhurst, 1991). For example, one of the Brazilian national gold companies was facing increasing controls and penalties on account of the toxic dust content in its processing plants. It therefore designed and introduced specialised dust precipitators. As a consequence, not only were the dust levels reduced but the extra gold values collected in the dust more than paid for the cost of buying and installing the new equipment. Homestake Gold Mining Company in California was another dynamic firm which turned regulatory pressure to clean up a cyanide seepage problem to its advantage. Its own R&D staff developed a proprietary biological technique to treat the effluent which led to the fast recovery of local fisheries and water quality in the mine's vicinity at Lead in Dakota (Crouch, 1990). This innovation is now being commercialised by the company to assist clean-up operations at other mines.

This environmental imperative could be seized as an opportunity to use and to develop further existing technological capabilities in DC engineering firms, suppliers and mining companies. Companies such as Buenaventura Engineering Mining Group of Peru for more than a decade have been undertaking investments and collaborating with engineering consultancy companies in several neighbouring Latin American countries (Nuñez, 1991). The growing demand for environmental engineering services in many mineral producing countries could therefore provide new investment opportunities, which would be enhanced through technological collaboration, in an otherwise depressed market. To ensure that regional firms as opposed to foreign ones play a major role, government incentive schemes could be set up, which include opening new lines of credit in national development banks for financing such activities and the establishment of a register of local engineering firms and the environmental services they offer. Organisations such as the Andean Pact could extend their already established register of regional capital goods suppliers to cover environmental services, and regional development banks such as the CAF (Corporación Andina de Fomento) could open new credit lines to promote regional collaboration in environmental technology development and diffusion.

New loans from the World Bank and Inter-American Development Bank to countries like Bolivia, Chile and Ghana already have portions dedicated to environmental management. Sometimes specific sums of money are allocated to co-finance with government the cleaning-up of existing mining pollution as a pre-requisite for new mineral investment, as in the case of Bolivia. Southern engineering and mining consultant companies are ideally suited to designing and undertaking such work.

4. Conclusions

This chapter has sought to draw out some new ideas about the potential and constraints of south-south co-operation to contribute to economic growth during the current new phase of mineral development. This phase is characterised by more complex patterns of investment, including joint ventures involving developing country enterprises, and a stimulus for innovation in the form of new environmental and economic imperatives. The discussion highlighted the common technological and development challenges faced by DC producers of similar types of minerals, particularly in neighbouring regions of the South. It pointed to the contribution that flexible technological collaboration, as opposed to market co-operation, could make to material economic growth. The potential learning effects that could be secured through joint ventures involving "third" parties from the industrialised world and their utility in building south-south partnerships was also raised. Lastly, the chapter noted the growing role and future potential of third world professionals in minerals projects, and also of local research organisations and mining, oil and engineering consultancy companies, and it stressed the need to develop new lines of credit to facilitate such collaborative investments, particularly to meet new environmental challenges.

For south-south co-operation to contribute to ensuring the economic future and environmental sustainability of mineral production in DCs, however, four major policy challenges will have to be met.

First, whether the new 'Environmental Imperative' offers an economic opportunity or threat to DCs will depend upon how those national companies (private or state owned) currently entering new phases of minerals development, plan and negotiate their **own** participation and environmental interests in new mining projects. Industrial strategy and environmental policy need to be developed in parallel, informed by the economic, social and political processes which both determine the need for environmental regulation, and condition company responses to it. Collaboration by policy makers in DC governments could contribute to the building of successful and consistent policy regimes and negotiating practices. Policies need to be in place which encourage the use of local services and expertise; this will require good information as well as new lines of credit to finance feasibility studies and technology search activities at a regional level.

Second, achieving and sustaining production efficiency in the DC context will be an important pre-requisite to achieving environmental efficiency, measured in terms of success at assimilating and adapting new less-hazardous technologies and improved environmental management practices. The achievement of improved production efficiency and environmental management will, in turn, be dependent upon the extent to which technology transfer and training clauses are built into joint ventures, investment arrangements or loan conditions with the aim of building-up engineering and managerial capabilities, and the extent to which local R&D centres are involved. Inter-governmental and inter-firm collaboration within regions could contribute substantially to this end. The lessons of success in this area from training programmes in South America should be built upon and used as an argument to raise finance to support further human resource development policies.

Third, environmental degradation from old, ongoing and new mining and mineral processing activities could be reduced and prevented through designing country-specific flexible regulatory frameworks. These should deal with the potential causes of degradation, not just the symptoms of pollution, by stimulating the development and diffusion of well-adapted innovative site-specific technological solutions, and 'best-practices' in environmental management based on an informed understanding of company behaviour in different economic and regulatory contexts. The sharing of information within a south-south context would play a useful role in diffusing these practices.

Fourth, whether a mineral producing economy can seize these potential environmentally-sound development opportunities, through the technological transformation promoted by the current environmental imperative, or suffers another debilitating round of technological dependency, will depend on its specific economic and historical conditions as well as policy frameworks, and the strategies of the mining companies investing there. South-south collaboration along the lines discussed in the previous section may help to strengthen the capabilities of DC mining companies as potential investors in Third World minerals development and of DC governments as hosts of new mineral projects using technology from the south.

Notes

1. The author would like to acknowledge the kind assistance of Gill Partridge for preparation of the manuscript, Hilary Webb for preparation of the tables, and Professor Lynn Mytelka for editing of the overall text and especially for her encouragement during the development of this paper.

2. For most of the non-ferrous minerals such as copper, silver and tin, these enterprises generally sell semi-processed material to state- or foreign-owned smelters and processing facilities located within their own countries, although gold is usually sold directly in the international metals markets.

3. Transnational Corporations in World Development. UNSTC/CTC/46, 1983, p. 293; quoted in Svetlicic (1986).

4. It might also be argued that investing abroad in mineral production would threaten a DC's hard-won market share. However, it is considered unlikely that such considerations would determine the behaviour of individual mining companies or entrepreneurs.

5. With UNDP support genetic engineering of the leaching bacteria was undertaken by Chilean university researchers with training in biotechnology, and the microbiological laboratory facilities established close ties with mining companies (through sustained collaboration in training and industrial application) (Warhurst 1990).

BELL, R.M. (1990), *The Thailand Institute of Scientific and Technological Research: Outline of a Project to Enhance its Productive Interaction with the Industrial Sector*, SPRN Working Paper, October.

BOMSEL, O. (1990), *Mining and Metallurgy Investment in the Third World: The End of Large Projects?*, OECD Development Centre, OECD, Paris.

CROUCH, D. (1990), *Personal Communication*, McLaughlin Mine, California.

DANIEL, P. (1986), Editorial: "Mineral Exporters in Boom and Slump", *IDS Bulletin*, Vol. 17, No. 4, October.

JORDAN, R. and WARHURST, A. (1992), "The Bolivian Mining Crisis" in *Resources Policy*, March, pp. 9-20.

KHAN, K.M. (1986), *Multinationals of the South: New Actors in the International Economy*, St. Martin's Press, New York.

MINING ANNUAL REVIEW (1989), published by Mining Journal Ltd., UK, London.

NANKANI, S. (1979), *Development Problems of Mineral Exporting Countries*, World Bank Staff Working Paper, No. 354, August.

NUÑEZ, A. (1991), "Heterogeneity of Production and Domestic Technological Capabilities in Mining and Mining Related Productive and Service Activities in Peru: Their Relevance for an Environmental Strategy", Research Proposal, Lima.

OMAN, C. *et al.* (1989), *New Forms of Investment in Developing Country Industries: Mining, Petrochemicals, Automobiles, Textiles and Food*, OECD Development Centre, Paris.

PEARSON, C.S. ed. (1987), *Multinational Corporations, Environment and the Third World*, Duke University Press, Durham.

PINTZ, W. (1987), "Environmental Negotiations in the OK Tedi Mine in Papua New Guinea", in Pearson, ed., *op. cit.*, pp. 35-63.

SVETLICIC, M. (1986), "Multinational production joint ventures of DCs, their economic development and specific features", in K.M. Khan *op. cit.*, pp. 67-87.

UNEP (1984), *Environmental Aspects of Selected Non-Ferrous Metals Industries: An Overview*, Industry and Environment Overview Series, United Nations Environmental Programme.

WARHURST, A. (1985), "Biotechnology for Metals Extraction: The Potential of an Emerging Technology, the Andean Pact Copper Project and Some Implications", *Development and Change*, Vol. 16, January.

WARHURST, A. (1986), "The Potential of Biotechnology for Mining in Developing Countries: the Case of the Andean Pact Copper Project", D.Phil. Thesis, Science Policy Research Unit, University of Sussex.

WARHURST, A. (1990), *Employment and Environmental Implications of Metals Biotechnology*, World Employment Research Working Paper (WEP) 2-22/WP, International Labour Office, Geneva, Switzerland, March.

WARHURST, A. (1991a), "Transfer of Technology and the Development of China's Offshore Oil Industry", *World Development*, Vol. 19, No. 8, pp. 1055-1073.

WARHURST, A. (1991b), "Environmental Degradation from Mining and Mineral Processing: Corporate Responses and National Policies". Draft of a study to be published by OECD Development Centre, Paris.

WARHURST, A. (1993), *Environmental Degradation from Mining and Mineral Processing in Developing Countries: Corporate Responses and National Policies*, Document on sale, OECD Development Centre, OECD, Paris (forthcoming).

Chapter 7

AN INNOVATION-DRIVEN MODEL OF REGIONAL CO-OPERATION
(Biotechnology and Sugar in the Caribbean)

Clive Thomas

Les modèles actuels de développement s'appuient, à tort, sur une vision étroite des produits de base provenant traditionnellement des pays du tiers monde, qui veut que chaque produit soit destiné à une utilisation unique. Ces produits sont considérés pour la plupart comme des «matières premières», destinées à être transformées en produits industriels ou en biens de consommation, et les questions relatives à leur production sont reléguées aux plus faibles niveaux d'intensité technologique et de savoir-faire. Les choix technologiques gravitent alors autour de l'une des trois options suivantes : amélioration de la production ou de la culture des matières premières ; amélioration de l'utilisation de leurs sous-produits à tous les stades de la production et de la transformation ; amélioration des procédés de transformation. Si aucune de ces options n'entraîne de gain de productivité significatif, la réponse logique est de chercher à diversifier la production en dehors des produits traditionnels, les produits tropicaux étant constamment menacés par la concurrence de substituts naturels ou synthétiques. Pourtant, la logique de l'innovation moderne plaide en faveur d'une approche plus large de la production de ressources et de matériaux, qui serait plus appropriée. Tous les produits devraient être perçus comme potentiellement complexes, avec différentes utilisations finales possibles, et l'innovation devrait être considérée comme s'appliquant à l'ensemble des phases de la chaîne de valeur ajoutée — qui s'étend de la recherche/développement à la production, la distribution, la commercialisation et la gestion. Ce chapitre retient cette conception de l'innovation et de l'utilisation des ressources, dans le cadre d'un modèle de coopération régionale fondé sur l'innovation technologique, à travers l'exemple de l'industrie sucrière des Caraïbes.

Current development models incorrectly adopt a monofocal perspective on traditional third world commodities according to which there is a "single" set of known uses for these products. As a result, technological issues affecting their production are relegated to the lower end of the technology/knowledge-intensity scale where these commodities are treated mainly as "raw materials" to be further processed into established industrial products or for final consumption uses. Technological choices then cluster around one of three options, namely, improved production/ cultivation of the raw material; better use of its by-products at all stages of production/cultivation and processing; and more efficient processing methods. If none of these yields significant productivity gains, then diversification away from the traditional commodities is the logical alternative, as tropical commodities face a perennial threat of real or synthetic substitutes. The logic of modern innovation, however, suggests a multi-focal view of resources and material output as more appropriate. All products should be conceived as potentially complex in their end uses and innovation treated as a process affecting all stages in their value-added chain, from R&D to production, distribution, marketing and management. It is this view of innovation and resource utilisation in an innovation-driven model of regional co-

operation which this chapter advances and illustrates with an analysis of sugar in the Caribbean.

1. Biotechnology, sugar and regional co-operation

a) Introduction

Compared to the successes of the European Community (EC), regional integration schemes started in the South during the 1960s and 1970s have not produced anything near the benefits originally anticipated. Many factors have influenced this result; some of these are discussed in Chapter 1. Of note, however, is that in a world of highly interdependent demand and supply structures, the emergence of acute internal and external disequilibria in many third world countries has led to an obsessive pre-occupation in current development theory and practice with solutions which focus on "structural adjustment", market liberalisation, open trade systems, and reduced roles for national planning and the public sector — the direct antithesis of the logic on which their co-operative arrangements were built. It is in view of such experiences that this chapter explores the possibility of a new rationale on which south-south co-operation might be constructed.

The argument is centred around three major propositions. First, that current development models incorrectly tend to be **monofocal** in their perspectives of traditional third world commodities (tropical agricultural products and minerals). There is an unstated presumption that there is a "single" set of known uses for these products with the consequent relegation of the technological issues affecting their production to the lower end of the technology/knowledge intensity scale where these commodities are treated mainly as "raw materials" to be further processed into established industrial products or for final consumption uses. Technological choices then cluster around three options, namely, improved production/cultivation of the raw material; better use of its by-products at all stages of production/cultivation and processing; and more efficient processing methods. If none of these yields significant productivity gains, then diversification away from the traditional commodities is the logical alternative, as tropical commodities face a perennial threat of real or synthetic substitutes. The logic of modern innovation, however, suggests a **multi-focal** view of resources and material output as more appropriate. All products should be conceived as potentially complex in their end uses and innovation treated as a process affecting all stages in their value-added chain, from R&D to production, distribution, marketing and management. It is this view of innovation and resource utilisation in an innovation-driven model of regional co-operation which the chapter advances.

Second, although there has been the phenomenon of the "widening technological gap" between North and South, there have been improvements in the South, albeit very unevenly distributed. The proposition is that there may be opportunities to use what has already been achieved in the South, to build upon these capabilities further and to link them together. It is these opportunities which the chapter also seeks to explore.

Third, the logic of an innovation-driven model suggests that organisational modes and actors, very different from those of the earlier third world co-operative arrangements, will be required to take centre stage. This chapter advances the case for a bottom-up model with a challenging role for new actors and institutions located in more open, inter-facing networking arrangements in which non-governmental organisations, private enterprises, and private initiatives may take the lead.

In order to combine fruitfully these theoretical/speculative propositions and concrete realities the analysis is presented around a case study of the scope for regional co-operation in biotechnology in the sugar sector of the Caribbean region, with a special emphasis on the Caribbean Community

(Caricom)[1]. The choice of case study is based on three principal considerations. First, the far reaching potential of biotechnology itself and the scope for its innovative application to sugar, in ways not widely recognised. Second, the importance of sugar on a world scale as a major tropical export staple, a major source of renewable biomass, and an important source of employment, income and foreign exchange earnings in certain third world countries. Third, among third world countries a strong case can be made for the comparatively advanced stage of the integration movement in Caricom, itself a major sugar producing region.

The remainder of this Section will elaborate on these considerations. Section 2 examines the scope for technology-driven co-operation in biotechnology and sugar. Section 3 looks at regional co-operation in Caricom, and the final Section deals with the "windows of opportunity" in support of the main thesis of this study.

b) Biotechnology and global transformation

There are strong reasons for supporting biotechnology as a central factor in promoting new forms of regional co-operation in the South. While many decry the fact that the early optimistic expectations about it have not yet materialised, there remains considerable support for the view that it would later, rather than sooner, produce changes commensurate in scope with those of the information revolution. While for centuries people have used micro-organisms, plants and animals for social purposes, in this text, biotechnology is seen as new in a two-fold sense: its capacity to manipulate living organisms through the artificial exchange of genetic material (recombinant DNA); and the emergence of techniques which have either widened the range of, or significantly improved on living organisms already in use (tissue culture, cloning, fermentation, embryo transfer)[2].

Certain revealed characteristics of the new biotechnology are of crucial importance to its development in the South. **First**, at the scientific level it has already exhibited a number of important features which put a heavy premium on human resources development and strong incentives for scientific discovery. One of these is a shift away from "one-shot" breakthroughs and a positive orientation towards the systematic exploitation of substantial gains in second-generation and later improvements in techniques. Thus, for example, the continuous up-scaling of the technique of reactor design, aseptic processes, and product recovery, has had a dramatic impact on the competitiveness of High Fructose Syrups (HFS) a major sugar substitute made principally from corn in the US, although other carbohydrate sources can be used, e.g. cassava. Also compared with traditional methods in agriculture where plant breeding trials can take upwards of a decade, the new biotechnology emphasizes the speed with which desired traits can be conferred on organisms and plants. This enables much of the innovation to focus on "designer-products" geared to highly specific end uses. Also, the new biotechnology is exceptional in its reliance on links between fundamental research and production and on a broad spectrum of scientific disciplines for its advances.

Second, across sectors the potential range of its application is wide, thereby permitting many points of entry: pharmaceuticals, agriculture and animal husbandry, energy, mining, chemicals, food processing, environment, forestry, marine resources, textiles. To date, however, the rate of diffusion has been very uneven, with the highest successes being in pharmaceuticals, followed by chemical and agricultural applications, and the rest lagging considerably behind[3]. The application of biotechnology in several of these sectors, however, has a direct bearing on the sugar industry.

Within **chemicals** a clear division has emerged between basic and specialty chemicals. With regard to the former, a major deterrent to the expansion of biotechnology has been the overwhelming global dependence on petroleum as the major chemical feedstock. It is estimated that at present costs the price of crude would have to triple to make bio-processes competitive. The importance of this to the sugar sector is dealt with later.

In **agriculture**, the rate of diffusion has been particularly disappointing given early expectations. While applications are focused on the genetic alteration of plants and crops and genetically engineered micro-organisms for application to plants and crops, so far no genetically engineered plant or plant inoculant has been approved for full scale commercial production, although about 50 genetically engineered plants have been successfully field tested (Godown, 1989), and six engineered micro-organisms had undergone small scale field testing in the USA (Sercovich and Leopold, 1991).

Food processing is the oldest and most traditional sector employing bio-processes. The major advances have been in the production of sugar substitutes e.g. HFS; cocoa butter substitutes which presently equal about one-quarter of world cocoa production; and the production of natural vanilla flavour from cell culture. More generally, however, plant tissue culture for particular agricultural strains is increasingly displacing traditional production in the South.

Third, because of the complex nature of the disciplines and processes which biotechnology encapsulates, it places a high premium not only on human resource development as indicated earlier, but also on institutional and management innovations both for product development and marketing. Many of these innovations, however, constitute severe impediments both to a "normal line" of "trickle down" from the North to the South, and to the promotion of traditional south-south forms of co-operation. For the purposes of this study the most important of these impediments are:

i) The increasing monopolisation of products and processes in a few countries and among a limited number of transnational enterprises, specialist biotechnology firms, and universities.

ii) Both as cause and effect of the above, the increasing extension of private property rights to processes and products developed in the life sciences. This has led to a decline of traditional agricultural research in public institutions, universities, and research centres and a reduced flow of agricultural research results into the public domain — methods of technology transfer on which many developing countries have traditionally relied.

iii) From the inception, universities, particularly those in the United States, have dominated R&D in biotechnology. They remain the leading patent holders in genetic manipulation and represent the crucial sector in fields such as molecular biology, bio-chemistry and medical research. This has forced universities into non-traditional roles requiring collaborative commercial arrangements with industrial firms. It has been reported that about one-fifth of all collaborative arrangements in biotechnology involve universities (Pisano *et al.*, 1988).

iv) Alongside the universities there have developed the dedicated biotechnology firms, originally conceived as a major channel for commercialising university research. There have been over 300 such new ventures in the United States since 1976. Their growth peaked in 1981 when 70 new companies were formed, but since then there has been a far lower entry rate reflecting increased risk, uncertainty, over-crowding, and reduced return[4].

v) The crucial role played by universities and research centres and the emergence of dedicated biotechnology firms reflect the earlier observation that to date genetic engineering, unlike other technologies, does not sustain a hard and fast distinction between basic discovery and commercial production.

vi) Expensive court cases, regulatory requirements, high development costs, and long delays associated with the commercialisation of biotechnology applications have resulted in enterprises relying on two primary strategies. One is pricing their product/process to ensure early recoupment of outlays, and the other is to spread their development costs through collaborative arrangements. For those outside the collaborative framework, and particularly developing countries, access is restricted and available only at very high costs.

While the universities and the dedicated enterprises have distinct advantages in R&D, both are weak in production capabilities and marketing skills, where high capital outlays, special expertise and know how for manufacturing, marketing, legalising, testing and certifying products and processes, are vital. It is here, however, that the established companies have sought to promote their own in-house research, while some of the universities and dedicated firms have moved into commercial production. Neither group, however, has been able to reproduce the advantage of the other, and **collaborative arrangements** between the sectors are the norm in the industry.

Of importance to third-world countries is the consideration that these collaborative arrangements operate through three broad governance structures: arms length contracts, vertical integration of enterprises from research to distribution, and joint-ventures on a product by product, area by area, basis. Arms length contracts are not highly favoured principally because of the difficulties of appropriating benefits in a technology where large areas of unclarity and uncertainty exist, especially as regards legal rights and the high costs of establishing these. From the South's point of view these problems of collaboration are far worse where enterprises have to cross national boundaries. It is not only that different legal systems exist, but severe imbalances in skills availability or inputs into the collaborative arrangement make mutually beneficial co-operation difficult. Further, the institutional innovation where the central position is given to inter-firm alliances as distinct from intra-firm relations is a paradigm shift in management and organisation. Indeed it has been claimed that the biotechnology sector will be to "strategic alliances" what the railroad industry was in the evolution of "modern management" (Pisano *et al.*, 1988). This shift displaces group structures as the primary relation, emphasizes bilateral relations, reduces the role of hierarchies, and limits the traditional claim by those who pay (the capital providers) to interfere in the direct management of operations. The emergence of these new forms is closely linked to the nature of the technology, as with few exceptions, biotechnology innovations are not "systemic in nature", so that compatibility with other production processes and products is not an overriding necessity. At the same time, it is a process technology and must therefore emphasize the transference of laboratory work to industry. It is this which impels collaboration, particularly when the laboratory work is initiated by non-traditional sectors with little or no experience in commercial applications, and often also with insufficient resources to exploit the market potential of the innovation.

In concluding this sub-section three final observations are appropriate. One is that on the present track, none of the elements outlined above suggests that the obvious needs of the developing countries, for example for cheap food, clothing and preventative medical care have played, or are likely to play a significant role in the evolution of biotechnology and its applications. There is, in other words, nothing inherently specific to the technology and its present institutional organisation which would give a natural advantage to the South. Indeed, already products of the South, such as sugar, vanilla, palm oil, cocoa are being displaced in world markets; and despite the prevalence of tropical diseases the amount of R&D expenditure on preventative health products for the South is minuscule, with the exception of a disease like Aids which is world-wide and profitable. In sum, therefore, the major incentive system is presently private profitability, and unless developing countries' needs can be mediated through the market, on this trajectory the prospects of biotechnology for the South would seem at best to be very limited, and at worst very disruptive, with widespread displacement of traditional products and processes. Secondly, experience suggests that a radical new technology will not be effectively or efficiently applied in the outdated forms of production and historically backward political and social structures which characterise many third world countries. This is even more relevant where reliance on human resource development and fundamental institutional and organisational changes in related economic processes are as crucial as they are with biotechnology. The basic challenge is, therefore, for major social changes to be put in place if the advances of biotechnology are to be effectively adopted in the South. Finally, as we shall see more fully later, a supply side incentive to go into biotechnology in the South exists, and already finds expression in a number of institutions in countries such as India, Brazil, Cuba, Mexico and Argentina. With rare exceptions, however, these institutions have very limited capacities.

c) Sugar as biomass and chemical feedstock

The global potential of sugar as biomass and chemical feedstock is the second major consideration behind this study. It is estimated that over 40 per cent of the world's manufacturing is based on biological materials. Taken as a whole the sugar cane plant is the world's largest source of annually renewable biomass traded in world markets. Sugar output at over 110 million tonnes annually, (70 million tonnes cane sugar and 40 million tonnes beet sugar) is also the world's largest output of a pure defined organic compound. Ordinary table sugar is so pure that it contains 99.96 per cent of the molecule sucrose, with more than one-half of the remainder being water. Sugar is so chemically versatile that it is technically possible to produce from it all the chemicals currently being produced from petroleum feedstock (Thomas, 1985). It is readily metabolised by micro-organisms, plants and animals, non-toxic and bio-degradable. It also produces energy and has bulk, unlike other alternate energy systems. Some of its characteristics are, however, more ambiguous; for example, being water soluble is both an asset and a disadvantage, depending on the chemical reactions sought[5].

Other things being equal, in light of the South's bio-resources and its limited scientific capacities it might well be that its best option is to enter biotechnology via agriculture; the reason being that in agriculture it draws on a very wide range of techniques and instruments of varying complexity thereby providing a range of potential entry points for the South. As we shall see later this holds particularly true for sugar where points of entry exist along a very wide range indeed: plant propagation, fermentation, fertilizer replacement, caloric and non-caloric sugar substitutes, sucro-chemicals, etc.

d) Sugar in the Caribbean and the global context

The strategic transformations of sugar in the world economy, its importance to the Caribbean, and the level of integration achieved in Caricom (see Section 3) together provide a major consideration in the choice of this case study. Sugar is the oldest surviving major tropical export staple and the largest existing agro-industry in the Caribbean. Originally its production was organised on slave plantations. With the abolition of slavery, it was later based on indentured immigration. The twentieth century saw control of the industry pass to transnational companies (TNCs) and, in a few countries, strong locally owned firms. In the post-independence period some of these TNCs were nationalised. More recently, with the world-wide drift to privatisation some of these same companies are in the process of being divested. Currently, therefore, the Caribbean countries have an amalgam of arrangements: state owned companies (Trinidad and Tobago); state companies with TNC management contracts (Guyana), private local plantations (Barbados) and joint-ventures (Jamaica). Small scale producers are everywhere, but their importance in total sugar output varies[6].

In 1960 the Caricom region produced 1.3 million tonnes of sugar; by 1990, however, sugar output was only 53 per cent of this figure (Table 1)[7]. The decline has been rapid and the survival of the industry in the region presently depends on a complex support network of protected markets in Europe (the Lomé Convention) and the US (the United States Sugar Quota), subsidies and administered prices. Yet it remains one of the region's largest foreign exchange earners and employers of labour, and in some countries (e.g. Guyana) the largest in both categories. The course of the industry's decline is revealed in Table 1 where dramatic falls in cane and sugar yields per acre, and the reduced efficiency of conversion from sugar cane to sugar, are indicated.

The dramatic fall in output reflects a severe disintegration of the industry rather than planned withdrawal or deliberate diversification. Several factors have been identified as causes (Thomas 1984, 1988): pests and diseases, poor husbandry, weather, deterioration of drainage and irrigation systems, poor ratoon and land replacement practices, factory inefficiency, a high proportion of extraneous matter in mechanically harvested cane, poor harvesting practices generally and particularly logistical delays in getting the reaped cane to the factory. In addition to declining output and escalating costs the industry also faces a hostile world market — despite the preferential sales arrangements referred to above.

In this almost chaotic situation the regional authorities leading the integration movement and in charge of sugar production have not shown signs of coping with the dramatic changes facing sugar. This includes a number of major transformations underway at the world level in sugar.

First, world output of high fructose syrups (HFS) has grown dramatically to a current output of over 8 million tonnes, about three times the volume produced in 1980. There are as many as 80 HFS plants world wide, with 80 per cent of the output in the United States. Although the growth of HFS has been exceptionally rapid, its sales have been severely constrained by administrative restraints on its distribution in the European Community (Thomas, 1985). In the US where there are few restrictions, marked centralisation of capital in the sector is taking place. Whereas in 1974, there were 14 sellers of HFS products, today three major ones (ADM, Staley and Cargill) account for about 75 per cent of the US market. A similar concentration is also taking place among the sugar millers in the US. In 1984 there were 30 separate sellers of refined sugar, today there are only 11 corporate entities, with three of these accounting for 60 per cent of the market. Significantly also, the major companies in the sweetener market hold major interests in all the important sweeteners: beet sugar, cane sugar, and high fructose syrups. In addition, major elements of these firms' facilities have "swing capability", i.e. the ability to move between HFS production, industrial starches, and ethanol (Thomas, 1985). The result is that third world countries face a situation where a small number of firms now have strategic control over which options are to be finally pursued in the world's largest national market.

Second, in addition to the many familiar problems facing tropical export staples on the world commodity markets, the world sugar market is undergoing special changes in its supply, demand and marketing conditions, most of which appear to be detrimental to the South. On the **supply** side there has been the emergence of the EC as a major exporter — while remaining a major importer; a definite trend towards self-sufficiency in sweetener production in the South (due to factors such as the strategic pursuit of food security, foreign exchange shortages, etc.); a technical revolution which has dramatically widened the range of competitive sweeteners both caloric (isoglucose) and non-caloric (aspartame); and an increasing concentration of export sales in only a few countries. Thus while in 1970 the share of the four largest exporters (European Community, Brazil, Cuba and Australia) was 46 per cent of gross exports, presently it is just under 60 per cent.

A few aspects of the technical revolution on the supply side should be noted for later analysis. One is that despite its rapid growth, the substitutability of HFS for sugar is limited by a number of technical constraints: namely, it is a liquid sweetener, it has to observe close temperature tolerances if its coloration and handling properties are not to be adversely affected, and it cannot be produced easily or cheaply in a crystalline form for home use. Its major growth has therefore been in industrial uses, particularly the soft drinks industry. Another is that second and later generation improvements in biotechnology have yielded impressive gains in the production of high fructose syrups, e.g. the replacement of batch reaction processes in enzyme technology with the techniques of enzyme immobilisation, the shift from first generation 42 per cent HFS to second generation 55 per cent, and the design of HFS plants with "swing capability". Further, the use of corn in HFS production in the US yields by-product credits which cover more than 50 per cent of the material cost of producing HFS. Significantly, each of these by-product credits, (corn oil, corn feed, and corn meal) serve relatively independently evolving markets. This gives US producers of HFS an unusually strong base for using corn as its basic raw material. Meanwhile, the commercial drive for technical improvements in non-caloric sweeteners continues unabated as the market potential is huge because of concern with weight control. Finally, the application of biotechnology to beet cultivation has yielded major gains compared to sugar cane cultivation, and this is an important factor in the rise of the EC as a major producer and exporter.

On the **demand** side, fundamental changes have also occurred, making the outlook for cane sugar bleak. Chief among these are: market acceptance of sweeteners which do not match sugar's profile; the growth of protectionist sentiment in the North; static or declining per capita sweetener consumption in the North, and in the South (where it is increasing) "other" considerations limiting the growth in demand for imported sweeteners.

The **marketing** of sugar has also been made more difficult by the movement towards flexible exchange rates, the separation of the market for "raw" and "white" sugar, and the rapid growth of "toll refining". Given that 90 per cent of the sugar trade is seaborne, the influence of freight charges on sugar marketing has also become considerable. Finally, because a rapidly decreasing fraction of world sugar output is traded internationally, and an even smaller proportion is actually traded in "free markets", the perverse world sugar cycle has become elongated. "Free market" prices are subject to adverse pressure for longer periods while price peaks have become shorter.

The result of the above is that in world markets, sugar is often portrayed as the supreme "political" crop. Its price in the world market bears little relation to production cost, and most of its output and export sales are based on special administrative and political arrangements.

Theoretically, the trade modifying effects of a new technology should operate through either the new trade created by totally new products for the world markets; the development of substitutes for previous products; the invention of new processes; or the utilisation of new inputs for existing products (Chesnais, 1988). In practice, these effects are being felt in sugar more than in any other agricultural output as a result of the emergence of high fructose syrups (new products), aspartame (substitute for saccharin), a number of fermentation products (new processes) and the use of corn (new input requirement for sweeteners). While previously it was observed that biotechnology can potentially have a positive impact on the third world, the effects thus far on the cane sugar industry have been overwhelmingly negative. In these circumstances several international institutions, e.g. UNIDO, UNESCO, and FAO, have taken the role of catalyst in securing third world entry into the new biotechnology, with the result that in regions like the Caribbean the process of biotechnology development is being supply-led and institutionally driven mainly through the work of the regional universities, research centres and R&D units in state enterprises, all of which are dependent, in one form or another, on international support. There are exceptions to the supply-led process, as in the case of Cuba where the process is "science-driven" and centred on interferon as a deliberate choice of product around which the country would build its skills. Brazil's ethanol programme is also an exception, it being a major example of a "market driven" model, the market, however, being modified, because while some claim that the social benefits of the programme exceed social costs, at prevailing market prices imported oil is still cheaper than ethanol (Sercovich and Leopold, 1991).

What, then, are the alternatives open to the Caribbean? The following section examines the technological options in sugar in order to identify potential points of entry and nodes of dynamism for regional co-operation.

a) The range of options

The ability to locate nodes of dynamism promoting regional co-operation in sugar will be in large measure dependent on the technical options which face the industry at the international, regional and national levels. At the global level the technical choices centre on cane sugar as one of several types of sweeteners. Here technical change and the competition this produces from other caloric and non-caloric sweeteners is the key, along with the possibility of non-traditional uses of sucrose and its by-products. At the regional (national) level the choices are more directly related to the efficient utilisation of resources already sunk in cane sugar production for the world market or their next best alternative uses. Here there are two broad choices. First, improving the productivity of resources already in sugar. This encompasses better yields from sugar cane lands, improved conversion efficiency in sugar mills, and better utilisation of all by-products. The second choice is diversification. This encompasses one or more of the following: withdrawing resources from sugar and agriculture altogether; substituting new crops; intercropping; a more systematic pursuit of by-product usage; treating the sugar cane plant as a complex multi-product entity using a production process which utilises the most commercially viable mix; cultivating the plant for its biomass, fibre and energy; alcohol production for later use either directly, as a petroleum enhancer, or as chemical feedstock; and the use of sucrose as a chemical feedstock.

Each of these diversification options is briefly reviewed in the remainder of this section.

2. Techno-logical options in sugar

b) *Efficiency in existing structures*

While performance varies from country to country, there is significant scope for improvement in the way sugar is presently produced in the region. Thus the observation has been made recently about Caribbean sugar factories:

"with minor improvements and improved operating techniques, it is possible to improve overall recovery rates from the present 65-85 per cent to 85-90 per cent... likewise modification of existing steam generating and mechanical systems... could reduce sugar cane factory fuel requirements by 30-40 per cent, thereby making surplus bagasse available for co-generation of electricity and other uses" (Rivero, 1989, 20)

Additional gains could be obtained by pursuing a multiple product approach in processing plants. Through an inter-governmental agreement with Germany, Jamaica has for some years now been developing a small scale plant designed to produce annually in one complex, amorphous sugar (2 500 tonnes), fancy molasses (3 000 tonnes), cane juice (1 800 tonnes) and charcoal briquettes (2 600 tonnes). Occasional sales have been made from the plant for many years and recently it has come on stream as a regular but small supplier of these products.

A similar situation exists in regard to land practices and is revealed in the decline in yields of the sugar cane plant shown in Table 1. The variety of forms of ownership/management in the regional sugar industry is a reflection of these difficulties and there is a need to search for improvements under each of these organisational regimes. Much of the R&D activity which takes place in sugar is focused on the development of plant varieties for commercial use, through the auspices of the Cane Breeding Station in Barbados which the Caribbean sugar producers jointly maintain. In preparing this study, several scientists have ventured the views that tissue culture can advance cane yields from 70-90 tonnes per hectare to 150-200 tonnes, through variety enhancement, improved resistance to pests and diseases, and so on. It has been pointed out also that in Brazil a bacterium capable of acting as a fertilizer in cane fields (Acetobacter diazotrophicus) is being developed to save on nitrogen based fertilizers. This could also lead to as much as a tripling of yields[8].

Table 1. **Caricom: sugar statistics**

	1960	1970	1980	1985	1990
Sugar Output (million tonnes)	1.30	1.04	0.88	0.76	0.69
Median Sugar yield/acre	3.2	2.6	2.2	2.0	1.9
Median Cane yield/acre	25.6	26.3	26.5	23.7	22.8
Median tonnes cane/tonnes sugar	10.2	10.3	11.9	12.6	11.2

c) *Diversifying out of sugar*

The process of abandoning sugar production altogether is already advanced in some territories. In Barbados property speculators alone are estimated to have taken over about one-quarter of the land previously in sugar (Thomas, 1988). In Barbados and elsewhere sugar lands have been alienated for tourist development and general urban uses. A significant amount of former sugar land lies idle, some of it being held with speculative intent as the pressures on land availability are immense in these small countries.

Governments in the region have promoted the diversification out of sugar and into alternative agricultural products such as either crops for domestic use to replace imports, e.g. rice, livestock, fish, or substituting with other staples, e.g. citrus, bananas, cocoa. None of these has achieved anything significant and the view is gaining widespread acceptance that given the high labour and land intensity of sugar cane cultivation, there is really no satisfactory substitute available to the region. Domestic markets are either too small or the export product which is to replace sugar does not face any better prospects in the world market. This view further encouraged the abandonment of sugar with no structured alternative, thus pointing to the need for the kind of reconceptualisation of sugar production outside of the traditional framework that is being attempted here.

d) Inter-cropping

Inter-cropping other plants with sugar cane has been subject to numerous trials both in the region and elsewhere. In Guyana the production of legumes, fish in the drainage/irrigation canals and livestock had been pursued after nationalisation of the industry in the early 1970s. For a number of reasons, including bad choice of product mix and lip-service effort in these initiatives, the results so far have been very disappointing, leading to a virtual abandonment of these projects, even as Mauritius field trials report hopeful results for inter-cropping with maize, potato, beans, and groundnuts (Biomass Users Network News, 1990).

e) Commercialising by-products

By-products have for long been central to the economics of sugar production. There is a long list of by-products produced in the making of sugar. On average, for every 100 tonnes of sugar cane ground the following is produced: i) 11.2 tonnes of raw sugar; ii) 5.0 tonnes of surplus bagasse (49 per cent moisture) = 1 300 kwh surplus electricity; iii) 2.7 tonnes of molasses; and iv) 30.0 tonnes of cane tops/trash. These are outlined below[9]:

Bagasse comprises cellulose used in making paper products, pentosans used in making furfural (a selected solvent in the production of lubricants, furfilic alcohol, and certain pharmaceuticals and pesticides), and lignin for making plastics. It is also used to produce fuel in many forms: electricity, charcoal briquettes and methane and producer gas. The use of bagasse to fuel sugar cane factories is nearly universal, making sugar production from the sugar cane plant energy self-sufficient. In some places such as Hawaii, surplus energy is sold. Over the past 30 years, average boiler capacity in Hawaii has increased more than eight-fold and sugar plantations produce about 10 percent of the state's electricity supply. In Hawaii and elsewhere bagasse has also been used as animal feed and in the making of a wide variety of miscellaneous products.

Molasses is a major by-product and is widely traded internationally. It is used in the preparation of fertilizer; animal feed; for distillation into rum, ethyl alcohol, rectified spirits, power alcohol and alcohol derivatives; other fermentation products (vinegar, acetic acid, acetone-butanol, citric acid, glycerine and yeast); and a variety of miscellaneous products (aconitic acid, monosodium glutamate, dextran). The principal uses are in animal feed and fermentation products. Beet molasses has a competitive edge over cane molasses in that it is higher in sucrose containing on average 48-55 per cent compared to 30-40 per cent. This makes it better suited for fermentation processes.

Cane tops and leaves make up the bulk of the by-products accounting for as much as 30 per cent of its weight, but the practice in the region is to burn this in the field to make harvesting easier. Research by ABA International Inc., for the Government of the Dominican Republic, however, suggests that the fuel potential of the cane tops is greater than that of the bagasse traditionally used. The main difficulty is the cost of collection.

In the wider Caribbean area, the most developed by-products are electricity, alcohol, and animal feeds. However, in Cuba pulp and paper products, yeasts, furfural and its derivatives, and agglutinated products from bagasse are produced. There, a special Institute of Sugar Cane By-Products supports a wide range of experimentation including the practice of commercial feedlot operations for cattle on sugar cane farms.

Brazil's alcohol programme is also exceptional attracting world wide attention in its use as an octane enhancer. Its current production is about 13 billion litres, up from 0.7 billion litres in the 1976/77 crop year. Brazil is also a significant exporter of the technology and equipment for ethanol production from sugar. There remains, however, a continuing problem of cost effectiveness that results from fluctuations in oil prices[10] and marketing problems, including US efforts to restrain the importation of Brazilian ethanol through claims of dumping.

Despite these difficulties research in ethanol production is advancing. Professor Gregor (1989) reports the development of a membrane process using ultrafiltration procedures for the cane juice and new micro-filters in the fermentation process which concentrates yeast cells and accelerates the process. Brazil has also made significant gains in its feed programmes through research to cheapen the treatment techniques to break down the resistant structure of bagasse lignocellulose and improve its digestibility as fodder. Autohydrolysis using steam and hydrolysis using Na_2O are already commercialised. Experimental work using urea in hydrolysis and oxidation using hydrogen peroxide and ozone is continuing. Recently it has been reported that Brazil is using "green yeast", a by-product obtained in the production of alcohol from sugar, which enhances the protein content of its cattle feed (Licht, 1991).

The wide range of possible by-products has allowed R&D and commercial development at a number of differing stages over the region. This indicates that the potential for gains from wider regional co-operation in at least selective areas could be combined with co-operative endeavours among the more closely related states already in the Caricom grouping.

f) Pursuing a multi-focal approach to sugar

The two principal areas for the development of a multi-focal approach to sugar are in exploiting sugar biomass potential and in using sugar as a chemical feedstock. The commercial potential of the biomass in the sugar cane plant has always been recognised in the industry, and the utilisation of bagasse and cane tops as by-products is evidence of this. A major technical option emerges, however, if the biomass potential is not portrayed as a by-product to sucrose production, but indeed the reverse — sucrose is a by-product to biomass production. The attractiveness of this option would be further reinforced if approached from the point of view of producing commercially from renewable resources, chemicals and energy, in amounts large enough to go a far way towards satisfying existing markets, in a form where, like petroleum, it can be easily stored and transported, but unlike petroleum, it is conservationist in relation to the environment. The environmental ideal would be production systems with "closed-loops", i.e. those in which the production of biomass yields its own replacement fertilizers as well as other by-products and does not require damaging agricultural and industrial practices in its production. Some scientists believe that the potential of the sugar cane plant is close to this ideal, giving support to the emphasis placed on it in this study.

In current practice, high sucrose plants have a bias against large ratios of biomass to sucrose. Indeed, cane with fibre content above about 15 per cent and large amounts of tops and leaves are discarded in cultivating varieties. Regional research indicates that the production cost of high fibre canes is about one-half that of normal cane, because after the first crop succeeding crops do not require herbicides or cultivation to produce six or more ratoons[11]. Green matter in excess of double that of traditional varieties and four times as much bagasse per acre have been obtained. The sugar content of these canes is expectedly low, 11.1 per cent of soluble solids compared to 16.1 per cent obtained in commercial varieties. The attraction therefore is to cultivate the sugar cane plant on a sustainable basis for the large quantities of ligno-cellusoic material that it contains.

Remarkably, an extraordinary project, from a scientific, commercial, and organisational standpoint, has been underway for some time now under the direction of Professor Alexander, at the University of Puerto Rico. The project commenced in 1986 and was planned to finish in 1993 — on the 500 year anniversary of Columbus bringing the plant to the region. The focus is on energy cane, i.e. the agricultural management of total biomass in cane cultivation. High tonnage varieties of up to 113 metric tonnes of green matter per acre (87 metric tonnes of millable cane) have already been achieved. This yields 45.8 metric tonnes of dry matter, 21.1 metric tonnes of trash, and 7 metric tonnes of sugar — about two and one half times that of standard varieties. The project focuses on the following objectives:

  i) cane field management as a high growth system for diverse products and cane using conservationist techniques to preserve the environment;

 ii) biomass productivity at the small family farm level, this being a deliberately chosen target[12];

iii) exploitation of cane botany and the native hardiness of the plant, which sucrose oriented cultivation has actively suppressed. Botanically it is believed that the plant's only preference would be to use its own sugar to pursue growth, and that therefore an ideal growth oriented cultivar could be developed;

 iv) to undermine the well entrenched but "flawed view" that the sugar cane plant is indissolubly linked to sugar as a sweetener. This has led to the widespread acceptance of the view in the region that "sugar cane for sugar's sake has all but disappeared as a credible farm commodity [and the] business sector's view that cane [is] a kind of dinosaur whose time has long passed"[13].

Organisationally, the project brings together scientists, land-owners and their hired labour in a voluntary grouping with no external institutional support. It finances itself from sales of the plant produced in trials, to local dairy farmers. Professor Alexander, the project leader, has described it as: "foremost a labour of love, faith, and personal convictions — features that sometimes blend poorly with institutional bureaucracy... it is substituting with time and perspiration what it lacks in financial resources"[14].

The project is low profile, perhaps too much so, as it risks negating one of its chief merits: leading by example. It is neither duplicated nor networked in any significant way within the region. As a "window of opportunity" it has not yet been seized upon. It remains however remains a brilliant illustration of the many different levels at which biotechnology can intervene in the cane sugar industry of the region, the potential for non-profit oriented R&D and scale up to commercialisation, and the scope for institutional and organisational innovation to support innovative research.

Another important initiative is the USAID funded Biomass Energy Systems and Technology Project (BEST), a follow up to an earlier project started in 1979. Its aim is to reduce petroleum import dependence in the Caribbean by promoting environmentally and financially sound biomass energy generated by sugar cane as well as rice and wood residues. The project draws on expertise in the US but encourages links with the local as well as US private sector both as investors in the project and sources and users of commercial technology. The project pays close attention to the dissemination of its results on the biomass option to farmers, processors, technology vendors, financiers and external aid donors. Research under its auspices has taken place at the Audubon Sugar Institute, Louisiana State University in the United States and the West Indies Cane Breeding Station located in Barbados. Trials on cultivars have yielded biomass output comparable to those cited earlier in the Alexander project.

In keeping with a multi-focal view of resources and products, the biomass approach, (particularly Alexander's) challenges the traditional pattern of cultivating and utilising the industry's **primary product**, i.e. the sugar cane plant, in the search for alternatives. One might also challenge the traditional uses of the industry's **end product**, i.e. sugar as a sweetener (Thomas, 1985). The former exploits the bulk potential of the sugar cane plant, the latter the bulk **and** purity of its end product, sucrose, as an organic chemical. To utilise sucrose commercially as a chemical it must be transformed into other products of greater value either by chemical or microbiological means. There are three routes in the transformation of sugar: microbial conversion, chemical degradation, and chemical synthesis.

Both microbial conversion, which is the traditional fermentation process, and chemical degradation are problematic. The use of micro-organisms in the conversion of one chemical product to another is relatively non-specific in the sense that after suitable treatment not only sugar but most carbohydrate sources can be made into a feedstock. Using this method would require therefore that a chemical industry based on sucrose be highly competitive, in terms of the cost of raw material, with other carbohydrate sources, e.g. corn, rice, wheat, potato, cassava. A similar problem is faced by the products of chemical degradation which are of a lower molecular weight, thereby permitting their synthesisation from cheaper sources of carbon, e.g. petroleum or even carbohydrate wastes.

Because micro-organisms are used in the microbial conversion process yields are inevitably low, since the micro-organisms must metabolise a proportion of the sucrose as a source of their energy. The process also has low reaction rates and requires large volumes of the product and long residence times. Although research is improving on these variables (as we noted in the case of isomerisation of corn to fructose where the use of immobilised enzymes has replaced the older batch production process), the cost of doing so relative to other processes, e.g. petro-chemicals, is a factor which has to be taken into account. The separation of the wanted product from the others in the microbial process also poses major technological problems whose solution inevitably raises costs.

In the case of chemical degradation, reactions proceed in a relatively "uncontrollable" fashion, thereby yielding a mixture of products from which the required product has to be then isolated. As Khan and Forage point out: "Despite extensive research in the past in degradation reactions of carbohydrates to yield a variety of products this approach, at present, is non-competitive."[15] The scope of economical application of sucrose through both the processes of microbial conversion and chemical degradation is therefore limited.

Despite these difficulties a wide range of products can be produced by microbial conversion: antibiotics and other pharmaceutical preparations; gluconic acid; biopolymers, the best known of these being dextran; D-araboascorbic acid (iso Vitamin C); kojic acid; fructose; and ethanol.

The real promise of sucrose as a chemical feedstock, however, is through the third route: directed synthesis. Unlike the two routes already considered, both of which basically seek to use sucrose as a source of simpler products, the approach of directed synthesis regards sucrose as a primary raw material itself and seeks to exploit the opportunities of synthesising it with other chemicals in order to produce higher value products. This approach makes use of sucrose in the form it is normally marketed, that is its pure anhydrous state.

Because sucrose is essentially a polyhydric alcohol, chemists point out that it has the potential to give rise to an almost unlimited range of derivatives. It will undergo all the typical reactions of alcohol. By function these are: esters, ethers, urethanes, zanthates and acetals[16].

A major obstacle in the development of synthetic sucrose derivatives is the "restricted solubility of the reactants in solvents other than those which are similar in reactivity to sucrose itself" (Parker, 1979). Some of the solvents used are very costly and this has encouraged the search for products that would require no solvents or products that can sell at a price to recoup the cost of such expensive solvents.

It is presently claimed that over 10 000 chemicals can be produced from sucrose and these products fall within the following broad market categories.

1. Foods	7. Solvents	13. Plasticisers
2. Feeds	8. Soil Conditioners	14. Plastics
3. Fuels	9. Fibres	15. Surface coating
4. Explosives	10. Adhesives	16. Surfactants
5. Elastomers	11. Paper	17. Medicines/Pharmaceuticals
6. Lubricants	12. Pesticides	18. Cosmetics

Within each of the broad categories there are high valued products which are produced in small volume and low valued products produced in large volumes. In the former, the chemical process is the key element in cost and selling price, as what is being sold is in fact a sophisticated chemical process rather than the raw material sucrose. Examples of these are expensive to develop systemic fungicides and certain pharmaceuticals. In the latter, sucrose is being sold as a cheap chemical and the processes used are not costly, e.g. sucroglycerides, animal feed additives, resins, plasticisers and even alcohol.

At present the categories with the most developed market potential are (1), (2), (3), (16) and (18). The leading enterprise in the field of sucrochemicals has been from the inception, Tate & Lyle, the British based transnational corporation. The initial stimulus for its R&D derived from the firm's long association with sugar and its traditional sugar base, and the high prices of petroleum products, particularly during the period 1974-81. They focused on surfactants for detergents and the food industry using the TAL process[17]. By 1980, however, Tate & Lyle acknowledged that

"To develop and make profitable a new chemicals technology is, we always acknowledged, to accept a major challenge — particularly at a time of acute depression in the chemicals market. With the added burden of heavy start up expenses, we have been in no position to make our planned impact on the market and incurred substantial losses in 1980. It is taking longer than we expected to commission the two new plants of our production complex at Knowsley, Merseyside. With our planned range of surfactant products we have encountered serious technical difficulties and have yet to prove our ability to produce these in volume and on a commercially viable basis. We are continuing our efforts to solve these problems but, in view of the high risk nature of this venture, have written our initial expenditure out of our balance sheet."[18]

The subsequent relative decline in petroleum prices combined with internal shifts in the Tate & Lyle power structure (occasioned by declining profitability) led to a major retreat from their sucro-chemical investments — after considerable outlays in this field. The crucial lesson is that the structure of the petroleum industry together with the deep entrenchment of petroleum as the world's principal chemical feedstock make for formidable barriers to the entry of new firms with a significant potential to challenge petroleum's hegemony.

To answer the question posed at the end of Section 2, this review suggests that quite a large number of technical options exist for the application of biotechnology to sugar. The points of entry vary in their complexity, sophistication and orientation, ranging from applications to upgrade the traditional product (tissue culture and the sugar cane plant) to a radical multifocal view of the plant as biomass, and its output, sucrose, as a chemical feedstock. The brief references to regional capabilities already indicate serious under-exploitation of this potential and considerable unevenness in the development of R&D and the commercialisation of non-traditional products from sugar. This, and the relatively limited development of co-operation in biotechnology and sugar, will be discussed in more detail in the next section.

3. Regional co-operation in and out of sugar

a) Caricom

The Caribbean Sea embraces the world's largest concentration of small and mini-states. This balkanised region has access to an exceptional number of preferential trading arrangements, including the Caribbean Basin Initiative (CBI), The Enterprise for the Americas, the EC — ACP protocols, and the Canada-West Indies Free Trade Arrangement and more recently the North American Free Trade Agreement. In addition several territories retain colonial or special arrangements to certain traditional metropolitan powers[19].

All of the states of this region have made regional co-operation a stated goal, but more often than not this is little more than a ritualistic assertion. In 1958 when the territories were still colonies, the British Government forged the formation of a West Indies Federation, mainly as a convenient administrative/governmental frame to deal with a large number of small and micro-states. The withdrawal of Jamaica from the Federation before its independence in 1962 led to its collapse. The idea of regional co-operation, however, survived the collapse and subsequently found expression in the Caribbean Free Trade Association (Carifta, 1968) later to become the Caribbean Community (Caricom, 1973). At present this is the most highly developed expression of co-operation in the region. This arrangement is not dissimilar in its essential form and content to other regional integration schemes in the South (see Chapter 1). Its basic mechanisms operate through two principal organs and a number of institutions, associated institutions, subsidiary committees and agencies. The two principal organs are the Heads of Government Conferences (scheduled to be held annually) and the Common Market Council of Ministers. The former has overall responsibility for the development of regional co-operation, while the latter supervises the operations of the common market which forms the essential core of the scheme. The main institutions comprise a number of Permanent Standing Committees of Ministers charged with the responsibilities for regional co-operation in their areas of competence. A number of regional bodies also have associate status, some of them established well before Caricom came into existence, e.g. the Universities of the West Indies and Guyana, and the Caribbean Development Bank. In 1981 a sub-regional grouping of seven smaller states was formed under the umbrella of the Organisation of Eastern Caribbean States. This is designed as a counter-weight to the influence of the larger states.

The organisational form of regional co-operation is, therefore, essentially that of an inter-governmental agreement empowered in a variety of inter-government institutions, both standing and ad hoc, operating through a regional bureaucracy (the Caricom Secretariat) located in Guyana. The principal actors are the governments and regional bureaucrats who administer the incentive arrangements within the scheme.

While the core of the Caricom system has been and remains the common market arrangements, intra-regional trade, as we saw in Chapter 1, has been only about 10 per cent of the region's overall trade, with a noticeable tendency to decline during the past decade, in the face of protracted economic difficulties in several countries (Guyana, Jamaica, Trinidad-Tobago and recently Barbados). A number of functional areas of co-operation also exist in the arrangements. Some of these, food, nutrition, agriculture and industry, are intended to create the scope for regional import substitution; others, education and shipping, for example, are intended to rationalise regional resource use and derive economies of scale. Unfortunately, so far none of these has become a major location of dynamic activity, and an earlier observation still remains true that:

> "although regional integration is essential if there is to be any permanent eradication of the systemic reproduction of poverty and powerlessness, Caricom's efforts in this direction have been disappointing"[20].

The crippling factor in the Caricom model of regional integration is that it is overly dependent on governments and the regional bureaucracy for its social energy in an age when the roles of these institutions are being reduced. Although the nature of Caricom's functional activities requires periodic involvement of other actors (NGOs, labour, farmers' organisations, private businesses, consumer associations, professionals) their roles remain essentially subsidiary and subject to institutional direction from above. Furthermore, much of their influence, where it exists, derives less from their own evolution within the region, than from growing pressures by donor countries and multilateral institutions for the involvement of such groups in the consultative processes. This has come about in response to the growing strength of lobbies in the North, especially in such sectors as labour, women, environment, the private sector and human rights. Even as the social energy of these non-traditional actors remains undeveloped, the Caricom model of regional co-operation offers few incentives for their growth and development. Indeed it might be argued that the existing model operates as a disincentive to forms of regional co-operation outside its formal ambit. There is a pressing need, therefore, for innovation in the forms of regional co-operation in order to take advantage of the new developments examined here and in Chapter 1.

b) Co-operation in sugar

Within Caricom, regional co-operation in sugar has not emerged as an area of particular focus. Not until the early 1970s was co-operation in agriculture promoted through a Regional Food Plan, later to become the Regional Food and Nutrition Strategy (RFNS). Under the RFNS the Caribbean Food Corporation (CFC) was established to encourage agri-businesses. Its subsidiary marketed non-traditional agriculture products on a joint basis for the region. In the area of agriculture research the Regional Research Council of colonial times was transformed into the Caribbean Agriculture Research and Development Institute. In addition, financing of agriculture through the Caribbean Development Bank and dissemination and training through the Caribbean Development and Advisory Training Service was also put in place. Sugar was not a central focus in these activities.

As a result of dissatisfaction with the overall development of regional agriculture a review of regional experiences was commenced in 1986 which led to the promotion of the Caribbean Community Programme for Agricultural Development (CCPAD). CCPAD embraced a regional action plan for the period 1989-1991[21]. This action plan which has already missed the original schedule, envisaged that the production of sugar,

> "a traditional export on which the region will be dependent for some time to come", is to be improved through "incremental increases in investment for the rehabilitation of existing production, the modernisation of plant, the introduction of cost saving methods in field and factory operations and the rationalisation of... marketing boards and producer associations"[22].

Further, joint marketing and joint-venture arrangements were to be pursued and diversification of by-products and the pursuit of new end uses for sucrose were recommended[23]. No action was taken to implement these objectives.

Outside the Caricom framework more attention has been paid to sugar. Prior to the creation of Caricom, for example, and going as far back as the nineteenth century the British government had encouraged co-operation in sugar marketing, sugar cane plant breeding, and the exchange of information on cultivation and factory processes. These have continued. At present the Sugar Association of the Caribbean (SAC), which replaced the former British West Indies Sugar Producers Association, later the West Indies Sugar Producers Association, performs these functions, and has done so since the territories became independent. SAC also co-operates within the wider regional framework of GEPLACEA, a grouping of sugar producing Caribbean and Central American countries and the Caribbean Basin Initiative (CBI) Sugar Group which has emerged out of the CBI arrangements.

GEPLACEA was established in 1974 as a grouping of 22 Latin America and Caribbean sugar producing territories, which accounts for about 28 per cent of world output and 45 per cent of world sugar exports. Its objectives are to develop regional capabilities in sugar production, to tackle significant local problems collaboratively, to encourage investments in sugar, and to undertake independent projects. Among the projects it is to encourage are the cultivation and exchange of sugar cane plant varieties, quarantine, pest and disease control, analytical techniques in determining sugar quality and control, by-product development, diversification, energy and fermentation. Although the range of projects is impressive, in practice the focus has been restricted to market protection for the traditional product, cane sugar, and exchanges on improvements in sugar cane production. Consultation and exchange on sugar cane varieties have taken place, while a number of publications, training courses and exchange of visits have also been accomplished. In late 1990, GEPLACEA encouraged the formation of the African Cane Producing Countries Association with broadly similar objectives.

The CBI group was formed in 1985 as an informal grouping of sugar producers in the Caribbean Basin whose objective is to protect the region's quotas in the US market and also to promote world wide free trade in sugar.

In addition to these, and outside their formal framework, a limited amount of regional and extra-regional net-working also takes place through the Biomass Users Network (BUN). This was formed in 1985 by 13 developing countries with its secretariat in Costa Rica, and presently it has 38 member countries. As the name suggests BUN focuses on Biomass in general. Sugar's role in this is obvious. It networks not only member governments, but NGOs, scientific and technical institutions, and private business sector interests. Its activities focus on training, dissemination, collective problem solving, resource rationalisation and diversification, knowledge transfer, management training and specialist studies in the technical, socio-economic, environmental and policy areas. However, apart from the irregular circulation of its newsletter in the region, it has not been influential.

In conclusion therefore, when we consider that sugar is a major employer, foreign exchange earner, and the most important activity in the rural sector of the region, we can appreciate the significance of the failure to date to focus on it meaningfully, as a locus of dynamic regional co-operation, development and transformation. The overwhelming thrust of existing collaborative arrangements has been on securing the already protected sugar markets to which the region has access. Co-operation in technology has been marginal and focused on routine concerns, such as field varieties, thereby taking the existing configuration of the industry as given. There has been no innovative work at the regional level to take the industry beyond its present confines. And so it continues to languish.

c) Co-operation in research

When taken in the context of the importance of biotechnology and the range of technical options outlined in the earlier sections, efforts to harness biotechnology at the national and regional levels in general and in sugar in particular have been far from adequate. In the broader Caribbean, with the exception of Cuba, most of the efforts in biotechnology were catalysed by international agencies particularly UNIDO, UNESCO, FAO, UNDP and the World Bank.

Through the sponsorship of a number of international agencies and under the aegis of Caricom, governments convened a meeting in 1986 to provide guidance on the way forward for the region in the two "new technologies": micro-electronics and biotechnology. The meeting recommended three major areas of focus: tissue culture; applied micro-biology and nitrogen fixation; a number of legislative changes and the promotion of international links. In all these areas, the importance of training, monitoring, dissemination and regional co-operation was stressed. The criteria laid down by the meeting for product focus were such as to encourage activity in sugar, with its diversification into an integrated rural development effort involving intercropping, bagasse, and energy development. Fermentation technology was also recommended as a major focus for the region's applied microbiology. Member territories were also encouraged to play an active role internationally by promoting institutional development especially through the International Centre for Genetic Engineering and BioTechnology (ICGEB), supporting the enactment of universally acceptable safety regulations and encouraging regional universities to be active in biotechnology and to network with extra-regional research centres. Following on this meeting a UNESCO/UNDP/UNIDO Regional Bio-Technology Programme for Latin America and the Caribbean began and was scheduled to cover the period 1987-1991.

Interviews with scientists in the region revealed that efforts by these international agencies have been successful in the following areas: i) creating awareness among policy makers; ii) getting national programmes started mainly through the establishing of science and technology agencies; iii) helping to identify key issues; iv) stimulating training programmes; v) creating opportunities for the region to receive equipment, scientific materials and personnel and thus to launch a few small R&D activities; vi) disseminating information on biotechnology; and vii) encouraging regional co-operation. They stress, however, that overall, programmes such as these have produced very modest results. This is primarily because the international institutions have placed comparatively more emphasis on research capabilities, than on diffusion and the involvement of potential producers and users of the technology in the region. No real linkages, therefore, have been forged between research and commercialisation, particularly in the private sector. Additionally, they have contributed little towards raising consumer influence on the course of biotechnology applications in the region. The exceptions are the two bilateral agreements, the German-Jamaica project and the USAID-BEST project, referred to earlier.

The Cuban case stands in direct contrast to the Caricom example. Cuba's efforts in biotechnology began about a decade ago and have involved a close linkage with its pharmaceuticals industry. Compared to the rest of the region it has enjoyed three immense advantages. First, its emphasis on education has produced an exceptionally impressive number and range of scientists. Second, its emphasis on health has also created an exceptional local demand for the products of the industry. Third, once the decision to go into biotechnology was made at the beginning of the 1980s, its centralised planning structure could redirect resources to such a venture in a way few developing countries could.

Although Cuba's effort initially focused around interferon, the objective was to use this as a point of entry into the new technology and a means for acquiring expertise in associated fields of purification, scale-up, chemical testing and even commercialisation. Cuban officials now claim that the country has gone well beyond that and has produced about 150-200 genetically engineered products. These include human growth hormone used to treat victims of Chernobyl, a variety of vaccines including those for meningitis B, hepatitis B, and dengue fever, several recombinant DNA proteins, and AIDs diagnostic kits. Cuba satisfies its own domestic market for about two-thirds of the generic drugs it uses and exports pharmaceutical and biotechnology products to a few Latin American countries (Brazil, Columbia and Venezuela) and the former Soviet Union. Organisationally, the Havana Biotechnology Institute established in 1986 is the flagship research institute. It co-operates with about a dozen other specialist research centres, including one for the Study of Biological Products in Sugar Cane[24].

The Cuban effort has been mainly supply-led but oriented towards the needs of its own population, especially in health. The critical hurdle which it now faces is how to move from significant technical innovation to the commercialisation of equipment and products it has innovated. While this would seem to require that Cuban industry forge strategic alliances with global TNCs as mass producers and marketing enterprises, south-south co-operation is also an important way to move ahead. This is particularly the case in areas where technical and commercial interests converge, as in the Caribbean, and where geography and culture might facilitate the search for mutual benefit, in strategic alliances across national frontiers. In view of Cuba's current need to find alternative partners, Cuba's strength in biotechnology may well provide a "window of opportunity" for co-operation in sugar within the wider Caribbean region.

4. Policies, proposals and participants

a) Introduction

From Sections 1, 2 and 3 it is clear that a large number of technical options of varying degrees of scientific complexity and sophistication for the application of biotechnology to the sugar sector seems presently to exist. Alongside this variation in knowledge intensity, there are significant revealed differences in the levels of capital intensity required by these points of entry, ranging from heavy investments in HFS plants with "swing capability" and those using genetic engineering processes, to knowledge intensive applications on a small scale level.

Despite the overwhelming concentration of the new biotechnology in the North, advances have been made in the South, and the potential there is often far greater than would be at first presumed. In some countries, e.g. Cuba,

Brazil and India, significant advances have been made. Scope for an innovative regional definition of the industry exists[25].

Although the profit motive is pre-eminent in biotechnology development, ethical concerns about the life sciences have spawned a number of private groups both in the North and South which operate outside this framework and which have dedicated a considerable amount of skill and time in promoting innovations on an altruistic basis. The Alexander project is a superb example of this, as it brings together personnel from the North and South in a South based project[26]. This creates a new social basis for action.

Lastly, a number of national and inter-governmental programmes with well meaning objectives are in the South — often coaxed into existence by international institutions. While in very few instances have major gains been obtained, these programmes should not be hastily discarded.

Exceptional opportunities have thus emerged out of present day systemic linkages between R&D, technology, organisational renewal, development of productive factors, growth in national output, development, and general relations within and between nation states. To seize these opportunities, however, will require an ordered programme for the removal of impediments to institutional and organisational renewal and the creation of incentives designed to encourage new actors to emerge as the leading social forces promoting regional co-operation. Without this the integration dynamic cannot be located, where it must, in the domain of innovation and in the building of regional capacity to participate competitively in the present international division of labour. Pursuing this objective, in what follows we set out some of the key elements in an innovation driven model of regional co-operation in biotechnology and a preliminary sketch of the vital mechanisms and modalities of its implementation.

b) Integral elements

Certain elements are key to an innovation-driven model of co-operation applied to biotechnology and sugar in the Caribbean. First in considering entry into the new technology, an explicit distinction must be made between entry into R&D and the commercialisation of biotechnology know-how. It has been widely and misleadingly claimed in the literature that entry into biotechnology, compared to the other radical new technologies of the past, is cheap. As Sercovich and Leopold (1991) point out this may be true for certain types of R&D, but not for the commercial production, distribution and marketing of biotechnology products. The Cuban case gives support to the position. Thus despite major technical gains, marketing and distribution of Cuban products and techniques lag far behind. To avoid the damaging consequences of such hype, innovative activities must be commercially driven rather than preeminently scientifically or technically driven, as is currently the case with many third world efforts. Because the forces of supply and demand are expected to prevail, entry into biotechnology in sugar must thus be narrowed to products and processes which have commercial prospects. One way of ensuring this is to establish an institutional mechanism for pre-feasibility testing, pre-investment surveys, determination of appropriate strategic alliances for commercialising know-how and the identification of possible sources of financing. Such activities will also require that greater attention be paid to human resource development and to the continuous improvement of indigenous technological and scientific capabilities within the region. We will return to this point in the discussion of mechanisms and modalities.

The importance of selectively focusing on specific products and processes is well brought out by Buckwell and Moxey (1990) with regard to biotechnology in agriculture. In contrast to the mechanical and chemical technologies with which it competes, biotechnology, they point out, is divisible and scale neutral, in that it affects highly divisible inputs (seeds, micro-biological applications). Furthermore, while it requires **higher** knowledge intensity for its application, it also requires **lower** complementary capital inputs than the chemical and mechanical technologies in agriculture. Its benefits are also very specific and can only be appropriated from farms which adopt it. Finally, its pattern of knowledge intensity in applications usually requires higher levels of management skills than other technologies. One obvious consequence of these considerations is that the diffusion of the technology is likely to be uneven — a phenomenon we have already observed in sugar. Buckwell and Moxey thus conclude that it:

> "seems unlikely at present that it will sweep rapidly over agriculture. Its effects will be patchy, affecting particular sectors and thus regions [consequently] it will be much more helpful to focus attention on a specific application of biotechnology, the sector it is going to affect and the issues just raised... there are no grounds for a grand strategy or policy for agricultural biotechnology"[27].

From our survey a number of important criteria for product and process selection can be derived. These include the need to take into account the:

— state of the art in the technology (globally, regionally and in different national territories);

— resource availability and current costs of production;

— local scientific tradition;

— scientific capabilities in the region and among non-residents working overseas;

— needs and demand, including market size and scope for commercialisation;

— potential support from external sources;

— scope for rationalising the region's scientific infrastructure;

— spill-over effects and externalities.

An innovation driven model of regional co-operation will, of necessity, encompass technology transfer and indigenous technological development, in both the traditional and non-traditional organisational forms which these can take. Much of the economic literature focuses on traditional organisational forms of technology transfer, which are generally mediated through the market place. A typical catalogue would include foreign direct investments in a variety of forms (subsidiaries of TNCs, joint ventures, equity holdings); direct transfers through licensing arrangements, purchase of patent rights, management contracts, technical consultancies and training; import of capital goods (sometimes linked to training); reverse engineering; turnkey projects; monitoring and screening of journals; visits to enterprises; training in overseas universities and research institutions. Little, if any, attention is paid to those non-traditional forms of technology transfer which are not commercially inspired and reflect other value systems expressed through like-minded networking institutions. In the approach adopted here these non-traditional forms play a crucial role, because in biotechnology the value systems inherent in the present process of relentless commercialisation of the life sciences has generated resistance at the ethical and moral level. It is our belief that the significance of this should not be understated as a motivating factor in the evolution of an alternative biotechnology. We have already seen the power of this motivation in the Alexander project.

Highlighting these concerns runs the risk of, but does not automatically lead to, "insensitivity" with regard to the requirement of commercial viability as the final validator of economic activities. What it requires is care in assessing risks and also ensuring that support from non-profit oriented individuals and institutions participating in this process is not pursued as a rejection of the requirement of positive real returns over a reasonable time horizon on assets committed to innovation.

Although the focus in this chapter has been mainly on technical innovation, one cannot treat this as a process unconnected to the socio-political context. To the contrary, an innovation driven model of regional co-operation emphasizes both the fundamental socio-political changes at the world level which are cause and effect of the new technologies and the local context of its application. Thus the repressive political arrangements which characterise many third world countries militate against the model by discouraging scientific inquiry, encouraging the brain drain, and creating unreceptive environments for innovation. Systematic efforts to promote an environment which favours R&D, innovation and entrepreneurial activity in scientific production as distinct from trading imported inputs, will be necessary for the model to work successfully. Social changes will therefore be needed to accommodate the new technology in the South as much as they already have been in the North[28]. Such changes do not mean that the established mode of co-operation which relies heavily on inter-governmental initiatives supported by a regional bureaucracy is entirely useless. Rather, incremental, if not radical and structural improvements in these arrangements are certainly possible and would complement the innovation driven model of regional co-operation proposed here. For example, in Caricom, the centuries of experience in sugar production and familiarity with the botany of the sugar cane plant, its cultivation and the processing of sugar, could give a head-start to the region as a "late-late-comer", much as some argue the centuries of experience in fermentation have given to Japan an edge in fermentation technology. Experience, however, shows that the ability to appropriate the gains from "leapfrogging" are dependent on the "social capability" of the region, especially in the area of skills and organisational flexibility; hence the need for improvements to existing regional arrangements so as to lay the basis for such developments.

c) Mechanisms and modalities

This brings us to the question of implementation. Certain mechanisms and modalities arise from the model's emphasis on user-oriented innovation. In what follows we will focus on three such mechanisms, namely a) those that centre on the potential of voluntary, non-profit, private initiatives both in the North and South, perhaps best typified in the flexible organisational form of NGO-type institutions operating in relation to both public and private sectors, b) the supportive role of governmental activism in the international arena, and c) a strategy of flexible relations with TNCs.

The strategic advantage of NGO type institutions is that they are better placed to access those in need, to be participatory, and to encourage development from the ground up. Importantly also, they usually bring to bear, in the process of co-operation, resources which are required for development but which are inherently self-generating, that is they do not diminish with use, but to the contrary, expand in use: commitment, dedication, involvement, altruism. This, as we have seen with the Alexander project, is not as "idealistic" as it might appear at first blush, for already we have noted that this is by far the best of the regional efforts to promote alternative technologies in sugar. Innovativeness, flexibility and open access systems are best developed in this sort of framework. Such structures are also potentially lower cost because of smaller overheads and a higher proportion of voluntary skilled labour. All these factors we believe are vital if new products and processes developed in the South are to be given a competitive edge in the global market place.

Linked to NGO-type structures is the increasingly ubiquitous organisational form of networks as an important mechanism of delivery. Networks, like the NGO organisations which are often constituent elements of them, can also be flexible. They, too, frequently require comparatively little initial investment, at least in such preliminary yet basic and important areas as information flows, inventories of skills, descriptions of local situations, interests and priorities. By their very nature they also favour decentralisation, while allowing their constituent elements to benefit from scale economies. Their participatory structures, which encourage reciprocal exchanges, would also help fight against the "dependency syndrome" which is said to be common to the region. Most importantly, however, they are the organisational mode best able to encourage a flow of skilled persons with a commitment to "the constituencies of the future", and sympathetic to the "public good" view of the life sciences — a perspective needed to redress the negative consequences of increasing privatisation in the field of biotechnology. Such institutions are not high profile and they often receive little more than patronising acknowledgement of their existence from governments. But there are grounds for believing that they have more potential than may yet be acknowledged.

Traditionally, technology transfer to the South has occurred through markets or Williamson-type hierarchies (Ernst, 1990). In these traditional forms, the receiving country was limited to "feedback" mechanisms to facilitate "local adaptations of the technology". Networks, however, can go beyond this and embrace the full spectrum from knowledge generation to commercial uses of the technology. As advanced here the idea of networks is of course not new, and has been a general proposal in the South going at least as far back as the "technical co-operation among developing countries" proposals made at the UN Conference on Science and Technology for Development (1979). Most of the networks coming out of these proposals, however, have laid considerable emphasis on the networking of governments and public institutions whereas our emphasis is on private individuals, private firms and institutions. This opens the possibility that needs in the South, even when incapable of being expressed as demand, will remain an impelling social consideration. It gives rise to the expectation, moreover, that initially mobilising commitment to Third World and Caribbean development of biotechnology through voluntary, non-profit networks will overwhelmingly involve the region's universities and research centres and will be directed towards entry into R&D (and perhaps some scale-up endeavours), monitoring scientific advance, enhancing negotiating capacity, and giving policy guidance on the legal and regulatory framework.

For such networks to be effective in ensuring entry into biotechnology, an activist supporting role for governments both at home, in terms of the requisite enabling legislation, and in the international arena will be needed.

In several Caribbean countries laws regulating visa requirements, work permits, currency transfers and so on constitute serious barriers to the mobility of NGO personnel and resources. Indeed there are not even laws expressly designed to give legal identity to NGOs and many are legally constituted through decades old laws on private companies, charitable organisations and co-operatives. Advocacy for enabling legislation in this area is a clear priority.

A second area for enabling legislation and new domestic initiatives is in education and training. Research programmes and courses in the new areas of sugar studies, sucrochemistry for example, need to be developed in regional training and research institutions, given the amount of regional resources committed to sugar. A start could be made in post graduate training awards and fellowships to develop a corps of persons equipped to offer training in these areas. In this way human resources deficiencies can be concretely tackled. This would be accompanied by efforts to build up the requisite laboratory and research facilities, while making fuller use of existing facilities in the region through networking and exchanges. Gaps in capabilities can then be filled through NGO networking. Networking these groups to facilitate continuous interaction across broad disciplinary fronts should also be a major objective of the regional consultation.

Countries in the region would also be required to support efforts to redress and shape international regulations to protect their interests. Coordinated efforts among governments in the region to respond to the political and economic pressures to comply with the new private property relations which are emerging in the life sciences pursuant to the Uruguay Round of GATT is a case in point. Support for an adequate international regulatory framework is another example. Current regulations governing the introduction of organisms into the environment are not universally applied, and among the leading countries they remain inconsistent (e.g. in the US the product is regulated while in the EC the process is)[29].

This troubled international situation is receiving international attention. Walgate (1990) reported on a recent USAID meeting which brought together participants from International Agricultural Research Centres, Universities and public Research Institutions in the North and South. Some of the points upon which they agreed are worthy of governmental support in international fora. For example:

— the need for more collaboration between North and South involving the private sectors and researchers;

— better regulations on the use of the South's territory for experimental work;

— the creation of an international institution to help the South negotiate proprietary matters in this field (the World Bank was suggested);

— more international effort in support of the commercialisation of the research advances made in laboratories in the South.

It should be noted that already the World Bank is a significant player. In 1989 it spent about $100 million on biotechnology. It has expressed the view that it should aid the South in this field and has proposed the creation of a skills pool for this purpose — a Biotechnology Transfer Unit. It also supports the early introduction of patent legislation in the South, a prominent role for the private sector, national and international regulation of experiments, products and processes, and the establishment of a special programme of support for "orphan commodities", that is those crops and animals for which there is no substantial commercial interest in the North.

While the TNCs' lead in biotechnology is indisputable, the South's choices in relation to them should not be artificially narrowed to those of conflict or surrender through unequal negotiation. There is a real alternative now in the form of strategic alliances within the South and with the North via the mechanisms of NGO-type institutions. This leaves room for marketing and large scale production links with TNCs — the areas where the South will remain weak for some time to come. The difference in the situation is that **potentially** the terms of engagement will be more favourable to the South because of the strength gained through prior R&D alliances advocated here. Furthermore, at this stage of the biotechnology revolution, TNCs are not a homogenous group with homogenous interests. The situation is too uncertain to allow this to occur. These differences create room for manoeuvre and open new windows of opportunity for North-South partnerships.

The shift in emphasis from intergovernmental structured integration arrangements supported by regional bureaucracies to networked arrangements centred on private enterprises and non-governmental structures, requires that the major private and public economic interests in sugar are brought together in the endeavour, and share the new vision. The key private interests are the sugar farmers (small, medium and large), millers, wage workers in field, factory and administration, local input suppliers, local users of the industry's output, financial institutions investing in the industry and the shareholding public. At present, there is no formal or informal grouping of these interests around common objectives. An urgent priority is to find a means for bringing this about, and to do so while keeping an innovation and entrepreneurial orientation to the group's activity. One way in which this might be done, and which at the same time could produce important R&D spin-offs, would be to centre efforts around the promotion of the Alexander project. A useful means for achieving this might well be the mounting of a travelling exhibit of the project's work throughout the region, culminating in a regional consultation where all the major interests in sugar, public and private, are brought together. Such an exhibit could play a tremendous role in public awareness, challenging the region with visions of sugar that are very different from these which presently dominate its consciousness. The regional consultation, moreover, would not be principally a celebratory occasion but one in which the opportunity is taken to identify and rank priorities for a regional effort in innovation. At that meeting the earlier proposal to establish a "feasibility, pre-investment unit" could be put into effect. This would become a sort of clearing house for regional R&D. The regional consultation would also be the locus for developing enabling legislation to stimulate the development of NGOs and it would provide a forum for networking these groups to facilitate continuous interaction across a broad user-producer interface.

There is a dearth of venture capital of this type in the region. Whether it is institutional weakness or unwillingness to take risks is not clear. It is therefore proposed that the financing of these activities could be drawn from two primary sources. First, a modest government cess on the output of all sugar could be introduced. These revenues would go into a Venture Capital Fund under industry control[30]. After World War II the colonial authorities, in fact, had done this as a way of forcing the companies to give priority to their modernisation and re-capitalisation. It turned out to be a major source of financing for the industry's mechanisation. Second, the region's capital markets could be approached in a systematic way as a likely source of equity capital for these ventures. Where possible, external capital markets should also be approached for funds on a joint-venture basis. Similarly, overseas firms could be explored with the aim of promoting strategic alliances for the commercialisation of local know-how.

A further proposal which touches on the area of financing linked to biotechnology and sugar is that support should be given in international fora for the proposal emanating from the BUN network, that "debt-for-nature" swaps, which are now largely confined to environmental projects, should also include investment in biomass projects for petroleum importing countries (*BUN Network News*, Vol. 4, No. 1, Jan.-Feb. 1990). In its proposal the network stresses that swaps should focus on investment in the exchange, thereby being supportive of the efforts of developing countries to **produce** their way out of debt, in a sound economic, social, environmental, and technical way.

1. Caricom embraces the following thirteen countries: Antigua and Barbuda, Bahamas, Barbados, Belize, Dominica, Grenada, Guyana, Jamaica, Montserrat, St Christopher-Nevis, St Lucia, St Vincent and the Grenadines, Trinidad and Tobago.

2. Some writers also distinguish between an "open process" and "closed process" use of biotechnology; the former being applicable to situations where natural resources are processed in the "open" and a broad range of techniques and disciplines are applied to optimise processes already taking place in nature, e.g. mineral leaching as discussed by Alyson Warhust in this volume, and the latter to "closed" manufacturing systems heavily reliant on sophisticated hi-tech.

3. Among the factors inhibiting a more rapid rate of diffusion are: the difficulty in going from laboratory to commercial production given the inherent complexity of the life sciences, legal difficulties, regulatory delays, public opinion, lack of the requisite skills, high prices, overcrowding of the market due to a large number of firms which produce a "swarming" effect that leads to high financial burn rates and low survival rates (F. Sercovich and M. Leopold, 1991, p. 36).

4. Of note is the fact that in the first half of 1991 their fortunes seemed to have revived, as reflected in the financial markets. Thus the Washington Post (15 April 1991) reports that: "The stocks of biotechnology companies have been hot properties on Wall Street since the beginning of this year... for years a sceptical Wall Street gave biotechnology companies the cold shoulder". While this caused several to go bankrupt, today "a crazy quilt of strategic alliances with pharmaceutical companies... venture capital companies and federal grants drum up the millions of dollars a biotechnology company needs for research and development".

5. It is also hygroscopic and forms complexes with some metal ions. It is an important raw material for microbial conversion processes and has traditionally been used this way. It is unstable to heat, creating problems in some chemical processes. Its molecules are somewhat unstable and sucrose hydroxyls are usually less reactive than water. The high ratio of oxygen to carbon also places a limit on the number of organic solvents that can be used. Furthermore, it has two manifest chemical reactions which are critical — hydrolysis and pyrolysis — and usually unwanted (Thomas, 1985).

6. They usually cultivate the plant and have it milled in factories controlled by one or other of the ownership/management forms mentioned above.

7. World output of beet and cane sugar averaged 57 million tonnes for the period 1961-65. By the crop year 1980/81 output had grown to 88 million tonnes. In the current crop year 1991/92 it is projected at 113 million tonnes. Cane sugar currently accounts for 66.3 million of this. In the larger Caribbean — Central American region output averaged 9 million tonnes for the years 1961-65 and 14 million tonnes for the years 1981-85. In the current crop year (1991/92) it is projected at 17 million tonnes. Of this total Cuba's, Mexico's and Guatemala's output is projected at 7, 4 and one million tonnes respectively. (The Czarnikow Sugar Review, 1991 issues).

8. About US$150 million is spent on nitrogen based fertilizers. The bacterium, discovered by Johanna Dobereimer, is found in roots, leaves and even cane residues. It absorbs nitrogen in the air and, using carbohydrates from the plant, transforms it through nitrogen fixation into ammonia. Previously it was not known that sugar cane could absorb atmospheric nitrogen.

9. In addition 3.0 tonnes of filter mud (80 per cent moisture), and 0.3 tonnes of furnace ash resulting from the burning of bagasse and usable as a building material are produced.

10. The competitive price for sucrose to be converted to ethanol for other uses is when the price of ethylene is over US$450 per tonne. In Brazil the energy is being produced at the equivalent of about US$34 per barrel of oil equivalent.

11. This is reported in *Biomass Users Network News*, March/April 1990.

12. It should be noted that there are two persistent criticisms of the Brazil programme. These are that the drive to put lands under sugar is severely disruptive to small holders, and that environmental pollution from distilleries is a serious threat.

13. *Ibid*, p. 2.

14. *Ibid*, p. 3.

15. R. Khan and A.J. Foraje (1979/80), p. 178.

16. Following Vlitos (1979) we can present these as follows with their potential industrial uses noted within parenthesis.

    Esters — monostearate (surfactant emulsifier), monoacetate (humectant), disterate (emulsifer), hexalinoleate (surface coatings), octa-acetate (denaturant plasticiser), octabenzoate (plasticiser), disobutyrate, hexa-acetable (viscosity modifier), monomethacrylkate (resin monomer), and polycarbonate (resin intermediate)

    Ethers — mono-octadecyl ether (surfactant), hepta-allyl (drying oil), octacyaneothly (dielectric), actahydroxypropyl (cross-linking agent in polyurethane resins), and tetracarboxyethyl (chelating agent)

Urethanes — N-alkylsulphonoyl (surfactants)

Xanthates — S-alkylmonozanthates (surfactant chelating agent)

Acetals — cetyloxyethyl (surfactants).

17. In the TAL process sucrose reacted directly with a triglyceride in the absence of a solvent, to produce surfactants with highly esteemed detergent properties (complete and rapid bio-degradability, non-toxicity to mammals, fish and micro-organisms, low foaming, non-irritating, non-allergenic, orthodermic, and with excellent surface active, emulsifying and oil dispersing detergent properties) and surfactants for use in the food industry, especially baking where excellent properties are also observed (improved surface appearance, improved wetting properties in reconstituted dried foods, delayed staling properties, improved oven spring, crumb softness, provision of gluten for non-wheaten flours, etc.), are the major products referred to in the quotation.

18. Tate & Lyle Ltd. (1980), p. 12.

19. For example, the United Kingdom, France, Holland and the United States (e.g. Montserrat, British Virgin Islands, Martinique, Guadeloupe, Aruba, Bonaire, Curacao, Puerto Rico, and US Virgin Islands).

20. C.Y. Thomas (1988), p. 323.

21. The aims of CCPAD are given as follows: the revitalisation of agriculture and fuller use of existing trade and production integration mechanisms, institutional strengthening in the areas of agriculture support services, mobilising funds and technical assistance for regional agriculture, stimulating private investment, bringing together all programmes and projects to ensure better linkage and prioritisation (*Agrocarib 2000*, pp. 7-8).

22. *Agrocarib 2000*, p. 14.

23. The author was a consultant to the Caricom Secretariat in the preparation of this programme and recommended the need to place emphasis in the commercialisation of new end uses for sugar, and indeed other tropical staples. I believe that the failure to take action over the period of the action plan is the significant point to be noted, not the declared support given to the proposal.

24. Included among these institutes are the following: Centre for Biological Research, Centre for Animal Breeding, Centre for Immunoassay, Centre for Genetic Engineering and Biotechnology in Camaginey Province, Sanctus Spiritus and Havanna, the Finlay Institute, Centre for Tropical Medicine, Centre for Animal and Plant Health and the Centre for the Biological Products of Sugar referred to in the text.

25. Within the South however, the same uneven distribution which exists between North and South is replicated, and this is true even in the small area of the Caribbean.

26. For a listing of many of the UN agencies and biotechnology networks, see C. Fowler *et al.*, (1988), "The Laws of Life, Another Development and the New Biotechnologies", *Development Dialogue*, 1-2 (Special Issue).

27. A. Buckwell and A. Moxey (1990), p. 56.

28. See the chapter by Carlota Perez for a more detailed discussion of these changes.

29. Given the changing nature of the technology, regulations are being outdated quickly.

30. Following an earlier proposal in Thomas, 1985.

Biomass Users Network News, Editorial, Vol. 4, No. 1, 1990.

Biomass Users Network News, "The Puerto Rico Sugar Cane Commemorative Project: The Next 500 Years", Vol. 4, No. 3, pp. 1-4, 1990.

BUCKWELL, A. and A. MOXEY (1990), "Biotechnology and Agriculture", *Food Policy*, February, p. 44-56.

Caribbean Community Secretariat, Agrocarib, 2000, Guyana, 1991.

Chemical Week, "Building War Brews for Connaught", 20 September 1989.

CHENAIS, F. (1988), "Biotechnology and the Agricultural Exports of Developing Countries: A Review of Trends and their Implications", Paper presented to the *Groupe de recherche sur l'État, internationalisation des techniques et le développement*, February.

Czarnikow Sugar Review, 1991.

ERNST, D. (1990), "Network Transactions and Technological Capabilities — Implications for South-South Co-operation, A Research Proposal", (mimeo), November.

FOWLER, C. *et al.*, (1988), "The Laws of Life (Another Development and the New Biotechnologies)", *Development Dialogue*, 1-2.

GODOWN, R.D. (1989), "Environmental Release: The Battles and the War on Two Fronts", *Biotechnology*, October.

GREGOR, H.P. (1989), "Cost Effective Biomass Conversion Techniques for the Future: Alcohol from Sugar Cane", *Biomass Users Network News*, Vol. 3, No. 3, May-June.

KHAN, R. and A.J. FORAJE (1979/80), "Carbohydrates as Chemical Feedstock", *Sugar Technology Review*, No. 7.

LICHT, F.O. (1991), International Sugar and Sweetener Report, Vol. 123, No. 35, Germany.

Office of Technology Assessment (1984), *Commercial Biotechnology: An International Analysis*, Pergamon Press, Oxford, UK.

PARKER, K.J. (1979a), "Carbohydrates and Chemistry", *World Sugar Journal*, 2(6), pp. 19-23.

PARKER, K.J. (1979b), "Sucrose as an Industrial Raw Material", Paper presented to International Sugar Organisation Conference, p. 18, London.

PISANO, G.P., W. SHAN and O.J. TEECE (1988), "Joint Ventures and Collaboration in the Biotechnology Industry", in D. Mowery ed., *International Collaborative Ventures in US Manufacturing*, Ballingen Publishing, Cambridge, Mass.

RIVERO, N. (1989), "The Latin American and Caribbean Sugar Industries: Facing the Challenge of the 21st Century", *Sugar Y Azucar*, November, pp. 17-22.

SERCOVICH, F.C. and M. LEOPOLD (1991), "Developing Countries and the New Biotechnology", IDRC, Ottawa.

TATE and LYLE (1980), Annual Report, PLC.

THOMAS, C.Y. (1984), "Plantations, Peasants and State: A Study of the Modes of Sugar Production in Guyana", University of California, Los Angeles.

THOMAS, C.Y. (1985), *Sugar: Threat or Challenge (An Assessment of the Impact of Technological Developments in the High Fructose Syrup and Sucro-chemicals Industry)*, IDRC, Ottawa.

THOMAS, C.Y. (1988), "The Poor and the Powerless: Economic Policy and Change in the Caribbean", Latin American Bureau and Monthly Review Press, London and New York.

VLITOS, A. (1979), "New Product Developments for Sugar-cane Carbohydrates", paper presented at the Symposium on Alternative Uses of Sugar Cane for Development, 26-27 March, p. 13, San Juan, Puerto Rico.

WALGATE, R. (1990), *Miracle or Menace? Biotechnology and the Third World*, Panos Institute, London.

WARHUST, A. (1987), "New Directions for Policy Research: Biotechnology and Natural Resources", *Development*, 4, pp. 68-70.

Chapitre 8

AU-DELÀ DES ÉCHANGES : INNOVATION, RÉSEAUX ET COOPÉRATION SUD-SUD

Lynn K. Mytelka

Au cours des années 70 et 80, qui ont vu la part de la valeur ajoutée intellectuelle dans la production de tous les secteurs augmenter et la concurrence s'internationaliser, la nécessité pour les pays en développement d'entamer un processus d'ajustement continu, susceptible de « transformer des atouts statiques en forces dynamiques »[1], est devenue plus manifeste que jamais. Néanmoins, le débat portant sur le rôle que doivent jouer les pays en développement dans l'économie internationale a rarement dépassé la théorie relativement conservatrice de l'approche statique en termes de gains commerciaux[2]. Articulé autour d'une vision dichotomique de l'économie mondiale, ce débat a mis en avant les signaux émis par les marchés internationaux, au détriment de ceux du marché intérieur, et encouragé la création d'un système d'échanges mondial, plutôt qu'un système d'accords de coopération entre les pays du sud. En d'autres termes, le débat opposait les partisans de l'« ajustement par les prix », le juste prix étant celui qui se pratique sur les marchés internationaux, et ceux pour qui les économies dynamiques d'Asie devaient leur succès aux mesures gouvernementales visant à modifier ces signaux et donc à « fausser les prix »[3].

Dans les années 90, tenants du multilatéralisme et partisans du régionalisme ont été amenés à modérer leur point de vue et à prendre en compte le contenu politique et les conséquences de chacune des deux approches. En effet, comme le fait remarquer Paul Krugman, les régimes commerciaux internationaux :

> « sont des instruments qui relèvent essentiellement de l'économie politique : ils sont conçus non seulement pour protéger les nations les unes des autres, mais également, et peut-être même surtout, pour protéger les nations de leurs propres groupes d'intérêts. C'est pourquoi tout débat sur le système commercial international implique nécessairement non pas de tenter de définir ce que devrait être la politique à suivre, mais d'étudier sous quelle forme elle se traduira dans le cadre d'une règle du jeu donnée » (Krugman, 1992, pp. n° 1-2).

Fixer les règles du jeu des échanges est en soi pour une large part un exercice politique qui, dans le cadre des projets d'intégration régionale, « impose inévitablement un certain degré d'arbitrage entre les institutions nationales, au même titre que sur les marchés de biens et de services » (de Melo, Panagariya & Rodrik, 1992, p. n°21). Cet exercice a certes des implications sur les flux commerciaux, mais il se répercute aussi sur une multitude de choix politiques touchant d'autres domaines et ne se limitant pas au strict cadre national. L'exemple de l'Afrique est particulièrement représentatif : comme les Communautés européennes (CE) l'ont récemment reconnu, il est impératif que les différents États signataires des accords commerciaux régionaux renforcent la coordination de leurs politiques, pour

**1. Faire
participer les
parties
concernées
au processus**

éviter que les dévaluations[4] entreprises dans le cadre des programmes d'ajustement structurel n'aient un effet d'« appauvrissement du voisin ».

Bien que certains économistes reconnaissent maintenant l'interdépendance étroite entre politique et économie dans l'élaboration et l'application des politiques commerciales, l'analyse économique et les recommandations qui en découlent interprètent souvent l'intégration régionale comme un ensemble d'accords commerciaux inter-gouvernementaux. Elles mettent donc l'accent sur la nécessité « d'atteindre des accords justes » et sur le renforcement des institutions inter-gouvernementales chargées de les mettre en œuvre.

Toutefois, comme le démontrent les articles de cet ouvrage, il est impossible de soutenir la libéralisation des échanges par des lois, de même qu'il est impossible de poursuivre durablement le processus de libéralisation des échanges sans un tel soutien. Deux des contributions militent en faveur de cette affirmation. D'un côté, à en croire l'analyse des modèles d'intégration « fondés sur les échanges » présentée au chapitre 1, le simple fait de signer des accords commerciaux préférentiels ne suffit pas à relancer les échanges. D'un autre côté, on constate parfois la situation inverse : dans la zone MERCOSUR ou l'ANASE par exemple, certaines sociétés multinationales se sont spécialisées dans la construction ou la vente d'automobiles, de pièces ou de composants automobiles avant la signature de tout accord préférentiel (et même, dans certains cas, sans qu'il y ait finalement d'accord). En nous intéressant à la façon dont certains acteurs ou certains intérêts s'associent pour soutenir ou s'opposer à certains efforts d'intégration, nous pouvons expliquer ces phénomènes paradoxaux. En s'attachant aux relations dynamiques qui existent entre les États et les autres acteurs socio-économiques, on comprend pourquoi « c'est seulement maintenant, dans les années 90 et après deux décennies de croissance économique fondée sur des stratégies nationales... que le développement des liens économiques régionaux au sein de l'ANASE... commence à s'accélérer » et, comme l'observe Linda Lim, pourquoi, bien que « la collaboration entre les gouvernements joue un rôle important dans ce processus... les relations qui peuvent se nouer au sein du secteur privé et la coopération entre secteurs privé et public semblent plus importantes encore ».

Néanmoins, à cette exception près, les intérêts, les capacités et les stratégies des acteurs nationaux sont rarement pris en compte. Comme l'observe Daniel Chudnovsky à propos de l'initiative d'intégration Argentine-Brésil de 1986, « l'annonce publique des accords... fit l'effet d'une surprise, leur signature n'ayant été précédée dans aucun des deux pays par un véritable débat ». Clive Thomas, qui s'est intéressé au cas de Caricom, une organisation inter-gouvernementale classique, fait remarquer que les organisations non gouvernementales, les syndicats de travailleurs et d'agriculteurs, les entreprises privées, les associations de consommateurs et les chercheurs ne sont dans la plupart des cas intégrés au processus que de manière sporadique, lorsque les activités fonctionnelles de l'organisation l'exigent. Même alors, « leur rôle reste accessoire et subordonné aux décisions des autorités institutionnelles... En fait, on pourrait même dire que le modèle actuel décourage toute forme de coopération régionale en dehors des structures officielles ». Ces structures sont de toute évidence anachroniques dans un contexte économique mondial où, comme Dieter Ernst, Carlota Perez et moi-même l'avons démontré, la compétitivité dépend de plus en plus de l'évolution de pratiques d'organisation qui impliquent des relations étroites entre les clients et les fournisseurs, une coopération entre les entreprises dans les activités de recherche, de développement, de production et de commercialisation, ainsi que l'organisation de réseaux entre les producteurs et les infrastructures scientifiques et techniques.

Si l'action institutionnelle demeure importante, il n'en est pas moins urgent d'innover en ce qui concerne les formes mêmes prises par l'intégration régionale en particulier et par la coopération sud-sud en général. Il faut notamment trouver une alternative à l'approche classique centrée sur l'État, qui intégrerait les parties concernées de manière plus significative au processus de coopération régionale. D'autre part, dès lors qu'on décide d'adopter une approche orientée sur les utilisateurs, il devient rapidement manifeste que la coopération sud-sud ne doit pas se limiter aux échanges.

2. Redonner la priorité à l'innovation dans la coopération sud-sud

S'il est impératif de remanier les structures institutionnelles de la coopération sud-sud, il l'est tout autant d'élargir et de redéfinir son contenu. Les articles regroupés dans cet ouvrage proposent un certain nombre d'orientations nouvelles. Toutes s'inspirent d'une même série d'observations concernant l'importance croissante de la « valeur ajoutée intellectuelle » dans le processus de production et le rôle joué par l'innovation dans la concurrence internationale. Dans cette perspective, la modernisation et la compétitivité ne sont plus nécessairement liées à des schémas d'industrialisation fondés sur la spécialisation à outrance et la production en série. Par ailleurs, le développement n'est plus considéré uniquement comme un processus qui consiste à passer de la production de matières premières à l'industrie manufacturière. Au contraire, les nouvelles technologies permettent aujourd'hui de valoriser l'ensemble des activités économiques, et non pas seulement les secteurs de pointe. Comme l'affirme Perez, « il est temps de s'intéresser sérieusement à une approche du développement fondée sur l'exploitation des ressources par des techniques à forte valeur ajoutée intellectuelle ».

C'est précisément ce que Clive Thomas a entrepris. En renonçant à étudier un seul aspect de certaines marchandises, telles que le sucre, il les a redéfinies comme des produits potentiellement complexes à utilisations finales multiples. Cette approche multiplie considérablement les maillons de la chaîne de valeur ajoutée dans lesquels peuvent intervenir les nouvelles technologies. Ce faisant, elle milite en faveur d'initiatives de coopération sud-sud destinées à « réhabiliter la valeur des ressources naturelles dans le processus du développement »[5].

De plus, si l'innovation constitue l'élément pivot des politiques de coopération, des « jeux à somme positive » sont possibles, même entre concurrents. En Amérique latine, par exemple, la collaboration entre les compagnies minières du secteur privé a donné l'occasion aux entreprises participantes d'améliorer considérablement leurs connaissances. D'après Alyson Warhurst, « si la coopération sud-sud n'est pas une panacée *a priori*, ces formes de partenariat ont présenté l'intérêt tout particulier de contribuer à la constitution d'un savoir-faire technologique et de capacités de gestion... [lesquels] ont à leur tour permis aux entreprises locales d'innover, d'utiliser des technologies nouvelles et, en aval, d'améliorer leurs performances économiques, qu'il s'agisse d'entreprises détenues en propriété exclusive ou de co-entreprises constituées avec d'autres sociétés des pays en développement ou avec des sociétés multinationales ».

Si l'on souhaite que la coopération régionale renforce la capacité d'adaptation des pays en développement aux évolutions des préférences, des prix et des conditions de la concurrence sur le plan international, un rôle central doit être donné à la constitution de réseaux favorisant l'innovation. Même si ces relations doivent d'abord être créées à l'intérieur de chaque pays et si le renforcement des systèmes d'innovation nationaux est donc très important[6], comme le font remarquer plusieurs articles, des liens plus étroits doivent également être tissés entre les pays : régionalement, du fait que la proximité est un facteur important dans les rapports utilisateur-producteur (Perez, Lim) ; entre les pays du sud, car ils sont confrontés à des problèmes communs, par exemple en ce qui concerne le traitement des minerais, la mise au point de technologies non polluantes (Warhurst) et l'agriculture (Thomas) ; et entre le nord et le sud, notamment dans les secteurs en évolution rapide tels que l'électronique (Ernst).

Il est plus aisé dans les années 90 que par le passé de mettre en œuvre des formes de coopération sud-sud fondées sur l'innovation, et ce pour deux raisons essentielles : tout d'abord, la nécessité de mettre en commun les ressources s'est imposée aux États et aux autres acteurs socio-économiques des pays du sud. Deuxièmement, comme le montre cette série d'articles, on constate un développement manifeste du patrimoine technologique des entreprises des secteurs public et privé, des instituts de recherche et des universités des pays d'Asie, d'Amérique latine et des Caraïbes, et ce dans de nombreux domaines, notamment les secteurs de l'exploitation des ressources naturelles, l'électronique, les machines-outils, les pièces automobiles et la biotechnologie.

En Afrique, les connaissances technologiques progressent également dans les établissements et les universités du secteur public et dans quelques entreprises privées, mais à un rythme beaucoup plus lent du fait de l'épuisement des ressources des gouvernements africains pendant les années 80. En ce qui concerne les entreprises, ce phénomène a essentiellement touché le secteur informel, qui s'est développé lorsque les dévaluations et la pénurie de devises ont rendu l'importation de pièces détachées et le transport difficiles. Le *Suame Magazine*, un groupement de quelque 5 000 artisans qui fabriquent des pièces détachées et réparent des véhicules dans des petits garages et des ateliers de Kumasi, au Ghana, est un exemple tout à fait représentatif de cette tendance.

Ce qu'il est particulièrement intéressant de noter, dans le cas de *Suame Magazine*, n'est pas tant que les mécaniciens locaux ont amélioré leurs qualifications, mais que « le gouvernement a soutenu ces techniciens locaux en mettant à leur disposition crédits, services et formation technique » (Banque mondiale, 1989, p. 121). Cette aide comprend plusieurs volets : des fonds publics destinés à l'Unité de formation technique intermédiaire (Intermediate Technology Training Unit) du Centre de conseil technique (Technology Consultancy Center) de l'Université des sciences et de la technologie de Kumasi et la multiplication des unités de formation dans l'ensemble du pays par le biais des Services technologiques régionaux appliqués à l'industrie du Ghana (Ghana Regional Appropriate Technology Industrial Services), qui dispensent une formation sur le lieu de travail dans le domaine du développement des produits. D'autre part, par le biais du Projet de rénovation des transports [des Instituts techniques de Kumasi] soutenu par l'AID, l'État développe les compétences des mécaniciens en organisant des cours dans le cadre d'ateliers informels, en leur enseignant les rudiments de la comptabilité et des méthodes de gestion [et a]... également participé à la mise en place d'un programme pilote de financement de petits projets [telle cette]... coopérative de mécaniciens qui achète et partage des équipements (tours et machines à rectifier les vilebrequins, etc.) » (Banque mondiale, 1989, p. 121). Ce type d'approche doit être généralisé.

En ce qui concerne les autres secteurs, le patrimoine technologique se développe essentiellement dans les instituts publics de recherche soutenus par les gouvernements locaux et les pays donateurs. Citons, à titre d'exemple, l'Institut international de recherche scientifique pour le développement de l'Afrique (International Institute for Scientific Research for the Development of Africa-IISDA), un centre récemment établi en Côte d'Ivoire et financé par le Canada, la France et le gouvernement ivoirien. Son programme de recherche actuel est tourné essentiellement sur l'amélioration des variétés d'igname et sur le traitement de la malaria. Pour ce qui est du premier domaine de recherche, une collaboration étroite est envisagée avec l'Institut international d'agriculture tropicale (International Institute for Tropical Agriculture) du Nigéria, qui est très actif dans le domaine de la culture des tissus pour la conservation du germen et de la distribution *in vitro* de semences saines d'igname et d'autres cultures (UNIDO, 1992, pp. 19, 27). La recherche biotechnologique se développe également en Éthiopie, où le Centre des ressources génétiques végétales (Plant Genetic Resources Centre) coordonne le Réseau des ressources génétiques de la Conférence ministérielle africaine sur l'environnement (African Ministerial Conference on Environment-AMCEN), (UNIDO, 1992, pp. 20).

Malheureusement, force est de constater que très peu de liens ont été établis entre ces activités de recherche et le secteur de la production (Rathgeber, 1991 ; Vitta, 1992). La contribution de la recherche à l'innovation reste donc limitée. Comme le montrent ces différents exemples, il est indispensable que les États et les institutions internationales accordent un intérêt plus grand aux mesures destinées à promouvoir une culture de l'innovation en Afrique et aux relations nationales, régionales et internationales qui en sont la garantie.

3. Le soutien des États et des institutions internationales

Comme la plupart des articles qui constituent cet ouvrage l'ont largement démontré, le modèle de coopération sud-sud fondé sur l'innovation technologique nécessite incontestablement l'entretien, voire la consolidation des liens nord-sud, car la technologie qui donnera l'impulsion au processus d'innovation viendra dans un premier temps principalement du nord. Dans la mesure où ces liens impliquent des transferts effectifs de technologie, ce sont les externalités de la coopération nord-sud qui sont susceptibles de procurer les gains de la coopération sud-sud[7]. Mais pour y parvenir, nouer des liens ne suffit pas : il faut également attacher une grande importance à « l'apprentissage et à la diffusion du savoir-faire disponible à l'échelle internationale, une possibilité qui n'a pas été suffisamment exploitée par la région dans le passé »[8]. C'est là que les institutions locales, gouvernementales ou non, ont un rôle décisif à jouer : elles doivent stimuler la demande d'innovation dans tous les secteurs[9] et avoir un effet catalyseur dans la création de liens entre utilisateurs et fournisseurs, aussi bien dans le système productif national que dans les infrastructures scientifiques et technologiques locales. Ces efforts sont complémentaires à l'établissement, au niveau régional, d'un réseau d'innovation, et les deux types d'activité constituent des domaines d'intervention importants pour les donateurs.

Au début des années 90, les donateurs ont pris conscience du fait que les capacités d'adaptation des pays en développement à l'évolution des conditions de la concurrence internationale étaient insuffisantes et qu'il convenait d'accorder une plus grande attention au développement des ressources humaines (Banque mondiale, 1991). La résolution 45/145 du 17 décembre 1991 de l'Assemblée générale des Nations Unies et le plan à moyen terme 1990-1995 de l'ONUDI (ONUDI, 1991) soulignent tous deux l'importance des activités de promotion de l'intégration économique régionale entre les pays en développement. Plusieurs organismes donateurs ont par ailleurs financé des réunions d'hommes d'affaires en Afrique occidentale[10] ou encore entre les acteurs des secteurs public et privé de l'Afrique australe et orientale[11]. Mais il y a encore beaucoup à faire, notamment dans le domaine de la promotion de l'innovation.

Le bref examen de deux programmes mis en œuvre en Amérique latine et des relations qui les unissent révèle que les pays donateurs peuvent jouer — et jouent déjà — de multiples rôles dans la promotion des modèles de coopération sud-sud fondés sur l'innovation en Amérique latine. Le premier, le *Centro de Gestión Tecnológica e Informática Industrial* (CEGESTI) du Costa Rica, a été mis sur pied par le PNUD et l'ONUDI pour répondre aux besoins des petites et moyennes entreprises (PME) en matière de formation, d'information technique et de conseils en management, de sorte qu'elles pensent en termes de stratégie et intègrent le concept d'innovation dans leurs perspectives de croissance. Le modèle CEGESTI est d'ores et déjà en cours d'application dans d'autres pays d'Amérique latine. Le second — le programme Simon Bolivar — s'inspire du programme européen EUREKA et concerne huit pays, dont le Costa Rica. Ses deux principaux objectifs sont les suivants : promouvoir l'innovation à l'échelle régionale en multipliant les interactions entre les instituts de recherche locaux et les entreprises dans les pays membres, et promouvoir l'intégration régionale en facilitant la création de relations de partenariat entre les entreprises et les instituts de recherche dans deux pays de la région au moins.

Le programme de formation du CEGESTI a pour principal objectif d'inciter les entreprises à innover. A cette fin, une série de petites expériences sont mises en pratique, qui fonctionnent comme des laboratoires d'apprentissage. Pour renforcer l'esprit novateur des PME, le programme costaricien a sélectionné neuf entreprises locales dans un large éventail de secteurs — chimie, industrie pharmaceutique, travail des métaux, logiciels — dans le but de renforcer leur capacité d'innovation. A cette fin, le CEGESTI a formé des équipes de deux personnes, principalement des ingénieurs industriels qualifiés en gestion technologique et employés comme conseillers auprès du directeur général. Ces équipes ont occupé ce poste pendant environ un an et demi et toutes les entreprises à l'exception d'une seule sont parvenues à mettre sur pied des projets de pré-investissement. Outre qu'elles doivent identifier les projets d'innovation potentiels au sein de l'entreprise, les équipes sont chargées d'établir des liens avec les universités locales et de gérer le projet de R-D correspondant. Au terme d'entretiens menés avec les directeurs des entreprises participantes, il est apparu que le programme avait eu les effets suivants :

— augmentation des ventes ;

— gains de productivité ;

— développement de nouveaux produits et services ;

— développement de nouveaux marchés ;

— développement de projets d'innovation, dont cinq ont obtenu l'autorisation d'être financés par l'État costaricien ;

— souhait exprimé par les entreprises d'embaucher l'équipe au terme de la période contractuelle.

Du fait même de sa conception, le programme du CEGESTI n'incite pas seulement les entreprises à innover : il ouvre la voie à des accords de partenariat stratégiques entre ces entreprises ou entre les entreprises et les instituts de recherche, tant à l'échelle nationale qu'à celle de l'Amérique latine[12].

Le lancement du programme Simon Bolivar a motivé la création de plusieurs accords de partenariat dans le domaine de la R-D sur l'ensemble du continent. En mars 1992, le programme a reçu un coup de pouce supplémentaire de la part de la Banque interaméricaine de développement, sous la forme d'une subvention à la coopération technique de 4.2 millions de dollars. A ces subventions s'ajoute une contribution de 3 millions de dollars de la part des États participant au programme. Ce budget total de 7.2 millions de dollars devrait suffire à couvrir pendant deux ans les coûts de mise en place et de fonctionnement d'un réseau régional de comités de coordination nationaux, et l'implantation à Caracas d'un secrétariat doté d'un effectif léger.

Les donateurs ne se contentent pas de soutenir ce programme financièrement : la DG XII des Communautés européennes, qui travaille avec l'actuelle présidence d'EUREKA, soutient un programme de formation destiné aux coordinateurs nationaux qui, dans le cadre du programme Simon Bolivar, seront les principaux responsables de l'identification des partenaires, de l'évaluation des projets et du financement du programme. Le gouvernement canadien soutient diverses initiatives visant à associer des consortiums canadiens spécialisés dans la R-D et des entreprises canadiennes à des projets conjoints entre le programme Bolivar et le Canada. La coopération nord-sud devra donc compléter les initiatives sud-sud dans le cadre du programme Bolivar.

4. La nécessité de créer un réseau pour l'innovation en Afrique

Si plusieurs programmes contribuent d'ores et déjà à l'élaboration effective de modèles de développement fondés sur l'innovation en Amérique latine, il n'en va pas de même pour l'Afrique. Or, il est indispensable d'encourager les entreprises africaines à résoudre leurs problèmes de restructuration et à innover au cours de cette période de réhabilitation afin de garantir un développement durable sur le continent. Compte tenu des difficultés financières actuelles de l'Afrique, les transferts de technologies depuis l'étranger, bien que vitaux, ne peuvent répondre à tous les besoins du continent. En outre, il s'agit d'un processus coûteux qui nécessite des dépenses répétées pour l'importation de biens d'équipement et de biens intermédiaires, et l'acquisition de compétences de gestion, de services de maintenance et d'un savoir-faire technique, dépenses que l'Afrique peut difficilement supporter à l'heure actuelle. Il devient donc impératif que les entreprises africaines soient mieux préparées à faire face à leurs propres difficultés et qu'elles suppriment les goulets d'étranglement qui handicapent le secteur productif.

Comme nous l'avons vu dans le cas du CEGESTI, dans un environnement où les entreprises n'ont pas l'habitude de raisonner en termes de stratégie ou d'intégrer l'innovation à leurs perspectives de croissance, l'innovation passera nécessairement par une dynamisation externe afin que s'engage un processus de résolution des problèmes, ce qui est inconcevable sans ressources financières et techniques. Ces ressources peuvent — et doivent — provenir de programmes de développement et de recherche en coopération avec d'autres intervenants des pays concernés, notamment les fournisseurs, les universités, les bureaux d'études et de conseil et les instituts de recherche. Néanmoins, la masse critique requise pour trouver ces solutions issues de l'innovation est rarement atteinte dans les pays africains[13]. La constitution de réseaux régionaux a donc un rôle crucial à jouer dans ce domaine.

Les pouvoirs publics des pays d'Afrique admettent la nécessité de développer des programmes de formation stimulant l'innovation. Ils s'efforcent également de mettre en place un cadre politique qui lui soit favorable. Pour compléter de telles initiatives, il faut instituer un mécanisme régional encourageant les entreprises à cerner les problèmes et à innover, d'une part, et permettant de canaliser les ressources locales pour soutenir cet effort d'autre part. L'Afrique disposant de ressources financières limitées, ce mécanisme pourrait également jouer un rôle de garantie financière important vis-à-vis des coûts et des risques afférents à l'innovation.

Dans le souci d'adapter au cas de l'Afrique les projets de collaboration fondés sur l'innovation existants dans d'autres régions, le Fonds pour l'innovation et le développement en Afrique pourrait, au travers d'une structure institutionnelle d'encadrement de projets basée sur un ensemble de réseaux locaux :

i) mettre l'accent sur le processus d'innovation technologique — plutôt que sur la recherche scientifique — dans les programmes d'enseignement et les instituts de recherche ;

ii) impliquer les utilisateurs dans les phases de lancement, de conception, de recherche et de développement de l'ensemble des projets et, par là même, s'assurer que leurs besoins sont véritablement satisfaits et qu'on peut compter sur leur soutien au processus d'innovation, ainsi que sur leur adhésion rapide aux résultats de la collaboration, pendant toute la durée du projet ;

iii) encourager la formation de consortiums sur le continent africain, à l'intérieur et au-delà des frontières nationales, afin d'atteindre la masse critique nécessaire, de réduire les coûts et de développer la pluridisciplinarité que requiert tout processus d'innovation ;

iv) encourager le développement d'une culture de l'innovation dans les entreprises africaines ;

v) enfin rendre l'industrie africaine compétitive, en faisant de la compétitivité un élément moteur du processus d'intégration et de coopération régionale.

S'il est encore trop tôt pour préciser le détail de ce mécanisme, on peut d'ores et déjà envisager un moyen de garantir son indépendance financière et administrative ainsi que son accès aux ressources technologiques hors d'Afrique : l'institutionnaliser sous forme d'un Fonds pour l'innovation et le développement en Afrique, dont les dotations proviendraient, dans des proportions égales, des entreprises les plus importantes et les plus novatrices du monde d'une part, et des subventions accordées par les agences gouvernementales et les institutions internationales d'autre part.

Bien que de nombreux fonds de « recherche » aient été mis en place par le passé, ils ont eu en général un faible impact commercial. Les différences de notre proposition par rapport aux initiatives précédentes sont les suivantes :

— on ne donne plus la priorité à la recherche en termes d'offre et l'identification et la sélection des projets ne se fait plus « d'en haut » (« top-down approach ») ;

— cette proposition repose sur une forme originale de partenariat entre les donateurs du secteur privé et du secteur public ;

— elle prévoit la constitution d'une structure en réseau reliant l'encadrement institutionnel aux organismes qui gèrent les projets.

En résumé, l'ampleur et la rapidité des progrès technologiques actuels nous imposent d'en finir avec la théorie et les pratiques traditionnelles en ce qui concerne les formes et la vocation de la coopération sud-sud. Les articles qui constituent cet ouvrage plaident en faveur d'une vision plus large des aspects à traiter. Ils soulignent notamment le bien-fondé des modèles de coopération sud-sud fondés sur l'innovation technologique et démontrent leur faisabilité au travers de nombreux exemples de projets actuellement en cours entre entreprises, entre l'université et l'industrie et entre les pouvoirs publics de différents pays. Pour soutenir ces initiatives, les états seront de plus en plus amenés à jouer un rôle directeur clé, même si la contribution et la participation active du secteur privé s'accroissent parallèlement. Il est indispensable d'instaurer des politiques destinées à promouvoir l'innovation et la diffusion des technologies, à créer un cadre institutionnel et juridique qui permette et même encourage l'établissement de réseaux d'innovation, et à favoriser le développement des infrastructures de télécommunications, de transports, de recherche et de formation sans lesquelles ces objectifs ne sauraient être atteints. De même, des solutions novatrices doivent être trouvées pour financer l'innovation. Il reste donc beaucoup à faire pour relancer la coopération sud-sud, mais on peut y parvenir à condition de concentrer les efforts sur l'organisation de réseaux encourageant l'innovation.

1. Un point sur lequel insiste Carlota Perez au chapitre 2.

2. Voir le chapitre 1 pour une présentation globale de ces débats.

3. Cette expression est d'Alice Amsden (1989).

4. Pour étayer cette affirmation, les CE citent deux exemples. Le premier est celui de la Gambie, qui a dévalué sa monnaie au moment où son voisin le Sénégal a relevé le prix de l'arachide, payable en francs CFA convertibles. En conséquence, la Gambie a essuyé une perte nette de près de la moitié de sa production au profit du Sénégal, d'où l'impossibilité pour la Gambie de tirer profit des avantages de la dévaluation. Deuxième exemple : après dix ans de surévaluation du naira, le Nigéria a procédé à une dévaluation radicale de sa monnaie entre 1986 et 1987, entraînant une déstabilisation notable des échanges informels avec le Bénin et le Niger (CE, 1990, 4). Voir également CE, 1988.

5. L'expression est empruntée à Perez (cf. chapitre 2).

6. Les articles de Lim et de Chudnowsky montrent qu'il est important de remettre l'économie nationale en ordre d'une manière générale.

7. Cet argument a été avancé une première fois par Mytelka (1973).

8. ECLAC, 1990, 14.

9. Pour la plupart des économistes, le soutien de l'État se justifie encore essentiellement dans des domaines tels que l'électronique et la biotechnologie. Aussi Laura Tyson écrit-elle : « presque tout le monde s'accorde désormais à reconnaître que l'avantage compétitif, dans le secteur des technologies de pointe, n'est pas inné : il faut le créer. Et partout dans le monde, les gouvernements lui accordent des mesures de soutien spécifiques » (Tyson, 1992, 9).

10. Ainsi, un séminaire sur le secteur privé en Afrique occidentale a été organisé en novembre 1991 avec l'aide du Club du Sahel de l'OCDE, du CILSS (Comité Permanent Inter-États de Lutte contre la Sécheresse dans le Sahel) et de l'USAID. Se sont rencontrés à cette occasion des représentants du monde des affaires, des établissements du secteur public et des organismes donateurs internationaux, issus de 15 pays d'Afrique occidentale (CILSS, 1992).

11. La Banque africaine de développement, la Banque mondiale et les CE soutiennent la création de groupes de travail techniques au sein desquels des représentants des secteurs public et privé établissent des recommandations dans les domaines de la politique d'investissement, de la politique commerciale, des finances et de la balance des paiements, et formulent des propositions visant le renforcement et/ou la création d'institutions.

12. Entretien avec Fernando Machado, Directeur, CEGESTI, Ottawa, 17 janvier 1992.

13. Bien entendu, le Nigéria et le Zimbabwe font exception.

Biblio-graphie

BANQUE MONDIALE (1989), *Rapport sur le développement dans le monde*, Washington, D.C.

BANQUE MONDIALE (1991), *Rapport sur le développement dans le monde*, Washington, D.C.

CILSS (1992), *The Private Operators' Perspective on an Agenda for Action*, February, Doc. N° SAH/D(92)388, Club du Sahel, OECD, Paris.

COMMISSION DES COMMUNAUTÉS EUROPÉENNES (1988), « Note de réflexion, ajustement structurel et coopération régionale », Direction générale du développement, juillet, Bruxelles.

COMMISSION DES COMMUNAUTÉS EUROPÉENNES (1990), *Cadre de référence pour les prochains travaux du CAD sur la coopération et l'intégration régionale*, 9 avril, Doc. n° AT/EG/ms, Bruxelles.

ECLAC (1990), *Changing Production Patterns with Social Equity*, United Nations Economic Commission for Latin America and the Carribean, Santiago, Chile.

KRUGMAN, Paul (1991), « Regionalism vs. Multilateralism: Analytical Notes », paper presented to the World Bank and CEPR Conference on New Dimensions in Regional Integration, 2-3 April, Washington, D.C.

MELO, Jaime de, Arvind PANAGARIYA et Dani RODRIK (1992), « The New Regionalism : A Country Perspective », paper presented to the World Bank and CEPR Conference on New Dimensions in Regional Integration, 2-3 April, Washington, D.C.

MYTELKA, Lynn K. (1973), « Foreign Aid and Regional Integration : The UDEAC Case », Journal of Common Market Studies, Vol. XII, n° 2, December, pp. 138-158.

ONUDI (1991), « Politiques de l'ONUDI : coopération économique et technique entre pays en développement », Doc. n° GC.4/7IDB.8/13, 14 juin, Vienne.

RATHGEBER, Eva M. (1991), « Knowledge Production and Use in Agriculture », International Institute for Educational Planning, 25 mars, Paris.

TYSON, Laura D'Andrea (1992), « Who's Bashing Whom? Trade Conflict in High-Technology Industries », Institute for International Economics, Washington, D.C.

UNIDO (1992), « Genetic Engineering and Bio-technology Monitor », n° 40, December, Vienna.

VITTA, Paul (1992), « Utility of Research in Sub-Saharan Africa: Beyond the Leap of Faith », *Science and Public Policy*, Vol. 19, n° 4, August, pp. 221-228.

Chapter 8

BEYOND TRADE: NETWORKING FOR INNOVATION THROUGH SOUTH-SOUTH CO-OPERATION

Lynn K. Mytelka

During the 1970s and 1980s, as the knowledge-intensity of production in all sectors increased and competition globalised, the need for developing countries to embark upon a continuous process of adjustment that "transforms static advantages into dynamic strengths"[1] became ever more apparent. Yet few of the debates concerning the role of developing countries in the international economy went much beyond a fairly orthodox view of the static gains from trade[2]. Most often couched in the form of opposing dichotomies, these debates assigned primacy to international rather than domestic market signals and favoured the creation of a global trading system over co-operative arrangements among countries in the south. Put in other terms the debate pitted those who favoured 'getting prices right', where the right prices were believed to be those prevailing in international markets, against those who saw successful past practice in the dynamic Asian economies as characterised by state policies to alter such signals or 'getting prices wrong'[3].

The 1990s brought a better balance to the debate over multilateralism versus regionalism by acknowledging the political content and consequences of both sorts of trading arrangements. Indeed, as Paul Krugman pointed out, international trading regimes:

> "are essentially devices of political economy; they are intended at least as much to protect nations from their own interest groups as they are to protect nations from each other. Thus any discussion of the international trading system necessarily involves an attempt to discuss not what policy ought to be, but what it actually will be under various rules of the game" (Krugman, 1992, pp. 1-2).

Setting the rules of the trading game is itself a highly politicised activity and within regional integration schemes inevitably "...enforces a certain degree of arbitrage among national institutions, just as it brings about arbitrage in markets for goods and services" (de Melo, Panagariya & Rodrik, 1992, p. 21). It thus has implications not only for trade flows but for a host of other policies and preferences and their extra-national impact. This became evident in Africa, for example, where, as the European Communities recently acknowledged, there is a need for greater policy co-ordination between states involved in regional trading arrangements in order to avoid the 'beggar-thy-neighbour' effects of currency devaluations[4] undertaken in the course of structural adjustment programmes.

Although some economists now recognise that politics and economics are intimately interwoven in the making and carrying out of trade policies, most economic analysis, and the prescriptions drawn from it, remain wedded

1. Putting participants into the process

to a vision of regional integration as a set of inter-governmental trading arrangements. The focus is thus on 'getting the agreement right' and strengthening the inter-governmental institutions through which it will be implemented.

As the papers in this volume illustrate, however, one cannot legislate support for free trade nor can one sustain a process of trade liberalisation without such support. Two developments described in this book give weight to this argument. First, the analysis of exchange-driven models of integration in Chapter 1 demonstrated that while states may sign preferential trading agreements, trade does not necessarily follow. Second, the reverse also occurs. In the MERCOSUR and in ASEAN, for example, multinational corporations moved towards specialisation and exchange in automobiles, auto parts and components either prior to or in the absence of a preferential trading agreement. By stressing the way in which various actors and interests combine to support or constrain particular integration efforts, we can make sense of such paradoxical phenomena. A focus on the dynamic interplay between states and other social and economic actors also makes it possible to understand why "only now, in the 1990s, after two decades of successful national-based economic growth...[is] the development of ASEAN regional economic linkages... beginning to accelerate" and more importantly, as Linda Lim observes, why, though "government-to-government policies are important to this process... private sector linkages and private-public sector co-operation appear to be assuming a more dominant role".

Elsewhere, however, the interests, capabilities and strategies of domestic actors are rarely taken into account. As Daniel Chudnovsky observed in the case of the Argentine-Brazil integration initiative of 1986, "...public announcement of the agreements... came as a surprise, and their signature was not preceded by a broad debate in either country". Writing of Caricom, a classic inter-governmental organisation, Clive Thomas notes that non-governmental organisations, labour and farmers' associations, private companies, consumer groups and researchers are brought into the process only sporadically, as the functional activities of the organisation requires it. Even then, he points out, "...their roles remain essentially subsidiary and subject to institutional direction from above... Indeed it might be argued that the existing model operates as a disincentive to forms of regional co-operation outside its formal ambit". Such structures are clearly anachronistic in a world economy in which, as Dieter Ernst, Carlota Perez and I have argued, competitiveness is increasingly a function of organisational changes that involve close linkages between clients and suppliers, collaboration between firms in R&D, production and marketing and networks between producers and the scientific and technological infrastructure.

While institution building clearly remains important, there is thus a pressing need to innovate in the very forms that regional integration, and south-south co-operation more generally, takes. In particular an alternative to the traditional state-centric view, one that brings participants more meaningfully into the process of regional co-operation, is needed. Once a user orientation is adopted, moreover, it quickly becomes apparent that there is more to south-south co-operation than trade.

2. Recentring south-south co-operation on innovation

Much as there is a need to reshape the institutional structures of south-south co-operation, so, too, is there a need to enlarge and refocus their content. The papers in this volume suggest a number of new directions which this might take. Each of these, however, begins from a set of common observations concerning the growing knowledge-intensity of production and the role of innovation in international competition. From this perspective, modernisation and competitiveness are no longer equated with narrowly specialised, mass production forms of industrialisation. Nor is development conceived solely as a process of moving away from raw materials production to manufacturing. To the contrary, new technologies are today capable of upgrading all economic activities and not only the high technology sectors. "The time has come" Perez thus argues, "to seriously reconsider resource-based knowledge-intensive development".

Clive Thomas has done precisely this by abandoning a monofocal approach to commodities such as sugar and reconceptualising them as potentially complex products with multiple end uses. This significantly enlarges the range of stages in the value chain to which new technologies can be applied and it enhances the prospect for co-operative south-south initiatives in "rescuing the development value of natural resources"[5].

With innovation as a focus, positive sum games are thus possible even among competitors. In Latin America, for example, collaboration between private sector mining companies has opened considerable learning opportunities for participating firms. "While south-south co-operation is not *a priori* a 'better thing'", Alyson Warhurst writes, "the particular advantage of these partnerships has been their ability to contribute to the building of technological and managerial capabilities...[which] in turn have enabled the local enterprise to innovate, to make technical changes and to improve its economic performance in subsequent operations, whether these are wholly owned or run as joint ventures with other DC firms or with multinational enterprises".

For regional co-operation to strengthen the ability of developing countries to adjust to continuous changes in international tastes, prices and competitive conditions, networking for innovation must become central to the process. Although, as several of the papers emphasize, such linkages begin at home and strengthening the domestic system of innovation is thus clearly important[6], increasingly ties must also be forged across national borders — regionally, because proximity is important for user-producer links (Perez, Lim); across the south because there are common problems in minerals processing, in the development of environmentally sound technologies (Warhurst) and in agriculture (Thomas), and between north and south, especially in dynamically evolving sectors such as electronics (Ernst).

Developing innovation-driven forms of south-south co-operation is more feasible in the 1990s than in the past for two important reasons. First, the need to pool resources has become evident to states and other social and economic actors in the south. Second, as these papers show, technological accumulation within Asian, Latin American and Caribbean public and private sector enterprises, research institutions and universities has progressed in a wide variety of sectors, including the resource industries, electronics, machine tools, auto parts and biotechnology.

At a much slower pace, a process of technological accumulation involving public sector institutions and universities and a few private enterprises is also taking place in Africa despite the shrinking resources available to African governments in the 1980s. With regard to the enterprise sector, this is most notable in the informal sector in Africa which expanded as devaluations and a shortage of foreign exchange made imports of spare parts for industry and transportation more difficult. The *Suame Magazine*, a grouping of some 5 000 craftsmen in small garages and workshops making spare parts for and repairing vehicles in Kumasi, Ghana is a case in point.

Of particular interest in the *Suame Magazine* case, however, is not merely that local mechanics have been developing their manufacturing skills but that "the government has supported these indigenous engineers through technology services, training, and credit" (World Bank, 1989, p. 121). These include government funding for the Intermediate Technology Training Unit of the Technology Consultancy Centre at the University of Science and

Technology in Kumasi and an extension of the training unit concept throughout the country via the Ghana Regional Appropriate Technology Industrial Services which provides on-site training in product development. In addition, through the Kumasi Technical Institutes' "...IDA-supported Transport Rehabilitation Project, the government is providing training to upgrade the skills of mechanics in informal workshops and to teach them basic accounting and management methods [and it]... has also helped to establish a pilot program to provide credit to small operators [such as]...a mechanics' co-operative established to purchase and share equipment such as lathes and crank-shaft grinders" (World Bank, 1989, p. 121). Such approaches must be generalised.

In other sectors, technological capabilities are mainly accumulating in public research institutions supported by local governments and donor countries. The International Institute for Scientific Research for the Development of Africa (IISDA), for example, is a newly established centre located in the Côte d'Ivoire and supported by Canada, France and the Ivorian government. Its current research programme is focused on the improvement of yam varieties and the treatment of malaria. With regard to the former, close collaboration is foreseen with the International Institute for Tropical Agriculture in Nigeria, which is already active in tissue culture for germplasm conservation and the *in vitro* distribution of disease-free planting material for yams and other corps (UNIDO, 1992, pp. 19, 27). Biotechnology research is also developing in Ethiopia where the Plant Genetic Resources Centre currently co-ordinates the Genetic Resources Network of the African Ministerial Conference on Environment (AMCEN), (UNIDO, 1992, p. 20).

On a less positive note, however, few linkages have been established between these research activities and production (Rathgeber, 1991; Vitta, 1992). The contribution of research to innovation has thus remained limited. As these examples demonstrate, there is a critical need for states and international institutions to refocus their attention on measures to promote a culture of innovation in Africa and on the national, regional and international linkages that sustain it.

3. A supporting role for states and international institutions

As many of the papers in this volume illustrate, there is no doubt that an innovation-driven model of south-south co-operation will require the maintenance and in some instances a strengthening of north-south ties, since much of the technology upon which such innovations will be based initially will come from the north. To the extent that these ties involve an effective transfer of technology, north-south co-operation could provide the externalities that make gains from south-south co-operation more likely[7]. For this to take place, however, these ties must be complemented by increased attention to "the learning and dissemination of internationally available know-how; a possibility which has not been sufficiently exploited by the region in the past"[8]. It is here that local, government and non-governmental institutions have a critical role to play in stimulating the demand for innovation in all sectors[9] and catalysing the creation of linkages between users and suppliers located in the domestic productive system and in the local science and technology infrastructure. Such efforts, moreover, are complementary to regional networking for innovation and both types of activity provide important areas for donor support.

By the early 1990s donors had come to recognise the need to strengthen the ability of developing countries to respond to changing international competitive conditions by developing human resources (World Bank, 1991). Both the United Nations General Assembly resolution 45/145 of 17 December 1991 and UNIDO's medium term plan for the years 1990-1995 (UNIDO, 1991) emphasize the importance of activities promoting regional economic integration among developing countries. Various donor agencies have also supported meetings among members of the business community from West African countries[10] and between private and public sector actors in Southern and Eastern Africa[11]. But much more needs to be done and it needs to be oriented towards the promotion of innovation.

A brief look at two Latin American programmes and the inter-relationship between them provides an example of the many different roles that donor countries have begun to play in promoting innovation-driven models of south-south co-operation in Latin America. The first, the *Centro de Gestion Tecnológica e Informática Industrial* (CEGESTI) in Costa Rica, funded by UNDP and UNIDO, is designed to provide the training, technical information and management consulting needed to stimulate small and medium-sized firms (SMEs) to think strategically and to incorporate innovation into their growth strategies. The CEGESTI model is already being diffused to other Latin American countries. The second, the Simon Bolivar Programme, is an eight-country initiative modeled after the European EUREKA programme. Costa Rica is a member. Its two main objectives are to promote innovation in the region by stimulating greater interaction between local research institutions and the enterprise sector in the member countries, and to promote regional integration by facilitating the establishment of partnerships between enterprises and research institutes in two or more countries of the region.

CEGESTI's training programme focuses on teaching firms to initiate changes via the creation of small experiments that operate as laboratories for apprenticeship. As part of a Costa Rican programme to foster innovative behaviour in SMEs, nine local firms were chosen from a variety of sectors — chemicals, pharmaceuticals, metalworking, software — with the intent of strengthening the firm's innovation capacity. For this purpose, CEGESTI trained a nucleus of two persons, mainly industrial engineers trained in technology management, who worked as advisers to the managing director. The nuclei have been in place for approximately a year and a half during which time all but one have been successfully developing pre-investment projects. In addition to identifying potential innovation projects within the firm, the nuclei are responsible for establishing linkages with local universities and managing the ensuing R&D project. In interviews with the directors of the participating firms, the impact of this programme has already been felt in the following areas:

— increased sales;

— productivity gains;

— development of new products and services;

— development of new markets;

— development of innovation projects, five of which have been approved for funding by the Costa Rican government; and

— an interest in hiring the nuclei at the end of the contract period.

By its very design, CEGESTI's programme not only induces firms to innovate but it lays the groundwork for strategic partnering among these firms and between firms and research institutions in both the domestic and the wider-Latin American environment[12].

Establishment of the Simon Bolivar Programme has given impetus to the creation of R&D partnerships across the continent. In March 1992, the programme was given further encouragement when the Inter-American Development Bank made $4.2 million in technical co-operation grants available to it. An additional $3 million was contributed by the member governments. The $7.2 million budget is expected to cover the set up and operating costs of a regional network of national co-ordinating committees and a lightly-staffed secretariat in Caracas over the next two years.

Financial support, however, is not the only form of assistance that donors are giving to this programme. DG XII of the European Communities, working with the current EUREKA Presidency, is supporting a training programme for national co-ordinators who will be the principal agents for partner identification, project evaluation and funding in the Simon Bolivar Programme. The Canadian government is supporting initiatives to link Canadian R&D consortia and Canadian firms as partners in joint Bolivar-Canada projects. North-south partnership will thus be a complement to south-south initiatives undertaken within the Bolivar programme.

4. The need for innovation networking in Africa

While a number of programmes that create building blocs for innovation-driven models of development are already operating in Latin America, initiatives such as these have still to emerge in Africa. Yet the need to stimulate firms in Africa to solve restructuring problems, and to innovate in the course of rehabilitation, is critical to the sustainability of development on that continent. Given current financial constraints, transfer of technology from abroad, while vital, cannot fulfil all of Africa's needs. Moreover, it is a costly process which generally requires recurrent expenditures for the import of capital and intermediate goods, management skills, maintenance services and technical know-how that Africa can ill afford at present. It has thus become imperative for the enterprise sector in Africa to strengthen its ability to solve its own problems and to overcome bottlenecks in production.

To engage in a process of problem-solving innovation in an environment where firms rarely think strategically or incorporate innovation into their growth strategies, as we saw in the CEGESTI case, requires outside stimulus and it cannot be done without access to financial and technological resources. These resources can and must come through a process of collaborative research and development involving other domestic actors including supplier firms, university faculties, engineering consultancy firms and research institutions. The critical density required for such problem-solving innovation is, however, rarely present in any single African country[13]. Regional networking is thus critical here.

African governments have acknowledged the need to develop training that promotes innovation. They are also attempting to put in place a policy environment that is conducive to innovation. To complement these initiatives, a mechanism through which enterprises are encouraged to identify problems and to innovate, and local resources are marshalled in support of that endeavour, will be needed. In view of Africa's limited financial resources, such a mechanism would also have an important financial role to play in underwriting the costs and risks of innovation.

Adapting principles derived from other innovation-driven regional collaborative schemes to the African context, the Fund for Innovation and Development in Africa should, through a locally-based networked institutional and project structure:

i) focus on the process of technological innovation rather than on scientific research in education and research institutions;

ii) involve users in the initiation, design, research and development phases of all projects thereby assuring that users' needs are being met and that user commitment to a process of innovation and to the rapid acceptance of the output of collaboration is built over the lifetime of the project;

iii) stimulate the formation of consortia within and across national frontiers in Africa thus creating the critical mass, reducing the costs and building the cross-disciplinarity needed for the innovation process;

iv) encourage the development of a culture of innovation in African enterprises; and

v) build competitiveness in African industry as one element in the movement toward regional integration and co-operation.

While it is premature to venture into too many details concerning the nature of this mechanism, one way of ensuring its financial and managerial independence and its access to technological resources outside of Africa is to institutionalise the mechanism as a Fund for Innovation and Development in Africa and to constitute it through an endowment of which 50 per cent might be solicited from among the world's largest and most innovative companies and the remaining 50 per cent be constituted by grants from governmental agencies and international institutions.

Although many funds for "research" have been created in the past, their commercial impact has generally been meagre. What differentiates the present proposal from these earlier initiatives is:

— its abandonment of a supply-driven focus on research and a top-down approach to project identification and selection;

— its unique private-public sector donor partnership, and

— its networked institutional and project structure.

In sum, in a period of intense and rapid technological change, breaking with traditional theory and practice concerning the form and function of south-south co-operation is essential. The papers in this volume have thus argued for a wider vision of what needs to be done. In particular, they provide a rationale for innovation-driven models of south-south co-operation and demonstrate their feasibility in the numerous examples of firm-to-firm, university-industry and government-to-government arrangements of this sort already underway. To strengthen these initiatives, states are increasingly being called upon to play a key steering role even as the private sector's contribution and active participation increases. Policies that promote innovation and technological diffusion, an institutional and legal framework that allows and indeed fosters networking for innovation, and the telecommunications, transportation, research and training infrastructure which support it, must be put in place. So, too, must creative solutions to the financing of innovation be developed. The agenda for south-south co-operation is thus long, but it is not inchoate if it remains firmly focused on the goal of networking for innovation.

Notes

1. A point emphasized by Carlota Perez in Chapter 2.

2. See Chapter 1 for an overview of these debates.

3. The latter phrase was coined by Alice Amsden (1989).

4. To illustrate the basis for its argument, the EC cites two examples. In the first, Gambia devalued its currency at the same time as in neighbouring Senegal the purchase price of peanuts, payable in convertible CFA francs, was raised. The net result was a loss of nearly half of Gambia's production to Senegal and hence the inability of the former to capture the benefits of devaluation. In the second example, after ten years of an overvalued naira, Nigeria radically devalued its currency in 1986-87 seriously destabilising informal trade along the Benin and Niger borders (EC, 1990, 4). See also EC, 1988.

5. The phrase is borrowed from Perez, Chapter 2.

6. Both the Lim and Chudnovsky papers also show the importance of getting one's economic house in order more generally.

7. A similar argument was first made in Mytelka, 1973.

8. ECLAC, 1990, 14.

9. Most economists continue to see the need for government support mainly in electronics and biotechnology. Thus Laura Tyson writes "[n]early everyone now concedes that competitive advantage in high-technology industries is created, not endowed by nature, and that governments the world over have earmarked them for special support" (Tyson, 1992, 9).

10. A seminar on the private sector in West Africa held in November 1991, for example, was supported by the OECD's Club du Sahel, the CILSS (Comité Permanent Inter-Etats de Lutte contre la Sécheresse dans le Sahel) and USAID. It brought together representatives from the business community, public sector bodies and international donor agencies from 15 West African countries (CILSS, 1992).

11. The African Development Bank, the World Bank and the EC are supporting the creation of Technical Working Groups that bring public and private sector nominees together to make recommendations in the area of investment policy, trade policy, finance and payments and proposals for the strengthening and/or creation of institutions.

12. Interview with Fernando Machado, Director, CEGESTI, Ottawa, 17 January 1992.

13. The exceptions are, of course, Nigeria and Zimbabwe.

COMMISSION DES COMMUNAUTÉS EUROPÉENNES (1990), Cadre de Référence pour les prochains travaux du CAD sur la coopération et l'intégration régionale, 9 avril, Doc. No. AT/EG/ms, Bruxelles.

COMMISSION DES COMMUNAUTÉS EUROPÉENNES (1988), "Note de réflexion, ajustement structurel et coopération régionale", Bruxelles, Direction Générale du Développement, juillet.

CLUB DU SAHEL (1992), The Private Operators' Perspective on an Agenda for Action, February, Doc. No. SAH/D(92)388, Club du Sahel, OECD, Paris.

ECLAC (1990), Changing Production Patterns with Social Equity, United Nations Economic Commission for Latin America and the Caribbean, Santiago, Chile.

KRUGMAN, Paul (1991), "Regionalism vs. Multilateralism: Analytical Notes", paper presented to the World Bank and CEPR Conference on New Dimensions in Regional Integration, 2-3 April, Washington, D.C.

MELO, Jaime de, Arvind PANAGARIYA and Dani RODRIK (1992), "The New Regionalism: A Country Perspective", paper presented to the World Bank and CEPR Conference on New Dimensions in Regional Integration, 2-3 April, Washington, D.C.

MYTELKA, Lynn K. (1973), "Foreign Aid and Regional Integration: The UDEAC Case", Journal of Common Market Studies, Vol. XII, No. 2, December, pp. 138-158.

RATHGEBER, Eva M. (1991), "Knowledge Production and Use in Agriculture", International Institute for Educational Planning, 25 March, Paris.

TYSON, Laura D'Andrea (1992), "Who's Bashing Whom? Trade Conflict in High-Technology Industries", Institute for International Economics, Washington, D.C.

UNIDO (1992), "Genetic Engineering and Bio-technology Monitor", No. 40, December.

UNIDO (1991), "Politiques de l'ÓNUDI : Coopération économique et technique entre pays en développement", Doc. No. GC.4/7IDB.8/13, 14 juin.

VITTA, Paul (1992), "Utility of Research in Sub-Saharan Africa: Beyond the Leap of Faith", Science and Public Policy, Vol. 19, No. 4, August, pp. 221-228.

WORLD BANK (1989), World Development Report, Washington, D.C.

WORLD BANK (1991), World Development Report, Washington, D.C.

MAIN SALES OUTLETS OF OECD PUBLICATIONS
PRINCIPAUX POINTS DE VENTE DES PUBLICATIONS DE L'OCDE

ARGENTINA – ARGENTINE
Carlos Hirsch S.R.L.
Galería Güemes, Florida 165, 4° Piso
1333 Buenos Aires   Tel. (1) 331.1787 y 331.2391
Telefax: (1) 331.1787

AUSTRALIA – AUSTRALIE
D.A. Information Services
648 Whitehorse Road, P.O.B 163
Mitcham, Victoria 3132   Tel. (03) 873.4411
Telefax: (03) 873.5679

AUSTRIA – AUTRICHE
Gerold & Co.
Graben 31
Wien I   Tel. (0222) 533.50.14

BELGIUM – BELGIQUE
Jean De Lannoy
Avenue du Roi 202
B-1060 Bruxelles   Tel. (02) 538.51.69/538.08.41
Telefax: (02) 538.08.41

CANADA
Renouf Publishing Company Ltd.
1294 Algoma Road
Ottawa, ON K1B 3W8   Tel. (613) 741.4333
Telefax: (613) 741.5439
Stores:
61 Sparks Street
Ottawa, ON K1P 5R1   Tel. (613) 238.8985
211 Yonge Street
Toronto, ON M5B 1M4   Tel. (416) 363.3171
Telefax: (416)363.59.63

Les Éditions La Liberté Inc.
3020 Chemin Sainte-Foy
Sainte-Foy, PQ G1X 3V6   Tel. (418) 658.3763
Telefax: (418) 658.3763

Federal Publications Inc.
165 University Avenue, Suite 701
Toronto, ON M5H 3B8   Tel. (416) 860.1611
Telefax: (416) 860.1608

Les Publications Fédérales
1185 Université
Montréal, QC H3B 3A7   Tel. (514) 954.1633
Telefax : (514) 954.1635

CHINA – CHINE
China National Publications Import
Export Corporation (CNPIEC)
16 Gongti E. Road, Chaoyang District
P.O. Box 88 or 50
Beijing 100704 PR   Tel. (01) 506.6688
Telefax: (01) 506.3101

DENMARK – DANEMARK
Munksgaard Book and Subscription Service
35, Nørre Søgade, P.O. Box 2148
DK-1016 København K   Tel. (33) 12.85.70
Telefax: (33) 12.93.87

FINLAND – FINLANDE
Akateeminen Kirjakauppa
Keskuskatu 1, P.O. Box 128
00100 Helsinki
Subscription Services/Agence d'abonnements :
P.O. Box 23
00371 Helsinki   Tel. (358 0) 12141
Telefax: (358 0) 121.4450

FRANCE
OECD/OCDE
Mail Orders/Commandes par correspondance:
2, rue André-Pascal
75775 Paris Cedex 16   Tel. (33-1) 45.24.82.00
Telefax: (33-1) 45.24.81.76 or (33-1) 45.24.85.00
Telex: 640048 OCDE

OECD Bookshop/Librairie de l'OCDE :
33, rue Octave-Feuillet
75016 Paris   Tel. (33-1) 45.24.81.67
(33-1) 45.24.81.81
Documentation Française
29, quai Voltaire
75007 Paris   Tel. 40.15.70.00
Gibert Jeune (Droit-Économie)
6, place Saint-Michel
75006 Paris   Tel. 43.25.91.19
Librairie du Commerce International
10, avenue d'Iéna
75016 Paris   Tel. 40.73.34.60
Librairie Dunod
Université Paris-Dauphine
Place du Maréchal de Lattre de Tassigny
75016 Paris   Tel. (1) 44.05.40.13
Librairie Lavoisier
11, rue Lavoisier
75008 Paris   Tel. 42.65.39.95
Librairie L.G.D.J. - Montchrestien
20, rue Soufflot
75005 Paris   Tel. 46.33.89.85
Librairie des Sciences Politiques
30, rue Saint-Guillaume
75007 Paris   Tel. 45.48.36.02
P.U.F.
49, boulevard Saint-Michel
75005 Paris   Tel. 43.25.83.40
Librairie de l'Université
12a, rue Nazareth
13100 Aix-en-Provence   Tel. (16) 42.26.18.08
Documentation Française
165, rue Garibaldi
69003 Lyon   Tel. (16) 78.63.32.23
Librairie Decitre
29, place Bellecour
69002 Lyon   Tel. (16) 72.40.54.54

GERMANY – ALLEMAGNE
OECD Publications and Information Centre
August-Bebel-Allee 6
D-53175 Bonn 2   Tel. (0228) 959.120
Telefax: (0228) 959.12.17

GREECE – GRÈCE
Librairie Kauffmann
Mavrokordatou 9
106 78 Athens   Tel. (01) 32.55.321
Telefax: (01) 36.33.967

HONG-KONG
Swindon Book Co. Ltd.
13–15 Lock Road
Kowloon, Hong Kong   Tel. 366.80.31
Telefax: 739.49.75

HUNGARY – HONGRIE
Euro Info Service
POB 1271
1464 Budapest   Tel. (1) 111.62.16
Telefax : (1) 111.60.61

ICELAND – ISLANDE
Mál Mog Menning
Laugavegi 18, Pósthólf 392
121 Reykjavik   Tel. 162.35.23

INDIA – INDE
Oxford Book and Stationery Co.
Scindia House
New Delhi 110001   Tel.(11) 331.5896/5308
Telefax: (11) 332.5993
17 Park Street
Calcutta 700016   Tel. 240832

INDONESIA – INDONÉSIE
Pdii-Lipi
P.O. Box 269/JKSMG/88
Jakarta 12790   Tel. 583467
Telex: 62 875

IRELAND – IRLANDE
TDC Publishers – Library Suppliers
12 North Frederick Street
Dublin 1   Tel. (01) 874.48.35
Telefax: (01) 874.84.16

ISRAEL
Electronic Publications only
Publications électroniques seulement
Sophist Systems Ltd.
71 Allenby Street
Tel-Aviv 65134   Tel. 3-29.00.21
Telefax: 3-29.92.39

ITALY – ITALIE
Libreria Commissionaria Sansoni
Via Duca di Calabria 1/1
50125 Firenze   Tel. (055) 64.54.15
Telefax: (055) 64.12.57
Via Bartolini 29
20155 Milano   Tel. (02) 36.50.83
Editrice e Libreria Herder
Piazza Montecitorio 120
00186 Roma   Tel. 679.46.28
Telefax: 678.47.51
Libreria Hoepli
Via Hoepli 5
20121 Milano   Tel. (02) 86.54.46
Telefax: (02) 805.28.86
Libreria Scientifica
Dott. Lucio de Biasio 'Aeiou'
Via Coronelli, 6
20146 Milano   Tel. (02) 48.95.45.52
Telefax: (02) 48.95.45.48

JAPAN – JAPON
OECD Publications and Information Centre
Landic Akasaka Building
2-3-4 Akasaka, Minato-ku
Tokyo 107   Tel. (81.3) 3586.2016
Telefax: (81.3) 3584.7929

KOREA – CORÉE
Kyobo Book Centre Co. Ltd.
P.O. Box 1658, Kwang Hwa Moon
Seoul   Tel. 730.78.91
Telefax: 735.00.30

MALAYSIA – MALAISIE
Co-operative Bookshop Ltd.
University of Malaya
P.O. Box 1127, Jalan Pantai Baru
59700 Kuala Lumpur
Malaysia   Tel. 756.5000/756.5425
Telefax: 757.3661

MEXICO – MEXIQUE
Revistas y Periodicos Internacionales S.A. de C.V.
Florencia 57 - 1004
Mexico, D.F. 06600   Tel. 207.81.00
Telefax : 208.39.79

NETHERLANDS – PAYS-BAS
SDU Uitgeverij Plantijnstraat
Externe Fondsen
Postbus 20014
2500 EA's-Gravenhage   Tel. (070) 37.89.880
Voor bestellingen: Telefax: (070) 34.75.778

OECD PUBLICATIONS, 2 rue André-Pascal, 75775 PARIS CEDEX 16
PRINTED IN FRANCE
(41 94 05 3) ISBN 92-64-04033-1 - No. 47136 1994